AN AMERICAN QUAKER
IN THE BRITISH ISLES

The Travel Journals of
Jabez Maud Fisher, 1775–1779

JABEZ MAUD FISHER
Painted by James Sharples of London (1751–1811)

RECORDS OF SOCIAL AND ECONOMIC HISTORY
NEW SERIES XVI

AN AMERICAN QUAKER IN THE BRITISH ISLES

The Travel Journals of
Jabez Maud Fisher, 1775–1779

EDITED BY

KENNETH MORGAN

Published *for* THE BRITISH ACADEMY
by OXFORD UNIVERSITY PRESS

Oxford University Press, Walton Street, Oxford OX2 6DP
Oxford New York Toronto
Delhi Bombay Calcutta Madras Karachi
Petaling Jaya Singapore Hong Kong Tokyo
Nairobi Dar es Salaam Cape Town
Melbourne Auckland
and associated companies in
Berlin Ibadan

Oxford is a trade mark of Oxford University Press

Published in the United States
by Oxford University Press, New York

British Library Cataloguing in Publication Data
Fisher, Jabez Maud
An American Quaker in the British Isles: the travel
journals of Jabez Maud Fisher, 1775–1779. — (Records of
social and economic history. New series, 16).
1. Great Britain. Description & travel, 1760–1830
I. Title II. Morgan, Kenneth III. British Academy
IV. Series
914.10473
ISBN 0–19–726096–9

Typeset by J&L Composition Ltd, Filey, North Yorkshire
Printed in Great Britain by
Bookcraft Ltd.
Midsomer Norton, Bath

To the memory of
MARIE-FRANÇOISE RENAULT

INTRODUCTORY NOTE

This sixteenth volume in the new series of *Records of Social and Economic History* widens its range in several respects. It pushes the series forward, for the first time, into the later eighteenth century, the records are American (while concerning Great Britain, with slight incursions into Ireland and continental Europe), and the diversity of the journals will appeal to a wider spectrum of interests than most previous books in the collection.

Jabez Fisher, as a young Philadelphian Quaker merchant on his first visit to Europe at the age of 25, was a serious tourist, above all as a diarist, so that this text is a fascinating addition to the corpus of 'travelogues' about Britain in this period — perhaps the most comprehensive between Celia Fiennes or Defoe and Torrington. Fisher was interested in country seats and landscapes no less than industrial plants, ports and mines. An important or fashionable scene of whatever provenance seldom escaped his eye or his pen as he criss-crossed the land. Historians of the eighteenth century will appreciate his personal encounters with so much that is familiar to them from other evidence; while his aesthetic responses accurately document the sensibilities of the period. There is a vivid sense of drama about such set pieces as his descent of the Dolcoath tin mine in Cornwall (pp. 107–108).

Apart from this general interest as a 'national gazetteer', which Dr Morgan has meticulously documented, the journals hold a more special appeal as an addition to Quaker historiography by documenting the extensive family networks through which Jabez Fisher's travels were structured. For economic historians the professional objectives of his visit are revealed through the detailed 'credit-ratings' given for many merchants particularly those who were actual or potential correspondents for Joshua Fisher and Sons (the family firm), and the astonishingly diverse lists of goods traded — a salutary reminder of the complexities of eighteenth-century industry and commerce.

January 1991

Peter Mathias
Chairman, Records of Social and Economic History Committee

Contents

List of Maps

List of Illustrations

with Acknowledgements

Abbreviations

Aedes Walpolianae	*Aedes Walpolianae: Or, A Description of the Collection of Pictures at Houghton Hall* (3rd edn., London, 1767)
Avery, *New Century Classical Handbook*	Catherine Avery, ed., *The New Century Classical Handbook* (London, 1962)
Bailey's *British Directory*	Bailey's *British Directory; or, Merchant's and Trader's Useful Companion, for the Year 1784* (4 vols., London, 1784)
Cassell's *Encyclopaedia*	Cassell's *Encyclopaedia of General Information* (10 vols., London, n.d.)
Cokayne, *Complete Peerage*	G. E. Cokayne, *The Complete Peerage* (2nd edn., London, 1910–)
Colvin, *History of the King's Works*	H. M. Colvin et al., eds., *A History of the King's Works* (5 vols., London, 1963–)
Corner and Booth, *Chain of Friendship*	Betsy C. Corner and Christopher C. Booth, eds., *Chain of Friendship: Selected Letters of Dr. John Fothergill of London, 1735–1780* Cambridge, Mass., 1971)
DNB	Sir Leslie Stephen and Sidney Lee, eds., *The Dictionary of National Biography* (22 vols., Oxford, reprinted 1959–1960)
Doerflinger, *Vigorous Spirit of Enterprise*	Thomas M. Doerflinger, *A Vigorous Spirit of Enterprise: Merchants and Economic Development in Revolutionary Philadelphia* (Chapel Hill, North Carolina, 1986)
Donaldson and Morpeth, *Dictionary of Scottish History*	Gordon Donaldson and Robert S. Morpeth, *A Dictionary of Scottish History* (Edinburgh, 1977)
DQB	Dictionary of Quaker Biography: Typescript at Friends' House, Euston Road, London
Emden, *Quakers in Commerce*	Paul H. Emden, *Quakers in Commerce: A Record of Business Achievement* (London, 1939)
Encyclopaedia Britannica	*The Encyclopaedia Britannica: A Dictionary of Arts, Sciences, Literature and General Information* (11th edn., New York, 1910)

FHL	Friends Historical Library, Swarthmore College, Pennsylvania
Flinn, *British Coal Industry: The Industrial Revolution*	Michael W. Flinn, *The History of the British Coal Industry, vol. 2: 1700–1830: The Industrial Revolution* (Oxford, 1984)
FLL	Friends' House Library, Euston Road, London
Frost, *Records and Recollections of James Jenkins*	J. William Frost, ed., *The Records and Recollections of James Jenkins* (New York, 1984)
Fry, *David & Charles Book of Castles*	Plantagenet Somerset Fry, *The David & Charles Book of Castles* (Newton Abbot, 1980)
Gifford et al., *Buildings of Scotland: Edinburgh*	John Gifford, Colin McWilliam and David Walker, *The Buildings of Scotland: Edinburgh* (London, 1984)
Gorton, *Topographical Dictionary of Great Britain and Ireland*	John Gorton (with G. N. Wright), *A Topographical Dictionary of Great Britain and Ireland* (3 vols., London, 1833)
Gummere, *Journal and Essays of John Woolman*	Amelia Mott Gummere, ed., *The Journal and Essays of John Woolman* (London, 1922)
Hadfield, *British Canals*	Charles Hadfield, *British Canals: An Illustrated History* (7th edn., Newton Abbot, 1984)
HMSO	Her Majesty's Stationary Office
Hodgson, *Society of Friends in Bradford*	H. R. Hodgson, *The Society of Friends in Bradford: A Record of 270 Years* (Bradford, 1926)
HSP	Historical Society of Pennsylvania, Philadelphia
JFHS	Journal of the Friends' Historical Society
Jones and Dixon, *Macmillan Dictionary of Biography*	Barry Jones and M. V. Dixon, *The Macmillan Dictionary of Biography* (rev. and updated edn., London, 1986)
Lewis, *Topographical Dictionary of England*	Samuel Lewis, *A Topographical Dictionary of England* (4 vols., London, 1831)
Lewis, *Topographical Dictionary of Wales*	Samuel Lewis, *A Topographical Dictionary of Wales* (3rd edn., 2 vols., London, 1843)
Lewis, *Topographical Dictionary of Ireland*	Samuel Lewis, *A Topographical Dictionary of Ireland* (2 vols., London, 1837)
Lewis, *Topographical Dictionary of Scotland*	Samuel Lewis, *A Topographical Dictionary of Scotland* (2 vols., London, 1841)
MM	Monthly Meeting
Moir, *Discovery of Britain*	Esther Moir, *The Discovery of Britain: The English Tourists* (London, 1964)

Morriss, *Royal Dockyards*	Roger Morriss, *The Royal Dockyards during the Revolutionary and Napoleonic Wars* (Leicester, 1983)
Murray, *New English Dictionary*	James A. H. Murray, ed., *A New English Dictionary on Historical Principles* (Oxford, 1888–)
Murray and Murray, *Dictionary of Art and Artists*	Peter Murray and Linda Murray, *The Penguin Dictionary of Art and Artists* (5th edn., London, 1983)
Namier and Brooke, *History of Parliament: The House of Commons, 1754–1790*	Sir Lewis Namier and John Brooke, *History of Parliament: The House of Commons, 1754–1790* (3 vols., London, 1964)
OED	*Oxford English Dictionary* (2nd edn., 20 vols., 1989)
Pen Pictures of London Yearly Meeting	Norman Penney, ed., *Pen Pictures of London Yearly Meeting, 1789–1833*, Journal of the Friends' Historical Society, Supplements nos. 16 and 17 (London, 1930)
Pevsner, *Buildings of England*	Sir Nikolaus Pevsner, *The Buildings of England*
PMHB	The Pennsylvania Magazine of History and Biography
QM	Quarterly Meeting
Raistrick, *Quakers in Science and Industry*	Arthur Raistrick, *Quakers in Science and Industry* (London, 1950)
RCHM	Royal Commission on Historical Monuments
TRE	Typed Register Extracts: typescripts at Friends' House, Euston Road, London
UBD	*Universal British Directory* (5 vols., London, 1791–)
VCH	*The Victoria County History of the Counties of England*
VCH: Cambridge	*Victoria County History: A History of the County of Cambridge and the Isle of Ely, vol. III: The City and University of Cambridge*, ed. J. P. C. Roach (London, 1959)

ABBREVIATED FAMILY TREE OF THE FISHER FAMILY

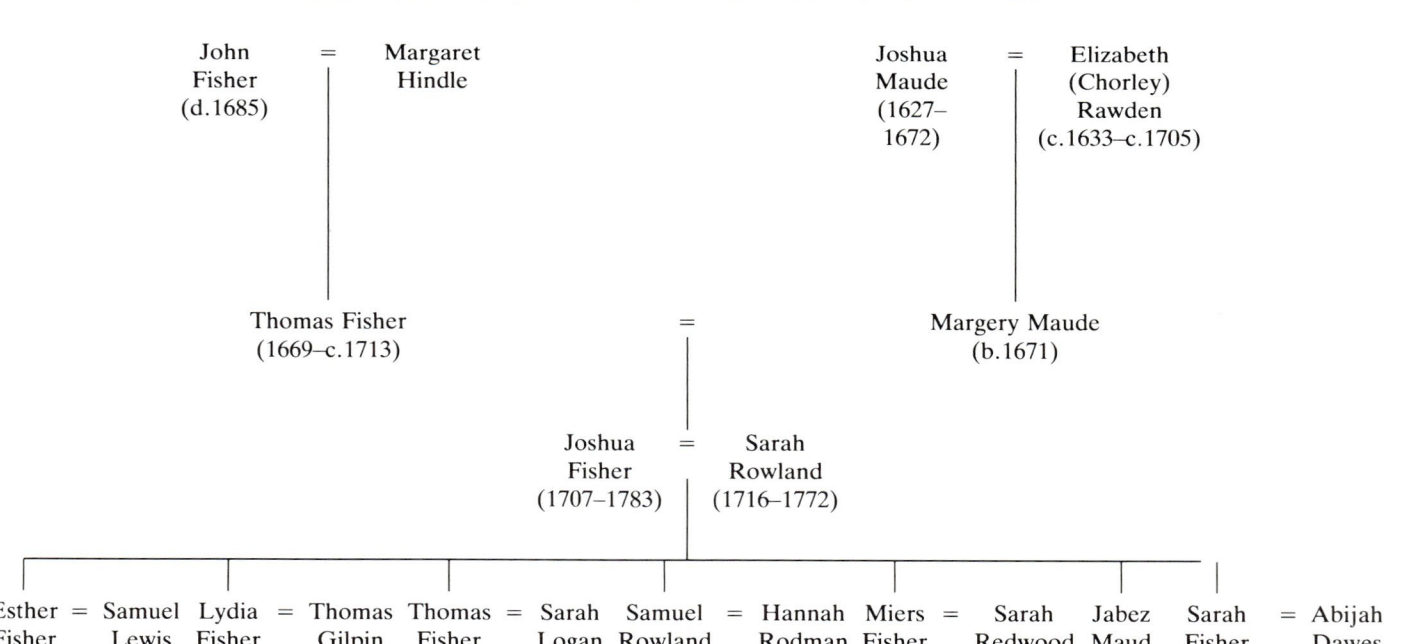

Sources: Anna Wharton Smith, *Genealogy of the Fisher Family, 1682–1896* (Philadelphia, 1896); William Wade Hinshaw, *Encyclopedia of American Quaker Genealogy* (Ann Arbor, 1938), volume 2; John W. Jordan, *Colonial Families of Philadelphia* (2 vols., New York and Chicago, 1911), I, pp. 664–669.

Introduction

The Fisher family of Philadelphia in the era of the American Revolution

Jabez Maud Fisher — the author of the journals presented in this edition – came from a Quaker family that had emigrated from England to America during the lifetime of William Penn, the founder of Pennsylvania.[1] His father, Joshua Fisher, settled at Lewes in Sussex County, Delaware, married in 1733, and became the father of seven children. After working for some years as a hatter, Joshua Fisher decided in 1745 to sell his property in Delaware in order to pursue a more prosperous livelihood in Philadelphia, which was rapidly becoming the largest city and biggest port in the British colonies in mainland America. At first the Fishers lived on the north side of Walnut Street, Philadelphia, just above Front Street, but in 1753 they moved to a lot at 110 South Front Street, which included a house plus a warehouse on Dock Street. This location was in the heart of the main commercial district in the city and close to the wharves and quays where vessels plying up and down the Delaware River would load and unload cargoes. Joshua Fisher soon took a keen interest in maritime commerce. He drafted the best eighteenth-century chart of the Delaware Bay and River and shortly after the move to Philadelphia the mercantile business of Joshua Fisher & Sons came into existence.[2]

Joshua Fisher & Sons was mainly involved in the distribution of dry goods — manufactured wares of all kinds — imported from Britain. It built up extensive connections with large English export firms such as William Reeve, Son & Hill of Bristol and Cooke, Lawrence & Relph, Neate &

---

[1] Jabez Maud Fisher presumably received his middle name in remembrance of his English grandmother, Margery Maud, from Wakefield in Yorkshire: see HSP, Samuel Rowland Fisher Journal, 5 Nov. 1783.

[2] These details are based on Anna Wharton Smith, *Genealogy of the Fisher Family, 1682–1896* (Philadelphia, 1896), pp. 22–24, 27, 34–35; Townsend Ward, 'South Second Street and its Associations,' *PMHB*, IV (1880), pp. 51–52; Hazel Shields Garrison, 'Cartography of Pennsylvania before 1800,' *PMHB*, LIX (1935), pp. 255–283; Lawrence C. Wroth, 'Joshua Fisher's "Chart of Delaware Bay and River",' *PMHB*, LXXIV (1950), pp. 90–109; Sophia Cadwalader, ed., *Recollections of Joshua Francis Fisher* (Boston, 1929), pp. 10–13.

Pigou, David & John Barclay, Harford & Powell, and Fludyer, Marsh & Hudson of London. It retailed dry goods in Philadelphia and in the prosperous Pennsylvania farming country that formed the hinterland to the city.[3] Joshua Fisher & Sons expanded its business to become probably the wealthiest Quaker merchant house in Philadelphia in the generation before the American Revolution.[4] In both 1769 and 1770 it earned a 10 per cent return on capital and in the latter year its net worth was £31,225 in Pennsylvania currency. The firm increased its wealth by substantial investment in iron manufacturing in New Jersey.[5] Business prosperity was accompanied by social status. Joshua Fisher was one of thirty-three Quaker grandees in Philadelphia in 1772 who owned a private equipage.[6] He had a genteel country seat, the Cliffs, built for him in Fairmount Park, then on the outskirts of the city.[7] He possessed substantial real estate holdings in Pennsylvania and Delaware,[8] and further strengthened his family's social and economic position through intermarriage with other leading Philadelphia Quakers.[9]

Joshua Fisher's four sons were all concerned with the world of business. Miers Fisher worked as a flour factor on the eastern shore of Maryland until 1766.[10] Though he later pursued a legal and political career, he joined his brothers Thomas and Samuel Rowland Fisher in a merchant firm that continued in trade with England after the death of their father.[11] Three of the Fisher brothers visited Britain as representatives of Joshua Fisher & Sons. Such trips helped to forge Anglo-American ties that were important in both a social and a business sense, and to sustain a transatlantic community of Friends held together by love, fellowship and a common

[3] HSP, Joshua Fisher & Sons Ledger (1769–1773), *passim.*

[4] Cadwalader, ed., *Recollections of Joshua Francis Fisher*, p. 10.

[5] Doerflinger, *Vigorous Spirit of Enterprise*, pp. 48, 153, 179.

[6] Frederick B. Tolles, *Meeting House and Counting House: The Quaker Merchants of Colonial Philadelphia, 1682–1763* (Chapel Hill, North Carolina, 1948), p. 131 n. 60.

[7] For black-and-white plates of the exterior and parlour of the Cliffs, built between 1770 and 1773, see Doerflinger, *Vigorous Spirit of Enterprise*, pp. 24–25. This fine Georgian house stayed in the possession of the Fisher family until 1868 (Richard Webster, *Philadelphia Preserved: Catalog of the Historic American Buildings Survey* [Philadelphia, 1976], pp. 229–230). The Cliffs survived intact until a few years ago, when it was gutted by fire.

[8] Doerflinger, *Vigorous Spirit of Enterprise*, p. 132.

[9] Nicholas B. Wainwright, ed., '"A Diary of Trifling Occurrences:" Philadelphia, 1776–1778,' *PMHB*, LXXXII (1958), p. 411. For biographical sketches of the Fisher family see Smith, *Genealogy of the Fisher Family, passim*; Cadwalader, ed., *Recollections of Joshua Francis Fisher*, pp. 3–34; and John W. Jordan, *Colonial Families of Philadelphia* (2 vols., New York and Chicago, 1911), I, pp. 664–669.

[10] Smith, *Genealogy of the Fisher Family*, p. 50.

[11] For evidence of this trade see HSP, Thomas, Samuel Rowland and Miers Fisher Journal (1792–1795).

faith.[12] These visits led to the compilation and preservation of written journals. Thomas Fisher stayed in Britain between 1764 and 1766 and kept journals outlining his visits to fellow Quakers and his observations on the state of manufacturing and trade in the mother country.[13] Samuel Rowland Fisher made two trips (in 1767–1768 and 1783–1784) and left a similarly informative commentary.[14] Jabez Maud Fisher spent over three years in the British Isles and parts of Northern Europe between 1775 and 1779 and compiled an extensive set of journals. These records, previously unpublished, are edited in this volume. They provide a fascinating insight into social and economic conditions in the British Isles at the beginnings of industrialisation.[15] To understand why Jabez Maud Fisher came to Britain and left such a detailed account of his tour, it is necessary to appreciate the difficult situation faced by his family during the American Revolution.

Many Philadelphia Quakers opposed the War of Independence because of their pacifist principles. In 1774 a few pious conservative Quaker merchants, including Joshua Fisher, turned their backs on any measure beyond asking the Pennsylvania Assembly to petition Britain for a redress of colonial grievances.[16] By August 1775, some eighty Friends had taken up arms in Philadelphia in support of the patriot cause, but they were a minority of the 800 Quaker families in the city.[17] Once the war began, most Friends tried to remain neutral and hoped for a British victory. In September 1776, the Philadelphia Yearly Meeting issued guidelines for uniformity of conduct and disowned Friends who were unfaithful to their principles.[18] Quakers were encouraged to oppose the war by withholding taxes, by refusing to perform military service, and by boycotting the

---

[12] This theme is explored in Frederick B. Tolles, *Quakers and the Atlantic Culture* (New York, 1960).

[13] Dickinson College, Thomas Fisher Journals (8 vols., 12 Dec. 1762–14 July 1764).

[14] HSP, Samuel Rowland Fisher Journals (2 vols., 1767–1768 and 1783–1784).

[15] This edition reproduces fourteen volumes of journals deposited at FHL and five volumes located at Dickinson College. The latter are referred to in Charles Coleman Sellers and Martha Calvert Slotten, eds., *Archives and Manuscript Collections of Dickinson College* (Carlisle, Pennsylvania, 1972), pp. 22–23.

[16] Richard Alan Ryerson, *The Revolution is Now Begun: The Radical Committees of Philadelphia, 1765–1776* (Philadelphia, 1978), p. 50.

[17] HSP, Samuel Rowland Fisher to Jabez Maud Fisher, 6 Aug. 1775, Box 21, Fisher Family Papers, 1761–1868, Collection no. 2094.

[18] Between 1775 and 1778 inclusive some 418 Philadelphia Friends were disowned; about one-fifth of the adult male Quakers in the city joined the American army or took places under the revolutionary government (Harry M. Tinkcom, 'The Revolutionary City, 1765–1783' in Russell F. Weigley, ed., *Philadelphia: A 300 Year History* [New York, 1982], pp. 131–132; Isaac Sharpless, *A History of Quaker Government in Pennsylvania: Vol. 2: The Quakers in the Revolution* [Philadelphia, 1899], p. 151).

Continental currency printed to finance the American army. One of the earliest boycotters was Samuel Rowland Fisher. Although the political power of the Quakers had waned since their temporary withdrawal from Pennsylvania politics in 1756, the fact that they comprised about one-seventh of the inhabitants of Philadelphia plus the fact that they were among the most wealthy and influential residents led to their being perceived as a threat by the Continental Congress, which was based in the city. The wrath of the patriots was aroused in 1776 when the Philadelphia Meeting for Sufferings, appalled by the fighting, issued a plea for retention of 'the happy connection' with Britain in a document entitled *The Ancient Testimony and Principles of the People called Quakers renewed with respect to the King and Government*.[19]

Jabez Maud Fisher was one of Philadelphia's most active conservatives in 1774. On 29 April 1775, he was publicly rebuked for submitting an anonymous letter to the *Pennsylvania Ledger* that questioned the commitment of a county in neighbouring Delaware to Congressional policy. The letter was also circulated in other newspapers in Pennsylvania and New York.[20] Joshua Fisher decided that his son would be safer outside the country until the political situation calmed down, so he sent him immediately on a trip to the British Isles. Jabez left Philadelphia for his first trip to England on the same day that he received public criticism. His father later supplied him with a set of instructions to follow carefully.[21] These directives specified that Jabez should settle the accounts of Joshua Fisher & Sons in England and establish commercial connections with merchants and manufacturers dealing in goods that could be marketed well in Philadelphia. They also recommended particular London merchants who might be suitable

[19] This summary of the Quaker position in revolutionary Philadelphia draws on Doerflinger, *Vigorous Spirit of Enterprise*, pp. 219–221; Jack D. Marietta, *The Reformation of American Quakerism, 1748–1783* (Philadelphia, 1984), pp. 269–270; Richard Bauman, *For the Reputation of Truth: Politics, Religion, and Conflict among the Pennsylvania Quakers, 1750–1800* (Baltimore, 1971), pp. 159–183; Robert F. Oaks, 'Philadelphians in Exile: The Problem of Loyalty during the American Revolution,' *PMHB*, XCVI (1972), pp. 299–301; and Hugh Barbour and J. William Frost, *The Quakers*, Denominations in America, no. 3 (Westport, Connecticut, 1988), pp. 140–143.

[20] Ryerson, *The Revolution is Now Begun*, pp. 45, 125; HSP, James & Drinker to Pigou & Booth, 9 Aug. 1774, James & Drinker Letterbook (1772–1786), Henry Drinker Papers. The letter is reprinted in Peter Force, ed., *American Archives: Fourth Series* (Washington, D.C., 1837), I, pp. 1270–1271.

[21] FLL, Thomas Pole Journal (1775–1776), p. 3 indicates that Jabez Maud Fisher left Philadelphia for England on 29 Apr. 1775.

business contacts.[22] Joshua Fisher advised his son to 'appear respectable to all our Correspondents,' adding that 'the way to do so is to acquaint thyself with our affairs how they are circumstanced, & be able to give them a full Ansre. to all their enquiries & likewise to acquaint thyself with everything necessary relative to them.'[23] There was no inkling, when these lines were penned, that the War of Independence would drag on, cutting off trade between the Quaker city and British ports for most of the next seven years.

Jabez Maud Fisher received further advice about his conduct in Britain. His father urged him to behave circumspectly, for 'we intreat thee as thou values our regard to avoid all places of Public resort & Licentiousness & study oeconomy & frugality in all thy proceedings.'[24] His brother Miers warned him about the delicate situation he would face and counselled him to eschew 'fairweather Friends' and spies.[25] Another Friend, George Logan, was anxious that Jabez should exercise caution in voicing his sentiments on the war, especially when among a large company of English Quakers.[26] These recommendations were offered with concern over the need to act in a prudent way. The problem was not that the Society of Friends in Britain and America differed over the matter of neutrality, for many British Quakers refused to support the war by payment of special taxes or military service.[27] It was rather that any outspokenness against Lord North's ministry might provoke a backlash of persecution.

Jabez Maud Fisher intended to avoid political controversy,[28] but took a close interest in Anglo-American relations. He was awaited eagerly at London coffee houses because he could repeat, almost verbatim, all the speeches of the preceding night in Parliament on American affairs at a time when the reporting of such matters in the newspapers was banned.[29] His

---

[22] See below, Appendix I, which is pieced together from two manuscript letters: FHL [Joshua Fisher & Sons] to Jabez Maud Fisher, 4 Sept. 1775, Fisher-Warner Papers, and HSP, Joshua Fisher & Sons to [Jabez Maud Fisher], n.d. Though these items are deposited in different archives, I believe that they are two unequal portions of one letter, with the second part beginning at the paragraph on Poole. I base this contention on similar handwriting and paper size and on the fact that the first letter is dated but unsigned whereas the second is signed but undated. Joshua Fisher & Sons' reference to being 'rather prolix' adds support to my viewpoint.

[23] HSP, [Joshua Fisher] to Jabez Maud Fisher, 13 May 1775, Box 21, Fisher Family Papers.

[24] *Ibid.*

[25] HSP, Miers Fisher to Jabez Maud Fisher, 14 May 1775, Joshua Francis Fisher Papers.

[26] HSP, George Logan to Jabez Maud Fisher, 20 Aug. 1775, Box 21, Fisher Family Papers.

[27] Anne T. Gary, 'The Political and Economic Relations of English and American Quakers, 1750–1785' (Oxford Univ. D.Phil. thesis, 1935), pp. 354–355.

[28] HSP, Jabez Maud Fisher to Samuel Coates, 29 Aug. 1775, Box 3a Folder 2, Sidney George Fisher Papers.

[29] Smith, *Genealogy of the Fisher Family*, p. 34.

written remarks emphasise his strong feelings of regret for the rifts caused by the Revolutionary War. 'I want words to express the pain I feel for the calamities of my Country,' he wrote in a letter after a few months in Britain. 'That a Contest so unnatural should continue only to the Destruction of both Parties,' he added, 'is a reflection so truly lamentable as takes from me the whole pleasure I receive from my visit here.'[30] In two other letters, he criticised the British government for arbitrary actions that displayed a lack of regard for the fate of the Empire.[31] His travel journals also contain one particularly eloquent outburst on the sad state of affairs between Britain and America.[32]

The Fisher family in Philadelphia suffered considerable distress while Jabez was staying in the British Isles. The commanding officers of the Continental army in Philadelphia seized goods from the warehouse of Joshua Fisher & Sons during a period of scarcity and ordered the wares to be sold at public vendue. The Fishers refused to accept Continental bills of credit as payment, an action that rendered them liable to conviction. On 15 February 1776, the Council of Safety confiscated the firm's ledgers and locked up their premises. Samuel Rowland and Miers Fisher, on grounds of conscience, refused to hand over the books or tell where they could be found. By this time, other Quakers had become isolated in Philadelphia and stubbornly resisted the war. The revolutionary government dealt with this threat to their authority by confining twenty people, mainly Quakers, in the Freemasons' Lodge in Philadelphia. They later sent the dissidents, including Samuel Rowland, Miers and Thomas Fisher, and five of their relatives, into exile at Winchester, Virginia. Samuel Rowland Fisher was released in 1779 but a letter written by him to his brother in England was intercepted and its contents pronounced inimical to the revolutionary government. He was arrested, put in gaol, tried, found not guilty twice by the jury, but then convicted of treason at a third trial and sentenced to two years' imprisonment.[33]

---

[30] FHL, Jabez Maud Fisher to Hannah Redwood, 5 Dec. 1775, Wharton Papers RG5.

[31] HSP, Jabez Maud Fisher to Samuel Coates, 29 Aug. 1775, Box 3a Folder 2, Sidney George Fisher Papers; and Jabez Maud Fisher to Dr Thomas Parke, 29 Aug. 1775, Pemberton Papers, vol. 28, f. 40.

[32] See below, p. 177.

[33] This paragraph is based on HSP, Thomas Fisher to Jabez Maud Fisher, 11 Mar. 1776, Box 21, Fisher Family Papers; Smith, *Genealogy of the Fisher Family*, pp. 27–31, 46–47; Wainwright, ed., '"A Diary of Trifling Occurrences,"' *PMHB*, LXXXII (1958), pp. 411–412; Anna Wharton Morris, ed., 'Journal of Samuel Rowland Fisher, of Philadelphia, 1779–1781,' *PMHB*, XLI (1917), pp. 145–148, 155–157; Thomas Gilpin, *Exiles in Virginia: with Observations on the Conduct of the Society of Friends during the Revolutionary War, comprising the Official Papers of the Government relating to that period, 1777–1778* (Philadelphia, 1848); Cadwalader, ed., *Recollections of Joshua Francis Fisher*, pp. 14–16.

Jabez Maud Fisher received news of his father's store being boarded up while he was touring Ireland in May 1776.[34] He was shocked about the imprisonment of his brothers and also missed the company of his fiancée, Hannah Redwood, who had remained in America.[35] Failure to receive letters from his family for many months increased his anxiety.[36] He therefore determined to return home as soon as possible. By August 1777 he hoped that General Howe's army would succeed in taking Philadelphia from the south and that the war would soon be over.[37] The occupation of Philadelphia by the British army on 25 September 1777, after a famous victory in a battle on the Brandywine, provided the incentive to organise a trip home.[38] During the autumn, Jabez Maud Fisher struck an agreement with three London merchant firms whereby a cargo of goods worth £30,000 would be assembled and sent to Philadelphia. Fisher and his associates agreed to purchase a ship (the *Live Oak*) to carry the goods and he himself intended to sail with the vessel and dispose of the cargo for a $7\frac{1}{2}$ per cent commission on sales and returns. Different commodities were ordered from suppliers all over England and by 1 December 1777 hopes were raised by news reaching London that the British army had taken Philadelphia. But a fortnight later a less favourable account of the situation filtered through to London and so Fisher delayed his trip.[39]

Jabez Maud Fisher's anxiety about the sufferings of his family and close relatives hardened his determination to return home.[40] He eventually set sail from Portsmouth in May 1778, keeping a journal on board ship with

[34] See below, p. 172. For some months he had known of the general treatment meted out by the revolutionary government to Friends in Philadelphia (FHL, George Logan to Jabez Maud Fisher, 27 Oct. 1775, Fisher-Warner Papers).

[35] FHL, Jabez Maud Fisher to Hannah Redwood, 10 Dec. 1777, Wharton Papers RG5. This collection contains nine letters from Fisher to Redwood spanning the period May 1775–March 1779. There are duplicate copies of four of these letters in HSP, Society Collection, Case 20 Box 7. For Fisher's strong reaction to the banishment of Philadelphia Friends by the Patriots see Haverford College Quaker Collection, Jabez Maud Fisher to Dr Thomas Parke, 10 Jan. 1778, Charles Roberts Autograph Letters Collection.

[36] HSP, Jabez Maud Fisher to Dr Thomas Parke, 3 Apr. 1777, Pemberton Papers.

[37] HSP, Jabez Maud Fisher to Robert Walker, 15 Aug. 1777, Joshua Francis Fisher Papers.

[38] HSP, Jabez Maud Fisher to Joshua Fisher & Sons, 23 Sept. 1777, Box 22, Fisher Family Papers; Sharpless, *History of Quaker Government in Pennsylvania, vol. 2: The Quakers in the Revolution*, pp. 146–147.

[39] Full details of these arrangements are given in FHL, Proceedings about goods to be shipped to Philadelphia (1777–1778).

[40] FHL, Jabez Maud Fisher to Hannah Redwood, 10 Jan. 1778, Wharton Papers RG5.

information on the British naval convoy in code.[41] He arrived at New York City in August only to find that the British troops, now led by Sir Henry Clinton, had evacuated Philadelphia several weeks previously when the probability of a French expeditionary force coming to America made the permanent occupation of the city impossible.[42] Jabez tried for six months to travel the hundred or so miles to Philadelphia from New York — the latter being still under British control — but realised that his personal safety would be at risk. Though he felt like 'a long absented Rambler' on a 'wearied Pilgrimage,' he reluctantly concluded that it was too difficult to reach Philadelphia and so he returned to Britain to settle his concerns there and to wait for the end of the war. His family wrote from America to urge him to retire to the north of England until the transatlantic mails were no longer interrupted.[43]

The Journals of Jabez Maud Fisher: General Observations

The Fisher Journals highlight three prominent features of eighteenth-century tours of the British Isles: the increasing popularity of travelling throughout the whole nation; the propensity for colonial Americans — notably Quakers — to visit the mother country; and the frequency of tours by foreign businessmen. Many tourists left impressions of the British Isles in travel diaries. Some accounts, notably Defoe's famous *Tour*, were not based on information acquired entirely from first-hand observation or from a single tour.[44] Most, however, were compiled by people who recorded what they saw and who registered a keen appreciation of country houses, landscape gardens, mountains and lakes, and the changing face of industry and agriculture.[45] Quakers were ubiquitous among the many colonial Americans who visited Britain for religious, scientific, political or business

---

[41] Dickinson College, Jabez Maud Fisher Journal (25 May–17 Aug. 1778). This volume also has some miscellaneous notes on the planets and on sixteenth century French history.

[42] Sharpless, *History of Quaker Government in Pennsylvania, vol. 2: The Quakers in the Revolution*, p. 148. For the organisation and conduct of local business while Philadelphia was in British hands see Willard O. Mishoff, 'Business in Philadelphia during the British Occupation,' *PMHB*, LXI (1937), pp. 165–181.

[43] FHL, Jabez Maud Fisher to Hannah Redwood, 3 Nov. 1778, Wharton Papers RG5; HSP, Joshua, Thomas and Samuel Rowland Fisher to Robert Walker, Isaac Wilson and William Rathbone, 22 Feb. 1779, Joshua Francis Fisher Papers; Smith, *Genealogy of the Fisher Family*, p. 34.

[44] Defoe's *Tour* was based on three general Tours and seventeen large circuits he had made prior to 1725 (Moir, *Discovery of Britain*, p. 35).

[45] A full account of these tourists appears in Moir, *Discovery of Britain*. Her bibliography of primary sources (pp. 159–178) lists 182 published and unpublished travel journals that

reasons.[46] Their lengthy journeys and extensive contacts with British Friends led to them being 'better informed about the region, and the ways of life and opinions of the people there, than any other colonial group.'[47] These Quakers invariably kept journals.[48] Foreign manufacturers — often French, Swedish and American industrial spies — also came to Britain in significant numbers to observe and record the technical innovations that were beginning to transform the economy.[49] All these travellers were fascinated by remnants of the past (castles, ruined abbeys, country houses) and by novelties that pointed to a prosperous future (factories, canals, technological inventions).

cover the eighteenth century. Extracts from some of these records appear in Robin Gard, ed., *The Observant Traveller: Diaries of Travel in England, Wales and Scotland in the County Record Offices of England and Wales* (HMSO, London, 1988). Among those which have been edited are James Joel Cartwright, ed., *The Travels through England of Dr Richard Pococke, successively Bishop of Meath and Ossory during 1750, 1751, and later years* (2 vols., Camden Society, 1888–1889); C. Bruyn Andrews, ed., *The Hon. John Byng: The Torrington Diaries: Tours made between the years 1781 and 1794* (4 vols., London, 1934–1938); G. D. H. Cole, ed., *Daniel Defoe: A Tour Thro' the Whole Island of Great Britain ...* (2 vols., London, 1927); Arthur Raistrick, ed., *The Hatchett Diary: A Tour through the Counties of England and Scotland in 1796 visiting their mines and manufactories* (Truro, 1967); J. D. Fleeman, ed., *Samuel Johnson, A Journey to the Western Islands of Scotland* (Oxford, 1985); Frederick A. Pottle and Charles H. Bennett, *Boswell's Journal of a Tour to the Hebrides with Samuel Johnson, LL.D.* (London, 1936); Christopher Morris, ed., *The Journeys of Celia Fiennes* (London, 1947); M. W. Thompson, ed., *The Journeys of Sir Richard Colt Hoare through Wales and England, 1793–1810* (Gloucester, 1984). The coverage of these journals is discussed in Malcolm Andrews, *The Search for the Picturesque: Landscape Aesthetics and Tourism in Britain, 1760–1800* (London, 1989), pp. 76–81.

[46] For a book-length discussion of these travellers see William L. Sachse, *The Colonial American in Britain* (Madison, Wisconsin, 1956).

[47] *Ibid.*, p. 87.

[48] E.g. FLL, Thomas Pole Journals (1775–1777) and Edmund Tolson Wedmore, ed., *Thomas Pole, M.D.* (*JFHS* Supplement no. 7, London, 1908); Henry J. Cadbury, *John Woolman in England, 1772: A Documentary Supplement* (*JFHS* Supplement no. 32, London, 1971); HSP, Richard Vaux Diaries (1779–1782); HSP, Robert Willis Journal (1770–1789); HSP, Samuel Shoemaker Diary (1783–1785); National Library of Wales, Aberystwyth, William Dillwyn Diary (1774–1775) and William Dillwyn Journal (1774–1775).

[49] See Gabriel Jars, *Voyages Metallurgiques* (3 vols., Paris, 1781); F. de St Fond, *Voyages en Angleterre ...* (Paris, 1797); Jean Chevalier, 'La Mission de Gabriel Jars dans les Mines et les Usines Britanniques en 1764,' *Transactions of the Newcomen Society*, XXVI (1947–1949), pp. 57–66; Michael W. Flinn, 'The Travel Diaries of Swedish Engineers of the Eighteenth Century as Sources of Technological History,' *ibid.*, XXI (1957–1959), pp. 95–106; Harold B. Hancock and Norman B. Wilkinson, 'Joshua Gilpin: An American Manufacturer in England and Wales, 1795–1801,' Parts 1 and 2, *ibid.*, XXXII (1959–1960), pp. 15–26 and *ibid.*, XXXIII (1960–1961), pp. 57–66; Harold B. Hancock and Norman B. Wilkinson, 'An American Manufacturer in Ireland, 1796,' *Journal of the Royal Society of Antiquaries of Ireland*, XCII (1962), pp. 125–137; S. G. Lindberg, ed., *Bengt Ferrner: Resa i Europa, En Astronom, Industriespion och Teaterhabitue Genom Denmark, Tyskland, Holland, England och Italien, 1758–1762* (Uppsala, 1956); W. O. Henderson, ed., *J. C. Fischer and his Diary of Industrial England 1814–51* (London, 1966); W. O. Henderson, ed., *Industrial Britain under*

Jabez Maud Fisher's Journals combine these interests, for he was an indefatigable tourist, a Quaker in close touch with his co-religionists, and an American businessman visiting the British Isles. 'England I am greatly delighted with,' he wrote to another Friend after a couple of months' residence in Britain. 'The Face of the Country, the Prospects, improvements in Art & Agriculture, the venerable old Ruins of our Forefathers, the hospitality of the inhabitants & the Fairness of the fair Celestials all impress me with the most favourable Sentiments.'[50] By this time, Fisher had already travelled 750 miles and at one stage he covered 600 miles in three weeks.[51] Altogether, his tour extended over several thousand miles. 'Thou may be truly called a Rambler,' a fellow Quaker remarked, for you are 'no sooner arrived from one expedition than parting away on another.'[52]

These excursions were mainly undertaken on horseback, and they naturally entailed a fair amount of physical discomfort, especially when riding for long distances over rugged terrain.[53] Fisher had to buy a new horse on two occasions, but only once was his money so reduced that he had to walk several miles rather than ride.[54] Sometimes he took a post chaise or whiskey when he wished to speed up the journey or when he was tired from too much time spent in the saddle.[55] On 3 January 1776, for instance, he took a series of post chaises to travel from Plymouth to Wellington in Somerset and paid 1 shilling for the driver, 2s. 6d. for tolls at turnpike gates, and £1 7s. 6d. for the use of the vehicles.[56] Post chaises proved satisfactory where roads were turnpiked or in good order but they were no guarantee of speedy travel. On one occasion Fisher spent eight hours in a chaise covering twenty-three miles between the two small Scottish towns of Kinghorn, near Leith, and Anstruther, across the Forth

the Regency: The Diaries of Escher, Bodmer, May and de Gallois 1814–18 (London, 1968); A. P. Woolrich, ed., *Ferrner's Journal 1759/1760: An Industrial Spy in Bath and Bristol* (Eindhoven, n.d.); T. C. Smout, ed., 'Journal of Henry Kalmeter's Travels in Scotland, 1719–1720,' *Scottish Industrial History: A Miscellany* (Scottish History Society, 4th series, XIV, Edinburgh, 1978), pp. 1–52; *Svedenstierna's Tour Great Britain 1802–3: The Travel Diary of an Industrial Spy* (Newton Abbot, 1973).

[50] HSP, Jabez Maud Fisher to Dr Thomas Parke, 29 Aug. 1775, Pemberton Papers. For further initial impressions of England see FHL, Jabez Maud Fisher to Hannah Redwood, 21 June 1775, Wharton Papers RG5.

[51] See below, p. 227; HSP, Jabez Maud Fisher to Samuel Coates, 29 Aug. 1775, Sidney George Fisher Papers.

[52] HSP, Robert Ormston to Jabez Maud Fisher, 4 March 1776, Fisher Family Papers.

[53] E.g., see below, p. 218.

[54] See below, pp. 66, 187, 218.

[55] See below, pp. 43, 47, 63, 84–85, 94, 96, 172, 175, 193, 238, 243.

[56] Dickinson College, Jabez Maud Fisher Expense Accounts (1775–1776). For the route followed see below, pp. 110–111.

in Fife — a journey that provoked the weary comment, 'such is the mode of travelling in Scotland.'[57] For longer trips, he took a stagecoach.[58]

Fisher rarely undertook expeditions alone. He usually travelled with one or more Friends — men such as Richard Philips or the Elam brothers of Leeds — who acted as guides and as contacts with fellow Quakers.[59] Sometimes larger groups assembled for a day trip to which Fisher was invited. Such gatherings included a party of sixteen who met for a visit to Greenwich and a group that set off from Samuel Elam's house in Leeds for a ride to Studley Royal and Hackfall, near Fountains Abbey, in Yorkshire.[60] Fisher was received hospitably wherever he called on Quakers and was usually able to lodge with them, only occasionally having to put up at an inn.[61] He had some letters of introduction, but even without a written recommendation he often obtained accommodation with Quaker families.[62] He was solicitous of fellow Friends, who held his conversation in high esteem and who reported that he always appeared to be 'the same chearful pleasing social companion.'[63] He was especially fond of the company of young Quaker women, whose presence was sufficient inducement for him to linger a litle longer than intended in some places.[64] At times he found it difficult to drag himself away from the hospitality he received.[65]

Fisher consolidated his Quaker contacts by meeting fellow expatriates from Philadelphia in London and by attending various Quaker meetings throughout the country.[66] Some of these gatherings were lengthy affairs such as the Northern Yearly Meeting at Keswick, which lasted for five days, and the London Yearly Meeting, which convened for a week.[67] These important assemblages were attended by representatives from all

---

[57] See below, p. 59.

[58] See below, pp. 41, 59, 191.

[59] See below, pp. 98, 121, 238, 269.

[60] See below, p. 194; HSP, Samuel Elam to Jabez Maud Fisher, 23 July 1777, Fisher Family Papers.

[61] E.g., see below, pp. 216–218, 220, 224. For Fisher's pleasure at the hospitality he received in the British Isles see Haverford College Quaker Collection, Jabez Maud Fisher to Dr Thomas Parke, 10 Jan. 1778, Charles Roberts Autograph Letters Collection.

[62] See below, pp. 34, 216.

[63] Joseph Gurney to Joseph Gurney Bevan, 27 Jan. 1776, in 'Letters from Joseph Gurney to Joseph Gurney Bevan,' *JFHS*, XX (1923), p. 113; HSP, Robert Ormston to Jabez Maud Fisher, 4 Mar. 1776, Fisher Family Papers; Smith, *Genealogy of the Fisher Family*, p. 34.

[64] HSP, Joseph Gurney to Jabez Maud Fisher, 5 Feb. 1776, Fisher Family Papers, and Jabez Maud Fisher to Dr Thomas Parke, 29 Aug. 1775, Pemberton Papers.

[65] HSP, Samuel Elam to Jabez Maud Fisher, 23 July 1777, Fisher Family Papers.

[66] See below pp. 43, 67, 130, 186, 201.

[67] See below, pp. 162, 191.

over the country who held sessions dealing with nationwide matters of concern to the Society of Friends.[68] While tapping this network of associations Fisher met some famous Quakers, including William Cookworthy, the translator of Swedenborg and discoverer of china clay; Dr Thomas Dimsdale, who had treated the Empress Catherine the Great in Russia; Benjamin West, the American portrait painter based in London; and Abraham Darby and Richard Reynolds, the well-known ironmasters of Coalbrookdale.[69] But he also came across many hundreds of other Friends and so his journals are almost a Who's Who of British Quakers during the American Revolution.

Jabez Maud Fisher approached his travelling in a convivial, outward-going, almost romantic spirit. Comparing a tour from Settle, in north Yorkshire, to see 'the wonders of the North' with the picaresque adventures of *Don Quixote*, he commented that 'we all mounted our Rosinante's, having a party of 3 Dulcineas and 4 Knights in quest of adventures.'[70] This mood is echoed on the title page of one of his journals which bears the inscription: 'The Travels & Surprising Adventures of Jabez Maud Fisher a Native of America & by Birth a Philadelphian.'[71] The adjective 'surprising' is apt because Fisher did not have a preconceived set of circuits such as we find in Defoe's *Tour*. His routes partly depended on the inclinations of his fellow travellers and partly on where he wished to attend Quaker meetings or deal with business affairs. Near the beginning of the tour, when about to set off from Leeds to Liverpool, Manchester and Scotland, he noted that 'for how long I shall be going & coming I cannot tell.'[72] He knew the trip would involve a roundabout route for 'my travels are very *zig zag*.'[73] He was, nevertheless, fully aware of the places he had described and of those he intended to visit and portray at a later stage.[74] He tried, wherever possible, to jot down the number of people and houses in different towns — invaluable information for the era before official censuses even if the estimates were, as Fisher suspected, sometimes under-calculated.[75] But he was not concerned to record everything. Thus the thorough, if prosaic, account of the colleges at Cambridge is matched by a cursory treatment of the Oxford colleges, for which the reader is referred to the guide books available.[76]

---

[68] Corner and Booth, *Chain of Friendship*, p. 30.
[69] See below, pp. 109–110, 119, 198, 265–266.
[70] See below, p. 184–185.
[71] Dickinson College, Jabez Maud Fisher Journal, 11–15 Aug. 1776.
[72] HSP, Jabez Maud Fisher to Samuel Coates, 29 Aug. 1775, Sidney George Fisher Papers.
[73] HSP, Jabez Maud Fisher to Dr Thomas Parke, 29 Aug. 1775, Pemberton Papers.
[74] See below, pp. 109, 123, 155, 158, 176, 178, 238.
[75] See below, pp. 39, 49, 51, 55, 62, 80, 82, 124, 142, 174, 211, 217, 242.
[76] See below, pp. 86, 134–140.

These travel journals were not kept for purposes of publication. Jabez Maud Fisher wrote them for his own pleasure, as a means of self-expression, and to record his observations on the British Isles in accordance with his father's instructions.[77] Entries in the journals are dated and it seems that several days' impressions were often recorded at once. On occasions Fisher fell behind with his account. He noted, for instance, on 20 May 1776 that he was '10 days behind hand' in his journal and that 'too much time has elapsed to be particular in my transactions all that time. So shall content myself with a Short Epitome of my Adventures.'[78] When the travelling ceased, so often did the writing. Thus in early 1776 Fisher spent five weeks enjoying London society without putting pen to paper.[79]

This resumé of how the journals were kept is a reminder that readers should not expect to find the literary polish and shapely construction that are hallmarks of Defoe's *Tour*, written over fifty years earlier. But Defoe's *Tour* was a consciously crafted set of journeys intended for publication and sale, written at leisure, and revised in various editions.[80] Fisher knew that finesse would be lacking to some extent from his own literary efforts.[81] Fortunately, however, his journals, despite some perfunctory passages, present a vivid, wide-ranging portrait of social and economic conditions in the British Isles on the eve of industrialisation. Much of their interest stems from a distinctive viewpoint, for Fisher combined a businessman's eye for the minutiae of commercial transactions with a well-developed aesthetic sensibility and the fresh perspective of an outsider.

His commentary in the journals was based mainly on first-hand observation and on conversations with acquaintances. But he was familiar with a number of antiquarian and topographical writers, to whom he refers at various points. The topographers included Thomas Pennant and William Hutchinson, who had respectively written popular accounts of Scotland and the Lake District just a few years earlier.[82] Camden's *Britannia*, an older topographical work, was also invoked when Fisher visited Ireland.[83] Among the antiquarians were Thomas Amory, under the guise of his pseudonym John Buncle, writing on the Lakes; Dr Thomas Percy, a

---

[77] See below, Appendix I, pp. 321–327.

[78] See below, p. 184.

[79] See below, p. 121.

[80] For discussion of Defoe's literary skill see Pat Rogers, 'The Guidebook as Epic: Reportage and Art in Defoe's *Tour*,' in his *Eighteenth-Century Encounters: Studies in Literature and Society in the Age of Walpole* (Brighton, 1985), pp. 115–150.

[81] See below, p. 196.

[82] See below, pp. 72, 160.

[83] See below, p. 173.

Northumberland poet whose compositions included *The Hermit of Warkworth*; and Charles Cotton, a Derbyshire poet who wrote about the Peak District.[84] Fisher's Journals also display considerable knowledge of English History — notably of Roman Britain and the Civil War period — and of Greek and Roman mythology.[85]

The Journals of Jabez Maud Fisher: A Commentary

The Fisher Journals combine a close interest in aesthetic matters (visits to country houses and gardens, appreciation of sublime and picturesque landscape) with a keen insight into social and economic affairs (the process of change in agriculture, manufacturing, trade, urban development, and living conditions). These two sets of interests are represented in almost equal proportions and only overlap fitfully — as if they were polarised in Jabez Fisher's mind. As we shall see, Fisher's judgements illustrate his eclectic tastes. His cultural outlook displays a sensitivity to the balance between intellectual satisfaction and emotional feeling and to the juxtaposition of art and nature, order and wildness. From a businessman's point of view, however, he was most impressed by signs of energy and improvement — 'oeconomy' and 'management' being two of his favourite terms of praise.[86]

Jabez Maud Fisher's appreciation of art and architecture was stimulated by visits to gentlemen's seats, including Blenheim Palace in Oxfordshire, Harewood House and Wentworth Woodhouse in Yorkshire, the Duke of Athol's residence at Dunkeld in Perthshire, and, in particular, a series of houses in Derbyshire, Nottinghamshire and Norfolk.[87] He also took stock of new architectural developments in cities such as Bath, Dublin and Edinburgh.[88] He usually commented on the internal decorations of houses — notably the prints, drawings and paintings — and was most impressed by the fine collection of Renaissance and Baroque masters acquired by Sir Robert Walpole for the Gallery at Houghton Hall in Norfolk.[89] His comments on buildings were grounded in contemporary taste. When visiting Bath he noted that connoisseurs were divided over whether to give the Royal Crescent or the King's Circus 'the Preference

---

[84] See below, pp. 53, 159, 184, 246–247.
[85] E.g., see below, pp. 77, 92, 173–174, 244.
[86] For examples of these terms see below, pp. 94, 110, 170, 228.
[87] See below, pp. 63, 86, 149–155, 186–189, 239–241.
[88] See below, pp. 56–58, 116–119, 165–167.
[89] See below, pp. 144–146. Cf. Moir, *Discovery of Britain*, pp. 72–73.

and I find it a Question difficult to resolve.'[90] He considered that the exterior of Holkham Hall, in Norfolk, was grand but that 'the inside is still more so and in point of convenience is allowed by *Conoseurs* to be preferable to any in the Kingdom.'[91]

Fisher sometimes offered a critical appraisal of country houses and gardens. He found certain buildings old-fashioned in style, including Sir George Savile's house at Rufford and the Earl of Portland's mansion, Welbeck Abbey, both in Nottinghamshire.[92] He referred to Lord Godolphin's estate in Cornwall as having a plain Gothic house and indifferent gardens.[93] He regarded Squire Fountain's residence at Narford, in Norfolk, as a 'good one, but by no means sufficiently attractive to be the object of view.'[94] And though Hardwick Hall, in County Durham, had impressive features, it was compared unfavourably with Studley Royal in Yorkshire. Fisher noted that Studley Royal had grounds five times as extensive as Hardwick, had twenty-five cascades of water compared with one at Hardwick, a greater variety of obelisks, rotundos and grottoes scattered throughout the grounds, and the added attraction of lying next to the ruins of Fountains Abbey.[95]

Enthusiasm for the eighteenth-century vogue for landscape gardening is much in evidence in Fisher's Journals. The gardens at Cobham in Surrey were praised for the artistry shown in the arrangement of artificial rivers, raised hills, clumps of trees, enchanting walks with meanders, avenues with temples, obelisks, columns, images, rotundos and a grotto.[96] The Elysian park and the objects in the grounds at Wentworth Woodhouse elicited the comment that 'Art and Nature have strove with uncommon efforts to outdo each other in charming the Spectator. Tis impossible to say which claims the Palm with greater Justice. If Art have been defective, tis only when Nature needed no Decoration. If Nature were wanting Art has so concealed her Defects as to leave you without suspecting wherein she was deficient.'[97] Fisher's response to the combination of wildness and order was exemplified at Chatsworth in Derbyshire where romantic aspects of the background such as a straggling wood with oaks and elms, a variety of objects 'which crowd upon the senses,' and a high mountain provided one kind of aesthetic nourishment, while the 'mechanism, order and

[90] See below, p. 116.
[91] See below, p. 147.
[92] See below, pp. 149, 153–154.
[93] See below, pp. 99–101.
[94] See below, p. 141.
[95] See below, pp. 179–181.
[96] See below, p. 199.
[97] See below, pp. 239–240.

Regularity' of the foreground, with tastefully placed objects and trees in uniform rows, offered another.[98]

Fisher's pleasure was always heightened when objects were carefully placed in landscaped gardens to create an atmosphere imbued with melancholy. He singled out in this regard two nearby houses and parks, Hagley and the Leasowes, a few miles to the south-west of Birmingham. The Leasowes was a modest farm with urns and other objects with Latin inscriptions scattered around the gardens. There were a number of walks, seats and verses 'inscribed from various authors suitable to the lonely, solitary and contemplative Scene.'[99] Similarly, the statues and alcoves at Hagley dedicated to various people and a Hermitage plus woods 'in ab origine disorder' also formed a scene 'exactly fitted for meditation.'[100] Fisher's enjoyment of these gardens — which were very popular among travellers by the mid-eighteenth century — was considerably enhanced by the imaginative stimulus of objects with literary and philosophical connections set in a landscape of carefully managed visual contrasts. Fisher particularly appreciated the pleasing melancholy and 'singularity' of lone, strikingly distinct objects at Hagley and the Leasowes, and in so doing he typified the cultivated sensibility of his age.[101]

Fisher also responded keenly to the associative power of ruins in the landscape. Like many of his contemporaries, he admired ruins not just for their magnificent architecture and historical value but also for their aesthetic appeal. Decayed castles, abbeys and Druid places of worship were appreciated for the gratification they provided to the senses. The time-worn remains of Chepstow Castle, covered with ivy, formed 'one of the grandest and most aw[e]ful objects,' while Caerphilly Castle was praised for being 'the most spacious Ruin in Great Britain.'[102] Fountains, Kirkstall, Whitby and Tintern were the most striking decayed abbeys.[103] Pride of place among the ruins, though, was accorded to Stonehenge where 'the ponderous imposts over our heads and the Chasms of Sky between the Jambs of the Cells' were likened to 'Quarries mounted in the Air, or the Bowells of a Mountain turnd

[98] See below, pp. 187–189.

[99] See below, pp. 258–260.

[100] See below, pp. 260–262.

[101] Moir, *Discovery of Britain*, ch. 7, esp. pp. 80, 83; John Dixon Hunt, *The Figure in the Landscape: Poetry, Painting and Gardening during the Eighteenth Century* (Baltimore, 1976), pp. 118–119; Barbara Maria Stafford, 'Toward Romantic Landscape Perception: Illustrated Travels and the Rise of "Singularity" as an Aesthetic Category,' *The Art Quarterly*, New Series, I (1977), pp. 89–124; and H. F. Clark, 'Eighteenth-Century Elysiums: The Role of "Association" in the Landscape Movement,' *Journal of the Warburg and Courtauld Institutes*, VI (1943), pp. 165–189.

[102] See below, pp. 205, 208.

[103] See below, p. 206.

inside out.'[104] The section on Stonehenge recalls the tours made by William Stukeley, an antiquarian with a passion for prehistoric and Roman remains, in the period 1710–1725.[105] And the commentary on ruins in general dwells on the nostalgic elements of a landscape of sensibility and on the visible reminders of the ancestry of land-based power.[106]

Other aspects of the landscape have a prominent place in the Fisher Journals. The wildness and scenic variety of the more rugged parts of the British Isles receive special attention. Jabez Maud Fisher's response here was partly triggered by comparisons with America. Some of the waterfalls in Wales recalled the falls at Niagara and on the St. Lawrence River, near Ottawa, which he had seen while on a trip to New York and Canada in 1773.[107] The American Alleghenies provided a yardstick by which to judge mountains in the Lake District.[108] And the hills and dales of Yorkshire were praised for having 'a vast deal of American grandeur.'[109] More important, however, was an absorption of the ideas which Edmund Burke had established in 1756 in the most famous aesthetic treatise of the eighteenth century. In Burke's formulation, the two classes of agreeable sensations inspired by scenic landscape were the 'beautiful' (a positive pleasure and social passion) and the 'sublime' (a selfish passion involving delight in perceptions of pain and danger, based on our instinct for self-preservation, when we are not actually in pain and danger).[110] Like other travellers in the British Isles a generation before the Romantic poets, Jabez Maud Fisher was directly affected by these sensations, especially when riding through the Peak District, the Lake District and Wales.[111]

Fisher's tour of the Peak District included visits to spa towns such as Buxton and Matlock but mainly focused on 'romantic and rude' scenery.[112] He felt a sense of wonder and astonishment in viewing the sights of Derbyshire.[113] He looked around several popular attractions —

---

[104] See below, p. 90.

[105] Moir, *Discovery of Britain*, ch. 5.

[106] Michel Baridon, 'Ruins as a Mental Construct,' *Journal of Garden History*, V (1985), pp. 84–96.

[107] See below, p. 222 and FHL, Jabez Maud Fisher's Journals of a Tour to New York and Canada (1773). A typescript of the latter is available at the Oneida County Historical Society, Utica, New York.

[108] See below, p. 161.

[109] See below, p. 181.

[110] For a helpful discussion of these ideas see James Sambrook, *The Eighteenth Century: The Intellectual and Cultural Context of English Literature, 1700–1789* (London, 1986), pp. 120–122. A third category of Beauty — the Picturesque — was defined by the Rev. William Gilpin in 1782, shortly after Fisher's tour.

[111] Cf. Moir, *Discovery of Britain*, ch. 10 and 11.

[112] See below, p. 189.

[113] See below, p. 251.

Devil's Peak Cavern, near Castleton, Elden Hole, Poole's Hole, and Mary Queen of Scots Pillow — and reacted to these sights with a mixture of pleasure and horror that was the quintessential element of the sublime.[114] He responded to the splendour of the Lake District — just becoming fashionable when he was touring — with much the same feeling. The sublimity of the 'stupendous' mountains surrounding the Lakes could only be felt by 'striking terror into the Beholder.'[115] Looking at the mountains above Kendal near Lake Windermere, he therefore observed that 'Beauty Grandeur and Horror unite in forming a variety of views, pastoral elegant and grotesque' and that the echoes of cascades of water 'reverberate with pleasing Awe.'[116] Although he felt Keswick had little charm, the mountains surrounding it were a different matter. They 'fill the Eye with wonder and lose the senses in a Maze of Perplexity' and exhibit 'beauty, immensity and horror' suitable for representation by the brushes of Claude, Poussin and Salvator Rosa.[117] These observations were influenced by knowledge of the imaginative landscapes created by these seventeenth-century Roman artists, but they were also stimulated by the change in contemporary taste that made mountains appear beautiful instead of hideous, a change that stemmed from the cultivation of the sublime as an aesthetic ideal. Mountains, far from being distasteful, were now appreciated for their grandeur and capacity to stir deep emotions in the beholder.[118]

Just as with the Lake District, so with Wales: rough-hewn landscape was accorded great admiration. The ride up the Wye Valley from Chepstow to Tintern was enjoyed for its 'prospects of the Sublime and beautiful.'[119] The mountains of North Wales, in Fisher's estimation, provided horrors for the imagination and terror for the mind, and were pleasingly varied with rocks, crags, streams and cataracts.[120] The mountains approaching Caddyr Idris rose in 'long successive Chains above the Clouds in the most aw[e]ful and sublime Stile,' while Caddyr Idris itself was praised for its 'irregularity and romanticity' and its descent applauded

[114] See below, pp. 243–246, 248–249.

[115] See below, pp. 158–159. The growth of interest in the Lakes for tourists is illustrated in Peter Bicknell, *The Picturesque Scenery of the Lake District* (Cambridge, 1987).

[116] See below, p. 158.

[117] See below, pp. 159–162.

[118] This is fully discussed in Marjorie Hope Nicholson, *Mountain Gloom and Mountain Glory: The Development of the Aesthetics of the Infinite* (Ithaca, New York, 1959). See also John Barrell, *The Idea of Landscape and the Sense of Place, 1730–1840* (Cambridge, 1972), ch. 1, and Keith Thomas, *Man and the Natural World: Changing Attitudes in England, 1500–1800* (London, 1983), pp. 258–262.

[119] See below, pp. 204–207.

[120] See below, pp. 220–223.

for producing a 'perturbation of mind.'[121] Even more awe inspiring were the mountains at the head of Cardigan Bay, on the border between the counties of Merioneth and Caernarvon. These mountains reared 'their crested heads in grand gradation, one beyond another, wrapping their Summits in the Smoaking Clouds' until they were capped by Snowden 'lifting his exulting Dome and raising the Envy of his Subject Hills, while they bow with humility before him conscious of their inferiority.'[122] As when touring the Lakes, the comments on scenery were partly based on an acquaintance with landscape painting; in this case, with prints by Richard Wilson, the Welshman who founded the English landscape school.[123]

To turn from the cultural aspects of the tour to the depiction of economic processes is a reminder that incipient romanticism was accompanied by the birth of industrialisation in late eighteenth century Britain. Urban sprawl and environmental squalor have become familiar by-products of the industrial revolution, but Fisher's tour took place when many of the new mechanical processes were getting under way in settings where they did not necessarily create a jarring effect. Thus the 'vast columns of thick Smoak' from the copper works at Swansea and Neath had 'a most pleasing effect on the Landscape.'[124] Fisher's remarks on new developments such as the White Cloth Hall at Leeds, the Leeds–Liverpool canal, and the iron bridge over the Severn at Coalbrookdale show his understanding of the burgeoning industrial economy of the time.[125] The one major disappointment in looking at such improvements was not being allowed by the proprietors to inspect Arkwright's mill at Cromford — 'the greatest Curiosity in the Mechanical Work in Great Britain.'[126]

Another type of improvement admired by Jabez Maud Fisher was the impact of enclosures — the hedges and fences and accompanying drainage — on agricultural cultivation. He set great store by the existence of enclosures in such diverse areas as the hinterland of Carlisle and the meadows of Somerset, and especially singled out the rural parts of Hertfordshire, Essex and Cambridgeshire, where he had 'not seen one spot of land lying useless' and where 'the whole is in high Cultivation and like one continued Garden.'[127] By contrast, he was critical of places where agriculture remained static. He felt that the lack of enclosures on the road from Edinburgh to Montrose reflected primarily the indolence of the

[121] See below, p. 221.
[122] See below, p. 223.
[123] See below, pp. 208, 221, 223.
[124] See below, p. 210.
[125] See below, pp. 42, 156–157, 238, 265–266.
[126] See below, p. 250.
[127] See below, pp. 76, 111–112, 132–134.

people.[128] He also noted a similar problem in rural Hampshire, between Romsey and Ringwood, despite good soil which was well watered, and reckoned it a pity that 'such tracts of land should remain unimproved and Provisions so scarce and dear.'[129] His view was that if the woods and heaths were better cultivated then England would no longer need to depend on imports of basic foodstuffs.[130]

Jabez Maud Fisher was also impressed with improvements to some of the major ports and dockyards. He selected Liverpool for particular comment, visiting the city twice. He observed that the Liverpool docks could take 3–4,000 ships and keep them afloat with ease and safety. In addition, the wharfs were convenient, there was an abundance of quays for the discharge of cargoes, and plenty of dry docks were available for careening vessels.[131] The docks at Port Glasgow drew similar praise for being suitably placed for the efficient unloading and storage of tobacco entering the Clyde.[132] Even more impressive was the scale and activity of the leading dockyards. The 'order, oeconomy, regularity and convenience of the Dock' at Plymouth maximised the facilities there for fitting out ships.[133] And the bustle of the King's Dock, Gosport was also worthy of note, with some 2,000 industrious workers and machines for large-scale shipbuilding all available on one site.[134]

Besides ports and dockyards, minerals and manufactures are documented in the Fisher Journals. There are several lengthy appraisals of industries in both rural and urban settings. Tin and copper mining in Cornwall is allocated the most space. Fisher was fascinated by the difference between tin and copper ores and by the technical processes involved in mining, and was able to see these features when exploring Dolcoath, near Redruth, one of the oldest and largest mines in the county.[135] He estimated that the Cornish tin and copper mines respectively furnished an annual yield of £250,000 and £180,000 in the 1770s, and that tin was vital for Cornish prosperity, 'creating subsistence for the Poor, affluence to the Landlord, besides a considerable Revenue to the Duke of Cornwal.'[136] Fisher realised, however, that Cornwall's economic resources were not being fully exploited. Employment in mining diverted labour

---

[128] See below, p. 60.
[129] See below, p. 124.
[130] *Ibid.*
[131] See below, pp. 81, 232.
[132] See below, pp. 72–73.
[133] See below, pp. 93–94.
[134] See below, pp. 126–127.
[135] See below, pp. 99–103, 105–108.
[136] See below, pp. 101, 106.

from other local industries and from agriculture, even though good corn was grown in parts of Cornwall. And lodes of iron ore lay largely unextracted because of the costs involved in transporting coal from the nearest supply area in South Wales.[137]

The three industrial cities to which Fisher devoted most attention were Sheffield, Manchester and Birmingham. 'No Sooner do we enter the Town of Sheffield,' he observed, 'than the voice of industry is heard in the Streets and every house is a manufactury where the hammers strike Unison with our horses feet.'[138] At the heart of Sheffield's industrial growth lay the making of cutlery, which was aided by water-powered mills that speeded up the slitting, tilting and grinding of metal. Fisher noted that the fine quality plate work resulted from the use of correct instruments and machines and from the division of labour, whereby a single article passed through 'a multitude of different hands, each a distinct trade.'[139]

Fisher was even more impressed with the rapidity of Manchester's growth and with the ingenuity and hard work of her artisans. Manchester 'as a manufacturing town,' he considered, 'rises superior to any in the Kingdom, both for the variety of Articles in which they are engaged, and the value of an enterprizing and Oeconomical Spirit [which] seems to pervade all its inhabitants.'[140] The choice of patterns among textile goods produced in the city was remarkable and the colours rivalled the famed East India cottons and muslins. Flax, cotton and silk were 'converted to a thousand uss' and to enumerate them would be as difficult a task as Linnaeus experienced in classifying species in the natural world.[141] Cotton handlooms, with their flying shuttles, rendered 'every Process so Simple and Labour ... of so little Utility, that it is almost time to call their Manufactures by some other name.'[142]

At Birmingham, Fisher admired the skill of papier mâché work and the range and quality of hardware being manufactured. In the warehouse of Boulton & Fothergill he saw colourful metalware 'more like the costly pageantry of some Eastern Court than the Toys of a Birmingham shop.'[143] A visit to Boulton & Watt's Soho engineering works, however, was the highlight of his stay in Birmingham. The inside of this manufactury was 'divided into hundreds of little apartments, all which like Bee hives are crowded with the Sons of Industry. The whole Scene is a Theatre of

---

[137] See below, pp. 103–105.
[138] See below, p. 155.
[139] See below, pp. 241–242.
[140] See below, p. 235.
[141] See below, p. 236.
[142] *Ibid.*
[143] See below, p. 255.

Business, all conducted like one piece of Mechanism, Men, Women and Children full of employment according to their Strength and Docility. The very Air buzzes with the Variety of Noises. All seems like one vast machine.'[144] The bustle of the workshops plus increasing urban growth and good canal connections with nearby coalfields made Birmingham, in Fisher's view, the most rapidly increasing city in England apart from Manchester.[145]

Fisher's tour of the British Isles did not just equip him to assess the nature of economic development; it also enabled him to observe different aspects of social life. He viewed the living conditions of ordinary people though the eyes of a cultivated traveller who was emphatically Anglophile and who expected standards of cleanliness, order and decency. For the most part, his observations on life in Scotland, Ireland and Wales are based on comparative judgements with a generally more affluent situation in England. The visual offensiveness of poverty was a recurrent theme.[146] Fisher pointed to poor housing in parts of Edinburgh, where families lived above one another and many streets were 'monstrous dirty, narrow and offensive,' with people living in 'gross darkness and buried in filth.'[147] In rural Scotland, he drew attention to poverty, dirty huts, barefooted women and children, and different dress from the English.[148] A Scotchman's parlour, he suggested, was less clean and neat than the Duke of Portland's stables at Welbeck Abbey.[149] No wonder he was relieved to find, on crossing the border between England and Scotland, that 'the country now wears a much more pleasing Aspect, the Fields and meadows skirted with hedge Inclosures, the Huts and Cottages of the Peasants more comfortable, the appearance of the Swains and Nymphs more clean and decent, the houses of the Inhabitants more convenient and elegant.'[150]

Similar impressions resulted from touring Ireland and Wales. Fisher admired some of Dublin's architecture but found himself staying in a dirty house which provided 'a striking contrast of the Neighbouring Kingdom' and at an inn which compared unfavourably with English inns on the London to Bath road.[151] He felt that Dublin's cultural facilities were 'but humble imitations of London refinements.'[152] As in Scotland, he was

[144] See below, p. 253.
[145] See below, pp. 252–257.
[146] Cf. Carole Fabricant, 'The Aesthetics and Politics of Landscape in the Eighteenth Century' in Ralph Cohen, ed., *Studies in Eighteenth-Century British Art and Aesthetics* (Berkeley and Los Angeles, 1985), pp. 62–63.
[147] See below, p. 58.
[148] See below, pp. 60–61, 69, 76.
[149] See below, p. 153.
[150] See below, p. 76.
[151] See below, pp. 164–168.
[152] See below, p. 168.

touched by the extent of poverty. He was offered little to eat or drink, or even a candle to read by, in rural areas where the doors of houses were filled with peasants who were 'humble supplicants of every distorted Feature and dreadful Malady.'[153]

Impressions of life in Wales were much the same. Fisher stayed at Welsh inns which had bed bugs and dirty conditions, poor stabling for horses, no access to window lights, and where it was difficult to procure a dish of tea for nourishment.[154] Once again, England served as the touchstone for his experience of Wales. Fisher mistook one of his Welsh landlords for an ostler 'and indeed an Englishman though an Ostler would be ashamed to appear half so shabby.'[155] He praised the recent introduction of turnpikes in Wales for being an imitation of similar road improvements in England.[156] He criticised the lack of charitable institutions and academies for the education of young people in Wales and thought that 'their Country would have been more highly cultivated, more populous, and the inhabitants would have long since emerged from that state of Barbarism and Ignorance which Candor obliges us to own are too predominant' if the Welsh had long ago allied themselves with the English.[157]

Though Fisher spent most of his tour in the British Isles, he also made a short trip to the continent in September and October 1776. After crossing the English Channel with his friend Richard Philips, he intended to visit Paris. This plan was soon abandoned, however, because Fisher knew he had insufficient time to explore the French capital.[158] Instead he followed a route along the northern coastline of France, Flanders and Holland, where he looked around a number of towns. He was impressed with the fortifications at Calais, Gravelines, Dunkirk and Nieuw porte and with the dykes, windmills and canals near Ostend, Bruges and Ghent.[159] His stay in Europe was too brief for a detailed commentary, but the pages of his journals dealing with this part of the tour are peppered with interesting reflections on the different behaviour, dress, customs and language of the people he met.[160] His fellow Quaker Robert Ormston concluded that Fisher's description of his continental trip was 'like thyself; fraught with excellent Sentiments. How just are thy remarks on everything, how hast thou studied the manners & customs of different countries thou has passed;

---

[153] See below, pp. 170–171.
[154] See below, pp. 217–218, 224, 228.
[155] See below, p. 219.
[156] *Ibid.*
[157] See below, p. 228.
[158] See below, p. 274.
[159] See below, pp. 270–280.
[160] *Ibid.*

& how proper thy reflections thereon.'[161] The reader of Fisher's travel journals will indeed find that the content is enlivened by the author's gift for metaphor, by his sense of humour, and by his capacity to evoke the curiosity and excitement engendered by the wonders of the age.

The List of Goods

Jabez Maud Fisher kept three notebooks in which he recorded comments on merchant firms that might prove good commercial connections for his father's business in Philadelphia after the end of the War of Independence. Two volumes cover inland and outport merchants; the third deals with London firms. Only some of the people listed were Quakers and all the merchants, except one, resided in England, for Fisher was unable to secure business contacts in Scotland.[162] These conspectuses are invaluable because no comparable material is known to survive for other eighteenth-century British or American merchants — though one imagines that such records were not at all unusual. The cameo portraits provide an interesting insight into the priorities esteemed by a businessman engaged in the transoceanic trade of the time.

Fisher recorded careful details in these journals about the price and quality of goods available at different places. He considered that Nottingham provided better quality fine hosiery than the coarser, higher-priced garments on sale at Leicester; that good quality textile goods at Norwich were better produced than similar wares in Durham and Yorkshire; that Great Yarmouth was the best port in England to secure a shipment of malt; and that fine hats could be bought more cheaply in the Bristol area than elsewhere.[163] Fisher was also concerned with finer points of difference between the commodities. The long lists of goods he appended to many merchants are a reminder of the intricacy of consumer demand for specific wares. By the 1770s, the North American market was already an extension of the consumer revolution in Britain and the prosperous Delaware Valley was an important region for the consumption of English manufactured exports. Merchants and farmers in Philadelphia and rural Pennsylvania eagerly scanned the lists of exports that were printed in American newspapers, with a close eye to quality, price and fashion.[164] Fisher's notebooks indicate which goods were unsuitable for

---

[161] HSP, Robert Ormston to Jabez Maud Fisher, 12 Nov. 1776, Box 21, Fisher Family Papers.

[162] For the exception see below, p. 292.

[163] See below, pp. 282, 289, 296, 305.

[164] For these developments see Neil McKendrick et al., *The Birth of a Consumer Society: The Commercialization of Eighteenth-Century England* (London, 1983) and Thomas

this particular market — printed linens and calicoes in general and expensive coarse white linen from Whitehaven in particular.[165] The impression conveyed by the lists is that Joshua Fisher & Sons were mainly interested in fashionable, varied textiles — notably East India muslins and cottons — plus a range of metalware and hardware.

Fisher was equally concerned with the size and standing of merchant houses. He tells us that Rawlinson & Chorley did more business than any other mercantile firm in Liverpool; that Edmund Radcliffe of Manchester was the greatest manufacturer in England and an extensive trader with Europe; that Wakefield, Pratt & Miers were the leading merchants in London handling Irish linen.[166] Individual businessmen were assessed according to a code of conduct prevalent among Quaker and other nonconformist traders — but found more widely too — a code which emphasised punctuality in supplying remittances, honesty and business stability, the building up of long-standing commercial connections, and the avoidance of debt.[167] Fisher recorded credit allowances, an important consideration because the business world — inland suppliers in Britain, merchants in British and American ports, customers in the colonies — depended on credit for virtually all commercial transactions.[168] Discounts were also noted, most being available from inland suppliers for payment with ready cash.[169]

Fisher noted with approval those merchants who already had good connections with his father's firm (for instance, John and Robert Barclay of London) or with Philadelphia generally (an example being Frank, Tucket & Waring of Bristol).[170] He was also drawn towards large London firms

M. Doerflinger, 'Farmers and Dry Goods in the Philadelphia Market Area, 1750–1800,' in Ronald Hoffman et al., eds., *The Economy of Early America: The Revolutionary Period, 1763–1790* (Charlottesville, Va., 1988), pp. 166–195.

[165] See below, pp. 293, 303.

[166] See below, pp. 284–286, 313.

[167] See below, pp. 289, 291, 301, 316. This code of conduct underpins the fortunes of the Quaker businessmen discussed in Jacob M. Price, 'The Great Quaker Business Families of Eighteenth-Century London: The Rise and Fall of a Sectarian Patriciate' in Richard S. Dunn and Mary Maples Dunn, eds., *The World of William Penn* (Philadelphia, 1986), pp. 363–399.

[168] Among many studies which analyse the supply of credit see Peter Mathias, *The Transformation of England: Essays in the Economic and Social History of England in the Eighteenth Century* (London, 1979), pp. 88–115; Jacob M. Price, *Capital and Credit in British Overseas Trade: The View from the Chesapeake, 1700–1776* (Cambridge, Mass., 1980); Kenneth Morgan, 'Bristol Merchants and the Colonial Trades, 1748–1783' (Oxford University D. Phil. thesis 1984), pp. 145–154, 187–192, 196; and Pat Hudson, *The Genesis of Industrial Capital: A Study of the West Riding Wool Textile Industry c. 1750–1850* (Cambridge, 1986), pp. 17, 111–119, 122, 124, 128, 156–160, 217.

[169] See below, pp. 294–295, 299, 318.

[170] See below, pp. 282, 307, 309–310, 316.

such as the Barclays, Du Bois & Lucas, and Wakefield, Pratt & Miers whose commercial eminence gave them the power to procure recommendations and goods from inland suppliers.[171] Finally, he put down brief remarks about merchants who might form shipping links with Philadelphia in terms of joint ownership of vessels or with a view to participation in the Anglo-American grain trade.[172] All these connections were forged in the wake of competition from other Americans who had visited Britain to solicit business from merchants.[173]

Conclusion

The value of the travel journals of Jabez Maud Fisher lies in their panoramic view of social, economic and cultural life in the British Isles in the early years of the American Revolution and the Industrial Revolution. The insights they provide into these processes are as valuable for historians as those found in Defoe's famous *Tour*. The distinctive flavour of Fisher's commentary stemmed from his combining a general tour with specific business intentions. By perambulating the country with this dual perspective, he was able to form a conception of the whole nation. He encapsulated both the cult of feeling that permeated polite taste in the mid-eighteenth century and the practical realism of a commercial traveller. One might anticipate that he eventually returned home to his fiancée, family and friends in Philadelphia. In fact, however, there was a sad ending to his tour. Jabez Maud Fisher died at the Leeds house of his friend Emanuel Elam on 1 December 1779 after about three weeks of slight indisposition and four days' illness with scarlet fever and an ulcerated sore throat. He had been absent from Philadelphia for four years and seven months and was aged twenty-nine.[174]

Checklist of the Journals of Jabez Maud Fisher

[171] See below, pp. 309–310, 313–314, 316–317.

[172] See below, pp. 282, 284, 303–304.

[173] See below, p. 304.

[174] Morris, ed., 'Journal of Samuel Rowland Fisher,' *PMHB*, XLI (1917), pp. 276–277. FHL, Wharton Papers RG5 includes a poem 'On the death of Jabez Maud Fisher' by Miss J. Head. Jabez Maud Fisher was buried in a grave adjoining the Friends Meeting House in

D. 16 December 1775–4 January 1776   70
E. 4 January–4 March 1776   63
F.   18–27 March 1776   50
G. 11–16 April 1776   46
H. 16–27 April 1776   46
I.   1–9 May 1776   45
J.   9 May–26 June 1776   60
K. 29 June–12 July 1776   56
L.   13–21 July 1776   86
M. 21 July–10 August 1776   56
N. 11–15 August 1776   57
O. 19–20 August 1776   42
P.   27 September–2 October 1776   47
Q. List of Goods, n.d., Volume 1   50
R. List of Goods, n.d., Volume 2   19
S.   List of Goods, n.d., Volume 3   44

N.B. Volumes A–D, F, H–J, L–M, O, Q–S are deposited at the Friends Historical Library, Swarthmore College, Pennsylvania. Volumes E, G, K, N, P are among the Special Collections at Dickinson College, Carlisle, Pennsylvania.

Editorial Method

The text of the journals presented in this edition was prepared from photocopies and checked word for word with the original manuscripts. Jabez Maud Fisher's handwriting is generally legible, so there were no major problems in deciphering words. The main editorial decision to be made was whether to follow a literal, expanded or modernised method of editing.[175] It seemed to me that a literal transcription would be unhelpful with regard to readability and that a modernised version would not give a feel of the age in which the journals were written. I have therefore opted for a middle course between these extremes by following the expanded method. Thus the text presented here retains irregularities in spelling, capitalisation of many substantives, occasional ambiguities in syntax, and

Leeds (HSP, Samuel Rowland Fisher Journal [7 Oct. 1783–23 Mar. 1784], 30 Oct. 1783). For a discussion of the 'sentimental revolution' in English manners see Paul Langford, *A Polite and Commercial People: England 1727–1783* (Oxford, 1989), ch. 10.

[175] Guidelines for these methods are given in Frank Freidel, ed., *Harvard Guide to American History* (rev. edn., 2 vols., Cambridge, Mass., 1974), I, pp. 27–36.

lack of commas in many subsidiary clauses – all of which were common in eighteenth-century manuscripts but which are relatively unfamiliar today. My mentor for the retention of such stylistic features is Dr. Johnson. Disapproving of Lord Hailes' modernised version of the works of John Hales of Eton, he remarked: 'An author's language, Sir ... is a characteristical part of his composition, and is also characteristical of the age in which he writes. Besides, Sir, when the language is changed we are not sure that the sense is the same.'[176]

The precise editorial rules are as follows:

1. *Spelling* is retained as written, but corrected in a footnote if it is unusual enough to obscure the meaning.

2. *Capitalisation* is retained as written. Every sentence begins with a capital letter. Where necessary, this has been supplied.

3. *Words underlined* in the manuscript are printed in italics.

4. *Omissions* in the text are left blank except where a suitable word or phrase can be inserted, in which case this is included within square brackets.

5. *Deleted passages* are generally omitted without notice.

6. *Paragraphing* is supplied in order to make the journals accessible to a modern reader. Sometimes long dashes in the Journals indicate where paragraphs occur; in many instances, however, my own judgement determines where the breaks should come.

7. *Slips of the pen* are retained as written, and are not marked by [sic]. If there is any ambiguity, a footnote is supplied.

8. *Abbreviations and contractions* are normally expanded. The ampersand is given as 'and' except in the form '&c' and in the names of business firms where '&' is retained. The thorn is rendered as 'th.' The tilde is replaced by the letters it represents. The tailed 'p' is expanded to 'per,' 'pre,' or 'pro.' Superscript letters are lowered to the line. Marks indicating repetition are replaced by 'ditto.' All words in which the apostrophe is used to indicate missing letters are expanded. However, initials of people who have not been identified are not expanded.

9. *Italics* are used for Quaker names where identification of a person is based on initials in the original manuscript.

10. *Fractions* at the beginning of sentences are spelt out.

11. *Punctuation* is retained as written. Where a sentence is not supplied with a period, a full-stop is inserted. Dashes used in place of commas, semicolons or colons are replaced by the appropriate marks.

12. *Minor cuts* are made in the text and a summary of the material left out is supplied in a footnote.

---

[176] James Boswell, *Life of Johnson*, ed. R. W. Chapman (Oxford, 1980), pp. 1308–1309.

13. *Footnotes* clarify textual passages and identify persons, places and events. Once a person has been identified, the documentation is not repeated. If a name cannot be traced in available records, there is no footnote. Reputable modern scholarly sources are used for citations wherever possible. In a number of cases, however, it has been necessary to cite older printed works. No references are provided for those footnotes that contain brief comments on people and places that should be familiar to the common reader.[177]

Maps are supplied to illustrate the routes followed by Fisher on his travels. They should be regarded as a vade-mecum to the text, not as an attempt to reproduce the detail of an atlas.

Acknowledgements

My work on this edition has been greatly aided by the help and support of various individuals and institutions. Peter Mathias was enthusiastic in the initial stages and has continued to act as a patient consulting editor. His counsel on this and other research ventures has been invaluable. Richard S. Dunn and Jacob M. Price have always been willing to share their knowledge of the first British Empire and to answer tricky questions that arose in editing these journals. Thomas M. Doerflinger provided expert guidance on manuscript material relating to Philadelphia merchant society in the era of the American Revolution. Jim Bradbury kindly checked my translations from Latin. D. C. Coleman, as general editor of the series, offered useful suggestions in the final stages of preparing the volume for the printers. Thomas L. Purvis drew on his editorial experience to advise on several aspects of presentation. Julie Braithwaite drew the maps. James Rivington guided the volume through the publication process and suggested one absolutely crucial change. Furthermore a number of people, acknowledged by name in the footnotes, responded to my queries on specific points. Needless to say, any errors in the finished product are mine.

I was fortunate in several ways while working on this project during a research trip to Pennsylvania in the summer of 1985. Marianne S. Wokeck and P. M. G. Harris kindly allowed me to use their Philadelphia town house as a base – just a few blocks from where the Fisher family had lived in that city. Albert W. Fowler was helpful in meeting my research demands

---

[177] Other editors might find it helpful to know that many of the topographical works cited in the footnotes can be speedily located in the Bodleian Library by use of Richard Gough, *A Catalogue of the Books, Relating to British Topography, and Saxon and Northern Literature, bequeathed to the Bodleian Library in the Year MDCCXCIX* (Oxford, 1814).

at the Friends Historical Library, Swarthmore College – and subsequently in dealing with requests made through correspondence – while Linda K. Stanley quickly directed me to major uncatalogued deposits of Fisher family papers at the Historical Society of Pennsylvania. Maurice Bric deserves a special word of thanks for alerting me to the journals of Jabez Maud Fisher that are located at Dickinson College: at the time I only knew of the volumes at Swarthmore. After I thought my work on the edition was finished, Pat O'Donnell helped me to locate important material in a newly deposited collection at the Friends Historical Library.

The British Academy has sponsored the publication of this book. I am very grateful to the Academy for providing the opportunity to prepare a fully annotated edition of the Fisher Journals and for the financial wherewithal that enabled me to undertake the necessary travel and research. The Staff Research Fund of the West London Institute of Higher Education helped with incidental expenses. For permission to cite manuscript material in their possession I wish to thank J. William Frost, Director of the Friends Historical Library at Swarthmore College; Martha C. Slotten, formerly Curator of Special Collections at Dickinson College; Edwin B. Bronner, formerly Curator of the Haverford College Quaker Collection; Peter J. Parker, formerly Director of the Historical Society of Pennsylvania; and Malcolm Thomas, Librarian at Friends' House Library, Euston Road, London. I would like to acknowledge assistance received from the staffs of the above institutions and of the other libraries where most of the research was carried out: the Institute of Historical Research and Senate House Library at London University; the British Library; Ealing Central Reference Library; the Bodleian Library, Oxford; Lincoln Central Library; the Avon County Reference Library, Bristol; and the Baillieu Library at the University of Melbourne.

During the time spent working on this edition, in between busy teaching schedules and changes of job, I have found encouragement and support from my non-historian family and friends —my parents and brother, Alan Beer, Steve and Lynne Coombs, Nigel Cousins, the late Marie-Françoise Renault, and Elsie Walsh. Finally I must thank the subject of this volume for presiding over an essential part of the work. When checking my transcription of these journals with the original manuscripts at Swarthmore, I realised, after some time, that the portrait on the wall opposite my desk was of none other than Jabez Maud Fisher himself. This is the picture reproduced at the front of this book.

THE TRAVEL JOURNALS OF
JABEZ MAUD FISHER

JABEZ MAUD FISHER'S TRAVELS, 30 JUNE - 29 OCTOBER 1775

JOURNAL A

30 June–23 September 1775

7th Day   June 30th

Accompanied by *Robert Barclay*[1] and *Thomas* Forthergill[2] I left London about 5 O Clock in the Evening, drank Tea 5 Miles out of London and lodged at Brentwood 18 Miles Distance. Early next morning I took leave of my Friends and riding through a delightful Country, full of Villages, many market Towns, beautiful Prospects, Hills, Vallies, Rich Improvements and elegant Country Seats, fine Roads, good Inns, extensive Views. Lodged at Bury,[3] a beautiful regular Town, wide Market, 2 large ancient Buildings of Gothic Structure and of noble appearance.[4] Next Day came through Bottledale,[5] Tatteshall[6] and about 5 O Clock in the Afternoon reached the favored City of Norwich. A noble hospital of that City lately built stands just without the Gates.[7]

    We enter the City thro a large high Gothic Gate and Tower supported

---

[1] Robert Barclay of Bury Hill (1751–1830) was born in Philadelphia but educated in England from 1763. He entered the business of his grandfather, David Barclay of Cheapside, returned to Philadelphia from 1771–1773, and came back to London in 1775. His wife was Rachel Gurney (1755–1794). The couple had fifteen children, of whom six died in infancy. Robert Barclay was in business in Cheapside until 1783 when the family firm was wound up. *DQB*; Hubert F. Barclay and Alice Wilson-Fox, *A History of the Barclay Family with Pedigrees from 1067 to 1933, Part 3: The Barclays in Scotland and England from 1610 to 1933* (London, 1934), pp. 273–277.

[2] Thomas Fothergill (1751–1822), a Quaker bachelor who settled as a lawyer in London. He was the son of Alexander Fothergill of Carr End, Wensleydale, Yorkshire. Corner and Booth, *Chain of Friendship*, p. 347n.

[3] Bury St. Edmunds.

[4] A reference to the surviving buildings of the abbey at Bury St. Edmunds, including the abbey church and cloister, a twelfth-century Norman Gate and a fourteenth-century Great Gate. Pevsner, *Buildings of England: North-East Norfolk and Norwich* (London, 1962), pp. 138–140.

[5] Botesdale.

[6] Tivetshall St. Margaret.

[7] The Norfolk and Norwich Hospital, built between 1770 and 1775. Pevsner, *Buildings of England: North-East Norfolk and Norwich*, p. 283.

by Columns of Stone.[8] This Town about as large as Philadelphia,[9] very irregular, Streets inconvenient. The River[10] divides it near the middle which has 5 Bridges over it. This City has 34 Churches in it besides a large Cathedral, Steeple 105 yards high.[11] Here stands on an Elevation a famous old Castle, now converted to a Prison.[12] My Friend N*athaniel* Springal,[13] to whom I had Letters, took me to his house where were P*riscilla* and C*hristiana* Gurney,[14] P*riscilla* Wakefield[15] and R*ichenda* Springal.[16] Here I met with John Griffits,[17] Samuel Spavold[18] and Friend Higginson[19] of distant Places; also *Joseph*

[8] From this account, it is impossible to specify which gate and tower is being referred to. The various gates and towers of medieval Norwich are listed in James Campbell, 'Norwich,' in M. D. Lobel, ed., *The Atlas of Historic Towns* (London, 1975), II, pp. 10–11, 25.

[9] The population of Norwich was c. 36,000 in 1750 and 41,000 in 1786. The population of Philadelphia was c. 20,000 in 1775. P. J. Corfield, *The Impact of English Towns 1700–1800* (Oxford, 1982), p. 111; Gary B. Nash and Billy G. Smith, 'The Population of Eighteenth-Century Philadelphia,' *PMHB*, XCIX (1975), p. 366.

[10] River Wensum.

[11] About 1095 Herbert de Losinga began to build a great cathedral and cathedral priory for sixty monks at Norwich. The monastic buildings lay to the south of the Cathedral; to the north, Losinga built a palace for himself. Campbell, 'Norwich,' p. 8.

[12] Norwich Castle was built immediately after the Norman Conquest (before 1075). It was the only royal castle in England until c. 1166. During the reign of Edward III, Norwich Castle became the public gaol of the county of Norfolk and the sheriff had custody to keep prisoners there. *Ibid.*, pp. 5, 8; *The History of the City and County of Norwich from the Earliest Accounts to the Present Time* (Norwich, 1768), p. 74.

[13] A merchant of St. Augustine's parish, Norwich. *Norwich Poll Book* (1780), p. 57.

[14] Priscilla Hannah Gurney (1757–1828), the daughter of Joseph (1729–1761qv) and Christiana Gurney (c. 1736–1796). *DQB*.

[15] Priscilla Wakefield (1750/1–1832) married Edward Wakefield (1750–1826), a Quaker mercer, in 1771. They lived at Tottenham, London. *Ibid.*; 'Letters from Joseph Gurney to Joseph Gurney Bevan,' *JFHS*, XX (1923), p. 114 n. 34.

[16] Richenda Springall was the wife of Nathaniel Springall of Norwich. She was the daughter of David Barclay of Cheapside. *JFHS*, XX, p. 86 n. 9; Lilian Clarke, *Family Chronicles* (Wellingborough, 1910), Section 1: Blecklys and Springalls, pp. 44–45.

[17] Probably John Griffith (1713–1776), a native of Radnorshire, Wales. He emigrated to America in 1726 and returned to Britain in 1751 after the death of his wife. He was an important minister and a strong advocate of the reform of the Society of Friends. He was living at Chelmsford in the 1770s. Corner and Booth, *Chain of Friendship*, p. 49.

[18] Originally a carpenter from Yorkshire who became a ship's captain, Samuel Spavold (1708–1795) travelled widely in the ministry and visited America in 1757. After 1750 he lived mainly at Hitchin and became a well-known preacher. *DQB*; Frost, *Records and Recollections of James Jenkins*, pp. 47, 86, 263–267; Gummere, *Journal and Essays of John Woolman*, p. 583.

[19] Edward Higginson (1703–1784), a frequent traveller in the Quaker ministry throughout England. He moved from Godmanchester, Huntingdonshire, to King's Lynn, Norfolk, some time between 1770 and 1778. *DQB*.

Oxley,[20] Friend Bland,[21] Ed*mund* Gurney[22] and several others of this Place.

July 14th 6th Day

Set off this Afternoon with *John* Gurney and his Wife,[23] R*ichenda* Springal, *Christiana* and *Priscilla* Gurney, David Springal[24] and David Lindoe[25] for Yarmouth which we reached at Dusk. Meeting with Rain I got well soaked. Here we found R*obert* Barclay and his intended *Rachel* Gurney. Here we made our home and spent the time till the second Day following very agreeably, every morning going in the Yarmouth Coaches,[26] a vehicle of curious Construction, to the Sea Side to bathe, leaving the Girls at a bathing house till our Return, generally taking a Ride to the Castle at the Mouth of the Harbour on the Deans,[27] a place covered with Grass, bounded on one Side by the Sea and on the other by the River [Bure], there being constantly in Sight a great Number of Vessels.

Took A Ride to Listoffe[28] a place famous only for a China Manufactory

[20] Either Joseph Oxley (1715–1775), a merchant of Magdalen Street, Norwich, who visited North America in 1770–1772, or his son Joseph Oxley (b. 1748). Bailey's *British Directory*, II, p. 857; Henry J. Cadbury, *John Woolman in England, 1772: A Documentary Supplement*, JFHS Supplement no. 32 (London, 1971), p. 5; *Journal of the Life and Gospel Labours of Joseph Oxley* (London, 1837), pp. 316–388; 'Letters from Joseph Gurney to Joseph Gurney Bevan,' *JFHS*, XX (1923), p. 84 n. 3.

[21] Probably Thomas Bland, merchant, Botolphs Street, Norwich. Bailey's *British Directory*, II, p. 845.

[22] Edmund Gurney (1723–1796), a worsted weaver in Norwich. *DQB*; Frost, *Records and Recollections of James Jenkins*, p. 281.

[23] John Gurney (1718–1779) and his second wife Ann Kendall (?1718–1803), whom he married in 1756. John Gurney and his brother Henry (1721–1777qv) followed their father in his worsted and banking interests. In 1775 they opened the Norwich and Norfolk Bank at Norwich. *DQB*; J. K. Edwards, 'The Gurneys and the Norwich Clothing Trade in the Eighteenth Century,' *JFHS*, L (1963), pp. 134–152; Raistrick, *Quakers in Science and Industry*, pp. 326–327; Emden, *Quakers in Commerce*, pp. 97–104.

[24] David Springall was one of the children of Nathaniel and Richenda Springall. *JFHS*, XX, p. 87 n. 25.

[25] Probably a member of Lindoe & Co., corn merchants and maltsters, Trouse Newton, Norwich. Bailey's *British Directory*, IV, p. 855.

[26] These vehicles, consisting of a low narrow cart drawn by a single horse, were popular with visitors to Yarmouth in the eighteenth century. *An Historical Guide to Great Yarmouth in Norfolk* ... (2nd edn., Yarmouth, 1817), p. 14.

[27] Yarmouth Castle was built in the reign of Henry III. It was demolished in 1621 and strong parapets were constructed in front of the town, and cannon placed on them, facing the sea. Lewis, *Topographical Dictionary of England*, IV, pp. 591–592.

[28] Lowestoft.

of no very great extent.[29] The ride to it is vastly pleasant along the Sea Side, commanding a very wide prospect. Here is a convenient place and convenient Machines for bathing. On our ride back we drank Tea at Websters a fine Country Seat.

Yarmouth is a beautiful Sea Port and a convenient Harbour. Water for Vessels of 16 feet at high Water, 4 Miles only from the Sea and the finest Key of any in England. The Vessels lade and unlade at the Wharfs, but there is a Bar, which renders it somewhat inconvenient getting over. The Town from the other Side the River looks very pretty. A great Number of Vessels are always here. There trade is chiefly in Fish of which they export vast Consequences.[30]

July 17th   2nd Day

We left this Place about 11 O Clock, regaled ourselves with Fruit and Cream at the Globe and got home to Dinner. Took a Ride to Baber, John Wagstaff's Mill,[31] and the next Morning, escorted by *Richenda* Springal and *Christiana* and *Priscilla* Gurney, *David Springal* and *Henry Kit*[32] to Dereham where I took leave of them and rode on not a little dejected with my lonely Situation, reflecting on the agreeable time I had spent at Norwich and Keswick and other Places with the inhabitants of that hospitable City.

Came through Swaffham, a pretty market town, a Curious Race a mile

[29] A small porcelain factory operated at Lowestoft from 1757 to c. 1799. Its products were of the variety known as soft-paste, an artificial type of porcelain fired at a lower temperature than the hard-paste or true porcelain produced by oriental potters or by most continental manufacturers. This establishment was apparently the only manufactory carried on at Lowestoft in the late eighteenth century. Geoffrey A. Godden, *Lowestoft Porcelains* (rev. edn., London, 1985), pp. 39, 43.

[30] Great Yarmouth was a centre for both the mackerel fishery and, more important, the herring fishery. Over half of the red herrings exported from England came from Yarmouth in the period 1771–1787. The main destinations for this top quality fish were Portugal, Spain and Italy. John Greaves Nall, *Great Yarmouth and Lowestoft* . . . (London, 1867), pp. 327, 331; A. R. Michell, 'The European Fisheries in Early Modern History' in E. E. Rich and C. H. Wilson, eds., *The Cambridge Economic History of Europe, Vol. V: The Economic Organization of Early Modern Europe* (Cambridge, 1977), pp. 136, 138–139, 144–146, 154, 176–178. Dr John Murphy of Copenhagen kindly helped me with this reference.

[31] John Wagstaffe (c. 1726–1808) was born in Hampshire and served an apprenticeship to a London baker. He studied science, especially Botany, in his leisure time. At the end of his apprenticeship he settled in Norwich, where he became a baker on his own account. He continued his study of natural history and, on his retirement to Bawburgh in Norfolk, he became distinguished for the practice of gardening and agriculture. He was among the first promoters of the setting of wheat. *DQB*.

[32] Henry Kett (b. 1744), merchant, St. Giles parish, Norwich. *Norwich Poll Book* (1780), p. 28; 'Letters from Joseph Gurney to Joseph Gurney Bevan,' *JFHS*, XX (1923), p. 114 n. 35.

distant,[33] and reached Downham that Evening. The next Morning came on to Wisbeach, a considerable town, navigable Water, a good bridge and the Ride from thence along a beautiful River[34] directly strait through a funny Country for many miles was a very new Sight to me. I dined at Peterborough with a great Number of great men, Lord Fitzwilliam at their head.[35] Here was to be a grand Race. At Peterborough stands a famous Cathedral 1100 years old.[36] Got to Stamford that Evening and the next Morning coming through Rutland breakfasted at Okam[37] their Capital famous for the birth of Dwarf Jeffry Hudson,[38] a town by no means elegant. Got to Milton to dine and reached Nottingham about 5 O Clock in the Afternoon. This Day traveld through a Country by no means rich but extremely beautiful. A great Number of extensive Prospect and innumerable Quantities of Sheep. Here I made my home at *John Leavers.*[39]

Nottingham is beautifully situated in a healthy Valley upon a rock.[40] It stands on the River Trent and a River of less Note[41] washes it at the Foot which also supplies the town by Water by a Conduit. It overlooks a long Chain of Meadows on one Side. It has a Number of houses hewn out of the rock and there are some Remains of antient Workmanship in the Rocks in Duke of NewCastles Park whose Seat an elegant Building stands on an Elevation and overlooks a fine Country.[42] In this house are a great Collection of fine historical Prints and the Walls of several

---

[33] A reference to the annual greyhound race on the heath on the north-west side of Swaffham. It was held in November and was organised like a horse race. Lewis, *Topographical Dictionary of England*, IV, p. 252.

[34] River Nene.

[35] William, Lord Fitzwilliam (1748–1833) was a member of the House of Lords from 1769. He was usually an adherent of the Whig Party and resided at Milton Park, near Peterborough. Cokayne, *Complete Peerage*, V, pp. 522–523, 527.

[36] A Benedictine monastery was founded on this site c. 650 and raised to cathedral rank by Henry VIII in 1541. Rebuilding of the current structure began in 1118. Pevsner, *Buildings of England: Bedfordshire and the County of Huntingdon and Peterborough* (London, 1968), pp. 305–325.

[37] Oakham.

[38] Jeffrey Hudson (1619–1682), a favourite of Queen Henrietta Maria. After reaching the age of seven, when he was eighteen inches high, he apparently did not grow at all until he was thirty, when he shot up to between three feet six to three feet nine inches. *DNB*, X, pp. 149–150.

[39] John Leaver (1711–1794), a grazier of Nottingham. *DQB*.

[40] I have cut some words Fisher jotted down from epitaphs in St. Nicholas Church, Nottingham.

[41] River Erewash.

[42] Nottingham Castle was originally built in the medieval period. In 1674 William Cavendish, 1st Duke of Newcastle, bought the site and built himself a palace on it (completed in 1679). Pevsner, *Buildings of England: Nottinghamshire* (London, 1951), pp. 130–131.

large Rooms are lind with Tapestry of curious Workmanship.[43] Here is a curious Passage into the Earth called Mortimers hole, described very justly by Drayton.[44]

July 31st 2nd Day

Left Nottingham past through a delightful Country along the River Trent to Newark a Considerable town. Got to Lincoln to Lodge, a large Town situate on the declivity of a steep hill. Here is a famous Gothic Cathedral or Minstral, large Arches and a Bell of monstrous Size.[45] Next to Gainsborough where I met with Gideon Wells,[46] through Brig[47] a pretty Town to Barton[48] and at 10 O Clock came over the Ferry.[49] 4 miles.

Hull is situate on the Conflux of the Humber and Hull. It has a Bridge over strong Fortification and they can bring Water all round the Town for 3 Miles. A fine Harbour for Ships but most of them lay aground. 75 Ships in Port. The Inhabitants are now digging out Dry Docks which when finishd will make Kingston an Island.[50] Half as large as Philadelphia trading

[43] The 4th Duke of Newcastle (d. 1768) beautified Nottingham Castle, wainscotting the rooms with cedar and creating a fine garden. But Thoresby, in his *History of Nottinghamshire* (1795), stated that 'here remains only some starved tapestry, in some of the rooms, that require notice.' John Hicklin, *The History of Nottingham Castle from the Danish Invasion to its Destruction by Rioters in 1831* (London, 1836), pp. 151–153, 157.

[44] Though the story may be apocryphal, the dramatic capture of Edward Mortimer and the guilty Queen Isabella in 1330 took place in Mortimer's Hole, a cave at Nottingham Castle. The incident is described in Michael Drayton's poem *Mortimeriados: The Lamentable Cruell Warres of Edward the Second and the Barons* (1596). The poem was dedicated to the Countess of Bedford. Pevsner, *Buildings of England: Nottinghamshire*, p. 130; J. W. Hebel, ed., *The Works of Michael Drayton* (Oxford, 1931), I, pp. 305–392.

[45] The building of Lincoln Cathedral began sometime between 1072 and 1075. The cathedral is a cruciform structure which is spectacularly situated on a steep hill. Building continued throughout the Middle Ages. The great bell of the Minster, 'Big Tom,' hangs in the north-west tower. Pevsner and John Harris, *Buildings of England: Lincolnshire* (London, 1964), pp. 81–128; J. H. Srawley, *The Story of Lincoln Minster* (London, 1933), p. 71.

[46] A merchant of Gainsborough, Lincolnshire. *UBD*, III, p. 143.

[47] Brigg.

[48] Barton upon Humber.

[49] There was a regular ferry service across the Humber between Hull and Barton, Lincolnshire. Battle's *Hull Directory, for the Year 1791* (reprinted Hull, 1885), p. 65.

[50] The first modern docks at Hull were built by the Hull Dock Company between 1775 and 1778. Gordon Jackson, *Hull in the Eighteenth Century: A Study in Social and Economic History* (London, 1972), pp. 243–248.

Town. River Humber. King Charles repulsd.[51] Statue of King William in the Market Place.[52]

August 6th   1st Day

Left it with *John* Proud[53] and came to Beverley, a large well built Place, a curious Church.[54] Many Antiquities here. Almost as large as Hull. Regular Streets. Many Statues and Monuments in the Church. Stayed there 1 Day and 2 Nights and

August 8th

Left it about 8 in the Morning. My horse being lame left him with *John* Dickinson[55] to be sent to me as soon as convenient. Came through several Towns and Villages. I reachd Scarborough about 7 in the Evening. This Day the Country began to wear the Face of Novelty: a continued Succession of Hills and Vallies and the Country very open and richly cultivated.

Scarborough is a very irregular Sea Port Town. Stands on a Promontory which stretches itself into the Sea. There is a noble Pier to defend the Ships from the Surge of the Sea.[56] They all lay aground at low Water on a hard Sand. There is now a very large Pier building of monstrous Stones where the old one is to be taken down.[57] Scarbro contains about 2000 Houses. The Inhabitants are chiefly supported by the Company which come every Season to drink of the Waters and to bathe for which it is very famous and

[51] On 23 Apr. 1642, several months before the 1st Civil War began, Charles I appeared before Hull with 300 horsemen and demanded admission. Sir John Hotham, the governor, refused to admit the king. Charles wanted to secure Hull as the most convenient landing port for foreign troops to disembark to aid his cause. Hull remained a Parliamentary stronghold throughout the Civil War. Charles Firth, *Oliver Cromwell and the Rule of the Puritans in England* (New York, 1900), pp. 64–65, 68; Peter Gaunt, *The Cromwellian Gazetteer* (Gloucester, 1987), p. 90.

[52] A statue of William III, erected by public subscription in 1734. The statue was by the Flemish sculptor Peter Scheemakers (1691–1781). *VCH: Yorkshire: East Riding*, ed. K. J. Allison (Oxford, 1969), I, p. 408.

[53] John Proud (b. 1746), son of William and Ann Proud of Wood End, Yorkshire. *TRE*.

[54] St. Mary's Church, one of the most beautiful parish churches in England. Its architectural history stretches from the twelfth century to the Reformation. Pevsner, *Buildings of England: York and the East Riding* (London, 1972), pp. 179–183.

[55] John Dickinson (d. 1786) was married to Mary Dickinson, who died in 1781 at the birth of their son. They lived at Beverley. *DQB* under 'Barnard Dickinson.'

[56] The new pier, known as Vincent's pier, was added to the old pier at Scarborough soon after 1732. There are now three piers at Scarborough. Pevsner, *Buildings of England: Yorkshire: the North Riding* (London, 1966), p. 328.

[57] Four acts of parliament were passed for the building of a new pier at Scarborough from 1732 onwards. Some 760 feet of the projected 1,200 feet of the new pier had been built by 1798. Thomas Hinderwell, *The History and Antiquities of Scarborough* (York, 1798), p. 164.

the Spa is a strong chalybeat.[58] Here is a famous Castle or rather Ruins standing on a high Hill which overlooks the whole Town, Harbour and Country round.[59] There are not a great many Vessels owned here.

August 17th 5th Day

Took a Ride with *Thomas* Corbin,[60] Wife and Daughter, *Samuel* Hoare[61] and Daughter, Nathaniel Newberrys Wife and B: Pettigree to Hackness, a little sequestered Vale about 7 Miles distant where we spent the Day.

August 18th 6th Day

After walking to the Spa and eating breakfast I left Scarborough about 10 O Clock and came along a very mountainous country close by the Sea, a Number of Vessels continually in Sight. Moors on the Summitts of the Hills, on the Declivity and in the Vallies rich Cultivations. Dined at Robin Hood Bay, a romantic Situation on the Sea and came into Whitby about 5 P.M.

Whitby is beautifully Situated on the Declivity of Two Hills and intersected by the River.[62] The Harbour is safe and commodious, but the ships all lay aground at low Water. They have some fine dry Docks[63] and the Vessels lay close along Side of the Warehouses. A fine fish Market.

---

[58] The *OED* (II, p. 255) defines 'chalybeate' as 'impregnated or flavoured with iron, especially as a mineral water or Spring; relating to such waters or preparations.' Chalybeate waters were recommended to be drunk at spas for people easily fatigued and suffering from poor health. In the early eighteenth century, Scarborough blossomed as a spa and as a coastal resort with sea-bathing facilities. From 1750 onwards, however, it declined as a spa, partly because improving communications made it easier for northern families to attend the southern resorts. Corner and Booth, *Chain of Friendship*, p. 50; Corfield, *The Impact of English Towns*, pp. 60–61.

[59] Scarborough had a Norman castle whose powerful keep was built between 1158 and 1169. Pevsner, *Buildings of England: Yorkshire: The North Riding*, pp. 324–326; Colvin, *History of the King's Works*, II, pp. 829–832.

[60] Thomas Corbyn (1711–1791) was a Quaker elder and London apothecary. *DQB*; Corner and Booth, *Chain of Friendship*, p. 200; Gummere, *Journal and Essays of John Woolman*, p. 571.

[61] Either Samuel Hoare (1716–1796), born in Cork, Ireland, but a London merchant living at Stoke Newington from 1748, or his son Samuel Hoare (1751–1825), apprenticed with Henry Gurney, banker at Norwich, in 1768 and later a partner with Bland and Barnett, bankers of Lombard Street, London. *DQB*; Raistrick, *Quakers in Science and Industry*, p. 332; F. R. Pryor, ed., *Memoirs of Samuel Hoare by his Daughter Sarah and his Widow Hannah* ... (London, 1911).

[62] River Esk.

[63] In 1734 three spacious dry docks were constructed on the east side of the Esk at Whitby. In 1757 some of the Whitby shipbuilders began to erect docks on the west side of the river. Thomas Allen, *A New and Complete History of the County of York* (3 vols., London, 1831), III, pp. 431–432.

Bridge across the River. Beautiful Prospect up the Stream and a good Prospect of the Fields from the River. Ruins of an Ancient Monastery.[64] Elegant Stone Piers of 200 yards each at the Mouth of the River.[65] Allum Works.[66] Sail Cloth Manufactory.[67]

August 21st   2nd Day

Having been met by *Emanuel Elam*[68] and William *Fisher*[69] at Whitby they prevaild on me to return to Scarborough through Robin Hood Bay. Rainy ride. At Scarborough we stayed till

August 27th   6th Day

Came in a Coach with *Jane Fisher*[70] and *Hannah Harris*[71] to Leeds and called at Castle Howard a fine Seat belonging to the Earl of Carlisle.[72] Nothing can exceed the Beauty and Grandeur of this splendid Building but the richness and Costliness of the Furniture, Tapestry, Marbles, Pictures Antique and modern, the images &c &c. Here is one room not yet finished which will cost £30,000. The Mausoleum a famous Pile of hewn Stone with 20 large Columns merely for depositing the deceased of the Family cost

---

[64] Whitby Abbey, founded by St. Hilda, abbess of Hartlepool, in 657. The monastery was for men and women and was destroyed by the Danes in 867. It was re-established c. 1078 and rebuilt in stages. The surviving ruins belong mainly to the thirteenth century. Pevsner, *Buildings of England: Yorkshire: The North Riding*, pp. 388–392; Alfred Clapham, *Whitby Abbey, Yorkshire* (HMSO, London, 1952), pp. 3–6.

[65] There were piers at Whitby in the time of Henry VIII. They have been regularly enlarged and it is not clear which of the several piers had caught Fisher's eye. Allen, *New and Complete History of the County of York*, III, pp. 434–435.

[66] In the early 1790s, there were three inland alum works at Whitby and six more on the coast, 'which employ a great number of industrious people.' *UBD*, IV, p. 740.

[67] Three sailcloth manufactories opened at Whitby between 1756 and 1759. By 1782, about 5,000 yards of sailcloth were made weekly at Whitby. Rev. George Young, *A History of Whitby* ... (2 vols., London, 1817), II, pp. 557–559.

[68] Emanuel Elam (1729–1796), a merchant in Leeds concerned in American trade with his brother Samuel. He retired from trade with upwards of £100,000. *DQB*; R. G. Wilson, *Gentlemen Merchants: The Merchant Community in Leeds, 1700–1830* (Manchester, 1971), Appendix B, p. 243.

[69] A Leeds merchant. Bailey's *British Directory*, III, p. 561.

[70] Jane Hustler of Bradford married William Fisher of Leeds in 1772. Hodgson, *Society of Friends in Bradford*, p. 114.

[71] Hannah Harris (1707–1784) was the wife of a shoemaker in Maryport, Cumberland. She had travelled in the Quaker ministry to Ireland and America. *DQB*.

[72] Castle Howard was designed by Vanbrugh in 1699 and executed with the help of Nicholas Hawksmoor. Frederick Howard (1748–1825) was the 8th Earl of Carlisle. Pevsner, *Buildings of England: Yorkshire: The North Riding*, pp. 106–118; Cokayne, *Complete Peerage*, III, pp. 36–37.

£30,000.[73] Here is a fine Lake Bridge Over it, Woods, Parks &c &c. Likewise a capital Inn near 300 feet front. We came to this Place through Malton, a pretty Town. Has an Inn which was formerly a Gentlemans Seat, vastly grand and commodious.[74]

We got to York this Evening and spent the next Morning in viewing the Town, Bridge, River, Cathedral, one of the finest Gothics in the World,[75] Monuments, Glass painted ancient and modern, fine Prison like a Palace,[76] a most elegant Court House,[77] a beautiful Walk along the River, ancient Castle in Ruins,[78] Walls all round the Town thick enough to ride or walk on.[79] The Gates are very grand, built of Brick. From York to Leeds where we arrived Tadcaster Inn. Fine.

August 28th   7th Day

Leeds is beautifully situated on the Aire which intersects it in the middle. The communication is by a fine Stone Bridge. Here are a great Number of Manufactures carried on here and a pretty fall of Water which affords Conveniences for 12 Mills, Fulling Mills, Grist Mills, Grinding Mills, Frize and Oil. Here is the greatest Cloth Market in England. Mixt Cloth Hall.[80] White Ditto[81] and one famous new building, a beautiful

[73] The Mausoleum at Castle Howard was designed by Hawksmoor in 1728–1729, begun in 1731, and finished in 1742 after his death. It was 'enormous in size and extremely noble in design.' Pevsner, *Buildings of England: Yorkshire: The North Riding*, pp. 117–118.

[74] The Talbot Hotel, formerly owned by the Strickland family. The Strickland mansion and estate was sold in 1739 to Lord Malton. The mansion is now the New Talbot Inn, alias the Talbot Hotel in Yorkgate. Pevsner, *Buildings of England: Yorkshire: The North Riding*, p. 236; N. A. Hudleston, *History of Malton and Norton* (Scarborough, 1962), p. 142.

[75] York Minster was originally founded on a Roman site by Edwin, King of Northumbria, in 627, but the present building consists of Norman and Gothic architecture from the period 1230–1475. Pevsner, *Buildings of England: Yorkshire: York and the East Riding*, pp. 75–112.

[76] The debtors' prison, erected in 1705; architect unknown but probably William Wakefield. *Ibid.*, p. 131.

[77] The Assize Courts at York, built between 1773 and 1777. *Ibid.*

[78] William the Conqueror built two castles at York. This refers to the second, whose remains still stand. *Ibid.*, p. 130; Colvin, *History of the King's Works*, II, pp. 889–894.

[79] There were walls at York during the Roman period when York (Eburacum) was the centre of a large legionary fortress. The walls at York span building carried out in the Roman, Saxon and medieval periods. Today they are the most complete historic walls of any city in England. *An Inventory of the Historical Monuments in the City of York, vol. 2: The Defences* (London, 1972), pp. 4, 7.

[80] This was built in 1755. The mixed cloths, in which the wool had been dyed before it was spun, were manufactured partly in the parish of Leeds but chiefly in the villages to the west of Leeds in the Aire Valley. Wilson, *Gentlemen Merchants*, pp. 54, 74.

[81] The White Cloth Hall was built in 1775. The manufacture of white (or undyed) cloths was concentrated in the Calder Valley. Though Wakefield was the focal point of the area, Leeds was the principal market for these cloths. The White Cloth Hall and the Mixed Cloth Hall were the two largest cloth halls in eighteenth-century Yorkshire. *Ibid.*, pp. 54–55, 74; Pevsner, *Buildings of England: Yorkshire: The West Riding* (2nd edn., London, 1979), p. 321.

infirmary.[82] The Streets are tolerably regular and paved middlingly. Fine Situations all round the Town. Took a Ride to Bradford a pretty Market Town for Stuffs &c. Spent a day with John Hursler.[83] He not at home. Took a walk with some young Folks to an hamlet about 3 Miles where stand the Remains of a fine Monastery covered over with Ivy, terraces &c &c.[84]

Took a ride to see R*obert* Walker[85] at Gildersome Meeting. On Return called at Fulnick a Beautiful Moravian Settlement in one of the finest Situations in the World: large Buildings, hanging Gardens, Burial Ground &c &c.[86] Jeremiah Clifford called on by D*aniel* Maud[87] of Wakefield. Went down with him in a Post Chaise.

Wakefield is a beautiful Town wide commodious Streets, elegantly paved, good houses and in a thriving Situation. It is situated on a hill in the midst of other Hills. Went out with E*manuel* E*lam* and W*illiam* F*isher* a coursing. Started but caught only one Hare. A Mile or two from Wakefield stands Heath the most beautiful Village in England. Several fine Seats and Ruins commanding a grand and rich Prospect. Took a Ride to Alverthorp, the Seat formerly of John Maud now of Sir William Lowther.[88] Went again to Wakefield and Heath. Left Leeds.

[82] The General Infirmary at Leeds, erected by public subscription, was built between 1768 and 1771. *A History of the Town and Parish of Leeds* ... (Leeds, 1797), pp. 24–25.

[83] John Hustler (1715–1790), variously described as a merchant, woolstapler, and woolcomber and sorter. He built Undercliffe House after buying an estate of 90 acres at Undercliffe, near Bradford. Hodgson, *Society of Friends in Bradford*, pp. 38–40; Raistrick, *Quakers in Science and Industry*, pp. 78–80.

[84] Probably Kirkstall Abbey: see below, p. 206 n. 17.

[85] Robert Walker (1716/7–1785), a clothier by trade who lived at Gildersome, near Leeds. He appeared in the Quaker ministry c. 1751 and became an eminent preacher. He made a religious visit to the Continental Congress in Philadelphia in 1775. His attempt to conciliate the delegates there failed because he was accused of being a British spy who had cunningly assumed the character of a Quaker preacher. *DQB*; Frost, *Records and Recollections of James Jenkins*, pp. 321–323; John M. Moore, 'An English Quaker Minister's Visit to Colonial America, 1773–1775', *Quaker History*, LXXVIII (1989), pp. 103–113.

[86] Fulnick, a village six miles east of Bradford, was entirely inhabited by Moravians until at least the early nineteenth century. There were two Moravian institutions there, one for men and one for women. Thomas Potts, *Gazetteer of England and Wales* ... (London, 1810), n. p.

[87] Daniel and Francis Maude, merchants, Wakefield. Bailey's *British Directory*, III, p. 728.

[88] Thomas Maude, the son of John Maude, sold all his inherited property, including Alverthorp Hall, near Wakefield, to his cousin the Rev. William Lowther in 1754. Sir William Lowther (1757–1844) was M.P. for Carlisle (1780), for Cumberland (1784), and for Rutland (1796). Joseph Foster, *Pedigrees of the County Families of Yorkshire* (4 vols., London, 1874), I and II, n.p.

September 7th   5th Day

At One O Clock in Company with S*amuel* Elam[89] I left Leeds, called on George Oates[90] at Chapel Town, a beautiful Village about 2 Miles from Leeds. Thence a fine rich Country to Harewood, an elegant Village in the neighbourhood of which stands Gawthorp a noble Seat belonging Ed*mund* Lascelles Esquire,[91] commanding a delightful View of the Country round about it; and at some Distance stand the Ruins of an ancient Castle.[92] Thence to Harrowgate where we drank Tea, a Place famous for Mineral Waters and where People of Quality resort in the Summer Months.[93] Here are one or two good Inns. But at upper Harrowgate are the most Capital where the better Sort station themselves. These places are Situate in Knareborough Forrest. A flat barren Country and nothing remarkable in View.

From Harrogate tis 5 Miles to Knaresborough, an indifferent built Town, though it be beautifuly situate on the River Nid[94] which forming a Curve surrounds it on almost every Side. On this River are a number of good Mills and some fine Cascades at the Dams. The River is prettily shaded with fine Trees on each Side, which thickly imbower it, and give it an elegant and pleasing Grace. On the side thereof under a perpendicular Rock stands a Number of Houses inhabited by the poor people. Here also is a Cave called St. Roberts Cave and about a Mile up the River stands

---

[89] Samuel Elam (d. 1797) was the brother of Emanuel Elam (see above, p. 41 n. 68). They were merchants in Leeds. Samuel Elam was apparently the most active American merchant in Leeds before 1776. Wilson, *Gentlemen Merchants*, Appendix B, p. 243; Herbert Heaton, 'Yorkshire Cloth Traders in the United States, 1770–1840,' *The Thoresby Miscellany*, vol. 2 (Publications of the Thoresby Society, XXXVII, Leeds, 1945), p. 240.

[90] George Oates & Sons, merchants and woolstaplers, Leeds. Bailey's *British Directory*, III, p. 563.

[91] *UBD*, III, p. 541 states that Mr. Lascelles was the former owner of Gawthorp Hall, about eight miles from Leeds. Edwin Lascelles (1712/3–1795) was M.P. for Scarborough (1744–1754), for Northallerton (1754–1761 and 1780–1790) and for Yorkshire (1761–1780). He was created 1st Baron Harewood in 1790 and his seat was Harewood House. Cokayne, *Complete Peerage*, VI, pp. 310–311; Namier and Brooke, *History of Parliament: The House of Commons 1754–1790*, III, pp. 22–23.

[92] Harewood Castle, on the site of Harewood House, was an oblong structure built in the twelfth century. In the Middle Ages Harewood was a flourishing market village protected by its castle, but by the sixteenth century it had decayed. Pevsner, *Buildings of England: Yorkshire: The West Riding*, pp. 244–245; David Hey, *Yorkshire from AD 1000* (London, 1986), p. 205.

[93] The chalybeate spring of the old spa in High Harrogate was discovered in 1571. The existence of mineral waters made Harrogate a fashionable resort from May to October each year. Lewis, *Topographical Dictionary of England*, II, p. 327.

[94] River Nidd.

St. Roberts Chapel,[95] a curious Gothic Room, carved out of a Solid Rock, an Altar, Images to represent the Trinity, and a Curious Image of Stone Guarding the Door from impetuous Robbers. Near this Place is a curious petrifying Spring which falls from a Rock about 15 feet high. Here is a curious collection of those things for Sale.

September 8th   6th Day

About 6 O Clock left Knaresborough came through the Forrest and some tolerable good Improvements to Ripley a small Market Town and from thence to Rippon a neat Spot a large Square in the middle with a high curious Cross.[96] This one of the largest Squares in England. Here is a noble Minstrel of the Gothic Structure.[97] Passed by Sir Slingsby's about 2 Miles from Knaresbrough, an elegant Seat.[98]

After breakfast at Rippon, we came to Studley, a grand Seat belonging to Aylesby Esquire, Member for Rippon.[99] The Cascades, natural and artificial, Canals, Lakes, Walks, Views, Groves, Shrubberies, Obelisks, temples, Rotundos, Images, Urns, Seats, Towers, Fields, Gardens, hedges, Lawns, Fields, Hills, Vallies, Rocks, Mountains, Islands, Avenues and Banqueting house which take up the Pleasure Grounds, are more astonishingly beautifull. The variety of Trees of various sorts and the grandeur of the whole is past all possible Description. Art and Nature have combined to make it an entire Elysium. The former has brought the latter out of Chaos and has given Mechanism to the whole Scene. There are also

[95] St. Robert's Chapel is a monument cut out of solid rock on the River Nidd near Knaresborough. Above it is a hermitage. St. Robert, the reputed founder of this chapel, was an anchorite of the thirteenth century. He is said to have performed many miracles. About a mile further down the river is St. Robert's Cave, another excavation in the rock, which is supposed to have been the same holy man's usual residence. Gorton, *Topographical Dictionary of Great Britain and Ireland*, II, p. 495.

[96] An obelisk, ninety feet high, erected in the centre of the market place at Ripon by John Aislabie, M.P. for Ripon and Chancellor of the Exchequer under George I. *Ibid.*, III, p. 271.

[97] Ripon Cathedral. The present structure began to be constructed in the late twelfth and early thirteenth centuries. It is a Gothic cathedral of fairly small size, being only 270 feet long. Pevsner, *Buildings of England: Yorkshire: The West Riding*, pp. 403–411.

[98] Sir Thomas-Turner Slingsby (d. 1806) of Scriven Park, near Knaresborough. Burke's *Peerage and Baronetage* (London, 1845), p. 911.

[99] Studley Royal, four miles from Ripon, was the seat of William Aislabie (?1699–1781). He controlled both parliamentary seats at Ripon and always returned a relation for the second seat. He was M.P. for Ripon from 1721 until his death. *UBD*, IV, pp. 316–317; Namier and Brooke, *History of Parliament: The House of Commons 1754–1790*, *II*, p. 14.

the Ruins of Fountains Abbey, the venerable appearance whereof beggars Description.[100]

We dined at Studley and came along a disagreeable romantic Ride to Hackfall, having missed our Way several times. This is one of the most beautiful and romantic Spots in Nature. Art has had little Care in bringing it into an Order. It is wild rurality. The Lusi Naturae sport here in the most luxuriant Stile. Here are ab origine Woods rude as the Land of Savages and except a number of delightful Walks through these umbrageous Groves one would imagine the Vestiges of Man had made no Traces. Here are a Tent, a Cave in the Grotto Order,[101] Several Seats, Ruins or rather imitations of Ruins.[102] Fisher's Hall, a curious Gothic Octagon house composed all within and without of Petrifications of Moss Leaves &c &c.[103] This stands directly in View of the River and several natural Cascades. No Spot can be more calculated to give delight. The Buildings, Ruins &c &c are all seen from each other, the Avenues through the Woods having been cut purposely. And at each of the Summer houses we have a view of one two three and sometimes more falls of Water.

The Bed of the River lays high and is constantly supplyd with a great Plenty of Water. It is here all in one Stream, but dividing itself into a variety of rills it runs rapidly down, sometimes a Perpendicular Fall of one, sometimes two, ten and sometimes 20 feet. Thus descending it forms a thousand different Cascades and at length again unites into one Stream, where runs foaming over the Rocks, 140 yards below the first height, astonishing the Imagination and filling the Spectator with wonder and admiration. Then we came to Masham where we lodged and

September 9th   7th Day

Breakfasted at Thirsk a little Market Town. Dined at North Allerton the great Thoroughfare from London to Edinburgh. It consists chiefly of one

---

[100] Fountains Abbey was founded by Cistercian monks. The earlier parts of the church date from 1135–1147 and from the 1170s. The dissolution took place in 1539. The setting of the abbey was landscaped after 1768 when it was incorporated into the grounds of Studley Royal House. Pevsner, *Buildings of England: Yorkshire: The West Riding*, pp. 203–213.

[101] Only the ruins of this grotto now survive. It was probably a garden seat rather than a grotto with waterworks. Edward S. Harwood, 'William Aislabie's Garden at Hackfall,' *Journal of Garden History*, VII (1987), pp. 342–343.

[102] The Ruin was a large folly with a tripartite entrance façade and three interior rooms. It was basically organised along Palladian lines and was probably completed in 1766. *Ibid.*, pp. 358, 395. Photographs of the ruin can be found on pp. 312, 359 and 362 of this article.

[103] Fisher's Hall is a gothic octagon named after William Fisher, the Aislabie's gardener until his death in 1743. It is a small, thatched structure, a mid-eighteenth century rustic-style hut. It was erected in 1750 and bears the initials 'W. A.' over the door. *Ibid.*, pp. 325, 334. Photographs of Fisher's Hall can be found on pp. 328, 329, 335, 337–339 of this article.

Street. Rode through a fine Country and got to Darlington in the Evening. Darlington is a neat, well built town. A number of good Streets. Lies on the River Skirn.[104] It has a large Square and a Market. Contains about 900 Houses.

September 11th 2nd Day

We went with James Backhouse junior[105] in Post Chaise to Stockton a neat clean Town containing about 800 houses, situate on the River Tees, navigable for small Sea Vessels up to the Town, but a Mile below is the chief Port. It has one noble Street running through it, perhaps much the widest of any in England, being 175 feet and strait from the Town Hall we see the Vessels in the Sea and the Country all round is a perfect Garden crowned with Hills of Yorkshire. Here is a manufactury of Sail Cloth. We returned to Darlington the same Evening. Huccabae and Camblets.

September 12th 3rd Day

Went to Meeting and in the afternoon took a Walk with B*etsey* and S*arah* Corbyn[106] to the Land of Promise and H*annah* Appleby.[107]

September 13th 4th Day

After Breakfast left Darlington and rode through a most delightful Country to Bishop Aukland, an illy built market town near which stands the Seat of the Bishop of Durham Castle.[108] The Park is extremely pleasant, the Situation fine and several Streams of Water run through it. The Deer house is very commodious. The gardens are not very extraordinary. His Chapel is small but extremely superb fine Tapestry and here is one most beautiful piece of Statuary of white Marble. Here are pictures in the Hall of all the Archbishops of Canterbury since the

---

[104] River Skerne.

[105] James Backhouse, Jr. (1757–1804), a Quaker born at Darlington. He was a flax dresser and linen manufacturer. In 1774, in conjunction with two of his sons, he established a bank at Darlington. For a long period he was the clerk to the Durham Quarterly Meeting and also for a time to the Stockton Monthly Meeting. He married in 1787. In later life he was active in the Quaker ministry. *DQB*; M. W. Kirby, *Men of Business and Politics: The Rise and Fall of the Quaker Pease Dynasty of North-East England, 1700–1943* (London, 1984), p. 3.

[106] Sarah Corbyn (1754–1819qv) and Elizabeth Corbyn (b. 1752/3) were the two daughters of Thomas Corbyn (see above, p. 40 n. 60). *DQB*.

[107] Hannah Appleby (d. 1818 aged c. 83) lived in Durham and was a member of Newcastle MM. FLL, Durham QM: Burials.

[108] The bishops of Durham have had a residence at Bishop Auckland since the twelfth century. The Bishop's Palace consists mainly of medieval buildings, though with seventeenth and eighteenth century additions. Pevsner, *Buildings of England: County Durham* (rev. edn., London, 1983), pp. 101–106.

Reformation. There is nothing peculiarly grand about his dwelling house. The Dining Room is adorned with the Pictures of Jacob and the 12 Patriarchs[109] and there are some other Rooms containing a variety of Historical Prints.

We dined at the Village and in the afternoon came to Durham. The rain all the way made our ride very disagreeable. We passed by a grand Seat within 4 miles of the Town.[110]

September 14th   5th Day

Breakfasted with John Starforth[111] and afterwards went with John Dodgson[112] and William Paxton[113] to view the Castle Abbey &c which stand on an Eminence and overlook the whole City. The Abbey is a grand Pile of Building chiefly of the Saxon Structure but the Altar and its appendages are Gothic.[114] The Organ is fine and the Bishops Seat is very rich. Here is a neat piece of Tapestry. The Library is large and curious. Here are remains of a large Collection of Statues &c with Roman inscriptions,[115] a number of curious Petrifications and here is a collection of

[109] A series of Jacob and the Patriarchs, painted by Zurbaran, was bought by Bishop Trevor in 1756 to adorn the Bishop's Palace. *Ibid.*, p. 106.

[110] There are a number of seats within a five mile radius of Durham, so it is not clear which one Fisher is referring to. But *UBD*, II, pp. 877–879, allots most space to Cocker Hall, the mansion of William Henry Lambton, M.P. for Durham.

[111] A partner in John & Gilbert Starforth, stuff and carpet manufacturers of Durham. They were substantial cloth manufacturers making 'all kinds of callimancoes, shalloons, wildbores, durants, tammies, plain and figured stuffs, German and common serges, plain Jerseys, strong kerseys, flannels' as well as 'carpets, which are now brought to a very great degree of perfection.' *UBD*, II, pp. 868, 875.

[112] Probably either John Dodshon (d. 1788 aged c. 74) or his namesake (d. 1794 aged c. 71). Both lived at Bishop Auckland and both were members of Darlington MM. FLL, Durham QM: Burials.

[113] William Paxton (b. 1750) was a member of Newcastle MM. FLL, Durham QM: Births.

[114] The site of Durham Abbey has been continuously occupied by a church since 995 but the cathedral church which stands today was begun in 1093. It took forty years to construct the main fabric of this Romanesque cathedral. The Nine Altars, behind the High Altar, were put up in the thirteenth century. *VCH: Durham*, III, ed. William Page (London, 1928), pp. 93–101; Pevsner, *Buildings of England: County Durham*, p. 189.

[115] The Durham Dean and Chapter collection of Roman inscribed stones is particularly from Lanchester in County Durham (collected by Christopher Hunter, 1675–1757) and from the Roman Wall area (collected by John Warburton, 1682–1759). The stones have now been moved to the Archaeology Museum, the Fulling Mill, the Cathedral Banks, Durham. F. J. Haverfield and W. Greenwell, *A Catalogue of the Sculptured and Inscribed Stones in the Cathedral Library, Durham* (Durham, 1899), pp. 1–40. I must thank Mr Roger Norris, Deputy Chapter Librarian, The Dean and Chapter Library, The College, Durham, for help with this note.

Pictures of the Apostles which were brought from Vigo, when that place was besieged.[116]

The livings annexed to the Abbey amount to £50,000. The Bishop has £15,000 per Annum. The Tower of this Church is large and commands a fine View of the City and the Country round. The Situation of this Place is vastly romantic. The chief Part of the Town is on a Peninsula, so that it is surrounded by water and the Hill on the Declivity of which it stands is high. The Streets are very narrow, dirty and irregular, the houses are low mean and old but the Situation fully compensates for these Disadvantages. The Walks about it are fine, the Prospect is exceeding Romantic and the Bridges are very curious having the largest Arches in England, about 70 feet horrizontal Distance between the Piers and each Bridge consists of 3 Arches. Here is a considerable Manufactury of Camblets, the Proprietor of which employs between 6 and 700 People.[117]

Accompanied by *John* Dodgshon and William Paxton about half way to Sunderland, we bid them Adieu and meeting with John and William Chapman[118] we went to their House and lodged and

September 15th   6th Day

Came to town. Sunderland is situated upon the Tees near the Mouth. Two large Stone Piers project into the Sea. The Tees intersects the town, taking about $\frac{1}{4}$ on the North Side. It is very considerable Sea Port. 300 Vessels belong to the Port and there are seldom less than 100 in. The Town is populous and contains about 1600 houses. Here is a manufactury of Sail Cloth and a Glass house, a Salt Manufactury.[119]

We crossed the Ferry and got into Shields about Dusk. North Shields is the first Entrance into Northumberland. The County of Durham is in general rich and highly cultivated, a Succession of Hills and Vallies but no mountains, a great number of Country Seats, Villages and fine Views.

---

[116] This seems like a small error: Fisher is probably referring to the paintings identified on p. 48 n. 109.

[117] Probably the business run by the Starforths: see pp. 48, n. 111, 299, n. 29.

[118] John & William Chapman, merchants and sailcloth manufacturers of Whitby. Bailey's *British Directory*, III, p. 729.

[119] Sailcloth was an important manufacture at Sunderland and Tyneside was one of the greatest centres of the British salt industry in the eighteenth century. In 1772 there were three green bottle-houses and one flint-glass house in Sunderland. A large manufacturing business in glass was carried on at Sunderland by the nineteenth century. Taylor Potts, *Sunderland: A History of the Town, Port, Trade and Commerce* (Sunderland, 1892), pp. 160–161, 172; Joyce Ellis, 'The Decline and Fall of The Tyneside Salt Industry, 1660–1790: A Re-Examination,' *Economic History Review*, 2nd Series, XXXIII (1980), pp. 45–58; *VCH: Durham*, Vol. 2, ed. William Page (London, 1907), p. 311.

Early this Morning we took a Walk to Tinemouth[120] a neat Village about 1 Mile Distant from the Town and the Castle which stands on a Point of Land commanding the mouth of the River. The Castle is now in Ruins[121] and also the monastery within the Walls which is very venerable.[122] We took a Walk after Breakfast through the Town. Shields is situated on the River Tyne near the Mouth and divided into North and South. North is much the largest. It is a very considerable Sea Port. 4 or 500 Vessels are sometimes in Port. Here it is that the Colliers load.[123] The Town is situate under a Hill. The Streets are narrow, dirty and inconvenient but there is a part of the Town on the Hill which is neat and well built. The Chief manufactury carried on here is the Ropery.[124]

September 17th   7th Day

Left Shields about 5 in the Evening and got to New Castle about 7 in the Evening. Found the Streets amazingly full of People.

There cleared out in one year from New Castle

3,585 Ships   689,000 Tons
350,000 Chaldrons of Coals
124 M.C. Lead
   for Coasters
363 Ships   49000 Tons
22 M Chaldrons Coals
30 M Lead
   Grindstones, Copper
     Foreign Exports

The Vessels chiefly load at Shields, though there is a great Number laying a breast of the Long Key, a fine Bridge over the River to the South Part of the Town. The Tyne intersects Newcastle. About $\frac{1}{4}$ lies on the South Side. The Town is irregular and in general illy built. Here is a neat infirmary of

---

[120] Tynemouth.

[121] A reference to the Gatehouse, the main defensive work of Tynemouth, built in the late fourteenth and early fifteenth centuries. Pevsner, *Buildings of England: Northumberland* (London, 1957), p. 301.

[122] A monastery seems to have existed on the promontory north of the Tyne as early as the seventh century. It was ravaged by the Danes in the ninth century and refounded as a Benedictine priory by Robert de Mowbray, Earl of Northumberland, c. 1090. *Ibid.*, pp. 300–301.

[123] Sea-going colliers loaded at North and South Shields because they were too large and unwieldy to penetrate far up the River Tyne to load directly near the coalfields. The Newcastle keels, or river vessels, were used instead. Flinn, *British Coal Industry: The Industrial Revolution*, pp. 19, 166.

[124] There was a considerable trade in ropes and sailcloth in County Durham until the early nineteenth century. *VCH: Durham*, Vol. 2, ed. William Page (London, 1907), p. 319.

hewn Stone,[125] on a fine Situation, one [of] the lightest and neatest Steeples in England,[126] a Castle built by William Rufus,[127] 6 Churches and many dissenters' Meeting houses.[128] Not above $\frac{1}{3}$ of the People are Episcopalians. There are about 40 Families of Friends and it is supposed there are 50,000 People in the Place. The Principal Manufactury here is Glass in all its various Branches.[129] Grindstones are made in the Neighbourhood. There is a considerable Iron Work near the Town[130] and a Lead mine not very distant.[131] The Key is very fine extending for $\frac{1}{2}$ a Mile along the water Side. Some few Vessels are built here.

The Country round about is vastly fine. A great Number of delightful Situations in the Neighbourhood and several elegant Seats.

September 19th

Took a Ride about 20 Miles round and called to see Gibside, a Seat belonging to Lord Strathmore, one of the Peers.[132] Here is a fine Collection of Capital Prints and Drawings. The Situation of this Place is uncommonly grand. The Prospects are extensive and rich. The house itself is old, elegant but not costly. But the pleasure Grounds are vastly fine. The Banqueting

[125] The Newcastle infirmary was erected in 1752. Lewis, *Topographical Dictionary of England*, III, p. 359.

[126] St. Nicholas Church was originally built in the fourteenth and fifteenth centuries. The height of its steeple is $193\frac{1}{2}$ feet. Pevsner, *Buildings of England: Northumberland*, pp. 224–228.

[127] This was originally a Norman castle built by Robert, son of William the Conqueror, in 1080. William Rufus took it by force in 1095 from Robert Mowbray, Earl of Northumberland. Colvin, *History of the King's Works, II: The Middle Ages*, pp. 745–748.

[128] Religious dissent was a thriving concern in Newcastle where, by the early nineteenth century, there were meeting houses for Unitarians, Methodists, Quakers, Presbyterians, Calvinist Baptists, Glassites and various independent congregations. *The Picture of Newcastle upon Tyne: Containing a Guide to the Town & Neighbourhood, An Account of the Roman Wall, and a Description of the Coal Mines* (Newcastle, 1807), pp. 36–38.

[129] There were extensive glassworks in and around Newcastle-upon-Tyne. In 1772 sixteen large glassworks were fully employed on the River Tyne, including one for plate glass, three crown glass houses, five for broad or common window glass, two for white or flint glass, and five bottle houses. *Ibid.*, pp. 105–106.

[130] This refers to the ironworks at Swalwill and Winlaton, two adjoining villages on the River Derwent, about three miles from Newcastle. These large ironworks — the largest in the Newcastle area before 1800 — were first begun by Ambrose Crowley in 1690. *Ibid.*, p. 97; M. W. Flinn, *Men of Iron: The Crowleys in the Early Iron Industry* (Edinburgh, 1962).

[131] There are various lead mines to the west of Newcastle, around Hexham. The ore was generally smelted near the mines and then conveyed to the River Tyne in pigs or bars. *Ibid.*, p. 101.

[132] The 7th Earl of Strathmore, John Lyon Bowes (1737–1776), acquired the Gibside estate, county Durham, in 1767 when he married Eleanor, daughter and heir of George Bowes, of Streatham Castle and Gibside. Cokayne, *Complete Peerage*, IX, pp. 532–533; Pevsner, *Buildings of England: County Durham*, pp. 292–295.

house and the beautiful ascent to it, the noble Terraces, the wild woods, the Images, the Bath are all very pleasing, and a noble Obelisk dedicated to the Goddess of Liberty with a splendid Figure on the Top richly gilt.

In the Evening took a Walk to Elswich and drank tea with the Girls at a Tea house. It is here that John Hodson lives who has an Estate of about 2500 per Annum.[133]

September 20th

Rose early this Morning and took a ride with R*obert* Ormston[134] to a Village about 6 Miles distant and breakfasted with Lamb[135] and his wife Sally Vaux, a Daughter of Warren Maud.[136] Thence to a fine Seat and Park belonging to Sir Thomas Avery. Here is a truly elegant building. The outside is plain and neat but the Rooms are rich and costly. A grand Collection of Prints and some original Paintings. The ride exhibits a constant Succession of fine Prospects. Dined with M Heaction.

September 22nd   6th Day

Accompanied by R*obert Ormston* we left Newcastle about 10 O Clock and called to see Hartley Pans a place cut of the Rocks for Shipping to come directly in from the Sea.[137] Here several vessels load at a time and the Carts of Coal coming immediately over the Vessel it is launched into the hold. By this means a Vessel may be loaded in a few hours. The Situation is exceedingly romantic, there being Steps down the Rocks quite down to the Sea where there is a Bath. Here are a number of Collieries in sight and a salt manufactury.[138]

We next came to Sir John Delavals Seat called Seaton Delaval.[139] The Situation is good. The house is elegant and the Stables, Riding Rooms, Groves, Images &c are genteel and fine. We dined at South Blyth, a neat

---

[133] Elswick House, about two miles west of Newcastle, was the seat of J. Hodgson Esq. *The Picture of Newcastle upon Tyne*, p. 73.

[134] Robert Ormston (1749–1836), a Quaker from Newcastle-upon-Tyne. *JFHS*, IX (1912), p. 124.

[135] Probably a partner in Ormston & Lamb: see below, p. 303.

[136] Warren Maud (d. 1779 aged c. 79) was a member of Newcastle MM. FLL, Durham QM: Burials.

[137] Hartley Pans is on the coast, a few miles north of Newcastle-upon-Tyne. During the second half of the eighteenth century, the owner of the Hartley colliery was Sir John Hussey Delaval. Flinn, *British Coal Industry: The Industrial Revolution*, p. 61.

[138] The salt works was owned by Lord Delaval. *UBD*, III, p. 134.

[139] Sir John Delaval (1728–1808), created baronet in 1761, succeeded to the family estates at Seaton Delaval, Northumberland in 1771. He was Tory M.P. for Berwick, 1765–1774 and 1780–1786. Seaton Delaval Hall was a sombre house of dark stone and Palladian design built by Vanbrugh in 1728–1729 for Admiral George Delaval. Cokayne, *Complete Peerage*, IV, pp. 138–139; Pevsner, *Buildings of England: Northumberland*, pp. 286–289.

Town on the Sea Side. 20 Vessels in Port loading with Coals, the Carriers for which are great being launched from above by a trough into the hold. From Blide we came along the Sea Coast on the beach and came into Warkworth, a small market town in which Stands the Castle, a noble and grand pile of building but now in Ruins belonging to the Earl of Northumberland.[140] Many of the appartments are elegant and a little Expence would make it quite habitable.

On the same Estate $\frac{1}{2}$ a mile up a beautiful River (Coquet) stands a most famous Pilgrimage.[141] The Situation is delightful being under a steep Hill of Rocks and having several apartments curiously cut out of the Rocks, Gothic Arches and Images. It has been described by Dr Percy in a poem called the Hermit of Warkworth.[142] It stands in Ruins. There is a Walk on the Top of the Hill which we ascend by steps in the Rock and below the Walk on a Terrace on the Grass under the fine Rocks and Trees is particularly fine. We lodged at Warkworth.

September 23rd   7th Day

Left Warkworth at 8 O Clock and came on to Alnwick, a neat small well built Market situate on the River Aln. Here is a neat Market built by the Duke of Northumberland[143] and near it a neat stone fountain, the water running out of a Lion's Mouth. On the North Side of the Town stand Alnwick Castle, a large fine Stone Building, the Mansion of the Duke.[144] We enter it through several Walls and large Gates. On the Top and all round it are a great Number of Stone Images, Goths, Vandals, Saxons, Picts, Russians, ancient Britons standing in various attitudes with Arms in their hands. The Entrance is through a hall where there is a beautiful Stone Stair Case with Iron Bannisters. The first Room we entered was a fine

[140] Warkworth Castle was built between the twelfth and fourteenth centuries. Hugh Smithson, afterwards Percy (1714/5–1786), 18th Earl of Northumberland from 1750, was created Earl Percy and 3rd Duke of Northumberland in 1766. Cokayne, *Complete Peerage*, IX, pp. 743–744; Pevsner, *Buildings of England: Northumberland*, pp. 313–318.

[141] A reference to a cave, called the Hermitage, cut into solid rock, about a mile from Warkworth, Northumberland. It included a chapel with an altar. It dates from the fourteenth century. Pevsner, *Buildings of England: Northumberland*, p. 318; *UBD*, V, pp. 236–237.

[142] Dr. Thomas Percy (1729–1811) was an antiquarian vicar who was interested in various literary undertakings, including the collection of old ballads. His ballad 'The Hermit of Warkworth' was published in 1771. *DNB*, XV, pp. 882–884.

[143] The 1st Duke of Northumberland was a notable 'improver' who rebuilt Alnwick Castle and the estate farms. He replaced a medieval bridge over the Aln in 1773 with the Lion Bridge, designed by John Adam, and also carried out other improvements in Alnwick. Edward Grierson, *The Companion Guide to Northumbria* (London, 1976), p. 157.

[144] This was originally a Norman motte-and-bailey castle with wooden buildings. Much of the present character of the castle is the result of building carried out between 1309 and 1352. Pevsner, *Buildings of England: Northumberland*, pp. 68–71.

Library, the Room long with several Carpets, the Ceiling superb, the Shelves rich, and a grand Collection of Books. We next go to the Chapel which is indeed splendid. The Breakfast Room contains much rich furniture. The dining Room has a Picture of My Lady Dutchess, the Drawing Room a looking Glass which cost £1000. The hall of this Castle is 1300 years old but is in good Repair. The Structure is a mixture of the Gothic and Saxon and the new Part is in imitation of the old.

September 23rd 1775

From Northumberland Castle we crossed over a little Bridge which has a happy effect from the Castle. Passed by a Cross which was erected for Malcom 3rd of Scotland who was killd there.[1] Dind at Belford a little market Town. Passed by an elegant Seat of Sir Thomas Aygerstons and crossed Berwick Bridge built by Queen Elizabeth containing 16 Arches[2] and arrived at Berwick about 8 O Clock.

September 24th   1st Day

Walked round the Walls of Berwick, which are 60 feet thick, a large Top thrown out, and all the Ground is Cannon Proof. There are a number of Battlements planted here and the Fortification is very strong. The Walls are a Mile round.[3] The City contains about 1200 houses indifferently built. We have a pretty view up the Banks of the Tweed and of the Sea. Here is a tolerable Pier at which Vessels load. The Town Hall is a very neat and elegant Building of hewn Stone.[4]

Breakfasted at Berwick and rode along a dreary Barren Continuation of Moors for 20 Miles with scarce a Cottage rising to the View. We met (half way) a curious Field Preacher whose Congregation was large. We came into Dunbar in the Evening. The Pier here is a nice piece of work. The vessels come in at a very small Passage but the Bason could contain a vast many. The Walls built to defend them from the Sea are 40 feet high.[5]

---

[1] Malcolm's Cross, near Alnwick Castle, where Malcolm Canmore, King of Scotland (1057–1093), was killed along with his eldest son after invading England in protest against William the Conqueror's attempt to make him a vassal. Leslie Godfrey, *Ward Lock Red Guide: Northumbria* (London, 1969), pp. 73–74, 76.

[2] Berwick Bridge has, in fact, fifteen arches. It connects the town of Berwick, on the northern bank of the River Tweed, with Tweedmouth, on the southern bank. The bridge was built in the reigns of James I and Charles I. Lewis, *Topographical Dictionary of Scotland*, I, p. 131.

[3] The stone walls at Berwick-upon-Tweed were originally built at the end of the thirteenth century, but those that now exist date from Elizabeth I's reign. Cassell's *Encyclopaedia*, II, p. 47.

[4] The town hall at Berwick was completed in 1760. *Ibid.*

[5] Dunbar was a heavily fortified town in the Middle Ages, when it was exposed to frequent attacks from the English. Its eastern pier was built or repaired at the time of Cromwell. Lewis, *Topographical Dictionary of Scotland*, I, pp. 322–323.

One side of the Pier is the Work of Art entirely, the other chiefly of Nature. The Stone running in the Columns almost perpendicular makes the appearance very curious. Near the Pier stand the Ruins of an ancient and strong Castle destroyed by Oliver Cromwell.[6] Here is a pierced Rock which makes the Scene particularly Romantic.

We lodged here and breakfasted at Haddington, the Capital of the Shire a tolerably well built Town for Scotland and got into Edinburgh about 2 O Clock. Took a walk over the Bridge into the new Town which is realy elegant and regular. The houses are extremely well built. Near it is a Square which is laid out for a walk.[7] The Bridge over the Valley is a neat piece of Workmanship with Arches to support the old bridge, having a few years ago fell down when several lives were lost.[8]

September 26th   3rd Day

We went to Holy Rood House formerly the Seat of the Scots Kings but now divided amongst a number of the Nobility.[9] The Duke of Hamiltons apartments[10] contain the Pictures of all the Kings of Scotland from Fergus[11] to James 6 or James 1st[12] of England. Here is a pretty Collection

---

[6] Dunbar Castle, destroyed by regent Murray in 1567, was already a famous stronghold in the middle of the ninth century. It was destroyed during the Battle of Dunbar, in which a victorious army under Cromwell defeated the Scots in September 1650. Cassell's *Encyclopaedia*, IV, p. 84; Charles Firth, *Oliver Cromwell and the Rule of the Puritans in England* (New York, 1900), pp. 280–284.

[7] St. Andrew Square, at the west end of Edinburgh New Town. The first house in the square was begun in 1768. By 1788, the square and the streets connected with it were almost complete. The Royal Commission on the Ancient Monuments of Scotland, *An Inventory of the Ancient and Historical Monuments of the City of Edinburgh* (HMSO, Edinburgh, 1951), p. lxxiv.

[8] The construction of the North Bridge was the first step in the building of Edinburgh New Town. In 1768, when the bridge was partially completed, its south abutment gave way, causing the death of five people and injury to others. The damage was put right and by 1772 the bridge was open for traffic. *Ibid.*; Gifford et al., *Buildings of Scotland: Edinburgh*, pp. 284–285.

[9] After the Act of Union in 1707 there was no Scottish Privy Council to occupy the Council Chamber at Holyrood House and no Scottish parliament or commissioner to occupy the Great Apartment, so Holyrood House became a tenement of exclusive flats for noblemen who had acquired grants to live there. Gifford et al., *Buildings of Scotland: Edinburgh*, pp. 127–128.

[10] The Duke of Hamilton took over the Queen's apartment at Holyrood c. 1682. (The Dukes of Hamilton and Argyll were hereditary keepers of the palace and of the household.) *Ibid.*, p. 128.

[11] According to legend, Fergus I was the first king of the Scots in Scotland in 330 B.C. The first authentic Fergus was the son of Erc, who led a party of Irish to settle in Argyll c. 500 A.D. Donaldson and Morpeth, *Dictionary of Scottish History*, p. 74.

[12] James VI of Scotland and James I of England (1566–1625) was the son of Mary, Queen of Scots, and Darnley. He began to direct policy in Scotland in 1585 and acceded to the English throne in 1603. *Ibid.*, p. 108.

of Tapestry and tolerable Furniture. Another part of the Palace is the Property of the Earl of Dunmore now Governor of Virginia.[13] This part is at present uninhabited but by a Person to take care of it. The Governor has removed all the Paintings out of it, except a Capital Painting of the King and Queen, in full Size, presented him by his Majesty. Another apartment belonging to the Duke of Burcleugh[14] contains a number of good Painting and some excellent Tapestry. Upstairs is a Stain on the Floor shed by some Villains who made their Way privately into the house of Mary Queen of Scots. Rizzio the Person slain[15] had come over from France a Servant and by his merit had rose to be principal Minister of State, and it was judged that he had too great an influence over the Queen. Here are several Paintings of Mary in the Dress in which she was beheaded. Here is the Earl of Strathmore's apartment who had taken an active Part in the last Rebellion and had lost all his Estate.[16]

We went to see the Royal Infirmary an Institution founded chiefly by George Drummond.[17] It is kept in fine Order and has everything such a Design can want. The Heriot Hospital, a beautiful elegant and large Building founded by Herriot a Goldsmith who built the whole at his own Expence and endowed it with such a Salary that it is now supported by, and has a number of Boys educated in one apartment dedicated to that

---

[13] John Murray (1730–1809), Earl of Dunmore from 1756, held various colonial appointments including the governorship of New York (1769–1770) and of Virginia (1770–1776). Cokayne, *Complete Peerage*, IV, p. 544.

[14] Henry Scott (1746–1812), 3rd Duke of Buccleuch from 1751. *Ibid.*, II, p. 369.

[15] Mary (1542–1587) was Queen of Scots between 1542 and 1567, when she was deposed in favour of her son. She sought asylum in England but Elizabeth I kept her as a prisoner until her death because she was a rallying point for English Catholics. David Rizzio (c. 1533–1566), an Italian musician, went to Scotland in 1561 and became Mary's favourite and secretary. He was murdered on the instructions of Mary's second husband, Darnley. Jones and Dixon, *Macmillan Dictionary of Biography*, pp. 556–557, 716.

[16] Thomas Lyon (1704–1753) became 8th Earl of Strathmore in 1735. Although his family were all out in the 1715 Jacobite Rebellion and suffered accordingly, there is no evidence that he took part in the '45. This reference alludes to the abolition of the heritable jurisdictions in Scotland in 1746, when Strathmore claimed compensation for the heritable constableship of the burghs of Forfar and Kincardine. Sir James Balfour Paul, ed., *The Scots Peerage* (Edinburgh, 1911), pp. 305–309; *A List of Persons concerned in the Rebellion, 1745–1746* (Scottish Historical Society, VIII, 1890), p. 199. Dr Eveline Cruickshanks, of the History of Parliament Trust, helpfully pointed me in the right direction for this note.

[17] George Drummond (?1687–1766), Lord Provost of Edinburgh six times between 1725 and 1764. He was much concerned with the improvements and new buildings which took place in Edinburgh New Town. He was largely responsible for getting subscribers to contribute to a fund for the Hospital for Sick Poor in Edinburgh, which opened in 1729. This was the first voluntary hospital in Scotland. From 1736 the hospital became known as the Royal Infirmary of Edinburgh. Donaldson and Morpeth, *Dictionary of Scottish History*, p. 60; Guenter B. Risse, *Hospital Life in Enlightenment Scotland: Care and Teaching at the Royal Infirmary of Edinburgh* (Cambridge, 1986), pp. 25–26, 29.

purpose.[18] Here is also a Chapel. We called to see a new Episcopal Church[19] containing in the Altar some fine Paintings, the Asention of our Saviour, Elias and Moses. Joining the Holy Rood Abbey are the Ruins of an ancient and superb Chappel in which most of the Kings of Scotland were deported and some fine Statues erected but some few years ago the Roof and part of the Walls fell in and the Students of the Colledge and some other Persons having free access carried off many of the Bones and Statuary.[20]

Edinburgh is situated on several Hills. The old Town consists chiefly of two long Streets. All the others are calld Windings or Closes which make into them. The principal Street (High) is wide well paved and the houses very high, some 8, 10 and 12 Stories. The Families live one above another and it is common to see one Story by itself. All the other Streets are monstrous dirty, narrow and offensive. The People live in gross darkness and buried in Filth. The Pavements are very good. On a hill at a little Distance they procure the Stones with which the London Streets are paved.[21] Here are several fine walks about the Town.

We took a Ride to Carron Works[22] along the Firth of Forth and called at the Queens Ferry. From thence went to the Earl of Hopeton's Seat,[23] the finest Building in Scotland. The pleasure Grounds are good and the Paintings are very capital, but the Rooms are too small. The Prospect it commands is grand and the Ride to it is beautiful.

Carron Works are on a River of that Name, a place exhibiting a striking Resemblance of what one would suppose were the infernal Regions. 1500

[18] George Heriot's School was begun in 1628 by William Wallace (principal master mason to the Crown from 1617) and finished c. 1700. Heriot, a royal goldsmith and banker, had left money in 1624 for the building of a hospital (i.e. a charity school). The chapel was erected in 1673 and fitted out from a similar structure at Leith Citadel. Gifford et al., *Buildings of Scotland: Edinburgh*, pp. 179–182.

[19] John Baxter's Cowgate Chapel (now St. Patrick, R.C.), built in 1771–1774 for a rich Episcopalian congregation. *Ibid.*, pp. 38, 169.

[20] David I founded Holyrood Abbey in 1128. By the fourteenth century, it was already a royal residence. It was pillaged and burned during the Earl of Hertford's invasion of 1544. *Ibid.*, pp. 125–141.

[21] A reference to freestone from the quarries at Humbie, about three miles from Queensferry. Lewis, *Topographical Dictionary of Scotland*, I, p. 396.

[22] The Carron Company was founded in 1759. Because of its size it quickly earned the reputation of being the chief foundry in Europe. It succeeded in the use of native ore, and was the first ironworks in Scotland to smelt iron with coke. The company's most famous product was ordnance. R. H. Campbell, *Scotland since 1707: the Rise of an Industrial Society* (Oxford, 1971), pp. 64–65; and R. H. Campbell, *Carron Company* (Edinbrugh, 1961).

[23] John Hope (1704–1781), 2nd Earl of Hopetoun, of Hopetoun House, near Edinburgh. The house was mainly built during the eighteenth century. Cokayne, *Complete Peerage*, VI, p. 573; Colin McWilliam, *The Buildings of Scotland: Lothian except Edinburgh* (London, 1978), pp. 251–258.

People are employed in the Carting Business. Here is a Mill to bore the Cannon, Furnaces, Fire Engines and every other implement and Convenience for casting and finishing Iron hollow Ware.

We lodged at Linlithgow where stand the Ruins of a Palace once in possession of the Scots Kings and inhabited by them and joining it an old Castle.[24] A beautiful Fountain stands in the Street near a Cross with a number of Images spouting Water from their Mouth.

September 29th   6th Day

In Company with W. Craig we took Coach and came to Leith, a place advantageously situated for Shipping. It is the port for Edinburgh, only a mile distance from it; and by having two noble Piers run out forms a safe and convenient Harbour for a great Number of Shipping who lay close to the Key and deliver and receive their Goods. We got a Boat and came over the Ferry 8 Miles to Kinghorn, where we took Chaise, came through CauCaudie,[25] a long dirty ill built Town consisting of one Street. It has a good Bason and a number of Shipping are ownd here. Came through several other Town to Anstruther a little dirty market where we lodged, not arriving till 1 O Clock in the Morning having been 8 hours travelling 23 Miles, such is the mode of travelling in Scotland.

September 30th   7th Day

We left Anstruther and got to St. Andrews to Breakfast. Went to view the Ruins of the old Monastery, which has been very large but there is little of it now left except two of the Towers and one fine Gothic Arch.[26] Here is also standing a Part of the first Church built in this Island for the Worship of Christians 1500 years ago[27] and part of the Castle on the Brow of the Hill built 200 years since,[28] but the Sea has made such Depredations as to wash away one half the Ground on which it stood and is daily going further

[24] Linlithgow Palace, in West Lothian, was originally a royal manor house from the time of David I (1124–1153). Much of it was burnt by the Duke of Cumberland's army as it marched out of Edinburgh on 31 January 1746. J. S. Richardson and James Beveridge, *Linlithgow Palace* (HMSO, Edinburgh, 1948), pp. 22, 33.

[25] Kirkcaldy.

[26] There was an early cathedral at St. Andrews of which part still stands, including the tower of St. Regulus (St. Rule's Tower). The cathedral was of Anglian type and was founded probably in 1162. Donaldson and Morpeth, *Dictionary of Scottish History*, p. 190; John Gifford, *The Buildings of Scotland: Fife* (London, 1988), pp. 361–367.

[27] St. Regulus' Church, built in the eleventh century to house St. Andrew's relics. It became a landmark for pilgrims. Gifford, *Buildings of Scotland: Fife*, pp. 359–361.

[28] St. Andrews Castle was built c. 1200 by Bishop Roger of St. Andrews Priory for himself and his successors. It has been mainly in ruins since the seventeenth century. Stewart Cruden, *St. Andrews Castle, Fife* (HMSO, Edinburgh, 1958), p. 3.

on. At low Water we see the Remains of an Abbey which formerly stood on the Top of the same Hill,[29] but this and several other Buildings are now buried in the Sea.

St. Andrews is an ancient Town famous for an university. It formerly had two Colledges but it has now but one.[30] This University is in no great Reputation. At the Chapel in the Colledge is a fine Gothic Arch with some neat carvd Work. In the Church is a curious Italian Figure of Bishop Sharp[31] who was murdered near this Place by some Gentleman in Disguise. He had been appointed by the Presbyterians to go to the King to pray for some Immunities but instead of endeavouring to obtain what he was appointed for, he was made a Bishop of the Roman Catholic Religion, and was coming down in a Coach and Six when he was stopped taken out of his Carreg and stabd and shot in an instant. His Daughter was with him and fell on her knees to prevent them from killing him but in vain.

From St. Andrews we came to Dundee where we crossed a Ferry of 3 Miles. Dundee is beautifully situated on the North Side of the River Tay. For Scotland 'tis a tolerably well built Town. Has one good Street in it. Several Kirks. The Town Hall is a good Building of hewn Stone.[32] We left it and came to Aberbrothick[33] where we lodged. Here are number of neat houses.

October 1st   1st Day

We rode to Montrose to breakfast having first to cross the River Esk about $\frac{1}{2}$ a Mile wide. Montrose is situated on the North Side of the Esk; is a neat well built town; several Kirks and a small but very neat Church. Our Ride from Edinburgh thus far has been through a Country by no means a bad Soil, but its whole Face discovers the Indolence of the People. The Country is all in Cultivation, and we have constantly before us an extensive Prospect but for the want of Inclosures. The richest views appear poor. The huts in which the Peasants live are low covered with Straw built sometimes of Stone and others of Turf. The Dress of the People is vastly

[29] Probably the remains of an abbey called the Kirkheuch, erected by Constantine II in the ninth century. Lewis, *Topographical Dictionary of Scotland*, I, p. 49.

[30] St. Salvator's College and St. Leonard's College were respectively founded in 1450 and 1512. They were united in 1747 and placed under the superintendence of one principal. *Ibid.*, p. 47; Gifford, *Buildings of Scotland: Fife*, p. 372.

[31] Bishop James Sharp (1613–1679) went to England on the Covenanters' triumph in 1638. He was appointed Archbishop of St. Andrews in 1661 and was murdered at Magnus Muir in 1679. *DNB*, XVII, pp. 1342–1345; Donaldson and Morpeth, *Dictionary of Scottish History*, p. 199.

[32] The Old Town Hall at Dundee was erected in 1734 after a design by Robert Adam. Lewis, *Topographical Dictionary of Scotland*, I, p. 330.

[33] Aberbrothock or Arbroath.

different from the English and the Children are intolerably dirty. The Men keep up the Prerogative over the women and make them do the greater Part of the Drudgery. The women often go barefoot, and the Children always.

After leaving Montrose we came over Waste Land and Barrens to Ury, where we were received by R*obert* B*arclay* with great Hospitality. Ury is delightfully situated on an Eminence surrounded by Hills. The house is venerable and has every appearance of Antiquity.[34] The Walls are thick, and it is in good Repair. The apartments are convenient and neat, not elegant. There are a number of out-houses and the Barn, Stable and Cow houses are vastly commodious. A number of trees surround the house for a considerable Space. The Gardens are more for Use than Beauty though there be several pretty Walks and terraces. At the foot runs a pretty Stream of Water whose Murmurs are heard at some distance. This place is much like America. The woods about it have a rude appearance and the prospect is very extensive. We breakfasted here and came to Aberdeen to Dinner.

A Bridge two Miles south of Aberdeen is very neat and the Ride from the Bridge to the Town is pretty. Aberdeen is conveniently situated on the River Dee, near the Sea. It is a tolerably well built regular Town. The Pavements are good and the main Street is wide and commodious. In the middle is a Cross with a Number of the Heads of the Scots Kings engraven.[35] Here too is the Walk for the Exchange, and one Side is the town house, a good Building, and on the other the Lodge, with a Spire which is a considerable Ornament to the City.[36] There is a Pier and it is a Port of some Consequence.

---

[34] Ury was the residence of the Barclay family in Kincardineshire. Robert Barclay-Allardice (1732–1797), 5th Laird of Ury, was an improver who spent much time studying the theory and practice of agriculture. He improved the land at Ury. He was also M.P. for Kincardineshire three times. He married twice: firstly, to his cousin Lucy, daughter of David Barclay of Cheapside; and secondly, in 1776, to Sarah Ann, only daughter of James Allardice, when he assumed the name of 'Barclay-Allardice.' Barclay and Wilson-Fox, *History of the Barclay Family*, Part III, pp. 215–218.

[35] Probably the market cross (1686) in Castlegate, 'an open-arched hexagonal structure, considered to be the most handsome of old crosses in Scotland.' *Encyclopaedia Britannica*, I, p. 30.

[36] The Exchange coffee house, at the west end of Castle Street, was opened in 1701. The first town house in Castlegate, the ancient forum of the burgh of Aberdeen, was built in 1394. It was superseded in 1622 by a square tower (surmounted by a steeple and spire in 1629). This is known as the Old Tolbooth. Macrie, *New Shell Guide to Scotland*, p. 310; William Kennedy, *Annals of Aberdeen* ... (London, 1818), II, p. 284; Alexander M. Munro, *Memorials of the Aldermen, Provosts, and Lord Provosts of Aberdeen, 1272–1895* (Aberdeen, 1897), pp. 198–199. Mr Peter Grant, the City Librarian of Aberdeen, provided valuable assistance with this reference.

We took a Ride to the old Town which is a Mile from the New. It is here the inhabitants repaired when the main Town was burnt down in the Reign of Edward 1st.[37] With the Librarian and Provost Ogilvie[38] we were introduced to the University, a good commodious Building. The Place which was formerly the Chapel is divided into two parts, one of which is fitted for a Library and contains about 8000 Volumes. The Quire now serves for the Chapel. Here is the Hall which contains a great Number of fine Portraiture Paintings, and a Museum containing a number of natural and artificial Curiosities.

At the mouth of the River Dee is a noble Pier now just begun which will cost £20,000.[39] It is to extend 1400 feet out, and all built of Stone. The Manufactures of this place amount to about £100,000, chiefly in the Stocking way.[40] The Town including the old contains 20,000 People, about 22,000 Houses.

October 3rd

This Morning we breakfasted with Francis Logie who introduced us to several Gentlemen and afterwards took a walk to the Town House, where were several of the Magistrates, where were taken into the Hall, and after drinking a few Glasses of Wine were presented with Diplomas making us Freemen of the City, and giving us *singularem favorem ac benivolentiam*.[41] We took post Chaise and got to Stone hive[42] a little village near the Sea to Dinner, where we met with R*obert* Barclay and several Lairds. Here we dined, came on to a Village to Tea, rode through Brechin, a pretty large village and got to Forfar about 2 O clock in the Morning, it being very dark. Here we lodged all Night and on

October 4th   4th Day

We rose early, came thro Glamis a little Village and got to Coupar to breakfast, a little Market town. The Country in this Neighbourhood is

---

[37] Edward I considered himself entitled to the throne of Scotland after the death of Alexander III. He invaded Scotland with a strong army and, having conquered the southern part of the kingdom, advanced with his forces to Aberdeen, took possession of the castle and plundered the town. Lewis, *Topographical Dictionary of Scotland*, I, p. 7.

[38] William Ogilvie (1736–1819), Professor of Philosophy at King's College, Aberdeen, 1762, and of Humanity, 1765. Donaldson and Morpeth, *Dictionary of Scottish History*, p. 165.

[39] In 1773 an act of parliament was obtained for a new pier to be built at Aberdeen, partly designed by John Smeaton. The pier was 1,200 feet long. Lewis, *Topographical Dictionary of Scotland*, I, p. 14.

[40] Stockings were a major manufacture at Aberdeen in the eighteenth century. Great quantities of knitted stockings were sent to Holland and Germany. *Ibid.*, p. 13; Ishbel C. M. Barnes, 'The Aberdeen Stocking Trade,' *Textile History* VIII (1977), pp. 77–98.

[41] Special favour and kindness.

[42] Stonehaven.

good and populous, but for want of inclosures its appearance is not rich. A number of small thatched houses are continually in Sight and the high hills appear at a Distance. We seldom pass a Seat of any elegance and the Churches everywhere are very indifferent.

We got to Perth to Dinner, crossed the River by a fine Bridge over the Tay. This Bridge has 9 Arches and is the first in Scotland.[43] Perth is a very neat Town of considerable Size. The Streets are regular, well paved and neat. The houses have a good appearance. At Perth we concluded to take a little Excursion to the High Lands and were informed that by going through Dunkeld to Blair Castle we should have a good Sample of the Highland mode of the Living, and see the Genius Customs Manners and dress of the People as if we went through the Kingdom. We took Post Chaise and rode through a most Romantic Hilly Country along the Waters of the Tay, crossed several Bridges and lodged at an Inn, about 1 Mile from Dunkeld. The Night was extremely Stormy and rainy. Our Carriage let the Rain in but at 9 O Clock we were safely housed.

October 5th 5th Day

Rose early this Morning, crossed a Ferry about 50 yards and took a Walk to the Duke of Athols Seat at Dunkeld.[44] The house is well situated in a Valley with Hills and Mountains on every side. It is not elegant, but neat. His outhouses are numerous. His Stables &c are commodious. His Gardens are laid out with great Taste and he has a number of Pineries and hot houses. He has a grand Collection of Prints in his house all pasted to the Walls, and disposed with great ingenuity on a Stone Coloured paper. He has some paintings on the Glass of his Windows, but few elsewhere. Near his house stand the Ruins of an ancient Church which have a good effect from the Gardens. Several Images and Objects make the Scene vastly pleasing. The pleasure walks extend for 10 Miles round through the wood and several Seats and Chinese Pagodas and Pavilions are interspersed.

Here is a beautiful Grotto on the Side of the River, with a vast number of fine inscriptions on the Rocks. Directly opposite this is a pretty Cascade of Water falling into the Tay. Here is a good Aviary and a number of Partridges and Pheasants of different kinds. The English are of a very fine plumage, but the Chinese are superior in Elegance and Beauty to any Bird I ever saw.

---

[43] This bridge, in fact, had ten arches. It was built in 1771 under the architectural guidance of John Smeaton, and was over 900 feet long and c. 22 feet wide between the parapets. Lewis, *Topographical Dictionary of Scotland*, II, p. 359.

[44] John Murray (1755–1830), 4th Duke of Atholl, resided at Dunkeld, Perthshire. Cokayne, *Complete Peerage*, I, pp. 320–321.

We rode on to a Tavern half way to Blair where we breakfasted. The Ride to it is on the Banks of the Tay, a most beautiful River through a fine rich Valley, with a number of Islands, and bounded on each Side by monstrous hills, down which as we ride along we see many Cascades of Water falling. The Huts here are small and mean, the People are dirty, their dress very different from any places we have been at, and sometimes it is difficult to tell the Boys from the Girls by their Appearance.

Through an amazingly romantic Country along side the River very rapid and a multitude of little Rivulets constantly running into the Tay, a fine rich Valley, vast mountains on either Side, a fine road on the Declivity of the Hill, with a Prospect extensive and charming we got to Athol Castle,[45] a delightful palace belonging to the Duke of Athol. The house outside is very plain but large. The outhouses are very extensive. Here are a great Number of fine Paintings and Images and Busts. The Rooms are mostly small, though there be some very grand and elegant. Here is a very fine Family Painting in the grand Room (of the Duke and Dutchess and even of her Children) besides a great Number of the Family. Here are some fine chimney pieces and some elegant marble Tables, a Bed of State very superb, and some beautiful Tapestry.

The Pleasure Grounds back of the house are pretty, some noble Images, and pine groves with walks through them, several Chinese Bridges and Temples, a high Tower with a Clock, a neat park with Deer, a white Tail Eagle &&c. Through a pretty walk leading through the Garden, where is a fine Pond with a number of little Islands, Summer houses and Images we go to the Banks of the River to a large Grotto, composed of marble Petrifactions &c, directly opposite to which a fine Cascade falls down a perpendicular Height of 25 Feet into the River. The Noise occasions an Echo in the Grotto, surprising.[46]

We dined at an Inn near Blair and about Sun Set came back to the halfway house. A fine moonlight Evening. Here we lodged and came to Dunkeld to breakfast through several Scots Villages consisting of very low dirty houses. After breakfast we went to see the Hermitage of the

---

[45] Blair Castle, the seat of the Dukes of Atholl since Celtic times. Situated in the village of Blair Atholl, it was remodelled in plain vernacular style by James Winter in 1747–1758 and renamed Atholl House. It is now known once again as Blair Castle. Maurice Lindsay, *The Castles of Scotland* (London, 1986), pp. 83–85.

[46] The gardens of the Duke of Atholl's residence at Dunkeld lie to the north-west of the house. They are described in Sir John Sinclair, ed., *The Statistical Account of Scotland 1791–1799, vol. 12: North and West Perthshire* (orig. pub. 1791–1799; reprinted Wakefield, 1977), pp. 343–344.

Duke,[47] by a pretty Walk on an exalted plain with a River on both Sides of us branching into several Streams and roaring as it falls, while the distant mountains seem to reach the Heavens. We ascended a very steep Summit to a Ruin built to form an object from some of the distant seats. Here we have a charming view through several vallies and see a vast number of high mountains.

From this we went through some rural Gardens to a little Summer house on the top of a steep Ridge of Rocks, directly opposite which a fine River presents itself, with a number of Cascades of different heights. At length pouring down with great rapidity it comes to a perpendicular Fall of near 30 Feet and 40 feet wide.[48] The water on the Brow of the Fall is deep, and a great [fall of] Water comes down. We have a pretty view of it from the Summer house, and the window contains several panes of stained Glass of different Colors, through which we see the Falls to great advantage. A yellow Pane makes the water of the most flaming appearance. The trees assume a dark Shade and the whole Firmament is like a blaze of Fire. A purple one makes the Scene very rich, a blue gives it a fine white appearance. In short this Scene is amazingly fine, and certainly the most beautiful Fall I have yet seen in this Island.[49]

A little way from this Place is a Bridge over the River from which we have a fine View of the Fall and the precipice below. On one Side (under the Rocks) is a fine Grotto, which is neatly ornamented with a Variety of Stones of different Kinds, Shells and Glass all laid in by the hands of the late Duke and Dutchess.[50] At the Entrance into this Grotto a fine fountain springs out of the Ground from 30 little Spouts and shoots up to the Top of the Roof. We walked from this place a mile along the Delightful River and got to Tulloch to Dinner at the house of Benjamin Swan from which we have a fine view of Perth, Scoon,[51] a palace where the Kings of Scotland sometimes dwelt and where the Regalia of state were always

[47] Ossian's Seat, or the Hermitage of the Duke of Atholl, is situated on the north bank of the River Bran near the village of Inver, Perthshire. This folly was built in 1758, converted to a mirrored waterfall room in 1783, largely destroyed by vandals in 1869, and is now restored and refurbished. Lewis, *Topographical Dictionary of Scotland*, I, p. 344; John Tomes, *Blue Guide: Scotland* (London, 1986), p. 270; Robin Prentice, *The National Trust for Scotland Guide* (3rd edn., London, 1981), pp. 201–202.

[48] Known as 'Rumbling Bridge.' Here water poured over a deep chasm in the River Bran. Lewis, *Topographical Dictionary of Scotland*, I, p. 344.

[49] I have cut a short passage on the Duke of Atholl.

[50] Ossian's Cave, an eighteenth-century folly, neatly using a group of boulders and claiming to represent the kind of place in which such a bard would have lived. John Tomes, *Blue Guide: Scotland*, p. 270.

[51] Scone.

deposited.[52] And beyond this we see the castle of MacBeth, where King Malcom 1st was slain.[53] We likewise see the Bridge, which has a good Effect. The Bridge cost £27,000 and was built by Lord [Kinnoull].[54] We stayed at Perth all Night and

October 7th   7th Day

We came on to Kingross[55] a little Market Town to breakfast, through a hilly Country, but the Vallies rich and finely watered. Passed by King Ross Lake, which is a beautiful piece of Water with several Islands, and at the same time see the meanders of several Rivers. There is a fine level Country on one Side and the other is mountainous.

On our getting here, finding our Finances were so reduced that we had not sufficient Cash to bring us to Edinburgh we concluded to ride only 10 Miles and walk the rest. We walked 6 Miles to Queen's ferry in 1½ hour (dinner time, but we had no Money) so we set off in a boat to Leith and came down the Firth the Distance of 10 Miles in about an hour where we borrowed some Money to pay our passage and got to Edinburgh about 4 O Clock. The Wind being high and our boat rather crank rendered our Passage somewhat dangerous. Both sides of the Bay exhibit very pleasing Scenes, the Land being good and richly cultivated. We passed by a Number of Seats, Lord Murray's[56] and Rosberry's[57] and several Villages. We have a number of Islands in view and the whole was vastly agreeable. At Queen's Ferry are the Pebble Stones of which London Streets are paved. On our getting into Edinburgh we found our Friends Jon*athan* Ormston[58] his daughters and N: Hogshon.

---

[52] Scone Abbey was founded as a priory by Alexander I c. 1120. The inaugural stone was preserved there until Edward I removed it in 1296 and placed it in Westminster Abbey. Donaldson and Morpeth, *Dictionary of Scottish History*, p. 193.

[53] A slip: it was Duncan who was killed by Macbeth in 1040.

[54] Thomas Hay, 9th Earl of Kinnoull, played a crucial part in financing this bridge, which was completed in 1772. Nowadays the bridge is called the Perth Bridge. Iain A. Robertson, 'The Earl of Kinnoull's Bridge: The Construction of the Bridge of Tay at Perth, 1763–1772,' *Scottish Economic and Social History*, VI (1986), pp. 18–32.

[55] Kinross.

[56] Francis Stuart (1737–1810), 24th Earl of Moray from 1767, was styled Lord Doune from 1739 to 1767. He was created Baron Stuart of Castle Stuart, Inverness-shire, in 1796. His other principal residences were Doune Lodge, Perthshire; Darnaway Castle, Morayshire; and Donibristle, Fife. Cokayne, *Complete Peerage*, IX, pp. 190–192.

[57] Neil Primrose (1729–1814), 3rd Earl of Rosebery from 1755, resided at Dalmeny Park, Linlithgow. *Ibid.*, XI, pp. 135, 139.

[58] Probably Jonathan Ormston (1708–1780), a Scotsman who settled at Newcastle-upon-Tyne. *JFHS*, IX (1912), p. 124.

October 8th   1st Day

Went to Meeting in the Morning. About 20 People present. Took a walk
on the Calton Hill where we have fine views of the Town, Country round,
Leith &c. This a publick walk lately laid out. Dined with Robert Miller and
in the evening took a Walk to the Botanical Garden but could not get to
see it.

October 9th   2nd Day

We took a ride this morning in Company with N and PO and N Hogshon to
Dalkeith a considerable Market Town 5 miles distant from Edinburgh,
near which stands Dalkeith Palace, an elegant Seat, belonging to the Duke
of Buccleuch.[59] There are some fine Views in the Park, terraces and walks
and a delightful Stream runs murmuring at the foot of a Valley between the
Park and a beautiful Wood. The house is very elegant though much
inferior to several I have seen. We enter in at a fine Hall, where is a choice
Collection of Paintings of Children at all their different amusements. There
are several Rooms below where the paintings are fine. We then go to the
Stair Case which is wainscoted with marble and all the way as we ascend for
two Stories we meet with very capital paintings: History, Landscapes,
Views, Ruins &c &c. There are several grand Rooms upstairs in which are
a variety of fancy Faces amazingly well executed. Some of these Rooms are
excellently furnished with Seats, Setties and Sophas.

We bid the good Girls Adieu and got up to Edinburgh to Dinner. After
Dinner went to view Duke of Hamiltons Apartments in the Abbey. Left
Edinburgh about 6 O Clock and came as far as the Queens Ferry to lodge
on our way to Glasgow.

October 10th   3rd Day

Rose early this morning and got to Burrowness a Market Town of some
Note to breakfast. Here is a Pier, several Collieries and a very considerable
manufactury of Salt.[60] Some ships are built here. Stopd at Carron Works
where they were casting Potts Cannon &c. We ride the greater part of the
way along side the River of Firth and the rest along the great Canal leading

---

[59] Dalkeith Palace, dating from c. 1700, was the residence of the Dukes of Buccleuch.
Donaldson and Morpeth, *Dictionary of Scottish History*, p. 52.

[60] Coal working along the shore of the Forth near Bo'ness was ancient. Several large
collieries at Bo'ness also had integrated saltworks by the late eighteenth century. Perhaps the
best known collieries there were Kinneil, owned by the Dukes of Hamilton, and the Grange,
leased by the Cadell family. Baron F. Duckham, *A History of the Scottish Coal Industry, Vol.
1: 1700–1815* (Newton Abbot, 1970), pp. 26, 42, 139, 177.

from a little Sea Port Town about a Scots mile from Carron to within 2 miles of Glascow.[61]

The Canal not being yet finished we saw several Fields of Corn not yet cut and passed by a very fine Seat but could not learn the Owners Name. After leaving Carron we came into a very fine Country hills and Vallies, richly cultivated, and prettily interspersed with Wood. The Road from Carron to Stirling was all alive with Cattle, a vast number of Flocks, amounting to many thousands being drove down from the High Lands to the Town in this Neighbourhood for Sale.[62] The people talk the Erst Language[63] and not one word of English. The Cattle are exceedingly small but generally look in good order. 27,000 Head are to be at Falkirk this Day.

We got to Stirling to Dinner a Town Capital of the Shire. This Town is situated on the Declivity of a Hill, consisting principally of one Street, rising all the Way for a Mile till we get to the Castle, which is built on a Rock. Every other way than by this Street inaccessible and perpendicular. This Building was formerly the Palace of the Scots Kings.[64] It has a number of Images, is very elegant besides being amazingly strong. It was founded above 1600 years ago and some part of it is now in Ruins. Here is some Cannon, and about 700 Stand of Arms. Within the Fortification is the old Parliament house, with a number of wooden Images of roman Heroes.[65] The Oak stands perfectly sound, though above 1000 years old.

At a little Distance from this Castle stands a Chapel in which several of

---

[61] This was the Forth and Clyde Canal, authorised by act of parliament in 1768. By 1775 the canal, built from the Forth end, had reached Stockingfield, three miles from Glasgow. Hadfield, *British Canals*, pp. 137–138.

[62] Many Highlanders paid their rents from the sale of the small shaggy black cattle, which were the most important and often the only money-producing item on a farm. At the end of August or September, when the animals were in peak condition, the drovers collected their herds and drove them to the fairs and markets at Crieff, Perth, Falkirk, or in the North of England. A. J. Youngson, *Beyond the Highland Line: Three Journals of Travel in Eighteenth-Century Scotland: Burt, Pennant, Thornton* (London, 1974), pp. 20–22.

[63] Erse is the name given by Scottish Lowlanders to the Gaelic dialect of the Highlands (which is of Irish origin), to the people speaking that dialect, and to their customs. In the eighteenth century, Erse was used in literary English as the ordinary designation of the Gaelic of Scotland. Murray, *New English Dictionary*, III, p. 278.

[64] Stirling Castle was of vital strategic importance. It was built during the reign of Alexander I (1107–1124), who died there. J. S. Richardson and Margaret E. Root, *Stirling Castle* (HMSO, 2nd edn., Edinburgh, 1948), p. 13.

[65] A reference to the oak medallions which adorned the compartmented ceiling of the Presence Chamber until the ceiling was dismantled in 1777. Some of these 'Stirling Heads' represented figures of history and mythology. Many survive and they are 'the most notable examples of Renaissance woodwork now known to exist in Scotland.' *Stirlingshire: An Inventory of the Ancient Monuments* (HMSO, Edinburgh, 1963), I, p. 202.

the Scottish Kings were interred.[66] From the Castle we have a view of the Country round beyond all Description beautiful. We see the winding of the River Forth in the most serpentine Form that is possible to imagine, and too beautiful and regular for the work of Nature. A little Village stands on one side of us which by the Road is only 4 miles distant. To go by Water is 24 and these meanders pass through a Country in the highest Cultivation interspersed with Trees, Gardens and houses, and the whole Valley exhibits the most beautiful Carpet while the Sides are composed of Cloud towering mountains, the Declivities of which are prettily improved, and a number of Villages planted here and there, while the Tops of the Hills mingling with the Clouds are naked wild and Craggy. The other Side exhibits a Scene amazingly fine but not equal to this.

Near the Castle stands an elegant Hospital[67] and fine Gothic Church,[68] part of which is in Ruins. We dined at Stirling and mounted our horses an hour before dark. No sooner mounted than the Rain began to pour, which continued incessant for several hours, and having been wet through in the morning found the more easy access to our Skins. After riding several miles over a very mountainous and stony Country (having got the wrong road) we lost our way, and were put right again by a man we met. Being very wet, and the Wind blowing high and chill, we stopped at a house after riding 9 Miles, but it being taken up with Company we could not lodge there, and our only Comfort was that we were obliged to ride to Killsithe[69] 5 Miles distant. A shocking road, windy, and rainy and dark as possible. We mounted and after riding that distance 'twas with difficulty we could procure a Bed. We at length got one and slept most comfortably.

October 11th   4th Day

We left Killsithe early this morning and came through a fine improved Country to Glascow. We overtook a vast many people going to Market. The road alive, the women mostly barefooted and bare legged while the men keep up the Prerogative, by wearing shoes and stockings. We got into Glascow to Breakfast, took a Walk to see the Town and called on several of our Friends.

Glascow is prettily situated on the River Clyde, over which there are

---

[66] The Chapel Royal, built by James VI in 1594, on the north side of the close of Stirling Castle. Richardson and Root, *Stirling Castle*, p. 11.

[67] Cowane's Hospital, built as an almshouse between 1637 and 1648 after a bequest from John Cowane, a prosperous Stirling merchant. *Stirlingshire: An Inventory of the Ancient Monuments*, II, pp. 289–293.

[68] Stirling parish church, which was originally the church of the Franciscan monastery founded by James IV in 1494. Lewis, *Topographical Dictionary of Scotland*, II, p. 491.

[69] Kilsyth.

two Bridges of Stone not very distant from each other. There is a regular stone Pier, at which the Vessels lie, but here is not sufficient Water for Sea Vessels.[70] The Town consists chiefly of two long wide strait Streets, with a few others of less Note crossing them at right Angles. The houses for the most part are built of a neat hewn Stone, and have an elegant Appearance. Here is a fine large gothic Cathedral with a neat Spire. This Building is converted into several Kirks with an appartment for the Synod to meet.[71] The Colledge is large, has a good Library and the Front is elegant.[72] There is a fine Walk back of it for the Students who amount to about 600. In this Colledge lives the University Printer. Here is a grand Collection of Paintings of the greatest Masters, Titian,[73] Rubens[74] &c &c.

Spent the Evening with James Wardrop[75] and Professor Richardson[76] and John Cross.

October 12th   5th Day

This Morning we took a ride to Hamilton a neat Market Town about 12 Miles from Glascow where we breakfasted and went to see the Palace of the Duke of Hamilton, which is one of the finest Seats in Scotland.[77] The Front of the house is grand but the ends and back nothing extraordinary. He has some good Pleasure Grounds and Images. In this Pallace is said to

[70] Only small craft could make their way upstream on the River Clyde to Glasgow before improved engineering techniques in the mid-eighteenth century made dredging and scouring possible. The building of Port Glasgow in the late seventeenth century had eased the problem and the quays, warehouses and docks built there led to Port Glasgow remaining the head port and principal customs station on the Clyde, with Glasgow and Greenock as its creeks, until 1815. J. R. Kellett, 'Glasgow' in *The Atlas of Historic Towns*, II, ed. M. D. Lobel (London, 1975), pp. 8–9.

[71] At the end of the sixteenth century Glasgow Cathedral had the lead stripped from its roofs, as well as losing most of its altars and statuary. The building was restored and rearranged as three Protestant churches — one each in the nave, chancel and crypt. Andor Gomme and David Walker, *Architecture of Glasgow* (rev. edn., London, 1987), p. 24.

[72] A reference to the University of Glasgow, founded in 1451. James Coutts, *A History of the University of Glasgow from its Foundation in 1451 to 1909* (Glasgow, 1909), p. 6.

[73] Titian (c. 1487/90–1576) specialised in portraits and erotic mythologies and helped to inaugurate the High Renaissance in Venice. Murray and Murray, *Penguin Dictionary of Art and Artists*, pp. 413–415

[74] Sir Peter Paul Rubens (1577–1640) spent most of his career as Court Painter to the Spanish Governors of the Netherlands. His output included ceiling paintings, altarpieces, landscapes, religious and mythological pictures, tapestry designs and book illustrations. *Ibid.*, pp. 364–366.

[75] John and James Wardrop, merchants, High Street, Glasgow. John Tait's *Directory for the City of Glasgow . . . from 15 May 1783 to 15 May 1784* (Glasgow, 1783), p. 67.

[76] William Richardson (b. 1743) who held the Chair of Humanity at Glasgow University from 1773 until 1814. Coutts, *History of the University of Glasgow*, pp. 309–310.

[77] Douglas Hamilton (1756–1799), 8th Duke of Hamilton, mainly resided at Hamilton Palace, Lanarkshire. Cokayne, *Complete Peerage*, VI, pp. 271–272, 277.

be the finest Collection of Painting in Britain, perhaps in Europe. They amount in number to 588, and among them are some of the most capital paintings of the best Masters: Daniel in the Lions Den,[78] Lord Denbigh[79] and some others by Rubens and several pieces of Titian. The rooms are many of them elegant, fine Wainscotts and Ceilings. The place is advantageously situated on the Waters of the Clyde which discovers some fine Meanders.

The Ride to this place is vastly fine, a succession of Hills and Vallies, and being inclosed makes a picturesque appearance. We pass by several Gentlemens Seats and crossed Bothwell Bridge a place famous for a bloody engagement between the Rebels and King's Forces.[80] Came to Town and went again to see the paintings in the Colledge. From thence to the Exchange, where there is a part of the Street set apart for the purpose, and paved with large flat Stones; and in rainy weather there is a Covering to walk under.[81] At the Exchange is a fine Statue of King William.[82]

We went in the afternoon to view the new Kirk which is a beautiful hewn stone building, the front supported by several large stone Columns. It has a good Spire, and is allowed to be the best Kirk in Scotland.[83]

October 13th   6th Day

After Breakfast we went with *John* Cross to the Hall and were presented with the Freedom of the City, and admitted to all the Priviledges and Immunities as if we had been born and resident there. In the great Room of the Town Hall are fine Portrait Paintings of all the Kings and Queens from James 1st to his present Majesty. Also a fine painting of the Duke of Argyle said to have cost £500.

---

[78] Rubens' painting of 'Daniel in the Lion's Den', in the Gallery at Hamilton Palace, was formerly in the collection of Charles I. The picture is described in G. F. Waagen, *Treasures of Art in Great Britain* (London, 1854), III, pp. 296–297.

[79] Van Dyck painted the portrait of William Fielding, 1st Earl of Denbigh (c. 1582–1643) in 1633 after Denbigh returned from an embassy to the Shah of Persia and the Great Mogul in India. The portrait may have been commissioned by, or given to, the Marquess of Hamilton, who had married Denbigh's daughter. The picture remained in the Hamilton Collection until 1919. Since 1945 it has been in the National Gallery. Oliver Millar, *Van Dyck in England* (London, 1982), colour plate IV, pp. 16–17 and no. 16, pp. 56–58.

[80] At the Battle of Bothwell Bridge (22 June 1679) the rebel covenanters of south-west Scotland were defeated by 10,000 men under the Duke of Monmouth.

[81] The Town Hall and Old Royal Exchange in Trongate Street, Glasgow, erected in 1636 and improved in 1740. Lewis, *Topographical Dictionary of Scotland*, I, p. 507.

[82] An equestrian statue of William III, presented to Glasgow in 1735 by James Macrae, a citizen of Glasgow and later Governor of the Presidency of Madras. *The Topographical, Statistical, and Historical Gazetteer of Scotland* (2 vols., Glasgow, 1842), I, p. 662.

[83] Probably St. Andrew's parish church, finished in 1756 and situated in the centre of St. Andrew's Square. Lewis, *Topographical Dictionary of Scotland*, I, p. 513.

About 12 O Clock we took leave of our Friends and left Glascow, crossed over the Bridge, and rode along the River Clyde through a fine Grass and Corn Country with a number of Gentleman's Seats and well cloathed with Trees to Course Hill where we dined. This place is opposite to Dumbarton Castle,[84] once a strong Fortification, built on a high Rock, which projects out into the Clyde, to which access can be had only by a long narrow Neck of Land, which at Times is overflowed. These Rocks are high and in the form of two Sugar Loaves. The Fortification is on the declivity and has a good Command of the River which is narrow here, so that it would be difficult for an Enemy to pass by. From this place we also see Dumbarton Town and at some distance a Monument of considerable Height raised to the Memory of Tobias Smollet,[85] the celebrated Historian who was born there. We also see an amazingly high Hill, said by Pennant to be 3360 Feet perpendicular height,[86] at the Foot of which commences the fine Lake of Lomond (call Loch Lomond), 24 Miles long and 12 broad. The Hills on both Sides out top the Clouds. They are on the Top bare craggy and wild, and the Declivities are in the finest Cultivation. The great Number of headlands, points, Bays &c &c make this one of the most pleasing Objects in Nature.

After dinner we rode through a hilly Country, with some rich Valleys, close by the Clyde to Port Glascow which stands on the South Side of the River, near two Miles wide. The Town is at the Foot of a high Hill, ill built, dirty and mean but it is a place of very great Trade. A vast number of Shipping are now here. They lay in a Bason formed by two Piers which project a good way out and almost meet each other. The greatest inconvenience is that at low Water they all lay aground, but they unload with great expedition laying alongside of the Pier. 45 to 48000 Hogsheads of Tobacco come into this Place annually. The present year 55000 are expected; upwards of 40000 Hogsheads are now in Port.[87] The Tobacco is landed on the Key and rolled to the Scale house where

---

[84] Dumbarton Castle was made a royal fortress at a very early date, and the town which had arisen under its protection was erected into a royal burgh by Alexander II in 1222. *Ibid.*, p. 314.

[85] Tobias George Smollett (1721–1771), a novelist from Dumbartonshire. He also wrote a large 'History of England' from the earliest times down to 1748. *DNB*, XVIII, pp. 582–591.

[86] Thomas Pennant states that Ben Lomond is 3,240 feet high from the surface of Loch Lomond (*A Tour in Scotland and Voyage to the Hebrides*, 1772 [London, 1774], I, p. 153.)

[87] Forty-six million pounds of tobacco were imported into Scotland in 1775. Virtually all of this import would have come to Glasgow and the Clyde. U.S. Bureau of the Census, *Historical Statistics of the United States, Colonial Times to 1970* (Washington D.C., 1975), Part 2, Series Z 449–456, p. 1190.

it is started, weighed and packed again. All this is done in 3 Minutes. From thence rolled into the Warehouses, which are contiguous.[88]

From Port Glascow we came to Greenock, a port of some Consequence about 3 Miles lower down the River, situate in a Cove with an excellent Bason. This is not a place of so much Consequence as Port Glascow but is a much neater Town. Indeed the Houses here are uncommonly elegant, and the Port is in a thriving Situation. Here is an excellent Church of hewn Stone. Port Glascow has a very fine Dry Dock all built of hewn Stone, which is a great Convenience to the Shipping.[89]

October 14th   7th Day

We rose early this Morning and set off from Greenock with a high wind in our Faces, which increased as we rode on through a mountainous wild romantic Country, for some distance in sight of the Firth of Clyde and afterwards along the Irish Sea, having within our View the Islands of Bute, Arran and several others of lesser Size. By the time we got to Largs (a little Village on the Sea Side) we were compleatly wet all over and had to strip and dry ourselves and our Cloaths before we could proceed. When we set off for Sealcots[90] some Rain but the wind much abated. We ride along the Beach the greater part of the Way, keeping the Islands in Sight. They as well as all the Land in View are hilly, craggy and mostly barren.

We dined at Sealcots and rode on to Irwin[91] a pretty large smuggling town,[92] with some Collieries in the Neighbourhood and some Ships employed in the Coal Trade. Here we drank Tea, and procuring a Guide we rode on in the Night to Air the Capital of the Shire, a considerable Town, intersected by the River Air, over which there is a good Stone

---

[88] A marginal note suggests population estimates of 80,000 for Edinburgh, 60,000 for Glasgow, and 20,000 for Aberdeen.

[89] The first graving dock in Scotland was built in 1762 at Port Glasgow. Groome, *Ordnance Gazetteer of Scotland*, p. 1342.

[90] Saltcoats.

[91] Irvine.

[92] The south-west coast of Scotland, especially Galloway and Ayrshire, was the great scene of smuggling in eighteenth-century Scotland. The cargoes smuggled consisted chiefly of tea, spirits, tobacco, snuff, East India goods, wine, drugs, lace, cambrics and silk — mainly commodities where duties were high. Coalmining in Scotland before 1800 was concentrated in Fifeshire, Ayrshire and the immediate vicinity of Glasgow. The main ports for shipment of coal from Ayrshire to Ireland were Irvine and Ayr. A. J. Youngson, *After the Forty-Five* (Edinburgh, 1973), pp. 117–119; Henry Hamilton, *The Industrial Revolution in Scotland* (new impression, London, 1966), p. 169; John Strawhorn, *The History of Irvine: Royal Burgh and New Town* (Edinburgh, 1985), pp. 67–68, 76–85.

Bridge with 4 large Arches.[93] It lays about a mile from the Sea, carries on the Smuggling, Coal and Fishing Trades. Here we lodged and

October 15th　1st Day

Set off about 7 O Clock, came for a few Miles along side the River Air, a pretty stream with high Banks on each Side and a number of well situated Seats, through an improveable Country, several Villages, Streams, Mills &c to Cumlock[94] a neat market Town in a fine sequestered Vale embowered with Trees, a Bridge, Church &c. This is a good object from the Country round. Breakfasted and set off for Sanchar.[95] A delightful morning, with scarce a cloud in view, a thing uncommon in this hilly Country, where there is almost continual Rain, the high mountains breaking every Cloud which passes over.

The approach of Winter is now visible over all the Face of the Country. The whole vegetable Creation shows its tarnished Features, yet their variegation seem to rival in beauty their former Verdures. We ride along the Declivity of a Ridge of Mountains half way between the Summit and a fine rich Valley, made alive with Cultivation, a beautiful Stream watering the fertile Soil, and the *Cattle of a thousand Hills* grazing around us.

We got to Sanchar to dinner a little dirty Town, but a good Situation. An old ruined Castle near it.[96] We left this place about Sun Set, a charming Road for many miles on the Bank of a pretty purling River shaded by fine Woods, with high mountains on each Side led us to Thorn Hill a little insignificant Town where we lodged in Sight of the Duke of Queensberry Palace,[97] a noble seat, advantageously situated for Soil and Prospect. This Day passed Lord Dumfries[98] and several other Seats.

October 16th　2nd Day

Rose at Day Break and came on to Dumfries through a very improveable Country, but where Cultivation hath not left many traces. The Country is

[93] The Auld Brig at Ayr, with four lofty strong-framed arches, was probably built at some time between 1470 and 1525. Groome, *Ordnance Gazetteer of Scotland*, p. 98.

[94] Cumnock.

[95] Sanquhar.

[96] Sanquhar Castle, in Dumfries and Galloway, begun by the Crichton family in the fifteenth century. It was a rectangular courtyard castle. Fry, *David & Charles Book of Castles*, p. 471.

[97] Either Drumlanrig, near Thornhill, a house modified between 1676 and 1689 for the 1st Duke of Queensberry, or Sanquhar Castle, Dumfriesshire, acquired by the same person in 1639. Donald Lomond Macrie, *The New Shell Guide to Scotland* (new version, London, 1977), p. 267; Donaldson and Morpeth, *Dictionary of Scottish History*, pp. 60, 192.

[98] Patrick MacDowall-Crichton (1726–1803), 6th Earl of Dumfries from 1768, resided at Dumfries House, Ayrshire. Cokayne, *Complete Peerage*, IV, p. 501.

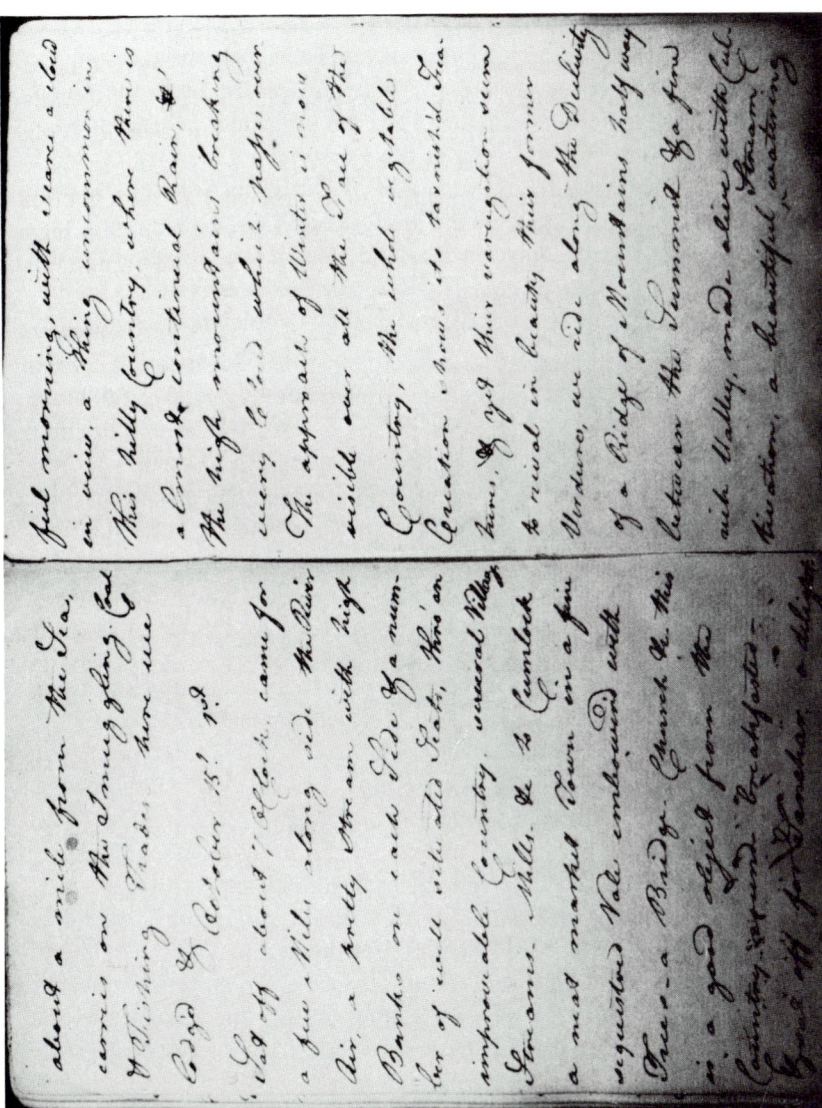

FIG. 1. Description of south-west Scotland (15 October 1775)

Hilly, not mountainous, several fine Streams of water pouring through the Valleys. We entered the Town by a large Bridge with 9 Arches over the River.[99]

Dumfries is a very neat well built Place of considerable Size, good Streets and many genteel houses of either Brick or Brick coloured Stone. In a heavy rain and tempestuous Wind in our Faces, which lasted all the time we were on horseback, losing our Way and getting upon the Quick Sands to Solway Firth and roads deep we got to Annan a little market Town when we found ourselves wet as if we had been under Water. Here we dined and finding it cleared up we left the Town about Sun Set and rode on to Longtown a little Village where we lodged.

Longtown is the first Village in England after leaving Scotland. Four miles beyond it is Gretna Green, standing on the Borders of Scotland, a place famous for uniting a number of young People from England in Hymen's bonds,[100] being the nearest Town to England in Scotland, where people may marry at a younger Age and where fewer Questions are asked of the Parties.[101] It is so common for that Purpose as to have become a Proverb. Near it is a Bridge across the River which divides the two Kingdoms. Here we bid Scotland a long long Adieu without the least expectation of ever visiting it again, or without a wish ever more to behold its Nakedness, Dirt and Customs. Here we lodged all Night and on

October 17th   3rd Day

We set off to Carlisle. The country now wears a much more pleasing Aspect, the Fields and meadows skirted with hedge Inclosures, the Huts and Cottages of the Peasants more comfortable and neat, the appearance of the Swains and the Nymphs more clean and decent, the houses of the Inhabitants more convenient and elegant. The Land shews the industry of the People instead of declaring their Negligence. The Dress and manners totally different. It should appear strange that so small a distance should make so essential a difference, especially when we consider that the Countries are not divided by any Sea, subject to the almost the same Constitution and Laws, and so closely connected by Commerce. This however must be remarked that the Ravages of the late Rebellion were great and tended so much to impoverish their

---

[99] The fifteenth-century Old Bridge over the River Nith at Dumfries. It originally had nine arches but now has six. Macrie, *New Shell Guide to Scotland*, p. 68.

[100] Originally the marriage song among the Greeks.

[101] Gretna Green, the nearest and most accessible point in Scotland from England, has long been a place for fugitive marriages.

Country.[102] However it is now fast recruiting. Great improvements are making in most of their capital Towns, new Land is inclosing, and manufactures and Trade increasing.

We got to Carlisle to Breakfast. This was once a flourishing City and a principal Station of the Romans.[103] Its Situation on the Conflux of 3 fine Rivers (the Eden, the Peterill and the Caude)[103a] is pleasing. It is a Sea Port but without Ships, Merchants or Trade; of an oblong Form, well built. It has a fine Gothic Cathedral of excellent Workmanship, with a window 48 feet high and some beautiful stained Glass.[104] Also a noble Castle above 1100 years old built of Stone and now in good repair.[105] It has undergone many Sieges and in the Rebellion a very severe one being in the Possession of the Rebels who held out a Nine Days siege against the Duke of Cumberland although he had two Armies, with a heavy train of Artillery, on Hills contiguous. His superior Force at length obliged them to surrender.[106]

Carlisle is the Key into England on the West as Berwick is on the East. Near it stands the Wall built by the Picts extending from Solway Firth to NewCastle crossing the Island in the narrowest Place 68 Miles.[107] This wall is to be seen in many Places, but it is mostly levelled with Ground. Here lives one Joseph Strong, now 44 Years of Age, blind from his Infancy. He weaves with great Ingenuity fine Coarse and figured Linnen and even

[102] A reference to the military encounters of the 1745 Jacobite Rebellion and, more specifically, to the pounding of the walls of Carlisle by the Duke of Cumberland's artillery between 28 and 30 Dec. 1745. W. A. Speck, *The Butcher: The Duke of Cumberland and the Suppression of the 45* (Oxford, 1981), pp. 101–102.

[103] Around 370 a fifth Roman province was created in Britain. It was called Valentia. Its precise location is unknown, but Carlisle may well have been its capital. John Wacher, *The Towns of Roman Britain* (London, 1974), p. 87.

[103a] i.e. Caldew.

[104] Carlisle Cathedral was founded in the reign of Henry I (c. 1102) and in 1133 Henry made the town the see of a bishop. Pevsner, *The Buildings of England: Cumberland and Westmorland* (London, 1967), pp. 88–96.

[105] Founded by William Rufus in 1092, Carlisle Castle occupies a triangular site at the northern end of the city which it dominated and guarded. The fortifications were probably completed by David, King of Scotland, who took possession of Carlisle in 1135 and resided there for several years. Lewis, *Topographical Dictionary of England*, I, p. 378; Colvin, *History of the King's Works, II: The Middle Ages*, pp. 595–600.

[106] William Augustus, Duke of Cumberland (1721–1765) commanded the forces that crushed the Jacobite Rebellion of 1745. Carlisle was the first obstacle in the path of the Jacobite army that headed south from Scotland. On 15 Nov. 1745 the town and castle of Carlisle surrendered to the rebels. Between 28 and 30 December, however, the Duke of Cumberland laid siege and the rebels were defeated. Speck, *The Butcher*, pp. 4, 79–80, 101–102.

[107] Fisher, like Camden in his *Britannia*, refers to Hadrian's Wall as the Picts' Wall. This was built c. 122–133 and it runs for 120 kilometres from Tyne to Solway. It was the main defence of the northern frontier of Roman Britain.

Letters on his Cloth, Coats, Waistcoats and Breeches without a Seem. He has several pieces of Clock Work: two Women fighting a Man dancing &c and a very curious Organ, all the work of his own hands. His Chairs, Tables and other Furniture are his own manufacture. He plays any Tune on the organ with great accuracy and precision; is extremely sensible in Conversation. He has no Idea of Colours, nor can form the least Conception of a persons being able at half a mile Distance to discern an object and tell its Shape and Quality. He gave me a hymn composed by himself at the end of this Volume.

We left Carlisle about One O'Clock and came on about 9 Miles to a little Villa where we dined and got to Penrith to lodge. A Mile before we enter the Town we descend a hill, which affords one of the richest Prospects in Nature. The Country for a great Distance is clear and in high cultivation with beautiful Inclosures and a sufficient Quantity of Wood to make it pleasing. The Town is prettily situated on a fine River, but indifferently built. We left this place early on the Morning of

October 18th   4th Day

The Country for a few Miles from this place is fine. Several Streams of Water and a sufficient Quantity of Wood. We pass by a very large round stone building where a large manufactury of Carpets is carried on by Sir James Lowther[108] and a few miles from this is building a long row of houses for carrying on a linnen Factury.[109] The Country now is rough hilly and barren. We ride many miles without seeing a single house except now and then in a valley at some distance. When we come within a few miles of Kendal we have a vastly extensive view of the Country round. We got to Kendal to dine.

October 19th   5th Day

We took a walk this morning to see the different manufactures that are carried on here: Cottons, Stockings, Silk Rugs; here are Fulling Mills,

---

[108] This building was erected at Lowther before 1700. In 1740–1741 it was a woollen factory; in 1742–1753, a linen and woollen factory; in July 1772–March 1774, a carpet factory; in 1793, a yarn-spinning (i.e. woollen) factory. Sir James Lowther (1736–1802), 5th Baronet, of Lowther, near Penrith, was reckoned the richest commoner in England before he came of age. He represented various constituencies in Cumberland and Westmorland, 1757–1784, and was created Earl of Lonsdale in 1784. J. F. Curwen, *The Later Records of North Westmorland* (Kendal, 1932), pp. 328–329; J. F. Haswell, *The Registers of Lowther 1540–1812* (Penrith, 1933), pp. 168–172; Namier and Brooke, *History of Parliament: The House of Commons, 1754–1790*, III, pp. 56–60. The carpet factory is described in William Hutchinson, *An Excursion to the Lakes, in Westmorland and Cumberland, August 1773* (London, 1774), pp. 59–61. I am indebted to the Cumbria Record Office for help with this reference.

[109] Manufactories of linen and cotton began to increase rapidly in Carlisle after 1750. William Hutchinson, *The History of the County of Cumberland . . .* (2 vols., Carlisle, 1794), II, p. 662.

Frizing Mills, Corn Mills &c. And in the Afternoon took a Ride to Lake [Windermere] about 8 Miles from Town over a rough rude craggy wild barren Country. The Situation of this Lake is remarkably fine, the high Mountains on either Side rising almost perpendicular from the Waters Edge; the multitude of little Islands. Took a walk to a Castle which stands on an eminence commanding the Town. This Castle is now in Ruins. It was partly thrown down by Oliver Cromwell who commanded a good Station from the opposite side, on an artificial Hill which he threw up in one Night.[110] At this place we stayed till

October 23rd   2nd Day

When taking Leave of our Friends accompanied by Jonathan Whitwell, George Braithwaite,[111] John Whitwell,[112] John Wilson[113] and E*manuel* Elam we left Kendal and about 7 Miles off Kendal took Leave of my companion S*amuel* Elam, who went strait to Leeds and whose place is supplied by Emanuel who met me here to go to London. Rode through a good Country, fine Roads, and got to Lancaster to dine.[114]

[110] An error. Kendal Castle was old and decayed by Elizabethan times. Though there was fighting between Scottish Royalist and Parliamentary forces in Cumberland and Westmorland in 1648, Cromwell participated in no military actions there and Kendal Castle was not attacked. Joseph Nicholson and Richard Burn, *The History and Antiquities of the Counties of Westmorland and Cumberland* (2 vols., London, 1777; reprinted Wakefield, 1976), I, p. 83; Peter Gaunt, *The Cromwellian Gazetteer* (Gloucester, 1987), p. 34.

[111] Either George Braithwaite, drysalter of Kendal, or a member of Braithwaite & Co., wholesale ironmongers and nail manufacturers. *UBD*, III, p. 474.

[112] John Whitwell was a linsey manufacturer in Kendal. Bailey's *British Directory*, III, p. 556.

[113] John Wilson (1748–1801) was a shearman-dyer of Kendal. *DQB*.

[114] I have cut 110 lines of religious reflections.

October 23rd 1775   2nd Day

Kendal is prettily situated on the River Can or Kent, which waters it on one Side and the other surrounded by hills. It consists chiefly of three Streets as the Letter Y with others communicating into them. The houses are all built of Stone and rough cast. It contains about 10,000 inhabitants. It is not the Capital of the Shire, but it is much larger and more considerable than Appleby. Its manufactures consist of Cottons, Linseys, hosiery, Silk Rugs and Saddle Cloth. The Church is large and beautiful and supported by 5 Rows of Pillars.[1] We came through Burton, a neat market Town.

October 24th   3rd Day

We took a Walk to see the Castle, Goal and Church at Lancaster. The Castle built in the reign of Edward 3rd is strong and is now in good repair.[2] The Church contiguous to it is a large Gothic Building.[3] From these Buildings situated on an eminence we have a good Prospect of the Town, River and Country. Lancaster is a well built Town, the houses of Stone either hewn or rough Cast. The Streets as well as those of Kendal are very clean and neat. Contains about 12,000 inhabitants. The Manufactories are Sail Cloth, Twine and Cabinet work for which latter they are very famous.[4]

---

[1] Holy Trinity Church, Kendal, a perfect rectangle with double aisles, built in the Perpendicular style. Pevsner, *Buildings of England: Cumberland and Westmorland* (London, 1967), pp. 253–254.

[2] This was a motte-and-bailey put up by the Normans; the Keep was built before 1102. Alterations were made throughout the Middle Ages and in the eighteenth and nineteenth centuries. Pevsner, *Buildings of England: Lancaster, vol. 2: The Rural North* (London, 1969), p. 156.

[3] St. Mary's Church, which originated in the foundation of a priory church on Lancaster Castle by Roger of Poitou in 1094. *Ibid.*, pp. 153–155.

[4] A reference to Gillows, a distinguished firm of English cabinet makers and furniture designers, based at Lancaster from 1731 and also operating from London after 1761. For a long period Gillows were the best-known makers of English furniture — Sheraton and Hepplewhite both designed for them. *Encyclopaedia Britannica*, XII, p. 23; R. S. Clouston, *English Furniture and Furniture Makers of the Eighteenth Century* (reprinted Wakefield, 1976), pp. 206–220.

They have an excellent stone Pier at which Vessels lade and unlade the greater part of their Cargoes with good Convenience. They have an harbour at a few miles distance from the City where Vessels generally lay for a fair wind.[5]

October 25th   4th Day

Left Lancaster before Sunrise. Came through Garstang, a little market Town. We came to Preston to Breakfast. Preston is a neat beautiful and large Town, the houses brick, the Streets wide and commodious. It has a large stone bridge over the Ribble, a pretty River, by which the Town is supplied with Coals. We passed by several Country Seats and Villages. Came over a Canal.[6] For several miles hereabouts the Country is overflowed, and as we see the Hedges, Trees and a Number of other objects raising their heads above the Surface of the water they have a pretty effect. The Flood has been much higher than it now is, as we see the hedges on the Road side in some places coverd with Straw, which the Water has left on them. The Country is good and a good deal of Woods.

We got to Ormskirk to dinner a neat Market Town famous for a bath in the Neighbourhood[7] and got in to Liverpool about 8 O Clock having rode several miles in the Dark and the road for a considerable distance overflowed.

October 26th   5th Day

This Morning we went to see the Docks, which are now uncommonly full of ships, about 1500 being in port. The wharfs are vastly convenient. Vessels load and unload at them and the Water being kept in during the Ebb they always lay afloat and lay nearly even with the Piers.[8] It is certainly by far the most convenient Port in Great Britain and there is perhaps none superior to it elsewhere.

---

[5] The port of Lancaster was subject to much inconvenience because of the difficulty of navigation of the River Lune, arising from the accumulation of sand in its channel. Ships discharged their cargoes at St. George's Quay, about five miles down the river from Lancaster. Lewis, *Topographical Dictionary of England*, III, p. 20.

[6] The Leeds and Liverpool Canal.

[7] Soft spring water is available in the neighbourhood of Ormskirk. The reference here is to Lathom spa, near Ormskirk. This spa was in existence by the seventeenth century. George Lea, *Illustrated Handbook to Ormskirk and the Neighbourhood* (2nd edn., Ormskirk, 1893), pp. 16–17; P. Smith, ed., *A Short History of Lathom* (St. Helens, n.d.), pp. 51–52. I received help with this note from the Ormskirk Library staff.

[8] Liverpool acquired all the attributes of a port from the reign of Queen Anne onwards. During the eighteenth century, five wet docks (excluding Duke's dock) were constructed at a cost of roughly £150,000. Francis E. Hyde, *Liverpool and the Mersey: An Economic History of a Port, 1700–1970* (Newton Abbot, 1971), ch. 2 and 5.

Liverpool is a large neat populous town. A great number of elegant houses and some excellent public buildings. The Exchange is a fine large Stone Building supported by a number of Pillars.[9] The Church is as elegant a building for its Size as any in England.[10] They have an infirmary which is a good building,[11] but the Alms house is a very spacious Pile of Brick in which 900 People are employed.[12] It is well situated near the Town. The River at high water opposite the Town is above a mile wide (it narrows much afterwards); at low water the width is much less. The Streets are tolerably regular, but dirty for the most part. This town contains about 6,000 houses and 80,000 Inhabitants. They carry on a great Affrican trade and have a vast deal of Connection with the West Indies.[13]

October 27th   6th Day

Accompanied by William Rathbone junior[14] we set out intending to go to RunCorn, but, after riding 15 miles by a bad road and losing our way, we got to the Ferry when the high wind and Tide prevented our crossing. This Ferry crosses over the Mercie where the grand Canal from Leeds empties into it.[15] We rode on to Warrington, a large neat well built populous town

---

[9] The Liverpool Town Hall, built in 1749–1754 by John Wood the Elder, was originally erected as an Exchange. Pevsner, *Buildings of England: Lancashire: The Industrial and Commercial South* (London, 1969), pp. 159–160.

[10] Consecrated in 1769 and 'built at the expence of the town.' *UBD*, III, p. 652.

[11] The Merchant Seaman's Hospital, built on ground belonging to Liverpool Infirmary in 1752, and intended for the support of decayed seamen of Liverpool and of their widows and children. *The Imperial Gazetteer*, II, p. 70.

[12] A poor house was opened in Liverpool in 1771 with accommodation intended for 600 inhabitants. By 1783, there were 920 poor people in this workhouse. J. Aikin, *A Description of the Country from Thirty to Forty Miles round Manchester* (London, 1795), pp. 342–343, 351.

[13] Liverpool was England's leading slave trading port from 1744 until the abolition of the British slave trade in 1807. Clearances of slave vessels from Liverpool to Africa reached over 90 a year in the early 1770s. By that time, Liverpool also had an extensive West India trade. Some 10,089 hogsheads, 1,513 tierces and 862 barrels of sugar were imported at Liverpool from the Caribbean in 1770. David Richardson, *The Bristol Slave Traders: A Collective Portrait* (Bristol Branch of the Historical Association, pamphlet no. 60, 1985), p. 3; Thomas Baines, *History of the Commerce and Town of Liverpool* (Liverpool, 1852), p. 714.

[14] William Rathbone IV (1757–1809) was a Liverpool merchant who worked with his father in a firm engaged in West Indian and American trade. *DQB*; Eleanor Rathbone, *William Rathbone: A Memoir* (London, 1905).

[15] This ferry was situated where the Leeds–Liverpool canal begins out of the River Mersey, just at the lower extremity of the town of Liverpool, by Back-hall, Bootle and Litherland. John Phillips, *A General History of Inland Navigation ...* (5th edn., London, 1805; reprinted 1970), pp. 90–91.

where the greatest quantity of Sail Cloth of any place in Great Britain is manufactured.[16] Here is a good Bridge over the Mercie.

October 28th   7th Day

This Morning we left Warrington and rode on through a fine Country to Worsley where we breakfasted. This place is composed of houses belonging to the Duke of Bridgwater: Mills, Forges, Furnaces &c. The Mill Dam here is upon an entire new but excellent construction. Instead of the water tumbling over the Earth raisd to keep it in there is a hole near the middle about 20 feet Diameter, the Sides walld up with Stone and whenever the water raises too high, it runs down this passage. This method will always prevent a Dam giving way. Near this place are the Duke's Coal Pits, which are brought by water from out of the Earth to Manchester.[17]

We got into a boat of great Length but narrow and went up a Passage above 1,000 yards cut out of a solid Rock above 100 feet below the Surface of the Ground.[18] In some places where the Rocks are loose they are supported by a Brick Arch just sufficient to let our heads go clear as we sat in the boat. After going up these 1,000 yards we got out of the boat and took a walk 160 yards to where the People were at work. This passage is on a right Line, and goes up several Miles further than we chose to venture. We took Candles to light us up this dark and gloomy road as not a single ray comes from without. We ride along the Canal 2 miles when we come to a fine aqueduct, where the Canal is led across a wide Valley and over a River. This Aquaduct is supported by a number of fine Arches and the Scene is realy beautiful. One River crossing over another so high above and boats sailing in each has a pretty Effect.[19]

[16] Warrington's prosperity in the second half of the eighteenth century was closely linked to the growth in the manufacture of sailcloth. A contemporary considered that 'this industry rose to such a height, that half of the heavy sailcloth used in the navy has been computed to be manufactured there.' Aikin, *A Description of the Country from Thirty to Forty Miles round Manchester* (London, 1795; reprinted Newton Abbot, 1968), p. 302.

[17] Francis Egerton, 3rd and last Duke of Bridgewater (1736–1803), constructed a famous canal from Worsley to Manchester. The canal opened in 1760. The Duke's coalpits at Worsley were the most valuable part of his estate. Before the Duke improved his mines, these coalpits suffered from flooding and from difficulties in overland transport to urban centres. *DNB*, VI, pp. 569–571; Hugh Malet, *Bridgewater: The Canal Duke, 1736–1803* (Manchester, 1977), p. 27.

[18] The Duke of Bridgewater was the first person to construct an underground canal system. Though initially expensive, it saved so much in winding coal to the surface and in costly draining of mine water that it proved a very profitable long-term investment. Malet, *Bridgewater: The Canal Duke*, pp. 78–92.

[19] Barton Bridge was three miles from the Duke of Bridgewater's coal pits at Worsley. The aqueduct built here by Brindley conveys the canal for more than 200 yards across the river and along a valley, forty feet above the navigable River Irwell. Phillips, *General History of Inland Navigation*, pp. 90–91. Further details on Brindley are given on p. 234.

From this place we came to Manchester to dinner, but not having it in our Power to wait to see the Town, Buildings, Manufactures &c I shall at present give no Account of it as I intend a more critical Survey hereafter.[20] We got to Rochdale in the Evening where we lodged all Night. This Town is the greatest Manufactury for Flannels Baize &c &c of any in England.[21] 'Tis well situated on the Declivity of two hills and intersected by a pretty Stream.

October 29th   1st Day

Left Rochdale very early and got to Halifax to breakfast. Halifax is an indifferently built Town but very populous and well situated, being within a mile of the Canal[22] by which it is supplied with Coal and enabled to send off the Manufactures at a small expence. It is a very considerable manufacturing Town for most sorts of Woolens, half thicks, broad and narrow Cloths and white plains.[23]

We rode through a fine country to Bradford, full of Hills and Vales and amazingly populous and as we have an extensive View continually before us we see an astonishing Number of little Huts and clusters of Buildings, scarcely intituled to the Name of Village. We dind at Undercliff, a place belonging to John Hurstler, and got to Leeds about 6 O Clock in the Evening.[24]

November 23rd   4th Day

Set off about 5 O Clock this morning in Post Chaise in Company with *Richard* Philips[25] and *Joseph Gurney* Bevan.[26] Left London Pavements

---

[20] See below, pp. 235–237.

[21] The principal branches of the woollen trade at Rochdale in the eighteenth century included baize and flannels (and also coatings, friezes and carpets). Lewis, *Topographical Dictionary of England*, III, p. 617; *VCH: Lancashire*, V, ed. William Farrer and J. Brownbill (London, 1911), p. 189.

[22] The Calder and Salterhebble Canal, built between 1758 and 1765. Arthur Raistrick, *The Making of the English Landscape: The West Riding of Yorkshire* (London, 1970), pp. 141–142.

[23] Lighter-weight cloths (shalloons, calimancoes, camblets, tammies) were produced at Halifax in the eighteenth century. The Halifax Piece Hall, built as a cloth market in 1775, had over 300 rooms. Pat Hudson, *The Genesis of Industrial Capital: A Study of the West Riding Wool Textile Industry c. 1750–1850* (Cambridge, 1986), p. 26; Pevsner, *Buildings of England: Yorkshire: The West Riding* (2nd edn., London, 1974), p. 231.

[24] An unfinished sentence has been cut here.

[25] Richard Phillips (1756–1836), a native of Swansea, a minister and evangelical Friend who was a regular attender at the London Yearly Meeting and who served for forty years in the British and Foreign Bible Society. *DQB*; Frost, *Records and Recollections of James Jenkins*, p. 528n; *Memoir of the Life of Richard Phillips* (London, 1841).

[26] Joseph Gurney Bevan (1753–1814), chemist and druggist of Plough Court, London. He joined his father in business at Plough Court in 1773. *DQB*; Audrey Nona Gamble, *A History of the Bevan Family* (London, 1924), pp. 41–42; *DNB*, II, pp. 445–446; Emden, *Quakers in Commerce*, p. 125.

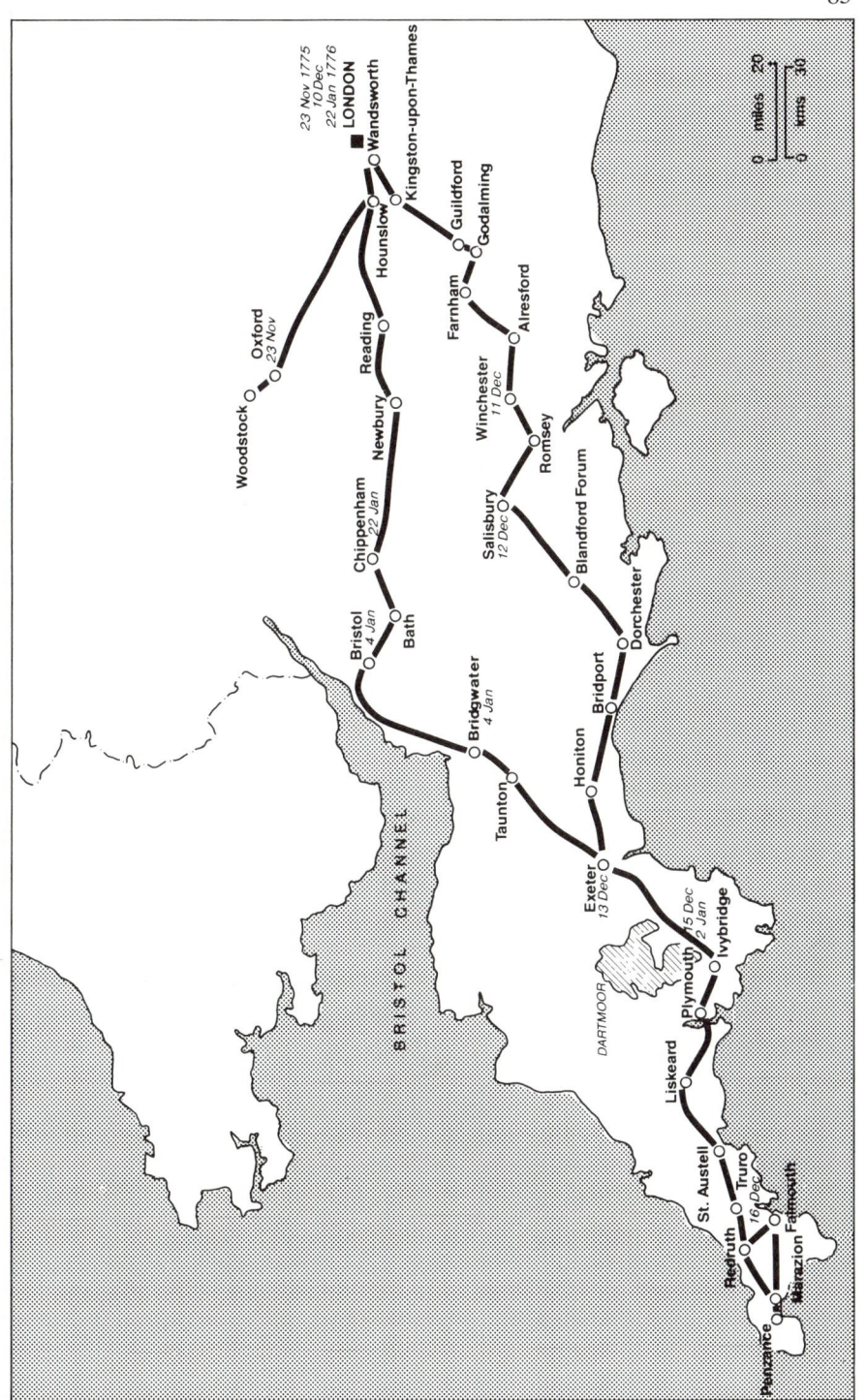

JABEZ MAUD FISHER'S TRAVELS, 23 NOVEMBER 1775 - 22 JANUARY 1776

about 6 and got to Hounslow, changed horses and got to Salt Hill to Breakfast. Dined at Oxford and took a walk after Dinner to see the Theatre,[27] Radcliffe Library[28] and some of the Colledges. This is [the] most magnificent Town in England. The great Number of superb Buildings, elegant and Beautiful Houses contribute to make its appearance particularly grand and majestic. See the Oxford guide which gives a full Account of the Buildings, Schools, Churches, Chapels, Libraries and Pictures.

November 24th   5th Day

Rose early this Morning and took a Walk to see the rest of the Buildings in this City and at Noon set off for Woodstock, where we dined. Here is the most magnificent Palace in Great Britain, belonging to the Duke of Marlborough.[29] The Park is quite an Elysium, finely watered, a noble Bridge across it and a number of Boats plying to and fro, full of Swans and Duck. A fine extensive View with beautiful Verdure, clusters of Trees, a multitude of Deer, a fine Column with a beautiful Image on the Top; in Short the whole Scene is amazingly fine.

December 10th   1st Day

Accompanied by *James* Philips[30] *John* Gurney and *Joseph Gurney* Bevan and R*ichard* Philips my companion we left London about 8 O Clock, came over London Bridge and rode through a delightful Country, passed through several towns, and a number of Gentlemans Seats, came through Wandsworth and got to Kingston to Mitching,[31] where we dined. About 3 O Clock took leave of *James* P*hilips* *John Gurney* and *Joseph Gurney* B*evan* and set off in Post Chaise with R*ichard* Philips, came through Cobham, Guilford,[32] the capital of Surrey, and got to

---

[27] The Sheldonian Theatre, built between 1663 and 1669, was Wren's first architectural work. It was a building erected for university ceremonies. Jennifer Sherwood and Pevsner, *Buildings of England: Oxfordshire* (London, 1974), pp. 255–256.

[28] The Radcliffe Camera, a library in the shape of a rotunda, was begun in 1737 and completed in 1749. The architect was James Gibbs. *Ibid.*, pp. 263–264.

[29] Blenheim Palace was built as a national monument and not as a home. The Royal Manor of Woodstock and funds to build a palace were presented by Queen Anne to John Churchill, Duke of Marlborough, as a token of the nation's gratitude for his defeat of the French army at Blenheim on the Danube in 1704. The architect of Blenheim was John Vanbrugh. *Ibid.*, pp. 459–475.

[30] James Phillips (1745–1799) was born in Cornwall. He settled in London by 1768, when he married Mary Whiting, and was described as a 'citizen and woolman' in the London and Middlesex Friends' marriage digest. He became a linendraper with John Dollin in London. *DQB*; Frost, *Records and Recollections of James Jenkins*, p. 211.

[31] Probably Mitcham.

[32] Guildford.

Goudalmin[33] to lodge. The Road all the way from London is delightful, a number of elegant Seats, fine Prospects, and pretty Villages, some land uninclosed, the Thames mostly in Sight, and nothing wanting but a good Season to perfect it. At this place is a good boarding School for young Women.

December 11th   2nd Day

Rose early left Godalmin and came to Farnham 14 miles to Breakfast. Thence to Alton, a tolerable good Market Town, to Alesford[34] where we only stopd to change Chaise and from thence to Winchester. The Country till we come within a few Miles of this Place is rich, well inclosed and finely wooded, but as we approach Winchester, it is more open, though the Land be good.

Winchester is a very ancient Town said to be founded several hundred years before Christ.[35] Its Appearance is curious. The houses are ancient and their form droll, though there are some new and elegant Buildings. They have a neat Market house, a Colledge[36] and several Public Buildings. There is a Wall round the City and the Gates are of fine Gothic Structure. Here is a very noble Cathedral partly Saxon and partly Gothic.[37] The Altar is one of the finest in England, [with] a vast Quantity of hewn Stone curiously decorated.[38] Here is the grave of William Rufus who was killed not very distant from this place,[39] and two of the finest Monuments in England, besides a Number of others of not a little curious Workmanship.

[33] Godalming.

[34] Alresford.

[35] Winchester is the successor of the British settlement of Caer Gwent, the Roman town of Venta Belgarum, and the Saxon Wintonceaster. It became the capital of Wessex in 519 and saw Egbert crowned as first king of all England in 827. Stuart Rossiter, *Blue Guide: England* (9th edn., London, 1980), p. 113.

[36] Winchester College was founded in 1382 by William of Wykeham. He was the first person to have a coherent idea of a system of tuition rising from school to college, and his two foundations, New College, Oxford and Winchester College, were on a scale unprecedented in England. William of Wykeham became Bishop of Winchester in 1366. Winchester College was built between 1380 and 1386 and it opened in 1394. Pevsner and David Lloyd, *Buildings of England: Hampshire and the Isle of Wight* (London, 1967), pp. 698–706.

[37] Winchester has the largest cathedral in England and Europe, its external length being 556 feet. It was mainly built at various points between 1070 and 1528. *Ibid.*, pp. 661–685.

[38] A reference to the sixteenth century screen above the altar. The screen was despoiled of all precious metals and its statuary destroyed during the Reformation, but the damage has been restored. *Ibid.*, pp. 677–678; E. G. Selwyn, *The Story of Winchester Cathedral* (London, 1934), p. 47.

[39] William II (c. 1056–1100) died from an accidental shot by his companion Walter Tirel while hunting in the New Forest.

This Cathedral was built first in the Sixth Century. The Work at the Entrance of the Choir is the Work of Inigo Jones.[40]

Here we dined and came through an open Country to Rumsey where we took up our abode with Michael Futcher.[41] At this place we went to see a fine Seat belonging to Lord Palmastone (Broad Lines).[42] A fine River[43] running near the house in a winding Direction, a great Number of Clusters of Trees and the pleasure Grounds are exceedingly beautiful. His Gardens are clever. The house was planned by the ingenious Architect Brown.[44] The Fronts are both supported by fine Stone Columns. The Rooms are grand, and here are some fine Pictures of Claude Lorain[45] and some other fine Masters — Poussaine,[46] Salvator Rosa.[47]

Rumsey[48] is situated on the River Tix[49] which runs through. It is a pretty large ancient Town, delightfully environed with woods, meadows &c. Here is a Church which was formerly a Monastery.[50] In the Neighbourhood of this Town is a famous Wood calld the New Forrest. Thirty miles in Circumference, it formerly had many villages in it and 36 Churches, but the whole was laid waste by William the Conqueror so that it

[40] Inigo Jones (1573–1652), theatrical designer, architect and Surveyor-General of the King's Works from 1615 until 1643. Howard Colvin, *A Biographical Dictionary of British Architects, 1600–1840*, (London, 1978), pp. 467–474.

[41] Michael Futcher, shalloon manufacturer and wine merchant, Romsey, Hants. Bailey's *British Directory*, II, p. 433.

[42] Henry Temple (1739–1802), 2nd Viscount Palmerston, of Broadlands, near Romsey, represented six different constituencies in southern England from 1762 until his death. He had literary and artistic interests, and rebuilt Broadlands and its grounds. Namier and Brooke, *History of Parliament: The House of Commons, 1754–1790*, III, pp. 519–520.

[43] River Test.

[44] Lancelot 'Capability' Brown (1715–1783), landscape gardener and architect, whose major aim was to bring out the undulating lines of the natural landscape. He laid out or remodelled the grounds at Kew, Blenheim, Nuneham Courtenay etc. *DNB*, III, p. 22.

[45] Claude Lorrain (1600–1682) was born in Nancy but mainly worked in Italy, where he acquired a big reputation as a painter of romanticised poetic landscapes. Murray and Murray, *Penguin Dictionary of Art and Artists*, pp. 80–81.

[46] Nicolas Poussin (1594–1665) was born in Normandy but mainly worked in Rome. He was famous for his depiction of Biblical and classical subjects, mythology, and landscapes based on solid geometry. *Ibid.*, pp. 329–330.

[47] Salvator Rosa (1615–1673), a prolific Italian painter whose early work consisted of battlepieces and of landscapes painted near Naples. From 1649 he was a religious and historical painter in Rome. *Ibid.*, pp. 369–370.

[48] Romsey.

[49] River Test.

[50] Romsey Abbey was founded as a Benedictine nunnery in 907 and refounded sixty years later. A general rebuilding took place between 1120 and about 1230. Pevsner and Lloyd, *Buildings of England: Hampshire and the Isle of Wight*, pp. 477–486.

might be a habitation for wild beasts for him to hunt.[51] But for this Act of Cruelty in driving the inhabitants away a Judgement followed for his two sons Richard[52] and William Rufus lost their lives, the first by a pestinential blast, the latter by an Arrow shot by Sir Walter Tyrrel at a Stag. Here is a tree paled in which was glanced by the Arrow when it killd Rufus.

December 12th   3rd Day

We left Rumsey early this Morning and got to Salisbury at 9 O Clock (the Capital of Wiltshire) having passed through Hampshire, one of the finest Counties in England for Timber. Salisbury is an Episcopal See, a large old City, the Streets regular crossing each other at right Angles. There are a number of Streams of Water watering every street. The Cathedral is one of the most elegant and regular in the Kingdom, the Spire in the Center being 410 feet high and the Isle of the church 452 feet by 205. It has as many Windows as there are Days in the Year, as many Doors and Chapels as Months, as many Pillars and Pilasters as hours, and as many panes of Glass as Minutes, which Circumstance gave occasion for the following Lines:

> As many days in 1 year there be
> So many windows in 1 church we see;
> As many marble pillars there appear;
> As through are hours throughout the fleeting year;
> As many panes there are brittle of Glass
> As minutes in one year away do pass
> As Many Gates as Morns one year does view
> Strange tale to tell, but not more strange than true.

This Cathedral is a noble Gothic structure and makes a grand appearance. Here are some good Cloisters and a number of elegant and capital Monuments.[53]

From Salisbury went about 6 Miles over an uninclosed open Country for Sheep to the magnificent Ruins of Stone Henge, an amazing pile of Building, in the investigation of which the virtuosi have taken great pains. It is situated on a great plain, and there is nothing to eclipse the view on

[51] Tradition has it that the New Forest was created at the instigation of William the Conqueror. 'The amount of devastation ... has perhaps been exaggerated, but certainly many villages were depopulated and there was doubtless some destruction of church property.' David C. Douglas, *William the Conqueror* (London, 1964), p. 371.

[52] Richard was accidentally killed in the New Forest at an early age (b. before 1056; d. c. ?1075). *Ibid.*, pp. 393–394.

[53] The foundation stones of Salisbury Cathedral were laid in 1220 and most of the building took place during the rest of the thirteenth century. There were later restorations. Salisbury has, at 404 feet, the highest spire of any English cathedral. Pevsner and Bridget Cherry, *Buildings of England: Wiltshire* (2nd edn., London, 1975), pp. 389–422.

any Side of us, the extravagant Grandeur of which is for a few Minutes somewhat abated by its being the only object on so wide a Theatre. However a little Contemplation soon rouses our astonishment.

Antiquarians have till lately been much divided in their opinions respecting the magnificent Structure, but it is now universally allowed to have been one of the grand Temples of the British Druids.[54] The Stones are natural, not factitious, and must not withstanding their enormous weight have been brought 16 Miles.

Our near approach to this stupendous Work is aweful, but its effects are much greater when you enter within.[55] It is inclosd in a circular Ditch, which we pass 35 yards before we enter the Building whose yawning ruins affect us in a manner not easy to be described. These Stones are of amazing magnitude. One of them though not the largest is fallen down and broken and weighs 40 tons. As we advance farther the ponderous imposts over our heads and the Chasms of Sky between the Jambs of the Cells together with the oddness of the Construction still more surprise us. We fancy Quarries mounted in the Air, or the Bowells of a Mountain turnd inside out.

It consists of 2 Ovals and 2 Circles respectively concentric. 17 of the upright Stones are standing, 33 feet in height, 3 in thickness and 9 in Width. The lesser Circle is 9 feet within the other, the Stones not so large. 11 of them are standing and 8 lie down. The walk between these two Circles is 300 feet in Circumference, grand and delightful. These enormous Stones, in height breadth and thickness, placd in such critical exactness create in the mind such emotions as cannot well be described. The Number of Stones now remaining is 140. Near this amazing work of Antiquity as well as in many other parts of this Country is a great Number of Elevations of Earth. These are Sepulchral Tumuli or Graves, where the ancient Britons deposited the Ashes of their Dead.[56]

From this place we went to Wilton, a considerable Market Town contiguous to which is Wilton House, a famous seat belonging to Lord Pembroke.[57] The house is ancient but embellishd by some modern

---

[54] Stonehenge is probably the most celebrated prehistoric monument in Europe. The stones belong to various Wessex cultures of the sixteenth and fifteenth centuries B.C. The site has been the target for antiquarian research and speculation since the seventeenth century. *Ibid.*, pp. 487–493.

[55] I have cut a couple of rough sketches of Stonehenge.

[56] These are the Stonehenge Barrow cemeteries, which have yielded some of the richest burials of the Wessex culture. Pevsner and Bridget Cherry, *Buildings of England and Wales: Wiltshire*, p. 493.

[57] Wilton House was originally part of an estate granted to the 1st Earl of Pembroke in 1544 and with various alterations since, especially by James Wyatt in the early nineteenth century. Henry Herbert (1734–1794) was 29th Earl of Pembroke from 1750. *Ibid.*, pp. 580–587; Cokayne, *Complete Peerage*, X, p. 426.

Architects, and the Rooms are spacious laid out with great Taste, and furnishd in the most superb and magnificent Stile. In the Court stands a Column of white Egyptian Granite of one piece weighing between 60 and 70 cwt. Julius Caesar set this up before the temple of Venus Genetrix.[58] There is in this house the greatest Collection of Antique Statuary by far of any in Great Britain. The Caesars, the Kings, the Great Orators of Rome and Greece and almost all the Gods and Goddesses of the Heathen. Here are also a fine parcel of very curious paintings by the best Artists: Raphael,[59] Poussin, Rubens, Vandyk,[60] Reynells[61] &c &c Guido[62] and Claude.

The River runs near the House through his pleasure Ground over which there is a noble Bridge. The Clusters of Trees, Walks, Images and other objects make the Scene exceedingly delightful. In the house are several large Marble and Granite Tables, a fine collection of Antique Alto and Basso Releivo Figures.[63] The Chimney Pieces by Inigo Jones are very capital. In short this (except the outside appearance of the house) is one of the finest Seats in England.

From Wilton we came to Blandford,[64] a smallish Market Town, drank Tea and came on that Evening into Dorsetshire. Wiltshire is a fine County tolerably well wooded, but there are some large Tracts without a Single [tree] for many Miles together. A vast number of Sheep are raised here and the Downs on which they feed are good.

We got into Dorchester about 8 O Clock where we supped and lodged.

[58] In the Court, before the grand front of Wilton House, stands a column of white Egyptian granite, out of the Arundel collection. 'Mr. Evelyn bought it for the Earl of Arundel at Rome, where Julius Caesar had set it up before the Temple of Venus Genetrix.' It was 13 feet high and had a diameter of 22 inches. James Kennedy, *A New Description of the Pictures, Statues, Bustos, Basso-Relievos, and other Curiosities at the Earl of Pembroke's House at Wilton . . .* (London, 1764), p. 1.

[59] Raphael (1483–1520) went to Rome around 1508 and became the principal master employed in the Vatican, with the sole exception of Michelangelo. Raphael is famous for his frescoes and for portraits based on religious themes. Murray and Murray, *Penguin Dictionary of Art and Artists*, pp. 340–342.

[60] Sir Anthony Van Dyck (1599–1641) worked in Italy (1621–1627), in Antwerp (1627–1632), and in England (1632–1641). He was a prolific portrait painter of great prestige at the court of Charles I, from whom he received a knighthood. *Ibid.*, pp. 122–124.

[61] Sir Joshua Reynolds (1723–1792) was mainly known as a portrait painter of nearly every famous person in England c. 1750–1790, but he also painted history pictures. *Ibid.*, pp. 349–351.

[62] Guido Reni (1575–1642) was born in Bologna and became one of the most prominent Baroque painters in Italy. His subjects were mainly mythological and Biblical. *Ibid.*, pp. 356–357.

[63] Alto Relievo is a form of sculpture or carving in high relief; basso relievo is low relief. Murray, *New English Dictionary*, I, pp. 259, 694.

[64] Blandford Forum.

This [is] a pretty large town and was a considerable Station of the Romans. They had a Camp[65] near it, the vestiges of which are still visible. It is situated on the Banks of the Frome. A Street of Romans is traced here and the Foundations of the Wall appear quite round the Town. Near this Place is an amphitheatre of the Romans, which now serves for a Walk for the Inhabitants.[66]

December 13th   4th Day

Left Dorchester early this Morning and came to Bridport to Breakfast. This was formerly a Sea Port of some Trade, but the Harbour is now quite choaked up. We next come to Honiton, the first Town in Devonshire. Dorsetshire is but an indifferent County, a great deal of broken Land tho the vallies are prettily laid out and afford a picturesque view. We rode many miles in Sight of the British Channel.

From Honiton we came to Exeter, a considerable City for Trade, Size Number and Wealth of its Inhabitants. It consists chiefly of one Street very strait, but rough Pavement. Into this run several other Streets but they are narrow and inconvenient. Here is a considerable Bridge over the River Ex with a number of houses built on it. This is a considerable See. The Cathedral[67] is but indifferent but they have besides 13 Churches and formerly had many others. Oliver [Cromwell] sold 14 of them and they were converted to other uses.[68] Here is also a pretty large Colledge.[69] There is [a] wall round the Town and several passages out of it.

We left this place at 7 O Clock, came to Chudleigh, changed horses and

[65] A reference to either Maiden Castle or Poundbury. Maiden Castle, on a hill above Dorchester, was originally a British hillfort erected in the early 1st century B.C. There are Roman remains at Maiden Castle, dating from much later, the closing years of the fourth century A.D. At the nearby Poundbury camp there is a Roman aqueduct, built in the late 1st century A.D., which carried water to Dorchester. Roger J. A. Wilson, *A Guide to the Roman Remains in Britain* (London, 1975), pp. 69–71, 73.

[66] The amphitheatre, known as Maumbury Rings, is on the southern side of Dorchester. The Romans carried out this project c. 70–80 A.D. The amphitheatre had an active life of between fifty and eighty years. *Ibid.*, p. 73.

[67] Exeter Cathedral stands on the site of a Benedictine monastery dedicated to St. Peter and founded in the seventh century. An entirely new cathedral was built in the twelfth century and rebuilt between the 1270s and the 1380s. Bridget Cherry and Pevsner, *Buildings of England: Devon* (2nd edn., London, 1989), pp. 364–387.

[68] A parliamentary army under Fairfax captured Exeter on 9 Apr. 1646. It ejected all the episcopal ministers from their cures. The cathedral was ransacked and thirteen of the parish churches in Exeter 'were exposed for sale, by the common cryer.' These actions were a punishment to the city of Exeter for supporting the Royalists. Alexander Jenkins, *The History and Description of the City of Exeter, and its Environs, Ancient and Modern* ... (Exeter, 1806), pp. 164–165.

[69] The Free Grammar School in Exeter, founded by the citizens before the date of the charter of Charles I. Lewis, *Topographical Dictionary of England*, II, pp. 156–157.

got to Ashburton, a pretty large but indifferently built Town where we lodged.

December 15th   5th day

Left Ashburton early in the Morning to Ivy Bridge a little paltry village where we changed horses and got to Plymouth to Breakfast. Plymouth is situated at the Conflux of the Plym and Tamar, was formerly only a fishing Town but is now including the Stone house and Stoke the latter of which is at the Royal Dock,[70] by much the largest in the Country. They have 2 Harbours capable of containing 1000 Sail of Vessels, which are as safe as any in the Kingdom. It is defended by several Forts mounting about 300 Guns, particularly by a Citadel of large Extent containing a magazine of Stores and 5 Bastions.[71] The Town is built on a hill falling every way. The Streets are irregular, very narrow. The houses outside cut but an indifferent Figure, though they be well finished within, all built of Limestone, and for the most part rough cast white.

An excellent Market for Fish, Meat and Vegetables about 1 Mile from Plymouth is Stoke, on one Side of which is the Royal Dock, a most noble and convenient Harbour for Men of War, a great Number being always stationd here, and many are built. Here are wet and Dry Docks, Mast Yards, Storehouses, Rope Walks, Timber yards, hemp houses, Wharves, Cranes; in short every Convenience for building, repairing, loading, fitting and careening and of an Extent incredible to an American. Here are four Ships now building, the Royal Sovereign of an 100 Guns, the Duke of 90 and two third Rates. The two former are in considerable Forwardness. 700 Ship Wrights are now at work here besides Smiths, Ropemakers, Joiners, Carvers &c &c. The house for the Officers of the Yard is a large elegant Building with Trees before the Door. The whole of this yard is on a solid marble Rock and the improvements now making are immense.

This inlet from the Sea is called the Hamouze and is commanded by a Castle on St. Nicholas island.[72] The prospect from the Dock is fine. The

---

[70] In 1692 William III established Plymouth Dockyard on the Hamoaze. The town of Dock (later Devonport) which grew around it was given its own fortifications in the eighteenth century. Plymouth Dockyard was greatly expanded and rebuilt from the 1760s onwards. It was second in importance only to Portsmouth Dockyard by the time of the American Revolution. Morriss, *Royal Dockyards*, p. 2; Cherry and Pevsner, *Buildings of England: Devon*, pp. 364–387.

[71] The Citadel was begun in 1666 by Charles II as a stronghold against attack from enemies. It remained the military headquarters of Plymouth until new buildings were provided at Devonport in the eighteenth century. Cherry and Pevsner, *Buildings of England: Devon*, pp. 648–649.

[72] St. Nicholas Island was fortified by Sir Francis Drake and remained in military occupation until 1956. The island is now generally known as Drake's Island. Brian Le Mesurier, *A Visitor's Guide to Devon* (Ashbourne, 1983), p. 69.

Harbour is dispersed with Men of War, about 35 now being in Port. Directly opposite is Lord Edgecombe's Seat[73] a large elegant Fabrick. In the Neighbourhood of the Dock is a Charity School and hospital[74] consisting of large Stone houses which make a magnificent appearance. The Order, Oeconomy, Regularity and Convenience of this Dock is on too large a Scale to be particularly described in a little epitome of my Travels. Suffice it for me to note that it was almost infinitely beyond any Idea I could have previously formed of it.

A little Distance from this and without the Dock Gate is the Gun Wharf, where [is] a noble Stand of Armoury and here all the Guns and Balls are deposited in the most compleat Order.[75] The Vessels are conducted in the Night safely by means of the Edystone Lighthouse, built on a Rock opposite the Harbour.[76]

December 16th   6th Day

About 12 O Clock left Plymouth, came to Saltash Ferry which divides Devonshire from Cornwall. We come into Saltash and for the present bid Devonshire goodbye. A good County it is, very different from any of the rest in this part of the Island. Hills and vallies, well wooded, nicely inclosed, rich Soil, and in every instance well cultivated. Black cattle graze in the Vallies and on the Hills skip the fleecy flocks, while the Declivities are converted to Arable. The whole County is excellently well waterd and excepting the western Side of the County, tis not excelled by many in the Kingdom.

Saltash is situated on a most rough steep, rocky side of an almost inaccessible Hill. Dirty streets, ill built houses, and poor wretched poor inhabitants. We here got Post Chaise and 4 miserable Quadrupeds, weak, lame and blind. But however made shift to get along 14 Miles over a terrible hilly Country to Liskerd, through which and another dirty

---

[73] The seat of the Earl of Mount Edgcumbe, Cornwall. It was built between 1547 and 1554, and was later laid out with English, Italian and French gardens. Pevsner and Enid Radcliffe, *Buildings of England: Cornwall* (2nd edn., London, 1970), pp. 123–124.

[74] The charity school was either Lady Rogers' charity school, in Tavistock Road, founded in 1773 for girls, or Lanyon's charity school, at North Hill, founded in 1632 for boys. The hospital is probably the Orphans' Aid Hospital, established in 1625 for the education and maintenance of ten boys. *The Imperial Gazetteer*, II, p. 626.

[75] The Gun wharf (or Morice Yard), an important department of the naval establishment, situated along the margin of Hamoaze. It was designed by Vanbrugh and laid out between 1719 and 1724. Cherry and Pevsner, *Buildings of England: Devon*, pp. 652–653.

[76] John Smeaton's Eddystone Lighthouse, fourteen miles south of the shore at Plymouth, was erected between 1756 and 1759. It replaced two previous lighthouses that had been destroyed. *Ibid.*, p. 656.

mean town (Lostwithail)[77] to St. Austale,[78] a place somewhat more comfortable than either of the former and here we took up our rest for this Night. So far of Cornwal the Country is good, well wooded, but tomorrow expect worse.

[77] Lostwithiel.
[78] St. Austell.

1775
December 16th   7th Day
Cornwal

We left St. Austale early in the Morning and got to Truro to Breakfast. This is a pretty large well built Town, tolerably regular and the Place from whence the Tin is shipd off, being brought here in Blocks of 3 cwt. each and left in the streets till an opportunity offer. We got to Redruth to Dinner and took up my abode with William Philips.[1] On 17 went to Meeting twice, very small, and on 18 and 19 stayd at home all Day to write, the Packet being about to sail for America.

December 20th

This Morning set off in Post Chaise with *Catherine* Philips[2] for Falmouth. We passed through Penryn and got to Falmouth about 10 Clock. Took up my abode with *Joseph* Fox.[3] Falmouth is situated a few Miles from the English Channel. The Harbour is good, well landlock and capable of holding a great Number of Vessels. There is a Bar at the Entrance, but Vessels of considerable Size may pass over without Inconvenience. They have two good Piers which form a good Bason, and load and unload with great Expedition, having Cranes and other Conveniences for Discharge. On this Wharf is the Custom House, an old ordinary building almost tumbling to Pieces.[4]

While we were here (a Ship which had arrived from Quebec and

---

[1] William Philips (d. 1785) was originally from Swansea but settled at Trewirgn, near Redruth. He was an agent to a copper company trading between Cornwall and South Wales. *DQB*; Isabel Grubb, *Quakerism and Industry before 1800* (London, 1930), p. 54.

[2] Catherine Philips (1726/7–1794qv) was the second wife of William Philips. *DQB*; Grubb, *Quakerism and Industry before 1800*, pp. 54–56; *Life of Catherine Phillips* (London, 1797).

[3] Joseph Fox (1758–1832), born at Falmouth, married in 1780 and moved to London in 1788. He was for many years a physician at the London Hospital. He and his wife returned to Cornwall c. 1802. *DQB*.

[4] The Custom House was established in Falmouth in 1650, when it was removed there from Penryn by the first Sir Peter Killigrew. Susan E. Gay, *Old Falmouth* (London, 1903), pp. 33, 229.

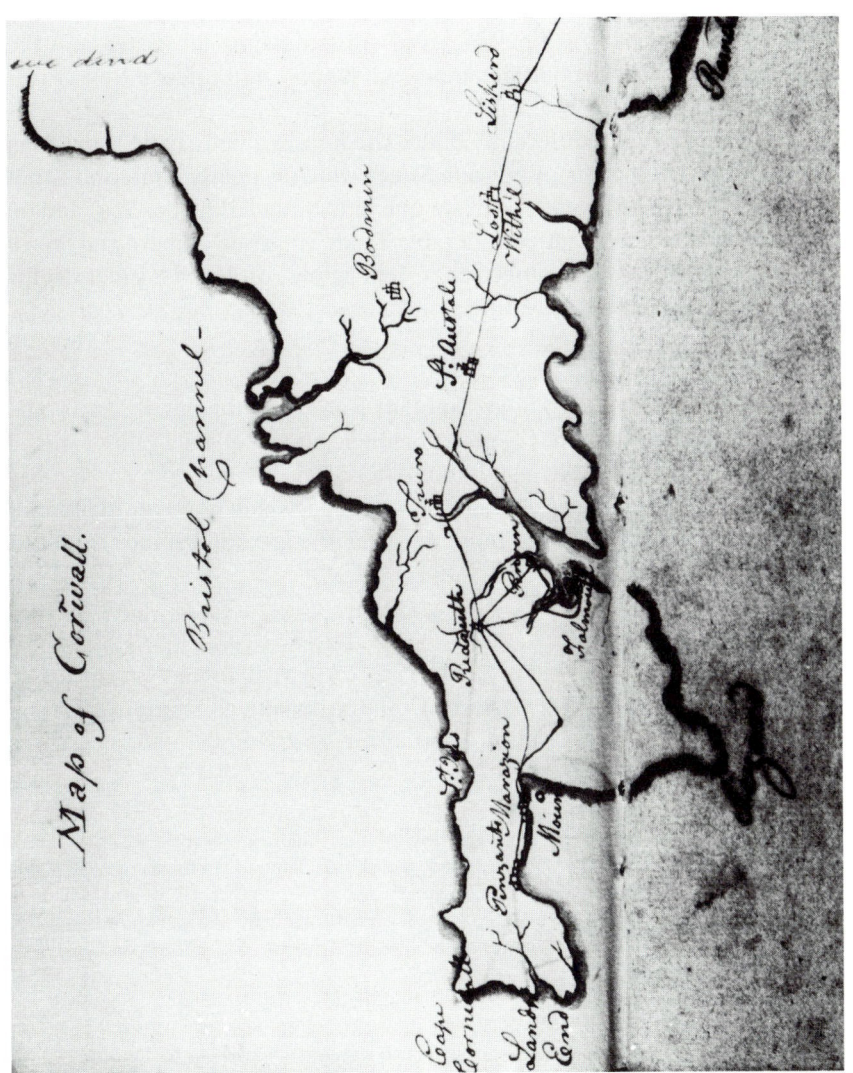

FIG. 2. Fisher's map of Cornwall

brought over Colonels Johnson and Closse, several other Officers and two
Indian Mohawk Chiefs) landed Allen an Officer in the Provincial Army,
and 34 other Prisoners, who were taken near Montreal on the first attack
on that place.[5] They were conducted in Irons to the Castle through a
considerable Mob to the Castle. This Castle is very strong, but a small
Garrison is kept here in time of peace. It commands the Town and the
Entrance into the Harbour was built by Henry 7 and attacked by Oliver
Cromwell, but he was beat off.[6]

The Town is but indifferently built. The houses chiefly two Stories high
and of Stone. It consists of but one Street which is nearly strait and is not
capable of being enlarged, as it is on one Side bounded by the Sea, and on
the other by a steep hill. A considerable Trade is carried on here and *few* of
the inhabitants have any objection to Smuggling, of which a great deal is
done here.[7] We stayed here till

December 22nd   6th Day

When I set out with Caty Phillips another Rode than the one we had come
and got to Penrin to dine, a place belonging to William Philips. In the
Evening we got home, having a rainy Afternoon. We passed by a Number
of Copper and Tin Mines, several Country Seats which however in point of
elegance are much inferior to those we meet at a greater distance from this
extremity of the Island.

December 23rd   7th Day

Richard Philips and myself this Morning on a visit to the Westward of
Redruth on horseback. We passed a Country, having its Share of Poverty,
though not without some fruitful Spots and a great Number of Mines, came

---

[5] This incident occurred at the beginning of the American War of Independence.
General Carleton had only 800 seasoned troops to defend Montreal against 2,000
Americans advancing northwards from Ticonderoga in September 1775. Fort Chambly
and Fort St John's both surrendered to the rebels and, by early November 1775,
Montreal was abandoned. Piers Mackesy, *The War for America, 1775–1783* (London, 1964),
p. 79.

[6] There were two substantial castles at Falmouth, one on the Pendennis promontory, the
other on the opposite headland at St. Mawes. Work began on these two forts in 1540. Two
castles were needed to defend the River Fal, which was a major harbour on the south coast.
Colvin, *History of the King's Works,* IV Part 2, pp. 595–602.

[7] The prosperity of Falmouth in the eighteenth century was based on the packet service
and the smuggling that grew up with it. Tea and spirits were the main commodities
smuggled. Falmouth was well positioned for the trade. It could meet East Indiamen reaching
the English Channel and obtain rich wares and tea, and runs were easy to the Channel
Islands, St. Malo or Roscoff. *VCH: Cornwall,* ed. William Page (London, 1906), I,
pp. 505–508.

along Side of the Place John Nancarrow[8] lived at, above Wheel Park. Got to Marazion to dine and went to see the Castle, called sometimes Cornish Mount.[9] This Castle is situated on a most romantic Rock which at high Water is an island, $\frac{1}{4}$ of a Mile from the main Land. But at low Water there is a small Neck of Land on which we may walk to it. This Rock is several hundred feet high, going near to a point at the Top, on which the Castle is built. The Ascent to it is steep, but a winding path leads up to it without much difficulty. There is a number of good Rooms and a Chapel and the Tour commands a most extensive view of the Channel and the Country round. This Island or Peninsula is said to have once been united with the Land, but the Sea has made such depredations as to have almost entirely disunited it.

There are several houses under one Side of the Rock next the Shore, two Piers which run out and form a good bason for Shipping, a number always lying here. It came on to rain hard, so were obliged to stay at Marazion that Night, the Wind high, squally and cold.

Cornwal
December 24th   1st Day

Set off this Morning for Penzants, a large trading town situate in Mounts Bay on the Beach. The Town is neat well built, chiefly Stone, a good Pier, and a number of Vessels chiefly employed in the Fishing Buisness, as are also the Vessels in Marazion and Falmouth at which last Place about 70 Thousand Hogsheads of Pilchards are caught annually. Went to Meeting at Penzants, dined there, and in the Evening came through Marazion to John Nancarrows (in the Rain) and lodged there that Evening.

Cornwal
December 25th   2nd Day

Took a ride this Morning to Lord Godolphins Park,[10] which is indeed a very curious one: no Grass, no Trees, but a large Tract of Moors, covered with Furze, and instead of Deer we see nothing but Asses. The house is a pretty large curious ancient Building, very plain of the Gothic Structure.

---

[8] John, son of John Nancarrow of Germow parish, married Anne Richards of Marazion in 1762. *TRE.*

[9] St. Michael's Mount, linked with Marazion by a causeway of boulders and pebbles passable at low tide. A cell of Benedictine monks was established there by c. 1087–1091. Pevsner and Enid Radliffe, *Buildings of England: Cornwall* (2nd edn., London, 1970), pp. 193–195. Fisher's drawing is reproduced overleaf.

[10] Godolphin Hall was the home of the Godolphins, who rose to prominence under Henry VIII. In 1766 the property descended to the Dukes of Leeds. *Ibid.,* p. 73; Robin Fedden and John Kenworthy-Browne, *The Country House Guide* (London, 1979), pp. 245–246.

100

Fɪɢ. 3. Fisher's sketch of St. Michael's Mount, Cornwall.

The Front is low with a Piazza at the Entrance supported by stone Columns. The Gardens but indifferent. The Land here is good and round the house is a number of fine Trees. From this place we went to Hayl, where there are several Capital Copper Works.[11] We stayd here a few hours, saw the Process of calcining, melting, casting &c[12] and in the Evening returned to John Nancarrows where we lodged.[13]

December 26th   2nd Day

Took a walk this Morning to see a number of the Tin and Copper Works. The land here, as far as we can behold, is turned inside out, all broken and an immense Number of Shafts sunk.[14] The Manner of finding where these *Shoals* or Veins of Mines are found is various, sometimes by observing the vapours which rise from the Earth, which never do in this Country where the Land is so dry. But when there is Ore of some Sort, sometimes plowing a field or digging ditches, a few pieces are found, and in this Case they never fail tracing the Mine to its Source. It is remarkable that Tin and Copper always run East and West and that Lead runs North and South. The Shafts or Pitts are sunk and as the Veins run downwards they trace them a great Depth, from 10 fathoms to 125 Fathoms and then run a considerable horizontal Distance. They have one passage for the Men to go up and down, another for the Buckets only. Whenever they go to a great Depth they are obliged to have a fire or Water Engine for keeping the Pitts clear of the Springs which would otherwise drown them.

The Tin Mines yield annually about £250,000 and the Copper Mines yield about £180,000. The Tin about 20,000 Blocks of 3 cwt. each, and the Copper 35,000 Tons annually. There are 13 Companies who are concerned in these Articles. They all preserve a great Harmony. Indeed the mode they adopt to buy their Ore is such that it does not admit of any Dispute arising on that Account. Each Day in a way there is a Sale at an Inn of the Ore, each Company being previously supplied by the Proprietors of the Mines with Samples and an Account of the Quantity that is to be sold, so

[11] The Hayle Copper Works were originally established at Entral, near Camborne, in 1754. After a few years they were moved to Hayle to eliminate the heavy costs of the land carriage of coal to a site at least four or five miles from tidewater. John Rowe, *Cornwall in the Age of the Industrial Revolution* (Liverpool, 1953), pp. 63–64.

[12] Calcination is the application of heat to an ore, or partially prepared metalliferous material, to alter its physical structure and/or expel a part of the material (e.g. water). The modern brassmaking process that uses metallic zinc and copper is known as melting, as no chemical change takes place in the materials used. Casting enables copper to cool and harden in a mould. Joan Day, *Bristol Brass: A History of the Industry* (Newton Abbot, 1973), pp. 195, 199; *OED*, II, p. 162.

[13] Fisher's drawing of John Nancarrow's house is reproduced overleaf.

[14] I have cut one page of loose jottings about the Cornish mines.

FIG. 4. Fisher's sketch of John Nancarrow's house.

that they have an opportunity to assay the Quality and determine on the Price they will give which they set down on a Ticket, and on the Day of the Sale hand them in to a Person appointed by the Purchasers who immediately reads out the Price and the Name of the Person that makes the Offer and the highest Bidder always has the Ore. If two of the Companies fix on one Price the Quantity is divided between them if it exceed 40 Tons, but if not the Person who bought the last parcel gives it up to the other. This just and equitable mode of Sale is well calculated to suit both Purchaser and Seller.[15]

The Tin Ore is taken from the Pit from which it is raised to a Stamping Mill of which they have great Numbers all over the County.[16] It is here broken into small pieces and washed sundry times till 42 Tons are reduced to two and then it is sold as above. From this place it is taken to the Works where it is twice melted and the 2 Tons are reduced to one. It is then cast into Blocks of 3 cwt. each and taken to the Places of Export.

The Copper is chiefly broken by the hand and the Mundick and Iron and Stones separated from it, when it is taken to the Melting Works, where it undergoes several purgations. It is first put into an Oven where the Mundick is evaporated. This process it goes through twice and thence it is taken to the Furnaces where it is many times melted before it attains a sufficient degree of purity.

If we confine ourselves to the Face of the Country in Cornwall we shall have but a very indifferent Idea of it, but such Riches are hidden beneath the Surface of the Earth as fully compensate for its apparent poverty, for besides the Copper and Tin got out of the Country, the Fish is far from being an inconsiderable object, yielding upwards of £50,000 per Annum. There is a small Quantity of Lead found here, some little parcels of Silver and now and then a trifle of Gold.

The People here being all more or less engaged in the Mining Business, they are diverted from any other Manufactury and even from Agriculture. But notwithstanding this, there are some very fine cultivated Spots of Land, and a Verdure which in this time of Year we only meet with here;

---

[15] Tin Mining in Cornwall was governed by customs and regulations. The stannaries came under protection, by charter, of their own laws, in return for which they paid taxes to the Duchy of Cornwall. The tin produced was taxed after smelting through a system of coinage. No tin could be sold until it had been coined. Under the coinage system, tin sales were only held once every three months. A. K. Hamilton Jenkin, *The Cornish Miner* (London, 1927), ch. 1; D. B. Barton, *A History of Tin Mining and Smelting in Cornwall* (Truro, 1967), pp. 18–19.

[16] The Cornish stamping mills owe their existence to the coinage system, in which the tin was stamped with the Duchy seal after the dues were paid. Barton, *History of Tin Mining and Smelting in Cornwall*, p. 18 n. 2.

and there is no where that Land produces Corn in greater abundance than in the improved parts of this County. The Features are uncommonly beautiful a continued Succession of Hills and Vallies without any Mountains; but in general the Face of the Country is so rough as to divest it of Charms. We dind with *John* Nancarrow and got to Redruth in the Evening.[17]

December 27th   3rd Day

We took a ride this Morning to Carnbri Castle and Ruins, situated on a high hill about 2 Miles from Redruth;[18] the Castle is on the highest Eminence of hill, and to the Westward of it is a plain of about an Acre of Ground; and from the enormous Stones some of which are erect, others fallen half way and resting on others of still more monstrous Size, and from the Basons hewn out of the Rock, and from a large inclosure of Stone not of the military but of the religious kind, there remains no Doubt but they are the Ruins of a Druid Temple.[19] And in the Spaces between these Rocks and on the Declivity of the Hill was a Grove of Oaks in the Memory of the last Generation. Now there are no Trees but the Traces where they have been are to be found.

> Consecrated hills
> Once girt with spreading Oaks, mysterious Rows
> Of rude enormous Obelisks, that rise
> Orb within orb, stupendous Monuments
> Of artless Architecture, such as now
> Oft times amaze the wondring Traveller;
> By the pale Moon discernd on Sarum plain.

The top of this hill is full of Ledges of Rocks. On the western Side are artificial Basons cut in the uppermost Rocks, their Figure circular, sometimes oblong and seemingly without aim at any regularity. The Castle on this hill is much the most modern thing to be seen, and what they call the parlour is floored with one Rock, in the Surface of which is a regular elliptical bason. In the West Side of the hill is a Cave, the Bottom of which is full of Water, and there are large Stones lying across the Entrance and

---

[17] Two illustrations are omitted here (A Cluster of Stones on Carnbrea Hill; North-East View of Carnbrea Castle).

[18] All that remains of Carn Brea Castle is a tower roughly 20 feet square which rises to a height of 40 feet. Frederick Wilkinson, *The Castles of England* (London, 1973), p. 51.

[19] For a detailed description of Carn Brea Hill, a Druid place of worship, see William Borlase, *Antiquities, Historical and Monumental, of the County of Cornwall* ...(London, 1769), pp. 117–121. Borlase quotes the same lines as Fisher gives here from part of the Druid monument.

here are a number of prodigious Stones now prostrate but seem once to have been placed on End. We find many Circles marked out by rude Stones of the Obelisk Form on this Hill: An Altar supposed for the Purpose of offering Human Victims and others of less importance made use of for occasions less solemn.

We came home to Dinner and then took a ride to the Cliffs on the Bristol Channel which exhibit an exceedingly frightful and Majestic Scene, being perpendicular or projecting and the Craggs loose, with several gloomy Caverns and Passages of considerable length through the Rocks. The Surf here is wild and high; it has made great Depredations on the Rocks and we see several small Islands near the Shore, from which their Resemblance to the Terra Firma must have been not long since united with it. Came home in the Evening.

The Metals found in Cornwal are Iron, Copper, Lead, Silver, Quicksilver and Tin. Of Iron and Gold considerable Quantities are found in working for Tin, and by the great Number of Chalybeate Springs there is no doubt but there are vast Bodies of it. Yet not one Iron Work has been carried with Success, though in some of them the Ore be very rich and near the Surface. Nor is any benefit expected to arise from the Iron Ore in this County till they can fall on some way of procuring coals cheaper.[20]

Of Copper there are various Sorts found in great plenty in all the Western Parts of the County. This supple, rich and useful metal Cornwall has for Ages been supposed to be in the possession of but no Experiments in collecting it turned out to advantage till about Eighty years ago. And it is now certain than there is no richer Copper, nor a greater variety of Ores anywhere than in Cornwall. The Ore which is most common is of a yellow brass colour; it is found adhering to Stones of all kinds but purest commonly in the white opake crystal, or in the white Clay, and according to the Quantity of the barren Stone intermixed is sold for a greater or less Price.

Of Green Coppers some are light as a Feather being more verdigris; others are heavy and rich. There is a blue Ore but this is found in such Small quantities that though very rich is not worth selecting from the Rubbish. The Grey Ore is very rich and contains more metal than the Yellow or Green. The Black Ore yields little metal. The Red Ore resembles Silver so much that it is with Difficulty good Judges can distinguish it from Silver. It is very ponderous and more valuable than any

---

[20] The nearest coalfield to Cornwall was across the Bristol Channel in South Wales. During the eighteenth century, the cross-channel colliers plied a steady trade between the Swansea area and the Cornish copper mines. Flinn, *British Coal Industry: The Industrial Revolution*, p. 11.

of the preceding. But the most perfect copper, from which the before mentioned are so many inferior and different Removes, is the Malleable. It is various combined and allayed, sometimes with crystal, sometimes with Clay, at other times with the rust of Iron. In shape various sometimes thin spread, shaped like leaves, now like Drops, now branched or fringed or twisted like Wire; sometimes blisterd and sometimes in solid Lumps of many pounds weight, maturated unmixed with rubbish and polished.

Silver is never found here alone. 'Tis usually mixed with all other metals. It has a corrosive Sulphur or Bitumen always attending it. Lead and Tin were formerly esteemed one and the same metal, but they are now proved to be specifically and materially different. Lead will dissolve in Acids, but Tin only in Aqua Regia, Lead being to water 11345 to 1000 and tin always 7321 to 1000. They are therefore radically different. Lead is in the mine of much the same Color as in its metallic State. There are many mines of it but not that have been workd to Proffit. It is said by Mineralists that where Copper is, there is always Quicksilver, but it is so mixd and entangled with other Bodies that the Miners have not thought it worth their while to separate it. As to Gold, little of it has been discovered and always in very small particles. But Tacitus was of opinion that the few samples of Gold found here was the Motive in the Romans to conquer Britain.[21]

Tin is the lightest of all metals. It is the peculiar and most valuable property of this County, creating subsistence for the Poor, affluence to the Landlord, besides a considerable Revenue to the Duke of Cornwal.[22] Tin is found either collected or loose and detached. In the first Case it is accumulated in a Lode or interspersed in Bunches in the natural Rock. In the 2nd Case it is in single separate Stones. The Lode being found 3 things are necessary to be considered: first, to dispose of the barren Earth; secondly to discharge the Water; thirdly to raise the Tin. These are easily performed when the works are near the Surface. But the difficulties increase with the Depth and Skill and Care become more and more necessary; and indeed all the Mechanic Powers, the most forcible Engines, and the greatest Sagacity of the Miners are often in vain when the Works are deep.[23]

---

[21] Section 12 of the *Agricola* notes that 'Britain contains gold and silver and other metals, as the prize of conquest.' A. J. Church and W. J. Brodribb, eds., *The Agricola and Germany of Tacitus* . . . (London, 1877), p. 13. Professor T. P. Wiseman, University of Exeter, pointed me in the right direction for this reference.

[22] H. R. H. George Augustus Frederick (1762–1830) was 20th Duke of Cornwall from 1762 until 1820, when he became George IV. Cokayne, *Complete Peerage,* III, p. 450.

[23] I have omitted the plan of Pool Mine, near Redruth, plus the brief notes that accompany it.

December 28th   5th Day

Stayed at home all Day, and in the Evening went to smoak a Pipe with William James.[24]

December 29th   6th Day

Took a Ride this Morning about 3 Miles to a Mine called Dolcoath[25] when after pulling off all our Cloaths and putting on dirty Flannel Shirts worn trousers and a Jacket made of Cloth of about 20 different Kinds, we entered upon a visit to the lower Regions. We first descend by a ladder alongside the fire Engine Shaft, on one Side rude rough Rocks behind and above us monstrous Logs and Timber in every direction to support the enormous Weight of Stones and Earth and Ore. On our left a view of a Gulph terminating in Darkness, the monstrous Rods which lift the Boxes of the Pump all in Motion and the dreadful Noise adding to the horrors of the Scene, still descending Ladder after Ladder by Staves half way worn through, some cracking, others loose, and some quite broken off, the way dark, gloomy, the air so thick and the Current so strong that with the Water falling down we found it difficult to keep our Candles lighted, some constantly out, and the others burning so faintly that the small Pittance of corrupted light was scarce sufficient to shew us where to put our Feet. The missing a Step or loosing our Grasp would in an instant deprive us of Existence. Now and then coming to a horrizontal path where the loose Rocks on our Sides and the prodigious pieces of Timber, gaping wide with Cracks and supported by others of still more huge Size served greatly to terrify us. Next crawling through a little hole, barely sufficient to admit us, then descending by other Ladders weak and dangerous.

After coming 124 Fathom (734 feet) we found ourselves in the most busy frightful Spot imaginable. Large Buckets coming down, others going up. The Grotto lighted with a vast Number of Candles carelessly stuck with Clay to the Sides. Men at work with Picks, Axes, Mauls, Wedges, Shovels &c &c. Fountains of Water spouting in many places and running in wild Meanders to the Bottom of the Engines where the Noise of the Pumps made the hollow Cavern resound with Echo. The Sides glittering with Ore, the Bottom deluged with Springs, our Heads covered with Timber drest the Scene in all

[24] William James (1738/9–1806) was a grocer at Redruth. He married twice and had nine children. He and his family moved to Bristol some time between 1774 and 1780 and in 1798 they moved to London. *DQB*.

[25] Dolcoath mine, just to the north-east of Camborne, was the deepest and most celebrated old mine in Cornwall. It was first worked from the 1720s or earlier, and was already 160 fathoms deep in 1778. It continued as a leading mine until 1917, but underground operations there were abandoned in 1920. D. B. Barton, *A Guide to the Mines of West Cornwall* (Truro, 1963), p. 28.

horrors; that excluding every Idea of the great depth from the Surface, the Place was too terrible to be viewed without Fright and Astonishment.

This Depth we gained in 50 Minutes seldom stopping one Minute to rest. We had now to ascend the great height, the thoughts of which almost frighted us from the attempt, being very warm and wet with Sweat. However, we summoned up our Resolution and exerting every effort we got up to the Surface by 52 different Ladders in good health and Spirits in 45 Minutes, pleased delighted and gratified with our Visit and filled with Reflections on the Lives the poor unhappy Victims to this dreadful Employment lead who go up and down without Thought or Care many times every Day; and notwithstanding this are as happy contented and chearful as the Sons of Luxury and Dalliance. 50 Minutes going, an hour down and 45 Minutes coming up.

We went to a house in the Neighbourhood, eat heartily of some choice beef Stakes, came home and fell asleep in our Chairs.

This is the Deepest Mine but one in all Cornwal and that but 2 fathom deeper. The Air below very warm and the Water still more so. Seven hundred people employed at these Works.

December 30th

Stayed all day at home.

December 31st   1st Day

Left Redruth about 6 O Clock, stopd at Truro to change horses. But notwithstanding Redruths insignificance and littleness, as it entertaind me in its Neighbourhood about a Fortnight I ought not to pass it over without the Tribute of Description. In the first place it is a small ill built Town, the houses for the most part of a Composition of Earth Sticks and Sand. These however are comfortable to the Body if not pleasing to the Eye. Limestone being scarce and dear in Cornwal they are under the Necessity of substituting these Materials in most parts of the County. The Roofs are chiefly thatched. Next the Situation is particularly unpleasant and inconvenient being on the Declivity of two hills, steep rough and dirty. At the foot of these hills runs a little very little Stream, over which there is a Bridge totally useless and seems to be placed there merely to hide the River which is a filthy Rill that a Child might step across in the Greatest Flood. Then their public buildings are of a quite original Stamp. The Exchange is small inconvenient and of but an indifferent appearance.[26]

---

[26] The Mining Exchange at Redruth was not built until 1880, but, prior to this, mining business was undertaken at Tabb's Hotel from 1726 onwards. Frank Michell, *Annals of an Ancient Cornish Town: Redruth* (2nd edn., Redruth, 1978), pp. 30, 180. This information was kindly provided by Joanne Hillman, librarian at the Cornwall Local Studies Library, Redruth.

However it answers the End of a Market house and boasts a Name no higher. The Church has all the Grandeur and Splendor that a Building of its Size, Age and Contrivance can well have, being very small, tumbling to pieces with Age, and a most wretched Form.[27] The Friends Meeting House was formerly a Coopers Shop but being too small for the Purpose and in a Situation too secluded it was judged eligible to convert it to its present use.[28]

The Land for a few Miles round this place is above all others most barren, in the midst of Country of Downs and Moors, the Bowells of which have been ransacked, turned inside out, and every particle of worth if it had any carried off. In no Spot is there less Appearance of Vegetation, as if the Genius of the place begrudged it footing. It has skulked away out of Sight and is no where to be found be the Search ever so diligent, except at the Bottom of the hills and there only when by mere chance there happens to flow a little Rill.

Came to St. Austale to Breakfast. Stopd to dine at Lostwithail, changed horses again at Liskerd, came to Tor Point in the Evening and crossed the Ferry over to Plymouth Dock, when having two Miles further to go, and could procure no Vehicle to transport me, I set off with my Luggage on my Shoulder moon light Night and waded in the Mud to Plymouth which I reached about 8 O Clock. Made William Cookworthys[29] house my home. The places I have this Day passd through have before describd and a second history of them is unecessary.[30]

January 1st 1776
2nd Day

Spent this whole Day from 9 O Clock in the Morning till half past 12 at Night with William Cookworthy, canvassing Politics, Religion, History &c &c &c. The most sensible Learned kind Man I ever knew. The History of every Nation is familiar to him. He has explored every Country,

---

[27] St. Euny, the parish church at Redruth, was built in 1756. Pevsner and Radcliffe, *Buildings of England: Cornwall*, p. 150.

[28] The first Friends' meeting house at Redruth was not constructed until 1790. The earliest reference to registers and recorded minutes of the Society of Friends in the town is 1700, so it is likely that the Quaker meeting place alluded to by Fisher was a private house. Michell, *Annals of an Ancient Cornish Town*, pp. 28, 55. Joanne Hillman provided this reference.

[29] William Cookworthy (1705–1780) entered business in Plymouth as a wholesale chemist. He was the friend of many scientific men. He discovered china clay in Cornwall and experimented with furnaces. From 1746 he travelled in the Quaker ministry and translated some of Swedenborg's works into English. Raistrick, *Quakers in Science and Industry*, pp. 193, 202–210; A. D. Selleck, *Cookworthy, 1705–80, and his Circle* (Plymouth, 1978); Emden, *Quakers in Commerce*, pp. 69–70.

[30] See above, pp. 93–95.

understands many Languages, an amazing Memory, excellent Delivery, and a Stile that we no where else meet with, catholic in the extreme, deep in Argument, meek, humble, and divested of the least particle of Vanity pedantry or any one disagreeable Sentiment; in short the most refind and accomplished Man and in his Discourses no less extraordinary. He is the Translator of several Performances of Emanuel Swoedenburgh,[31] a Man of amazing Genius and the greatest Metaphoriser of Scripture that hath ever appeared. His Visions and some other extraordinary parts of his Works have obtained for him the Character of an Enthusiast and by some is suspected of insanity. However William Cookworthy has the most implicit Confidence in all his Writings and having personally known him gives him the most amiable and accomplished Character.

January 2nd   3rd Day

Took a ride this Morning to Plymouth Dock, where I got a boat and went out in the Harbour to see some of the Men of War. Went first on board the Ocean a fine ship of 90 Guns now in Commission, then went on board the Royal George, the largest and finest Ship in the World, mounting 110 Guns. Her Length of Keel is 180 feet. A Ship is one of the greatest Improvements and Inventions of Man and these Monstrous floating Islands make so noble an appearance that it is impossible to conceive anything more grand. The harbour is altogether a fine Object, on every Side the Land rising gradually from the Water to a great height. One Side Plymouth Buildings Store houses &c, the yard alive with Industry. On the other Side Lord Edgcome's Seat, allowed to be equal to any in England for extent and variety of Prospect; and the Lake below so dispersed with Shipping that it is one of the most pleasing Scenes imaginable.

The Order Regularity and Oeconomy on board these Ships are astonishing. The Life Action and Employment of the People make it a little World of Buisness. The Cabbin Furniture &c &c are splendid Superb and grand.

January 3rd   4th Day

In Company with James Fox[32] of Plymouth I set off in Post Chaise this Morning about 7 O Clock, changed Chaise at Ivy Bridge and got to Ashburton to Breakfast. We changed Chaise at Chudleigh. We now leave

---

[31] Emanuel Swedenborg (1688–1772) was a Swedish scientist and theologian. By the 1740s his enquiries as a scientist — into all kinds of mathematical subjects, geology, anatomy etc. — were beginning to merge with his visionary speculations as a seer. Jones and Dixon, *Macmillan Dictionary of Biography,* pp. 806–807.

[32] Probably James Fox, grocer, Pike Street, Plymouth. Bailey's *British Directory,* II, p. 422.

a Country indifferently shaking of the rough and rugged and now come into a most picturesque and delightful Country. A few Miles before we reach Exeter the Prospect is enchanting, Hills and Vallies laughing and smiling on every Side, and a Prospect of interminable Extent not giving the Sight of a single uncultivated Spot; and the whole divided into innumerable inclosures and the most beautiful Variety of Objects; Towns, Villages, Seats, Rivers, and the Sea all striving to outrival each other in Charms.

This Succession of Beauty is kept up till we get to Cullompton a little Market Town on the Borders of Devonshire, near Somerset, when we get into a most soft rural and pastoral Country dissected by a few inclosures into the most delightful Pastures. We come to Wellington, a considerable Manufacturing Town for Serges and other Goods for the Holland and German Trade.[33] We lodged at the house of Thomas Ware[34] and on the Morning of

January 4th   5th Day

After Breakfast mounted the Chaise and came through Taunton to Bridge Water. Taunton is a very large Borough Town, beautifully situated on the River Tone, a place of great Note for the Manufactury of Serges and Duroys and Sagathies.[35] The Tone is made navigable to this Place. The Streets are spacious; the houses good; a neat market house; an elegant Church; large hospital.[36]

Bridgewater is a very considerable Town and a great Thoroughfare. It has a Castle built by Briwere who also founded St. John's Hospital.[37] At

---

[33] The manufacture of druggets and serges was a considerable industry at Wellington. The Were family carried on a large woollen trade with Dutch and German ports. A new partnership called Weres & Co was formed in 1772. Lewis, *Topographical Dictionary of England*, IV, p. 417; Joseph Hoyland Fox, *The Woollen Manufacture at Wellington, Somerset* (London, 1914), pp. 8–10, 39, 42.

[34] Either Thomas Were senior (d. 1776 aged 81) or his son Thomas Were (d. 1781 aged 58). Both lived at Wellington. FLL, Bristol and Somerset QM: Burials.

[35] Woollen manufacture had flourished in Taunton since c. 1336. By the 1780s it had decayed 'and its success has been in great measure translated to the neighbouring town of Wellington.' John Collinson, *The History and Antiquities of the County of Somerset* (3 vols., 1791; reprinted Gloucester, 1983), III, p. 226.

[36] The Market House is a redbrick building of 1770–1772 in the centre of Taunton. The church is probably St. Mary Magdalene, a Perpendicular structure with a 163 feet high tower. The County Hospital in Taunton was founded in 1772. *Ibid.*, p. 240; Pevsner, *Buildings of England: South and West Somerset* (London, 1958), pp. 312, 314.

[37] Bridgwater Castle was built by William Brewer in the reign of King John. St. John's Hospital was also founded by Brewer, in the reign of Henry II, for a master, brethren, and thirteen poor persons of the order of St. Augustine. Colvin, *History of the King's Works, II: The Middle Ages* (London, 1963), p. 576; Lewis, *Topographical Dictionary of England*, I, p. 251.

this place a number of Topsail Vessels lay. Though the River be very narrow and at low Water almost dry, the Tide rises 22 feet. Ships of 200 Tons may come up. This Town was once famous for a wool Manufactury but now chiefly for Leather.[38] The Spire of this Church is the third loftiest in England.[39] Here is a large Free School.[40]

From this place we came to Cross a little Village where we dined, and in the Evening got to Bristol. Nothing can exceed the Beauty of the Country all the way from Bristol to Exeter. Devonshire has a great number of Hills and Vallies, but the Soil is rich, abounding with Streams and most charmingly cultivated, so many Trees that many People burn Wood instead of Coals. Somerset is one continued Garden, every Spot highly improved, abounding with lofty Trees, rising in the Hedges or in Clusters, some fine Seats and the Land exceedingly rich. Innumerable Cattle and Sheep graze here. In short it is without exception the finest Country I ever saw, exceedingly populous, abounding with Manufacturies and the inhabitants rich.

At Bristol I made John Dowells[41] house my home.[42]

---

[38] Woollen manufacture had almost finished at Bridgwater by the end of the eighteenth century. Sydney Gardner Jarman, *A History of Bridgwater* (London, 1889), p. 109.

[39] This church, founded c. 1292 and dedicated to St. Mary, is a large, handsome structure. Its spire and tower are 174 feet high. Collinson, *History and Antiquities of the County of Somerset*, III, p. 88; Pevsner, *Buildings of England: South and West Somerset*, pp. 94–96.

[40] The free grammar school at Bridgwater, endowed by Elizabeth I, was founded in 1561. Lewis, *Topographical Dictionary of England*, I, p. 252.

[41] See below, p. 282.

[42] I have omitted six drawings of Cornish scenes plus some loose jottings.

JOURNAL E
4 January–4 March 1776

Bristol arrived at
January 4th   5th Day 1776 Evening

Bristol is by some esteemed the Second by others the third in Great Britain for Trade and Number of Inhabitants. Tis irregular, the Streets but indifferently paved one or two excepted. 7 Mile in Circumference; the houses not extraordinary. A vast number of Shipping lie here in a very narrow dirty River and at low Water dry, some of them along Side the Keys which are convenient and on which there are excellent Cranes for the discharge of Ships.[1] This River (Frome) divides the Town and on one Side of it are commodious dry Docks.[2] There is a good draw Bridge over the River which makes the communication from one Side of the Town very convenient.[3] Half a mile from this there is the Conflux of the Avon with this.

Here is a pretty large Cathedral but nothing in it worthy of Observation.[4] Redcliffe Church is a fine Structure in the Gothic Taste.[5] The Workmanship of this Church is excellent, the Roof finely vaulted with

[1] The quays at Bristol were in the centre of the city. The great tidal range of 45 feet on the River Avon severely restricted the periods during which ships could come up to the quays. Most of the wharfs had cranes for unloading ships. By 1774, it was reported that there were fourteen cranes available. Walter Minchinton, 'The Port of Bristol in the Eighteenth Century' in Patrick McGrath, ed., *Bristol in the Eighteenth Century* (Newton Abbot, 1972), pp. 141, 146.

[2] William Champion built a wet dock at Rownham, Bristol in 1765; alongside this were two graving docks suitable for shipbuilding. *Ibid.*, pp. 139–140.

[3] The Drawbridge on St. Augustine's Back was first erected for the defence of the western side of Bristol c. 1239–1240, when the modern course of the River Frome was cut. During the eighteenth century, the original drawbridge was replaced by two structures on the same spot, one built in 1714 and the other, a bascule bridge, constructed in 1755. Charles Wells, *A Short History of the Port of Bristol* (Bristol, 1909), pp. 4, 20, 33; George Frederick Stone, *Bristol: As it was — and as it is* (Bristol, 1909,) p. 7.

[4] Bristol was given cathedral rank by Henry VIII in 1542. Until then the church formed part of the Augustinian abbey founded on the site by Robert Fitzharding in 1140. Pevsner, *Buildings of England: North Somerset and Bristol* (London, 1958), pp. 371–386.

[5] St. Mary Redcliffe Church, which Elizabeth I called 'the fairest, goodliest, and most famous parish church in England.' The present building contains work from the early thirteenth century to the fifteenth century. *Ibid.*, pp. 395–404.

Stone and the Tower is high. In this Church is the Tomb Stone of Admiral Penn[6] Father to the first Proprietor of Pennsylvania. Its Altar piece is well painted by Thornhill[7] and decorated by three grand paintings representing the Burial, Resurrection and Ascension of our Saviour by Hogarth.[8] Here are many other Churches besides. Here are two Squares in this Place, King and Queen.[9] The Second has a fine Statue of William 3rd.[10] This is encircled by a number of good Buildings as is also King Square. Five hospitals are also in this place well endowed and clever to appearance.[11] Also several others of less note.

Here is a good Stone Bridge over the Avon with four broad Arches. This bridge is narrow and inconvenient and subject to a heavy Toll.[12] The

---

[6] This is in the north aisle. Sir William Penn (1621–1670) was the father of William Penn, the Quaker founder of Pennsylvania. William Barrett, *The History and Antiquities of the City of Bristol* (Bristol, 1789; facsimile reprint, Gloucester, 1982), pp. 585–586.

[7] Fisher must have been mistaken, since there is no record of any painting by Thornhill having been at St. Mary Redcliffe. Some confusion may have arisen because Thornhill was Hogarth's father-in-law. The Hogarth altarpiece did replace an earlier one by a mysterious and otherwise unknown artist called Holmes in 1709. This may still have been in existence when Fisher visited Bristol, and it could have been executed in what he took to be Thornhill's manner. Information kindly supplied by Mr M. J. H. Liversidge, University of Bristol.

[8] William Hogarth (d. 1764) was invited in 1755 by the Vestry of St. Mary Redcliffe to paint an altarpiece for the church. He accepted the commission and in the following year completed three large paintings which form a triptych depicting 'The Ascension' flanked by 'The Sealing of the Sepulchre' and 'The Three Marys at the Tomb.' The altarpiece remained in St. Mary Redcliffe until 1858, and is now displayed in St. Nicholas Church Museum, Bristol. M. J. H. Liversidge, *William Hogarth's Bristol Altarpiece* (Bristol, 1980), pp. 8, 16, 17.

[9] The introduction of squares into eighteenth-century Bristol was a planning innovation in imitation of London and with improved health in view. Queen Square was the first of these to be built; it was begun in 1699. King's Square on Kingsdown was laid out between 1755 and 1769. M. D. Lobel and E. M. Carus-Wilson, 'Bristol' in *The Atlas of Historic Towns*, II, ed. M. D. Lobel (London, 1975), p. 23.

[10] A bronze equestrian statue by Rysbrack made between 1732 and 1736. Pevsner, *Buildings of England: North Somerset and Bristol*, p. 431.

[11] There were five 'hospitals,' or endowed charitable institutions, in Bristol by the 1770s. Queen Elizabeth's Hospital and Colston's Hospital (now Colston's Boys School) were grammar schools for boys. The Hospital of St. Mark (or The Gaunt's Hospital) was a medieval institution with provision for poor people. Trinity Hospital and Temple Hospital were almshouses. F. H. Tovill, 'Bristol Charities, Past and Present' in C. M. MacInnes and W. F. Whittard, eds., *Bristol and its Adjoining Counties* (Bristol, 1955), pp. 293–294.

[12] The new Bristol Bridge was completed in 1768 and was to be paid for by means of a house tax, wharfage tax, and a toll. By the Bridge Act, tolls were to be collected until an excess of £2,000 had accumulated, and then to cease immediately. Mark Harrison, '"To Raise and Dare Resentment": The Bristol Bridge Riot of 1793 Re-examined,' *The Historical Journal*, XXVI (1983), p. 566.

Walls of this City though raised in the Reign of William Rufus[13] in part remain.

The Guildhall and the Mayor and Sheriffs Courts are in Broad Street and adjoining thereto is a spacious lofty Room.[14] In the front of the Guildhall is a Statue of Charles 2nd.[15]

The Exchange here[16] is a fine Stone Building about 2 thirds as large as the Royal Exchange, London. There are 4 Entrances into it, Rooms for Shops over it. As we enter this Exchange on the Left is a good Coffee house and on the other Side Rooms for the Bank &c. This Structure is all of Free Stone & very compleat.

At Colledge Green is a Stately high Cross of Gothic Structure with the Effigies of several Kings.[17] The Hot Well about a Mile from the City down the River is much frequented in July and August.[18] Near this place are found the Bristol Stones.[19] Jacob's Well is a Mile from the Hot Well much frequented in the Spring and elegant lodgings for Gentlemen contiguous.

[13] Bristol was fortified with walls in 1089 by Geoffrey, Bishop of Coutances, who had assembled his forces there to take part in a confederacy against William Rufus and to raise his elder brother Robert to the throne. Lewis, *Topographical Dictionary of England,* I, p. 261.

[14] The earliest mention of the Bristol Guildhall was in 1311 during the reign of Edward II. It was the civic centre of Bristol until 1551 when a Council House was built on the site of the old one in Broad Street. The Guildhall came to be used for law courts as well as for meetings of the most important guilds and the City Council. Max Barnes, *Bristol A–Z* (Bristol, 1970), n.p.; Bryan Little, *Bristol: The Public View* (Bristol, 1982), pp. 8–10; Elizabeth Ralph, *Government of Bristol 1373–1973* (Bristol, 1973), p. 49.

[15] John Harry, a stone cutter, was admitted as a freeman by the Bristol Common Council in 1666 and in return offered to present the city with a statue of Charles II. Latimer states that this 'poor piece of statuary' is to be found in the Guildhall. John Latimer, *The Annals of Bristol in the Seventeenth Century* (Bristol, 1900), p. 340.

[16] Designed by John Wood the Elder and built between 1740 and 1743. It included a place for merchants to meet under cover. *UBD,* II, p. 121; Pevsner, *Buildings of England: North Somerset and Bristol,* pp. 415–416.

[17] A monumental cross which, according to tradition, was erected in 1373 to commemorate Edward III's charter which conferred the status of a county upon Bristol in its own right. But possibly the High Cross is of fifteenth-century origin. Until 1733 it stood in the older part of Bristol at the intersection of Broad and High Streets with Wine and Corn Streets. It was dismantled and between 1736 and 1762 it was sited in the centre of College Green. It was taken down again and found a new site overlooking the lake at Stourhead, Wiltshire, where it has remained since 1765. M. J. H. Liversidge, *The Bristol High Cross* (Bristol, 1978), pp. 1–3, 10–11.

[18] The Bristol Hotwell was a spa resort that became fashionable during the eighteenth century. A tepid medicinal spring issued from the rocks on the right bank of the River Avon, near St. Vincent's Rocks. This water had medicinal properties which were supposed to be therapeutic in the treatment of various diseases, including diabetes and tuberculosis. Arrowsmith's *Dictionary of Bristol* (Bristol, 1906), pp. 226–227, and Vincent Waite, 'The Bristol Hotwell' in McGrath, ed., *Bristol in the Eighteenth Century* (Newton Abbot, 1972), pp. 109–126.

[19] These were the Bristol 'diamonds' (or ornamental rocks) found near St. Vincent's Rock, fine specimens of which decorate Goldney's grotto, Clifton Hill, Bristol. P. K. Stembridge, *Goldney: A House and a Family* (Bristol, 1969), p. 21.

These places I visited with *Susannah Cookworthy*[20] and M*ary* Hobson[21] with whom and S*arah* Champion[22] I took a ride to Bath, the most beautiful and elegant Town I had ever seen. Nothing can exceed the uniformity and neatness of these Buildings and being all built of one kind of Stone and that of a beautiful Color has a most happy effect. In every Street the Buildings are of a particular plan but in each Street alike.

The Crescent[23] contains 30 houses of 26 feet front each, the houses except the two Wings exactly of one Size and plan and all elegant having from the Top of the lower to the Top of Attic Story an Ionic $\frac{3}{4}$ Column $2\frac{1}{2}$ feet between each Window. The Cornice is vastly neat. Each house has two Windows and a Door in front. The Form of the Crescent is not any part of a Circle, but the Arches of three Triangles. The Prospect from the Front is most grand and pleasing: a long Continuation of Hill and Valley, the Avon not distant, and the Country richly improved and in the highest Cultivation. The View from the back is greatly confined but is not much less beautiful than the other. There is an inclosure before every house of Iron Pallisadoes and a passage with Rails on each Side to the Doors. Before this a Pavement of 20 feet of large square flat Stones. Still further on a wide Street for Carriages, elegantly paved and bounded by a Rail of Iron in a Row paralel with the Form of the Crescent. Then commence the Fields, inclosures, Gardens and a variegated Prospect almost interminable and one of the finest Landscapes in the World.

Beautiful as this Scene is, Conoosurs are divided whether to give this or the Circus[24] the Preference and I find it a Question difficult to resolve. The Circus is more compleat being an entire Round of houses separated only by three Avenues leading into it. The Elegance, Neatness and Uniformity of

---

[20] Susannah Cookworthy (1743–1810) was the younger daughter of William Cookworthy. She and Mary Hobson and Sarah Champion enjoyed each other's company on a trip to Bristol in 1775. Susannah was married to George Harrison (1747–1827), a banker and influential London Quaker. A. Douglas Selleck, *Cookworthy, 1705–80, and his Circle* (Plymouth, 1978), pp. 205, 208–209, 222, 274.

[21] Mary Hobson (1740–1809) was the daughter of William Cookworthy. She was crippled from youth. She married a non-Friend, Dr. Benjamin Hobson (d. ?1774). *Ibid.*, pp. 204, 274.

[22] Sarah Champion (1740–1811) was the eldest of the three children of Joseph and Elizabeth Champion of Bristol. She was a sister of Richard Champion and married Charles Fox, a Plymouth banker, in 1790. *DQB;* Hugh Owen, *Two Centuries of Ceramic Art in Bristol ...* (Gloucester, 1873), pp. 273, 284.

[23] The Royal Crescent was built between 1767 and 1774 by John Wood the Younger. It is a large half-ellipse facing down a grassy slope. It has a completely plain ground floor and giant Ionic columns above. Pevsner, *Buildings of England: North Somerset and Bristol,* p. 130.

[24] The King's Circus dates from 1754–1758. It is the most monumental work designed by John Wood the Elder (though it was completed by his son). It has one architectural motif, coupled columns in three orders (Tuscan, Ionic, Corinthian), then a top balustrade. *Ibid.*, pp. 128–129.

this perfect Circle are unparalleled. Of one Age, Size, Form and plan. The nicest Stone. Well proportioned Columns in the Front. The fine Pavement for Passengers and the openess and light that every house enjoys are to be met with only at Bath.

The Streets leading into this place are grand and uniform and from the Center of the Circus where is a watch house we have a fine View down each Avenue by which we see the City is situated in a Valley overcrowded by an amphiteatrical Circle of Hills finely improved to the Summit. The Circus is about 1000 Feet in Circumference. The same Number of houses and the same Width of those in the Crescent.

The town was famous in the Time of the Romans for its medicinal Waters.[25] Its Baths are The King's Bath, the Queen's bath, the Cross Bath, the hot Bath, the cold bath and Lepers Bath.[26] In the King's Bath is a Statue of King Bladud with an inscription importing that he discovered the Use of these Baths 300 years before Christ.[27] This Bath has a neat Pump Room where the Company meet to drink the Water which is conveyed to it almost boiling hot by a Pipe from the bottom of the Springs.[28] Tis grateful to the Stomachs, has a Sulphureous Steely Taste, strengthens the Bowells, by renewing the vital heat and restoring the lost Tone.

The Water of the Queen's bath is not so hot as that of the Kings.[29] Here also are Pumps and pumping Rooms for pouring the hot Streams on any

[25] Bath was one of the leading therapeutic establishments in the Roman Empire. It was a place to which sufferers from rheumatic and allied diseases travelled all over Gaul and Britain. The Roman baths were founded in Flavian times, very early in the era of Roman occupation. *Ibid.*, pp. 97–99.

[26] The King's and Queen's Baths are situated on the south-west side of the Abbey churchyard. The Queen's Bath is named after Anne, the wife of James I. The Cross Bath is on the west side of Stall Street. A little way southwards are the Hot Bath and the adjoining Leper's Bath. John Collinson, *The History and Antiquities of the County of Somerset* (3 vols., 1791; reprinted Gloucester, 1983), I, pp. 39–42; Jean Manco, 'The Cross Bath,' *Bath History,* II (1988), pp. 49–84.

[27] Bladud was a mythical king mentioned in Geoffrey of Monmouth's *Historia Regnum Britanniae* (c. 1135). According to this tale, Bladud built baths around a spring with medicinal qualities at Bath. Barry Cunliffe, *Roman Bath Discovered* (rev. edn., London, 1984), pp. 3–4.

[28] The Pump Room, on the north side of the King's Bath, was erected in 1704, enlarged in 1751, and redesigned between 1789 and 1799. *UBD*, II, pp. 88–90; Pevsner, *Buildings of England: North Somerset and Bristol,* pp. 112–113.

[29] The temperature of the King's Bath was 103 degrees fahrenheit in its warmest part and 100 degrees at its coolest part. The Queen's Bath was supplied with water from the same spring, so the same temperature should have been present in its water. Fisher's reference to the lesser heat of the Queen's Bath is therefore a little puzzling. Possibly, however, he was referring to the Cross Bath (so called from a cross erected in it after James II's Queen had conceived after using its waters). The temperature of the water in the Cross Bath was 93–94 degrees fahrenheit. *Ibid.*, II, p. 89; Collinson, *History and Antiquities of the County of Somerset,* I, pp. 39–41.

part of the Body. In the South West part of the Town are the Hot Bath and the Cross Bath, whose Waters rise near the Level of the Streets and the overflowing of the Cross Bath forms the Lepers. At the Cross Bath is a Monument whose inscriptions are erased representing the Holy Ghost attended by Angels.[30] The eucharist, the Pillar and all the Ornaments are of fine Marble. This Bath is most frequented by People of Quality, was covered by the Earl of Marlborough, has a Gallery on one Side where people stand to converse with their Friends in the Bath, and on the other a Balcony for the Music which plays all the Time they are bathing. The Two Seasons are Spring and Autumn: the first beginning with April and ending with June; the Autumn with September and ends at the Beginning of January.[31]

The City has a Bridge over the Avon which washes it on the South West. Its Walls are almost entire and said to be the Work of the Romans.[32] The Ground which these Walls inclose is in the Form of a pentagon with Gates and a Postern. The Stone of which these houses are built is dug out of Quarries not very distant, and brought to the City by a Curious Machine at Cheap rate invented for the Purpose.[33] The Grove near the Abbey is called Orange Square in complement to the Prince of Orange and a Stone erected importing that he had his health restored by drinking these Waters.[34]

Over the Market House is the Town-hall, a fine Stone Building erected on 20 Pillars. Here are also the Effigies of several ancient Kings.[35] St.

---

[30] A reference to the cross which gives the bath its name (see above note).

[31] Bath had two seasons — a health season from March to June, and a pleasure season from September to December. *A Companion to the Watering and Bathing Places of England* (London, 1800), p. 1.

[32] The Romans surrounded Bath with walls twenty feet in height and of great thickness. In the walls were four gates terminating the principal streets, from which they constructed roads leading to neighbouring stations. Lewis, *Topographical Dictionary of England*, I, p. 109.

[33] These quarries were owned by Ralph Allen who took a keen interest in the rebuilding of eighteenth-century Bath. The quarries were on Combe Down, near Bath, and they produced Bath stone. Since they were one and a half miles from the River Avon and 400 feet above it, the problem of transporting stone down to Allen's yard and wharf was met with practical ideas including a crane for loading and unloading timber waggons moving on iron wheels. Benjamin Boyce, *The Benevolent Man: A Life of Ralph Allen of Bath* (Cambridge, Mass., 1967), pp. 31–32.

[34] In 1734 the Prince of Orange visited Bath and received great benefit from the use of the waters, which Beau Nash recorded on an obelisk erected at his own expense in the grove afterwards called the Orange Grove. *A Picturesque Guide to Bath, Bristol Hotwells, the River Avon, and the Adjacent Country* ... (London, 1793), p. 69.

[35] There were deposited at the Town Hall, Bath, several altars, columns, friezes and other antiques from the Roman ruins of the city plus the head of Minerva. Collinson, *History and Antiquities of the County of Somerset*, I, p. 51.

Peters Cathedral is supposed to be built on the Spot where stood the Roman Temple of Minerva, the Patroness of Baths.[36] Tis a venerable and lofty Pile.

January 13th 6th Day

Being met by Doctor Dimsdale[37] last Evening with whom I had appointed to go to London, we rose about 4 O Clock, a most dismal Morning, the Wind high and snowing fast. Were obliged to procure a Chaise and 4, but the Snow being so deep we found it difficult in many places to plunge through and sometimes were fast and not without Expectation of being obliged to leave our Chaise and walk off. At length we reached an almost unbeaten Track. We reached [it] in three hours.

January 21st 1st Day

Till this Day we have been detained here by such a Snow as was not remembered by the oldest Man. All Intercourse between one City and another has been suspended. The Post stopped for four Days. Carriages stopped up. Some left till the Weather abated, others dug out, Men and Beast suffering grievously, but the poor Sheep most. The People in England seldom meeting with this kind of inclemency are not prepared to encounter it and of course suffer much more than we do in America. But England in the Winter Season has greatly the advantage of us for while we are buried in Snow and a Frost so severe and for many weeks together that our Sheep Cattle and horses must be fed within doors, while here the Verdure is so fine (in general) and the Air so temperate that they may graze unhurt and unattended.

Nor are the Advantages they reap in Summer over us inferior to these. While we are all parched and burnt with excessive heat our Meadows dressed in Russet brown and our Pastures in Mourning, their repeated rains chear and enliven the whole vegetative Class and all Nature blooms afresh. But our Fall and Spring by no means yield to them. We have much more Sky, less rain and fog and Mist and after a long cold Winter when the whole Face of the Earth has been covered with Snow and all Vegetation disrobed of its Beauty, tis impossible to say how pleasing and acceptable is the Spring. And in the Fall while they have nothing but Rain and Mists, now and then 'tis true Phoebus[38] does peep out from the Clouds. But this

---

[36] This temple has gradually been recovered by archaeological excavations over the past 300 years. There is still a great deal hidden under the paving of Bath Abbey yard and the adjacent streets and buildings. Excavations in 1981–1983 led to the temple being visible for the first time in 1,500 years. Cunliffe, *Roman Bath Discovered*, ch. 2.

[37] Dr. Joseph Dimsdale: see below, p. 120.

[38] In late Greek mythology, Apollo in his aspect of sun god and dispenser of light.

not often (particularly in the gloomy month of November). We have a pure serene Sky and frequently Weeks together without a Drop of Rain, the Dew yielding sufficient Moisture to paint the Fields. And for want of this Sky and Sun many kinds of Fruit here are inferior to ours in derision of all the Art and all the expensive artificial heats they can procure.

And though on the whole it must be granted the Advantages of Winter here over us are considerable yet ours are more healthy. Though we have it keen and piercing, they have it raw and damp and a Sky we have that England cannot boast. Here we seldom can see the Sun. He hides behind the Clouds, or skulks beneath the mist ashamed of himself. But greatly to my Surprise and delight my Countryman paid us a visit this Day and shone several hours. His Company was so agreeable that I wish he would stay with us a few Days. But this Wish is too unreasonable to be granted, too improbable to happen. I must be content with getting a Glance at him as he passes, but I do not expect this Winter to see him in half American Royalty and Splendor.

The Roads being now passable by means of several hundred people employed to dig away the Snow, we set off about 6 O Clock in the Evening with Doctor Jos*eph* Dimsdale and we got to Bath, spent the Evening in the Crescent at Doctor Watson's[39] with my two Sisters Pris*cilla* and Chris*tiana*[40] and early on the Morn of

January 22nd   2nd Day

We set off from Bath, changed horses at Chippenham and got to Marlborough to breakfast. The Inns from London to Bath are the finest in England. The Conveniences for travellers are not perhaps to be equalled in the World, and the Castle at this place is the best of them all, a large building, high Stories, grand Stair Cases, the Ceilings Stuccoed, Wainscots carved, and the furniture particularly elegant, with fine Gardens, Walks, Images and fountains. A beautiful Mount with a Spiral Walk to the Summit. This place was once a Noblemans Seat. Belongs now to Lord Harford.[41] Its situation on a pretty River[42] adds much to its beauty and Convenience.

Thence to Newbury and got to Reading to dine. Here too is a fine Inn next to Maidenhead. Here is an Inn where they make 80 Beds. The

---

[39] William Watson (1744–1824), a deeply religious man, was the third husband of Christiana Barclay. They settled at Bath. *JFHS*, XX, p. 113 n. 31; *DQB*.

[40] Priscilla and Christiana Gurney (see above, p. 34).

[41] The Castle Inn was known as Marlborough Mount when it was the seat of the late Earl of Hertford, afterwards Duke of Somerset. *The Traveller's Pocket Book; or Ogilby's and Morgan's Book of the Roads* (London, 1770), n.p.

[42] River Kennet.

Chamber Maid pays £3 per Annum for her berth. Then to Hounslow and through Kensington to London which we reached about 12 at Night, having come from Bath in a day, distance 108 Miles. Such are the Conveniences for Travelling in England, notwithstanding the Badness of the Roads and the Coldness of the Weather. As they have every thing in London they have *hotels* so being late to go to our several homes we went to an hotel and lodged and on

January 23rd   3rd Day

We got a Coach and came home. In the Afternoon took a trip to Hyde Park where is a fine Stream of Water frozen over, and with about a thousand others with Barclay and Bell, we skated an hour or two. As all Buisnesses are followed in London and a hundred Ways of getting money, without following any Buisness at all, we found people here ready to furnish us with Skates, in fine Order, and had nothing to do but sit down in a Chair on the Ice and have them fixed to one's Mind.

February 28th   4th Day

After having rested about 5 Weeks (from travelling) in London and enjoyed a great Share of Gossip, I left the little Village for a while intending to go as far as Pool and on my return pay a Visit to Portsmouth. This Morning with Emanuel Elam I set off on Favourite, and if We had not missed our Road and got 3 or 4 Miles out of the Way we should have breakfasted at Hounslow, but thinking more Politics than our Journey we got into a different road and only came to Brentford to Breakfast. This is famous for an Election between Wilkes and Luttrel, when the latter prevailed though very inferior in Number of Votes.[43]

Through Hounslow and Hounslow Heath, a place famous for Robbers and where a number of them are hanging in Chains, to Stains, a neat little Market Town on the Banks of the Thames, and soon after we leave this we get into Bagshot Heath, at the Commencement of which is the Duke of Cumberland's Seat, with a number of fine Objects in View, Towers, Obelisks, Columns &c, &c, a fine Park and beautifully situated.[44]

[43] In 1768 John Wilkes (1725–1797), politician, agitator and journalist, returned from exile on the continent, and tried to secure re-election to parliament (he had been M.P. for Aylesbury from 1757 to 1764). He was defeated in London but elected for Middlesex four times in 1768–1769. Nevertheless, he was expelled from the Commons on the grounds that he was an outlaw and, after a last re-election, the House declared his defeated opponent, Henry Luttrell, the duly elected member. George Rudé, *Wilkes and Liberty: A Social Study of 1763 to 1774* (Oxford, 1962), ch. 4.

[44] Cumberland Lodge in Windsor Great Park, built at the time of Charles II and inhabited in the mid-eighteenth century by the Duke of Cumberland, who was Ranger of Windsor Park. Pevsner, *Buildings of England: Berkshire* (London, 1966), p. 297.

JABEZ MAUD FISHER'S TRAVELS, 28 FEBRUARY - 5 MARCH 1776

After riding near 12 Miles over a Country where the hand of Cultivation has left no mark we come to a Seat of Admiral Keppele's.[45] Here the Forrest ends and joining to Keppele's Ground is the Village of Bagshot where we made an excellent Dinner the last stage being 19 Miles and the roads very wet and for Turnpike very heavy but the Roads from thence to Murrell Green are the finest in England. But the whole Country is uninhabited and almost uninhabitable. For many miles we see not a Cottage rising to the View and as seldom meet with a Tree. But leaving Surrey and coming into Hampshire we find the Creation wears a very different Complexion. Here are Groves and Fields and Meadows in abundance. At Murrell Green a Town consisting of one house and its appendages we lodged this Night.

February 29th   Fifth Day   76

Memorandum: Tis Leap Year. We mounted early this Morning and rode to Basingstoke to Breakfast. Here lives Dr. Portsmouth.[46] From thence we got on, having a tolerable Sky over our heads to Winchester to Dinner. The Country we passed through to Day is fine, much wood, a good Deal of Hopland, large Sheep Grounds and well interspersed with Water. We passed by the Seat of his Grace the Duke of Bedford.[47]

Winchester I have been at before, and have described it in a preceded Volume, as well as the Road from it to Rumsey, where we intend to go to Night.[48]

Basingstoke is a clever little Market Town a number of neat houses and prettily Situated. At Winchester is a fine Palace built by George 2nd but he dying before it was finished it remains incompleat.[49] It is of very large Scale, exceedingly elegant and commands a very beautiful View. We spent the Evening with our Friend Joseph Merryweather[50] and took a bed at Michael Futchers.

[45] Augustus Keppel (1725–1786) was a famous naval admiral, active in both the Seven Years' War and the American War of Independence. He was M.P. for Chichester (1755) and Windsor (1761–1780). He came into the possession of Bagshot Park in 1772 and lived there for the rest of his life. Owen Manning, *The History and Antiquities of the County of Surrey* (3 vols., London, 1809), III, pp. 84–85.

[46] Dr. Henry Portsmouth (1703–1780), a Quaker doctor who lived at Basingstoke. *JFHS*, XIII (1916), p. 155 and Persons Index.

[47] Francis Russell (1765–1802), 8th Duke and 11th Earl of Bedford from 1771, was a well-known Whig politician whose seat was Chenies in Bucks. Cokayne, *Complete Peerage,* II, p. 84.

[48] See above, pp. 87–88.

[49] Fisher has mistaken George II for Charles II, who wanted to make Winchester his summer residence and retreat. Building began in 1683, but the palace was never completed. Colvin, *History of the King's Works,* V, pp. 304–313.

[50] Joseph Merryweather (1727–1777), from Ringwood, Hants., paid many visits to London and to the western, southern and eastern counties in the service of the Quaker ministry. *DQB*.

March 1st   6th Day

Spring opened with as fine a Morning as possible. A clear Sky and scarce a breath of Air to disturb the Surface of the Water. We left Rumsey and got to Ringwood to dinner, 17 Miles. The Country all the way either Woods or Heaths. Hardly one improvement. And if we were to judge of its Population by the Number of People we meet on the road we might suppose it almost wholly unhabited, though there be many Parts capable of fine Cultivation, the Soil being good and in many places well watered. Tis a Pity such Tracts of Land should remain unimproved and Provisions be so scarce and dear. Were the Owners of these Lands disposed to cultivate one half the Ground, which now lies useless, England would want no Provision from abroad whereas they are now dependent on the Countries for the Staff of Life.[51]

Ringwood is a pretty large Market Town consisting of one Street and situated in a valley on the River Eden.[52] We went from this Place to Pool through an open Country as barren and uninhabited as the High Lands of Scotland, or the Barrens of Cornwal. Pool is on a Peninsula at the bottom of a Bay, well secured from the Sea by several Islands and Promontories which effectually landlock it. Tis about 4 Miles from the British Channel. It has a large Trade chiefly in the Newfoundland Fishery, having an 100 Vessels in that Employ.[53] The Fish are taken from Newfoundland to Portugal Spain and up the Mediterranean. The Oil is brought here. 1200 Tons of Cod Oil and 300 Tons of Seal Oil. The Harbour is uncommonly convenient as it has a long range of Keys, at which Vessels lay to discharge. The Tide does not rise and fall above 6 to 8 feet and it has one peculiar Property unknown to any other place. There is a Flood Tide every 6 hours occasioned by the Ebb in the Channel meeting the Ebb in this Arm of the Sea, which causes such an Eddy as to rise the water as much as the real Tide. They build some fine Vessels here. The Town is tolerably regular, consisting of about 800 houses, some of which are neat and elegant. Here is not a single public Building of any note. An amphitheatre of Hills surrounds it, which adds to its beauty and defends it from the Winds.

---

[51] Until the mid-eighteenth century, most of England's basic foodstuffs were produced at home. After 1750, however, the rapidly growing population quickly absorbed food surpluses and turned England in two decades from a large corn exporter to a substantial importer. Ralph Davis, 'English Foreign Trade, 1700–1774', in W. E. Minchinton, ed., *The Growth of English Overseas Trade in the Seventeenth and Eighteenth Centuries* (London, 1969), pp. 108–109.

[52] An error: River Avon.

[53] Poole was one of the ports in Devon and Dorset that specialised in the Newfoundland cod trade. In 1763, for instance, vessels from Poole took 8,770 of the 56,365 quintals of fish exported from St. John's, Newfoundland. Harold A. Innis, *The Cod Fisheries: The History of an International Economy* (New Haven, 1940), p. 146.

March 2nd   7th Day

We spent most of this Day in viewing the Town and harbour and in the Evening set off on our return for Ringwood. A most delightful Night with the moon nearly full accompanied us all the way. We lodged at Ringwood and on

March 3rd   1st Day

We decamped early came over a woody Country, through several Villages, to Red Bridge, a place of some little Trade and from thence to Southampton, a Place which from its Situation, Elegance and Neatness may be ranked next to Bath. It stands between two Rivers the Itching and the [Test] which fall into that called Southampton Waters. It has a wall almost round it. The principal Street is one of the broadest in England and contains a great Number of good houses. Here is the prettiest Market Place in the Kingdom. It has two good Stone Keys at which Vessels load and discharge and several temporary ones. It carries on a considerable Trade.

In the vicinities of this Town are the most advantageous Situations for Gentlemans Seats, which have not been neglected. There is a great Number of very capital and grand Structures and Grounds in the nicest Culture. Southampton is a place of great Resort in the Summer Months, and the most compleat accommodations for Bathing &c are to be had.

Passed through Bottel,[54] Titchfield and Fareham, soon after which it came on to rain hard and blow furiously, in which we rode 9 Miles to Portsmouth and found ourselves compleatly wet by the adventure.

March 4th   2nd Day

Spent this Morning in viewing the Towns of Portsmouth and Common, the Fortification, Docks, Ship Yards &c.[55] Portsmouth is the great Key of England, stands at the Entrance of a Creek on the Island of Portsea about 12 Miles in Circumference. The Fortification has every thing about it that Art can give, Regularity, Strength and Beauty. With a large body of Forces 'tis impregnable. The Motes round it are wide and deep and overflowed in a few minutes by the lifting up of a Flood Gate. This fortification affords a delightful Walk round the Town, abounding on every Side with all that can ornament and aggrandize a prospect. The beauty of the harbour is

---

[54] Botley.

[55] Although naval works began there in 1495, it was not until the eighteenth century that Portsmouth predominated amongst the dockyards. By the second half of that century, Portsmouth and Plymouth were the most important dockyards in Britain. R. J. B. Knight, ed., *Portsmouth Dockyard Papers 1774–1783: The American War* (Portsmouth, 1987), p. xvii.

nowhere to be equalled, besides having constantly a great Number of Shipping.

This Town is also defended by South Sea Castle,[56] Block house Castle[57] and a Chain that goes across the harbour from the round Tower to the opposite Shore. This is the narrowest point of Entrance to a safe harbour. The whole Island of Portsea is one continued Village, the Town including what they call the Common and the Kings and other public Buildings is larger than any City in Great Britain London excepted. The houses are mostly new and continuing to increase with the most rapid Progress. The Streets are clean and tolerably strait. From it we have a perfect view of Gosport on one side and the Isle of Wight on the other.

Gosport is a place of great Trade, very populous and has every advantage for Shipping. The Isle of Wight is about 4 Miles distant, 22 Miles long and 12 broad. The air of it is universally allowed to be as pure and healthy as any in the Kingdom, and the Soil is so rich that it produces Corn enough in one year to last them Seven. Through the middle of the Island runs a ridge of Mountains which not only afford plentiful pasture but a fine Prospect of the Sea. The Vales below consist of the richest Meadows and most stately Cornfields. The extremities of the Coast of the South and West are rocky and West not far from the Shore are the Needles. At both these Places the Island is inaccessible; and where it is level it is fortified by Art. In this Island are several principal Towns Vizt. New Port and Cowes, both considerable in Trade and convenient for Navigation.

The Kings Dock is sufficient to strike Terror into the Enemies of England.[58] Nothing can give one an higher Idea of its Strength and Power. Rope Makers, Smiths, Ship Wrights, Mastmakers: all seem to move by Clock work. They are all busy, all industry, but you see no Bustle, hear no Noise. Look at the Timber yard and you will think there is enough Materials to furnish all Europe and the whole is placed in such order, and so well sorted, that we forget tis piles of Timber. They are laid out in such exactness that we think them Streets. If we go to the Ropehouse we think

---

[56] Southsea Castle was built in 1544 at the southernmost point of Portsea Island, the principal entrance to Portsmouth harbour. Henry VIII wanted the castle to be a protection against French attack. The castle was repaired from time to time during the second half of the sixteenth century and since then it has been much modified. Colvin, *History of the King's Works*, IV Part 2, pp. 557–563.

[57] A battery was erected at the Blockhouse on the Gosport side of Portsmouth Harbour entrance in the period c. 1660–1750. Pevsner and David Lloyd, *Buildings of England: Hampshire and the Isle of Wight* (London, 1967), p. 419.

[58] Portsmouth was already a dockyard of some size by the time of Henry VIII. There was an extensive programme of construction from 1698 and the yard was pre-eminent by 1739 and continued as such until the end of the eighteenth century. *Ibid.*, pp. 407–418; Morriss, *Royal Dockyards*, pp. 1–2.

we are entering a Palace; a noble Building meets us, 1080 feet by 70, of brick, and uniform. When we enter it we see the most busy Scene imaginable, like a Beehive, all moving, and each in his proper Sphere. Here they can manufacture 5 Tons of hemp in a day. The Smiths Department is not less curious. Here Vulcan reigns in all his horrors and presents a Scene frightful to the imagination. Such a Number of Furnaces, so many men with their dreadful weapons and such a Din and Clash of Arms with flashes of heated Iron flying around us as beggar description.

The multitude of houses taken up for the purposes of Boatbuilding and mast making, and the People employed in these Branches are surprising. But all these collateral occupations are trifling compared to the great Object of Ship-Building. Here is an occupation which no other place will give an Idea of but in Miniature. The Conveniences for this business are in every respect compleat. Innumerable Machines for hoisting, moving, transporting the timber. The finest Docks wet and dry in the world. Reservoirs of water for holding the Masts and timber. Other conveniences for receiving the water from the Docks, when the Tide does not afford an opportunity to discharge them. These and all the Docks are walled with fine hewn Portland Stone. Besides all these, very considerable additions are daily making to enlarge the plan. Nineteen Acres of Land have been lately taken in from the Sea. The Sides walled with heavy Stone, Earth brought to fill it up and Piles are drove for a Foundation wherever a Building is erected. The many large houses here, the Store Rooms, the palaces in which the Officers reside and other large Structures within these walls give the whole a magnificent appearance and 2000 People employed make it sufficiently full of inhabitants.

A little distance from this is a very commodious and elegant hospital[59] and on the other Side is the Gun Wharf, a place well fortified and inclosed with very capital Store Houses and apartments for Balls, Bombs, Mortars, Cannon and every other implement of Mars.

After viewing these surprising works of Art we made a comfortable Dinner and set off for Chichester through a rich thick settled Country finely watered and variegated with Woods, Meadows and Cornfields. Chichester stands near an Arm of the Sea. Is a neat small City, walled in the greater part. In the Center is a most splendid and elegant Cross.[60] Here

---

[59] The Royal Naval Hospital at Haslar was begun in 1746, opened in 1754 and completed in 1762. Pevsner and Lloyd, *Buildings of England: Hampshire and the Isle of Wight*, pp. 243–245.

[60] This beautiful market cross was erected c.1500 by Edward Story, Bishop of Chichester (1478–1503). It is an octagon structure of Caen stone, having a central shaft above which is a cupola, supported by eight flying buttresses. *VCH: Sussex*, III, ed. L. F. Salzman (London, 1935), p. 73.

is a fine Gothic Cathedral with the Dean's Prebendaries and vicars houses and the Bishop's Palace.[61] A mile from this place on the road to London is a Roman Camp[62] of an oblong Square and 2 miles further on is an old Camp of Circular Form, supposed to be Danish.[63]

We left Chichester about the going down of the Sun. Cynthia[64] filled his Place to our Comfort and Convenience and under her Guidance we rode along through a fine open Country about 11 Miles to Midhurst, a Borough Town by whose Foot runs a pretty Stream over which there is a Dam and Causeway and several mills supplied with the Contents. Here we lodged. Though a Borough and Market Town Midhurst is but an indifferent Place, illy paved and shabby houses. In its suburbs is a famous Seat of Lord Montagu in a very old and Gothic Stile.[65] It is spacious but not regular, grand without elegance. The pleasure grounds and woods about it are delightful.

March 5th   3rd Day

We bid Midhurst Adieu early and rode on through a fine hill and Valley Country to Godalmin 18 Miles to breakfast. We leave Sussex about 5 miles before we reach this Place. That part of the Country we have seen is charming, in the highest Cultivation, and full of falling rills. Surrey being nearer to London is more richly improved, and better calculated for Gentlemans Seats.

As soon as we leave Godalmin we have Seat after Seat without Number. We pass through Guildford, a fine large well built Borough Town, and then come to Lord Onslow's[66] the Situation and Improvements of which are beautiful. From this Place to Epsom, we have a Chain of Seats, rich improvements, fine Prospects, good roads and every thing that a Traveller can desire. Epsom furnished us with a good Beef Stake in

---

[61] The Bishop's Palace is situated to the south-west of Chichester Cathedral. Most of its building took place at various stages from the Norman period to the eighteenth century. Ian Nairn and Pevsner, *Buildings of England: Sussex* (London, 1965), pp. 163–166.

[62] Chichester was the capital of the ancient Regni and the headquarters of Florius Vespasian. A strongly walled Roman station was built on the site and a subordinate station formed almost a mile to the north. *The Imperial Gazetteer of England and Wales,* I, p. 422.

[63] The remains of a circular Danish camp were situated on St. Roche's Hill, Chichester. The citizens of Chichester repelled the Danes in 876 and 900. *Ibid.;* Lewis, *Topographical Dictionary of England,* I, p. 441.

[64] Epithet of Artemis.

[65] The family home of Anthony Joseph Browne, Viscount Montagu (1728–1814), was Cowdray estate, the house of which was destroyed by fire in 1793. Cokayne, *Complete Peerage,* IX, pp. 97, 102.

[66] George Onslow (1731–1814), 4th Baron Onslow. The family seat was Clandon Place, near Guildford. *Ibid.,* X, pp. 69–71; *UBD,* III, p. 202.

gratitude to it. I must say that it is well situated for Air; and its Mineral Waters are in much vogue; that its form is semi-circular; that it lies open to a spacious Downs where the Sheep bleet sweetly; in short that Nature has done a great deal to make it clever and some generous Citizens of London have made it much cleverer by filling it with good houses and planting it with Trees that yield the utile and the dulci.

JOURNAL F

18–27 March 1776

March 18th 1776   1st Day

In Company with Thomas Weston junior[1] left London about 8 O Clock, came to Stamford Hill to Breakfast, went to Tottenham Meeting and came through Edmunton[2] and several other Towns to Hodsdown[3] where we dind. The Road all the way from London to this place is one continued Street of houses. We got to Hertford where we put our horses and took a walk to the Village of Bangor [i.e. Bengeo] where were kindly received by *Priscilla* Barclay[4] and her Niece Lucy. Goodwins the Name of this house is finely situated on a hill which overlooks the Town of Bangor and the Country round about, which is rich and beautiful. This is a most delightful Spot, and rendered famous by being the Residence of the celebrated Lucy. Hertford is a prettily situated Town with a fine Stream running thro it.

March 19th 1776   2nd Day

We left Bangor early and rode thro a fine Country, full of rich Prospect, to Youngsbury, the Seat of David Barclay.[5] The House here is in a plain but elegant Stile and the plan very convenient. His out houses, Stables &c are large and neat. The Features of the Country round are vastly fine. A beautiful Stream runs near the House and from it there a gentle Ascent. Here the Lawn is charmingly interspersed with Clusters of Trees. This view tho not extensive is particularly beautiful. His Gardens are laid out with great Taste and Judgement and in short every thing is in the nicest Order.

[1] Possibly a partner in Thomas Weston & Son, tobacconists, 19 Coleman Street, London. Kent's *London Directory* (1777), p. 188.

[2] Edmonton.

[3] Hoddesdon.

[4] Priscilla Barclay was the daughter of John Freame, a London banker. She was married to David Barclay. On the death of her brother John in 1766, Priscilla became the sole heiress of the banking business in Lombard Street, London, now Barclays Bank. Charles Wright Barclay, Hubert F. Barclay and Alice Wilson-Fox, *A History of the Barclay Family . . . from 1066 to 1924* (London, 1924–1934), III, p. 243.

[5] David Barclay the Younger (1729–1809) was a London merchant who closed his business trading with the American colonies at the outbreak of the American War of Independence. *DQB*; Jacob M. Price, 'The Great Quaker Business Families of Eighteenth-Century London: The Rise and Fall of a Sectarian Patriciate' in Richard S. Dunn and Mary Maples Dunn, eds., *The World of William Penn* (Philadelphia, 1986), pp. 367–368.

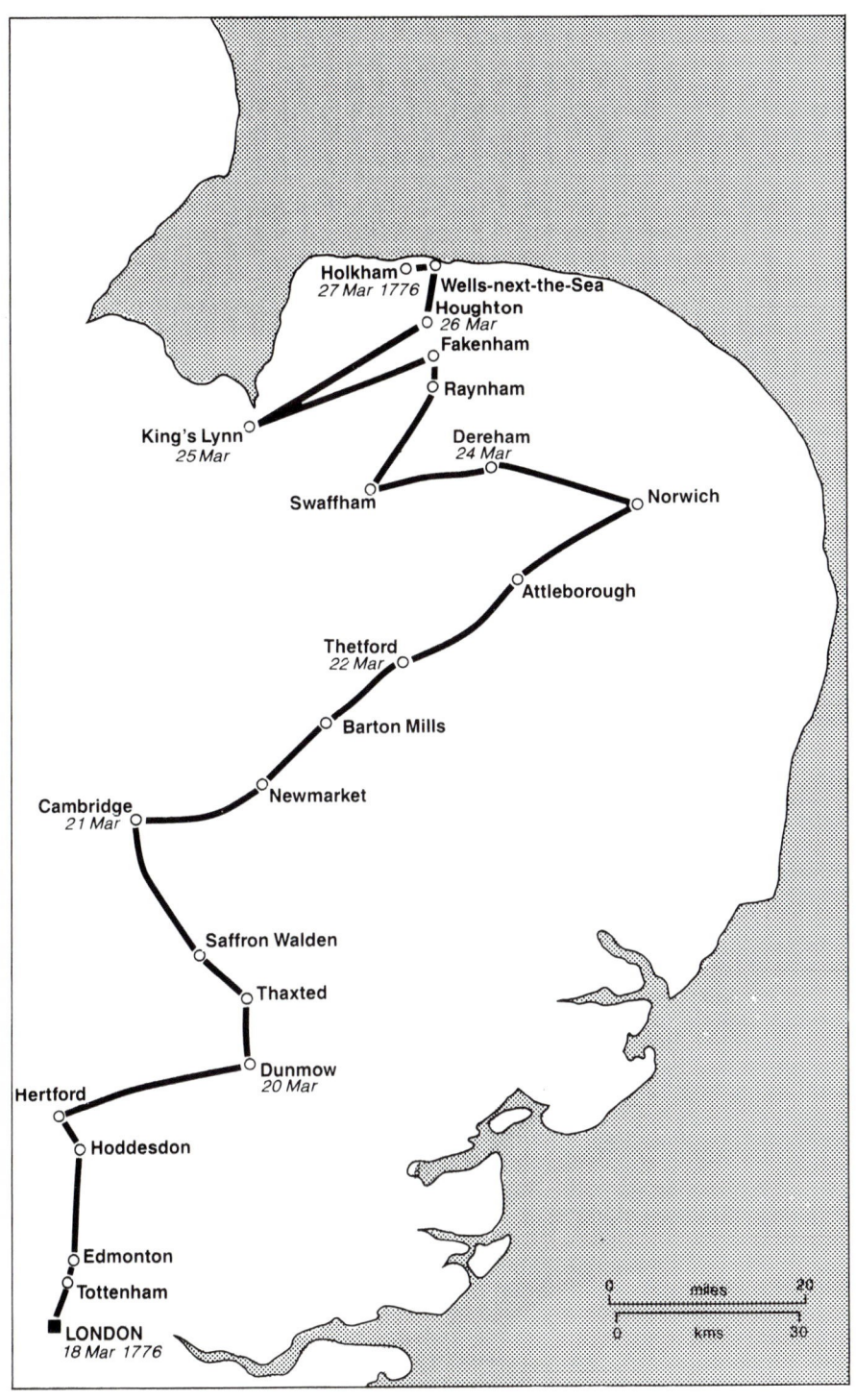

King's Lynn
25 Mar

Holkham
27 Mar 1776

Wells-next-the-Sea

Houghton
26 Mar

Fakenham

Raynham

Dereham
24 Mar

Norwich

Swaffham

Attleborough

Thetford
22 Mar

Barton Mills

Cambridge
21 Mar

Newmarket

Saffron Walden

Thaxted

Dunmow
20 Mar

Hertford

Hoddesdon

Edmonton

Tottenham

LONDON
18 Mar 1776

JABEZ MAUD FISHER'S TRAVELS, 18 - 27 MARCH 1776

We spent the greater part of the Day in strolling up and down the Hills and in the Evening took a delightful Ride thro the Fields and Park to Goodwins and came back to Youngsbury where we lodged.

March 20th   3rd Day

We left Youngsbury early and travelled along a Country richly abounding with picturesque and beautiful Prospects without a Spot of uncultivated Land and passed by some fine Seats and a number of villages and Towns besides Ware, where we called to see the improvements of John Scott, the celebrated Author of the four Elegies on the Seasons. And a beautiful Seat he has got, laid out with great Taste and commanding a very fine view.[6] His Grotto is vastly capital, consisting of a number of different Rooms communicating with each other per narrow passage cut thro a rock of Chalk. He has discovered nice Judgement in the disposition of the Shells as well as in the choice. The further Cave is supported by a fine Pillar planted thick with a very glassy and rich Mussel. This is about 50 feet under the Surface. The passage to it is laid with flint Stones and the floor of each Cell is neatly covered with fine pebbles and just sufficient Light to find the way to and fro peeps here and there thro a round passage for the purpose.[7] We came to Hockrill[8] to breakfast. We now leave Hertfordshire, a most fine County and the most famous for Corn and for the manufactury of Flour in the Kingdom. There is a constant succession of Hill and Valley but no mountains. The Land is well watered and inclosed.

We next got to Dunmow a tolerable Market Town, and pretty well situated for Prospect. This place is famous for an institution of Henry 3rd who decreed that whatever married Persons who did not repent of their marriage after 1 year and a Day should be intituled to a Flitch of Bacon.[9] But to procure it they are obliged to go down on their marrow bones on sharp Stones and repeat the following Oath at the Priory of Dunmow:

> You shall swear by the Custom of confession
> That you never made nuptial Transgression

[6] *Amwell: A Descriptive Poem* (1776) is the best-known work of the minor Quaker poet John Scott (1730–1783). Amwell is in Hertfordshire. John Butt (edited and completed by Geoffrey Carnall), *The Oxford History of English Literature, VIII: The Mid-Eighteenth Century* (Oxford, 1979), pp. 130, 639.

[7] Like many eighteenth-century poets, Scott was interested in gardening and in building a grotto. The excavations took at least fifteen years, but the grotto at Amwell was completed by the summer of 1773. Lawrence D. Stewart, *John Scott of Amwell* (Berkeley and Los Angeles, 1956), pp. 31–36; R. T. Andrews, 'Scott's Grotto, Amwell,' *East Hertfordshire Archaeological Society Transactions,* I (1899), pp. 15–31.

[8] Hockerill.

[9] Great Dunmow was made a market town by Henry III in 1250. Lewis, *Topographical Dictionary of England,* II, p. 83.

Since you were married to your wife
By household brawls or contentious strife:
Or otherwise at bed or in board
Offended each other in deed or in word:
Or since the Parish Clerk said Amen
Wished yourselves unmarried again.
Or in a twelvemonth and a day
Repented not in Thought any way
But continued true and in desire
As when you joined hands in holy quire
If to these conditions without all fear
Of your own accord you will freely swear
A gammon of bacon you shall receive
And bear it hence with love and good leave
For this is our Custom at Dunmow well known
Tho the Sport be ours the bacon's your own.

The words of this place mention no less than three Matrimonial Heroes who in the Space of 5 hundred Years laid Claim and carried off the Prize. Tradition says several hundreds did intend to get possession of it, but disqualified themselves by some act in the preparation. One good Man whose wife was coming with him took it into head that She knew the way better than her husband, which brought on such a Contention, as did permit their saving their bacon.

At this place I met with my Cousin and Fellow Passenger *George* Logan[10] with whom we agreed to procure a Dish sometimes eaten in America but often in France. This was neither more nor less than a Mess of Bull Frogs which I caught with a hand net in a Pond at the Foot of the Garden. This unfashionable Frikasee we thought very excellent. After Dinner we set out from Dunmow and got to Thaxstead to Tea and came to Saffron Walden where we took up our abode for the Night.

March 21st   4th Day

We mounted early and came on thro a fine Champaign country to Cambridge. We leave Essex 10 Miles before we get here. Essex is a fine inclosed Country producing an abundance of Wheat and Barley. We have now travelled from London in the Zig Zag way about 90 Miles and have

---

[10] George Logan (1753–1821), an American-born Quaker. After an unsatisfactory period in a Philadelphia merchant's counting house, he decided to follow a medical career. He set sail for England in 1775. Corner and Booth, *Chain of Friendship,* pp. 460–461; F. B. Tolles, *George Logan of Philadelphia* (Oxford, 1953).

not seen one Spot of Land lying useless. The whole is in high Cultivation and like one continued Garden.

Cambridge tho in some Respects inferior to Oxford is a most beautiful place, made so by its Situation and the multitude of Spacious and magnificent Colledges, Churches, walks, Bridges, and from its good Discipline, plentiful revenues and other necessaries for the advancement of Literature may challenge equality with any of the Universities in Europe. It is built on the banks of the Cam. The houses in general are but indifferent and the Streets by no means pleasing. Its appearance is however exceedingly grand from the number of Spires and Towers which it contains. It stands on a fruitful plain, is about 1 Mile in length and half a Mile in width. The River[11] which runs thro is realy beautiful, being on one Side walled up and on the other the banks are shelving and the Grass grows to the Edge of the Water. It is navigable thus far. There [are] 9 Bridges over it of good Architecture and you see most of them from one Spot. The Market Place is spacious and well supplied. Near it stands a neat stone Fountain built by one Hobson, formerly a Carrier from this place. This Hobson was famous in his Day for hiring horses and he made it an invariable Rule to let each horse have an Equal Share of rest and would never let one go, out of his turn. Hence the Proverb of *Hobson's Choice: this or none.*[12]

There are fourteen Churches, besides a number of other public buildings. The Senate house is a magnificent and elegant building, in Front 101 by 42 and the height 32 feet.[13] The Sides and Galleries are of Oak finely adorned and the Ceiling is beauteously stuccoed. Here are 4 fine Statues: George 1st and 2nd and the Duke of Somerset and an Italian Statue representing Victory.[14] One Side of this Square remains unfinished

---

[11] River Cam.

[12] A proverb attributed to Thomas Hobson (?1544–1631), a carrier of Cambridge. He let out horses for hire from his stables 'and the pertinacity with which he refused to allow any horse to be taken from them except in its proper turn is said to have given rise to the proverb, "Hobson's choice," i.e. "this or none."' *DNB*, IX, p. 946. I have omitted a drawing of the Gibbs' Building at King's College, Cambridge.

[13] The Senate House at Cambridge was built between 1722 and 1730 and was designed by James Gibbs. Pevsner, *Buildings of England: Cambridgeshire* (2nd edn., London, 1970), pp. 202–203.

[14] The statue of Charles Seymour, 6th Duke of Somerset, Chancellor, 1689–1748, is by Rysbrack (1756). A figure representing Academic Glory, by Giovanni Baratta, is now removed and is in the Fitzwilliam Museum. The statues of George I and II are, in fact, in the Squire Law Library in the Schools Building. That of George I is by Rysbrack and was carved between 1736 and 1739. The statue of George II is by Joseph Wilton and was first placed in the Senate House in 1766. Both are white marble statues crowned with wreaths and clad in classical armour and toga. RCHM, *An Inventory of the Historical Monuments in the City of Cambridge*, Part I, pp. 9, 11, 18 and plates 73, 80, 81.

but 'tis intended to have the opposite Side to answer the Front of this, which is very grand, having fluted Columns between each Window. The whole height of the Building and the Doors are fine. The west Side of this square is taken up with the Schools and public Library. This Library contains upwards of 90,000 Volumes.[15] Here is a Mummy of 2,000 years Preservation, also a Chinese Pagod composed of Rice, hard as Marble and heavy as metal, and a volume of Manuscript written on Reeds bound together like a Baker's Tallies (in the arabic Language).

St. Peter's Colledge is the most ancient, consists of two Courts separated by a Cloister and Gallery.[16] The Chapel is a good building with an handsome Altar piece and a window of painted Glass.[17] Clare Hall Colledge[18] is on the bank of the River over which it has an elegant Stone bridge leading to a beautiful Vista, beyond which is a delightful Lawn, surrounded by lofty Elms and Corn fields without termination. This Colledge consists of one grand Court with two noble Portico's, thro which we see the Vista to the Fields. The Court is 150 feet by 111.[19] The Front of this Colledge is noble. The whole Building has a fine effect from the Field. The Chapel of this Colledge is elegant.[20] The Hall is a fine Room as is also the Combination Room where are fine Portraits of Marquis of Granby and his horse full Size by Sir Joshua[21] and the Duke of Somerset by Dance.[22]

[15] Cambridge University Library was originally erected at the charge of Rotherham, Archbishop of York, and Tunstal, Bishop of Durham, c. 1480. The east front, containing the New Library, was rebuilt by subscription prior to 1769. The university library was originally in the Schools Building. *Ibid.*, pp. 11–12; James Dugdale, *The New British Traveller; Or, Modern Panorama of England and Wales* ... (4 vols., London, 1819), I, p. 237.

[16] Peterhouse was founded in 1280 by Hugh de Balsham, Bishop of Ely. The College was removed to its present site in 1284. The north range of Old Court was being built in 1424–5 but the lower part of the Gallery, linked to the north range, has been assigned to c. 1350. First Court was later added, as were arcaded walks with galleries dated 1625–1635. RCHM, *Inventory of the Historical Monuments in the City of Cambridge,* Part 2, pp. 156–157.

[17] The first mention of a chapel at Peterhouse was in 1388. The master, scholars and residents had the bishop's licence to hold services in the chapel. *VCH: Cambridge,* p. 335.

[18] Clare College was endowed in the 1330s by Lady Elizabeth de Clare, Widow of John de Burgh, but a society existed on the site from at least 1326. *Ibid.,* p. 340.

[19] The quadrangular court at Clare College was completed probably within fifteen years of the rebuilding of the college after 1521. It was rebuilt in the seventeenth century and further modifications were added down to 1815. *Ibid.,* p. 342.

[20] The first permanent chapel at Clare College arose after a Papal licence was granted in 1363. During the rebuilding of the college in the 1520s and 1530s, the first chapel gave way to a new one with a library above. This structure was demolished in 1763 and the present chapel was built between 1763 and 1769. *Ibid.,* pp. 342–343.

[21] A slight error: this full-length life-size standing figure of John Manners, Marquess of Granby, by Sir Joshua Reynolds, is in Trinity College not Clare College. *Ibid.,* p. 470.

[22] Sir Nathaniel Dance-Holland (1735–1811) was best known as a portrait painter. He was a frequent exhibitor of portraits and historical pieces before 1776. *DNB,* IX, p. 1045.

Pembroke Colledge consists of two Courts.[23] The Chapel is elegant, well proportioned, built by Christopher Wren.[24] The Library is capital; the Garden large and well laid out.[25] Benet Colledge and Chapel are tolerable; the Altar piece of the latter is good.[26] Trinity Hall is one of the prettiest Colledges in the University, a pretty Chapel but small.[27] Colledge of Caius or Key's consists of 3 neat Courts. The middle one is a neat piece of Architecture.[28] The Chapel is not large, but very beautiful.[29] The Hall is clever.[30]

Kings Colledge is on many Accounts deemed the most magnificent in Europe.[31] It contains several large piles of Building detached from each other. The old Court is 120 by 90 feet. The new Court forms a Quadrangle with the help of the Chapel. This Quadrangle is 300 feet each way.[32] The Chapel is allowed to be the finest piece of Gothic Architecture now remaining in Europe. 304 by 74 feet and not a single Pillar to sustain the Roofs. The Roof is of Stone fine wrought. There are 26 beautiful Pinnacles

[23] The Old Court is the oldest part of Pembroke College, and was built between c.1351 and 1398. It was partly demolished in the late nineteenth century to make way for the present First Court. Ivy Court was begun in 1614 but not completed until after the Restoration. RCHM, *Inventory of the Historical Monuments in the City of Cambridge,* Part 2, pp, 147–156.

[24] The Old Chapel at Pembroke College dates from the fourteenth century, but a new chapel, designed by Wren, was begun in 1662 and consecrated three years later. *Ibid.,* pp. 147–148.

[25] Laurence Booth, Master of Pembroke College from 1450 to 1480, built a library over the foundress's hall. Books from this library were removed into a new library established in the old chapel in 1690. *VCH: Cambridge,* p. 350.

[26] i.e. Corpus Christi College, founded in 1352. In 1519 a separate and spacious college chapel was built. This replaced earlier chapels of the period 1478–1515. The altarpiece was erected in the 1750s 'at the Expence of Sir Jacob Astley, Bart., who was educated here.' *Ibid.,* pp. 371, 373; *Cantabrigia Depicta: A Concise and Accurate Description of the University and Town of Cambridge, and its Environs ...* (Cambridge, 1763), pp. 38–39.

[27] Trinity Hall was founded in 1350 as a college for scholars of the Canon and Civil Law. The chapel was built by 1366 and was completely redecorated in 1729–1730. Despite later additions, the chapel still keeps the general appearance given to it in 1730. *VCH: Cambridge,* pp. 362, 368–369.

[28] The three courts are Gonville Court, the west range of which was built in 1441 and the east range c. 1490; Caius Court, built to the south of Gonville Court by Dr. Caius, 1565–1569; and Tree Court, built between 1617 and 1619. RCHM, *Inventory of Historical Monuments in the City of Cambridge,* Part 1, pp. 72–73; *VCH: Cambridge,* p. 359.

[29] This chapel was constructed during the period of the second master, William Rougham, c. 1360–1393. The building was not formally consecrated until 1494. In 1637 the chapel was lengthened eastwards and repaired. It was encased in freestone, partly rebuilt, and entirely redecorated between 1718 and 1726. *VCH: Cambridge,* pp. 357–359.

[30] The Hall at Caius College belongs to the time of the sixth master, Thomas Attwood, 1441–1444. *Ibid.,* p. 357.

[31] King's College was founded by Henry VI in 1441. *Ibid.,* p. 376.

[32] The new court was constructed between 1724 and 1732. It is only partially complete. *Ibid.,* p. 392.

of which the four principal are 150 feet high and are seen at a great Distance. There is a profusion of carved work seldom to be paralleled. The various pieces of Scripture History painted on the 26 Windows entire, not extraordinary.[33] The new Building is beautiful and magnificent, 236 feet by 46, built with Portland Stone. The apartments grand and commodious.[34] There are several Gardens and Orchards belonging to this College and besides a River that runs thro them there are some Canals with Groves of Elm, which make the avenues to the Colledge pleasant.

Queens Colledge contains two Courts and a pile of Building near the Garden.[35] Each Court is about 100 feet every way. The Chapel makes a good appearance.[36] The Hall is large and the Library well stored.[37] The Grove and Garden are vastly charming taking in both Sides of the River and including several neat Bridges. Catherine Hall has one of the most extensive and regular Fronts in the University.[38] The Entrance is thro a handsome portico that leads into a Court 180 by 120 feet.[39] In the middle is a flower Garden. The Chapel is a fine piece of Architecture.[40] The Hall is midling.[41]

Jesus Colledge is surrounded by Groves Gardens and fine Meadows. We enter it by a magnificent Gate.[42] The principle Court is 141 by 120 feet.[43]

---

[33] Work on King's College Chapel began in the 1450s but was not completed until 1515. *Ibid.*, pp. 389–391.

[34] The new building, designed by James Gibbs, is in the partially complete New Court. *Ibid.*

[35] These courts could be any two of the following: the Old Court, built in two stages in 1448–1449; the Cloister Court, 1460–1495; the Pump Court, 1756; and the Walnut Tree Court, begun in 1616. Mason, *Blue Guide: Oxford and Cambridge*, pp. 141–142.

[36] The foundation stone of this chapel was laid in 1448 and the chapel was redecorated in 1775. It is now used as a reading room, a new chapel having been built in 1889–1891. *VCH: Cambridge*, p. 410.

[37] The Hall at Queens' College began to be constructed in 1449. It received its present panelling and flat ceiling in 1732–1734. The library at Queens', on the north side of the front court, was already in existence by 1472. *Ibid.*, pp. 409–411.

[38] St. Catherine's College was founded by Robert Woodlark (or Wodelark), Provost of King's College, on St. Catherine's Day, 25 November 1473. Until 1860 it was known as Catherine Hall. *Ibid.*, p. 415.

[39] The three-sided front court, closed on the Trumpington Street side only by iron railings, was built in various stages between 1675 and 1757. Mason, *Blue Guide: Oxford and Cambridge*, p. 140.

[40] The chapel walls and roof were completed by 1676, but lack of funds prevented the furnishing of the interior until 1704. *VCH: Cambridge*, p. 418.

[41] This dates from 1675. *Ibid.*

[42] The Gatetower is of three storeys, and was built c. 1500–1507. RCHM, *Inventory of the Historical Monuments in the City of Cambridge*, Part I, p. 84.

[43] Cloister Court, the heart of the old nunnery, to which Bishop Alcock added the third storey, a timber ceiling for the cloisters, and his rebus. Mason, *Blue Guide: Oxford and Cambridge*, p. 132.

The Chapel is so so; the Hall handsome; the Cloisters are as usual. The Grove is extensive and much admired.[44]

Christ's Colledge has a grand Court 138 and 120, is a uniform pile of Stone.[45] The Chapel well adorned.[46] The Hall is an handsome Room.[47] The Garden is one of the pleasantest: shady Walks, beautiful Alcoves, Summer houses and a bowling Green besides Baths.

St. John Colledge consists of 3 Courts, one of which is adorned by 4 tall Towers and is 228 feet by 216 broad, another 270 by 240.[48] The Hall and the Chapel are like most of the rest.[49] The Library is clever.[50] St. Mary Magdalens Colledge I shall say little of because tis like the rest and because I am tired of the Subject.[51] But Trinity Colledge is too capital to be omitted.[52] It contains two spacious and beautiful Quadrangles. The first is 344 by 325, the other 287 by 256. It has a grand Gate with an observatory over it, by which we enter, and another Gate with 4 lofty Towers.[53] There

[44] Jesus College Chapel was originally a conventual church for the Nunnery of St. Radegund (established in 1135). It was modified first by Bishop Alcock, the founder of the college (c. 1496), and many later alterations took place. The Grove and the Cloisters are remnants of the nunnery. Alcock rebuilt the nuns' refectory to form the first hall in Cambridge to be placed upstairs. *Ibid.*, pp. 130, 132–133; Pevsner, *Buildings of England: Cambridgeshire*, pp. 83–84.

[45] Christ's College was an enlargement of God's House, instituted in 1439 by a London parish priest, William Byngham, for training grammar school masters. It was refounded as Christ's College c. 1506. *VCH: Cambridge*, pp. 429, 431.

[46] God's House had a chapel of its own, which was enlarged for Christ's College and reconsecrated in 1510. *Ibid.*, p. 432.

[47] The Hall dates from c. 1506. *Ibid.*, p. 431.

[48] The First Court was built between 1511 and 1520, but was much altered during the eighteenth century. The second and third courts were built in 1598 and 1624 respectively. Mason, *Blue Guide: Oxford and Cambridge*, pp. 124, 126.

[49] The Hall is in the west range of First Court, opened in 1516. The old chapel (demolished in the 1860s) dated back at least to the end of the thirteenth century. RCHM, *Inventory of the Historical Monuments in the City of Cambridge*, Part 2, pp. 187–188.

[50] St. John's College Library, on the north side of the third court, was built in 1623–1625. *Ibid.*, p. 188.

[51] Magdalene College was founded by Thomas, Lord Audley, Lord Chancellor of England, in 1542. *VCH: Cambridge*, p. 450.

[52] Trinity College was founded by Henry VIII in 1546. He amalgamated two existing colleges, the King's Hall and Michaelhouse, together with various small hostels attached to them, and added to their revenues substantial endowments from the dissolved monasteries. R. Robson, *Trinity College* (Norwich, 1982), n.p.

[53] The Great Court, the largest college court in Oxford or Cambridge, and Nevile Court were constructed as part of the rebuilding of the college between 1595 and 1605. The Great Gate, now the principal entrance to the College, was built originally for the King's Hall in several stages between 1490 and 1535. The Observatory was put on the Great Gate in 1706 and taken down in 1797. The Clock Tower, like the Great Gate, was built for the King's Hall and moved to a position twenty yards north of its original site in 1599. *Ibid.*; *VCH: Cambridge*, p. 464.

is a pretty Conduit in the middle which supplies the Colledge with water conveyed thither by an aquaduct 1 Mile in length. The other Court is most elegant, encompassed on three sides by a spacious Piazza, over which are the Library and Students apartments.[54]

The Chapel is large and handsome 204 by 33 feet.[55] It is adorned with a neat Altar piece, Stalls and an Organ Gallery. On each Side the Altar are two good Paintings. In the outer Chapel is a very fine Statue of Sir Isaac Newton,[56] with a Prism in his hand. The Attitude is good and the execution very capital. The Hall is exceedingly pretty adorned with fine bow Windows, but the Library which takes up a whole Side of the Quadrangle is the grandest Structure of the Sort in the Island. 198 feet front 40 deep and 38 high. You ascend it at one End by a rich black marble Staircase. The room at first Entrance is very striking. It is divided into 30 Apartments and over each are the Busts of the Great Poets and Philosophers — on the left the antients, on the right the moderns — done by different Masters but all excellent. Here are likewise several good Portraits by Van dyke.[57] The Ceiling is a good piece of Stucco work.[58] At the End is a fine bow Window and a most rich and beautiful piece of Stained Glass representing his Majesty George 3rd with Britannia behind him and the Genius of the Place introducing Sir Isaac Newton to him who has a Globe under his Arm.[59] Bacon[60] is under the Throne with a book and Pen in his hand. On the East Front of this Library is a good piece of Alto Releivo representing Law, Physic and Divinity and [Mathematics].[61] Under the Library is a Piazza which makes a spacious walk.

The many agreeable Walks about this and the other Colledges render the Scene particularly pleasing; being laid out with good Taste, Shaded by

[54] The Wren Library, on the west side of Nevile's Court, was built during the years 1672–1677. Robson, *Trinity College,* n.p.

[55] Trinity College Chapel was constructed straight after the founding of the college in 1546. *Ibid.,* p. 465.

[56] This piece of statuary was by Roubiliac. Dugdale, *New British Traveller,* I, p. 232.

[57] A mistake. Dr. R. Robson of Trinity College, Cambridge informs me that guide books to the college in 1763 and 1781 do not mention any portraits by Van Dyck.

[58] Wren designed the interior of the library as well as the outside.

[59] This bust of the natural philosopher Sir Isaac Newton (1642–1727) was completed by Roubiliac in 1751. There is also a statue of Newton in the ante-chapel at Trinity College. *DNB,* XIV, pp. 370–393.

[60] Sir Francis Bacon (1561–1626), lawyer, scientist, essayist, philosopher and Lord Chancellor from 1618. *DNB,* I, pp. 800–832.

[61] The alto relievo is a keystone projecting as a scroll-bracket rising to the soffit of the main entablature. It shows Ptolemy II receiving the Septuagint from the translators. There are four statues on top of the library representing Divinity, Law, Physic and Mathematics. Robson, *Trinity College,* n.p.; RCHM, *Inventory of the Historical Monuments in the City of Cambridge,* Part 2, pp. 237–238.

stately Elms, forming nice Avenues, and nothing more heightens the Scene than the River which runs thro it and the pretty Bridges which are over it. Emmanuel Colledge[62] has several Courts and a Hall and a Garden and a Walk and would be worth description but it is done by referring to the others, to which it is very similar. The same may be said of Sidney Sussex Colledge.[63]

We left Cambridge and soon after got out of those rich Improvements which had accompanied us the last 100 Miles. We got to NewMarket to Tea. This is the grand Resort of the Lovers of Sport. Near it is the celebrated Heath for Racing, being the finest Ground in the Kingdom for the purpose.[64] We drank Tea here and rode on over Downs which afforded us an interminable view with a Hut or inclosure to Barton Mills, a little village, at which we took our Repose for the Night.

March 22nd   5th Day

We decamped soon as Phoebus would permit us and came over a barren heath to Thetford. But as no Spot in England is without some use or other those parts of this Heath which do not yield sufficient vegetation for the grazing of the wooly Tribe are inhabited by miriads of Rabbits who burrow here with little molestation.

Thetford is a little Market Town of no Consideration except its having the Ruins of a Priory which are scarcely worth viewing.[65] We dont get [out] of this desolate Country till we arrive within a few miles of Attlebro'[66] where we dind and now intend to see the favourd City of Norwich in a few hours, having a fine Sky overhead, which has attended us all the way from London for 5 Days — a thing so uncommon in this part of the world and at this Season as to merit observation.

March 23rd   6th Day

We came to Town last Night and on my arrival found my old Land Lord Springal in a melancholy Situation on account of the Death of her

[62] Emmanuel College was founded by Sir Walter Mildmay, Chancellor of the Exchequer to Elizabeth I, in 1583. *VCH: Cambridge,* p. 474.

[63] Sidney Sussex College was founded as a result of the bequest by Lady Frances Sidney, Countess of Sussex, in 1595. *Ibid.,* p. 481.

[64] The reputation of Newmarket for horse racing seems to have originated during the reign of Edward I. The fame of the racecourse greatly increased during the reign of Charles II, who frequently attended the races. Lewis, *Topographical Dictionary of England,* III, p. 367.

[65] The Priory of Our Lady, founded for Cluniac monks from Lewes, the earliest Cluniac settlement in England, in 1103–1104. Pevsner, *Buildings of England: North-West and South Norfolk* (London, 1962), pp. 342–344.

[66] Attleborough.

Daughter Patty, so I deserted my old Lodgings and took up my abode with the Widow Gurney.[67] About 5 in the Afternoon we set off with the addition of Joseph Gurney to our Party on the Norfolk Tour. By bright Cinthia's good Auspices we came to Deerham and lodged.

March 24th   7th Day

Under an azure Canopy undecked by a single Cloud, we rode from Deerham to Swaffham where we breakfasted. Tis the neatest town in the County, healthfully situated in a champaign Country and good Neighbourhood, having some great Seats contiguous to it. From Swaffham we jogged on to Narford the Seat of Squire Fountain.[68] The house is a good one, but by no means sufficiently attractive to be the object of view. Its curiosities however are very striking, particularly a curious cabinet of earthenware done after the designs of Raphael. This collection is particularly grand, consisting of a great variety of Urns, Vases, Images &c &c, mostly of a useless kind, for which Fountain has been offered £5,000.

Here are a few pieces of antique Sculpture, a number of fine Family Portraits and some few good pieces of History, Landscapes, Sea pieces and some miniatures. From this we went to Rainham,[69] a fine seat belonging to Lord Townsend.[70] The house is large, partly brick and partly Stone. The Stone is modern, the rest of the building old. It cannot be entituled to the Name of Magnificence, tho it be spacious and commodious. The Hall is a very large Room, well proportioned, adorned with Pilasters and Columns and prettily decorated with Stucco on the Ceiling. The Rooms are generally well furnished and adorned, but cut up into small apartments. There is a most capital Collection of Family Portraits and some admirably finished, a few historical paintings, among which is a vastly fine one of Bellisarius.[71] The Library is a good Room, and large.

In the vicinity of the house and in view from the upper Story we have a

---

[67] Elizabeth Gurney (d. 1788) was the widow of John Gurney of Norwich (1716–1770). *DQB*.

[68] The estate at Narford was bought in 1690 by the collector Sir Andrew Fountaine. Narford Hall was built in stages between c.1700 and the 1860s. Pevsner, *Buildings of England: North-West and South Norfolk*, pp. 265–266.

[69] Raynham.

[70] Raynham Hall was a seventeenth-century house, but most of the interior was remodelled by Kent in the 1720s. George Townshend (1723/4–1807) was 4th Viscount Townshend of Raynham from 1764. Pevsner, *Buildings of England: North West and South Norfolk*, pp. 148–151; Cokayne, *Complete Peerage*, XII Part 1, pp. 808–809.

[71] Bellisarius (c. 505–565) was a brilliant and successful general in the service of the Byzantine Emperor Justinian. His most important campaigns were fought when he was trying to regain the former territories of the Roman Empire in Italy and Africa. Jones and Dixon, *Macmillan Dictionary of Biography*, p. 69.

fine lake and there is a pretty Collection of Woods Groves and
Shrubberies, Lawns, Vistas, walk &c &c. We dind at an Inn near Fairham
and very soon afterwards took a Dish of Tea and after Night mounted and
got on to Fakenham where we lodged.

March 25th   1st Day

Fakenham is a clever little Town. We stayed at it till after Dinner when we
marched thro a trackless Country over hedges and Ditches and thro Gates
to Lyn,[72] stopping on our way to regale ourselves with a Dish of Tea at
Houghton, a pretty Village in the Vicinity of Houghton Hall,[73] for an
account of which I must refer to the Negociations of tomorrow.[74]

Lyn is a large rich and populous thriving town, on the East Side of the
River Ouze. Contains about 2500 houses and only about 10,000 People (as
the inhabitants say). But this like all the Towns in England are under
calculated. There is one good Street and a number of good houses. St.
Margaret's Church is a large piece of Gothic Structure and very grand.[75]
The Court House, Goal and Assembly Room are all under one Roof.[76]
The Front is a curious piece of rustic work, being chequered with Flint
Stones cut square and a nice hewn stone like Portland. The Market place is
a fine Area of 3 Acres well paved. The Market is a neat built and well
contrived place, being a Sort of Piazza supported by columns and of a
circular Figure. Here is likewise a beautiful Cross of modern Architecture
adorned with Statues and other Embellishments.[77] The new Walk is
beautiful being 340 yards in length and 11 in width, planted on each Side
with thick set hedges and here and there a Seat. It is likewise shaded by 2
Rows of Stately Trees and it is terminated by a Stone Walk containing
three grand Arches.[78]

[72] King's Lynn.

[73] Designed by Colen Campbell and executed by Thomas Ripley in Yorkshire stone in the
1720s and 1730s for Sir Robert Walpole. Pevsner, *Buildings of England: North-West and
South Norfolk,* pp. 207–210.

[74] See below, pp. 143–146.

[75] This Norman church dates from the twelfth century. Pevsner, *Buildings of England:
North-West and South Norfolk,* pp. 221–226.

[76] The Town Hall or Guildhall at King's Lynn is made up of four buildings, including a
prison, a hall for the county quarter sessions, and an assembly rooms built in 1766. William
Richards, *The History of Lynn . . .* (2 vols., Lynn, 1812), pp. 1173–1174; Pevsner, *Buildings of
England: North West and South Norfolk,* p. 230. I am grateful to Katherine Brown, curator at
the Lynn Museum, for assistance with this reference.

[77] A domed octagon built between 1707 and 1710 and now pulled down. Pevsner,
Buildings of England: North-West and South Norfolk, p. 234.

[78] New walks were laid out and trees planted in King's Lynn in 1753. In the centre of 'the
Walks' is Red Mount chapel, completed in 1485 and surrounded by avenues of chestnuts and
limes. Richards, *History of Lynn,* II, p. 1209. Katherine Brown supplied this reference.

In the Neighbourhood of this Place are the ruins of several Priories, Oratories and religious houses, and some Remains of a Fortification.[79] The walls are partly gone, but the Gates thro which we enter the Town are entire and grand. The River is navigable for Ships of 16 feet.

March 26th 2nd Day

Missing the way and coming out of the wrong Gate we got into a road which parted from the one we should have gone by 90 degrees. We attempted by exploring a new way to gain the right path, and for this purpose bid defiance to hedges, ditches and every other impediment, having horses nicely calculated for the purpose. But for want of a more accurate knowledge in the Geography of the Country we were continually getting wrong and the people we meet as ignorant as ourselves were incapable of giving us any information. However, guessing at the bearing of our port, though we were quite out of our Latitude, after riding 22 instead of 12 Miles we found ourselves in the neighbourhood of Houghton — a little village the property of the Earl of Orford,[80] Grandson to the Great Minister Sir Robert Walpole,[81] who built the Hall which gives Name to this Village.

Houghton Hall is less than half a Mile from the Road. We enter the Park thro a good Lodge. There begins our Astonishment and Admiration: a great Number of fine Groves, artlessly disposed, Vistas and Avenues, a thousand Deer grazing on the Verdure and hares without Number. The openings which are judiciously left in many places to let in the view of more distant woods changes the Shade and gives them that solemn Brown which always has a great effect. Two things only are wanting to make this Scene perfect: Rising Ground and Water. The first is in some Measure remedied by the disposition of the Groves which appear in different Shades one beyond another to a prodigious Extent. The Extent of this Building is 450 feet exclusive of the Colonnades 166 feet. It is all of Portland Stone and crowned with an entablature of the Ionic Order on which is a Balustrade. You first enter the hall a Cube of 40 feet. The Elegance and Magnificence of this strike one with Wonder though all of White Stone and every

---

[79] These buildings were mainly associated with the mendicant friars who had a strong presence in King's Lynn in the later Middle Ages. Scanty fragments of the Blackfriars, Austin Friars and Whitefriars survive, but a fair amount of the Greyfriars is intact. Lynn was a fortified town by 1271. The buildings of the Red Mount, a kind of fortress, existed by the mid-fifteenth century. Pevsner, *Buildings of England: North West and South Norfolk,* p. 221; Richards, *History of Lynn,* II, pp. 1189, 1191.

[80] George Walpole (1730–1791), 4th Earl of Orford from 1751. He was Lord Lieutenant of Norfolk from 1757 until his death. Cokayne, *Complete Peerage,* X, p. 86.

[81] Sir Robert Walpole (1676–1745), 1st Earl of Orford, was M.P. for Castle Rising (1700–1702) and for King's Lynn (1702–1745) and 'prime' minister between 1721 and 1742. *DNB,* XX, pp. 635–664.

decoration that can add beauty to Grandeur. Next we enter the Saloon, which is one of the finest Rooms in the World. It is 40 by 30 feet and 40 high. Then come the dressing and 20 Rooms more all fitted up in the most splendid and magnificent Stile and contain a collection of Pictures which most unquestionably is the first in England.

Here are all the great Masters shining with uncommon Lustre: Vandyck, Wooton,[82] Kneller,[83] Zuchero,[84] Le Brun,[85] Salvator Rosa, Viviani,[86] Rembrandt,[87] Rubens, Cignani,[88] Teniers,[89] Lilly,[90] Sacchi,[91] Vanloo,[92] Raphael, Titian, Guido, Claude, Rosalba,[93] Jordano,[94] Sarto,[95]

[82] John Wootton (?1678–1765) was an animal and landscape painter. Five of his pictures belonged to Sir Robert Walpole. *Ibid.*, XXI, p. 911.

[83] Sir Godfrey Kneller (1646–1723): original name Gottfried Kniller. Born in Lübeck, north Germany, he worked in England from 1675, mainly as a portrait painter. He was appointed principal painter to William III, knighted in 1691, and continued in this office under Queen Anne. *Ibid.*, XI, pp. 240–243.

[84] Taddeo Zuccaro (1529–1566) mainly worked in Rome, but there are many portraits attributed to him in English houses. His works represent the end of the Mannerist tradition. Murray and Murray, *Penguin Dictionary of Art and Artists*, pp. 455–456.

[85] Charles Lebrun (1619–1690), the virtual dictator of the arts in France under Louis XIV until the death of his protector Colbert in 1683. His most important paintings are at Versailles. *Ibid.*, p. 227.

[86] Antonio Viviani, called Codagora, flourished in Rome c. 1650. He excelled in painting architectural ruins. There were two pieces of ruins by him over the second and third doors in the Common Parlour at Houghton. Bryan's *Dictionary of Painters and Engravers* (new edn., London, 1927), V, p. 316; R. Beatniffe, *The Norfolk Tour: Or, Traveller's Pocket Companion . . .* (Norwich, 1777), p. 55.

[87] Rembrandt van Ryn (1606–1669) worked mainly in Leiden and Amsterdam. He painted many portraits, notably self-portraits, as well as Biblical subjects, landscapes, and studies of the Jews. Murray and Murray, *Penguin Dictionary of Art and Artists*, pp. 344–346.

[88] Carlo Cignani (1628–1719) was a late Baroque painter of the Bolognese school. *Ibid.*, p. 78.

[89] David Teniers I (1582–1649) was a painter of religious pictures and some landscapes with peasants similar to those by his son David II (1610–1690), the most famous member of the family and the one probably referred to here. David Teniers III (1638–1685) was also a painter. *Ibid.*, p. 417.

[90] Sir Peter Lely (1618–1680), a portrait painter born in Westphalia of a Dutch family, and trained at Haarlem. He came to London c. 1643 and was appointed principal painter to Charles II at the Restoration in 1660. *Ibid.*, pp. 236–237.

[91] Andrea Sacchi (1599–1661) was the chief representative of the classic strain of Algardi and Poussin in Roman Baroque painting. *Ibid.*, p. 370.

[92] The Van Loos were a family of painters of Flemish descent working in France. The eldest was Jean Baptiste (1684–1745). *Ibid.*, p. 239.

[93] Rosalba Carriera (1675–1757), a Venetian woman panellist who had a great vogue among English tourists. *Ibid.*, p. 75.

[94] Luca Giordano called Fra Presto (1632–1705), a painter of religious and mythological subjects. He was mainly active in Italy and Spain. *Ibid.*, pp. 174–175.

[95] Cornelius Dusart (1660–1704), a Dutch painter of peasant scenes. Harold Osborne, *The Oxford Companion to Art* (Oxford, 1970), p. 340.

Le Sueur,[96] Morrellio,[97] Carlo Maratt,[98] Pousin and Tivoli[99] &c and a Number of inferior Paintings. This Collection is invaluable. The Marble Parlour which has two Alcoves supported by Columns of Plymouth Marble contains over the Chimney a fine piece of Alto Releivo in Statuary Marble by Rysbrack.[100] Thro the Hall which is full of Statues and Busts we go to the Gallery which has a Cabinet of Paintings that no other Room in the World can boast.[101] This Gallery is 73 feet by 30, 21 feet high, windows all round near the Ceiling to shew the Painting to Advantage. Among these very capital ones are the following still more capital: A Lioness and two Lions by Rubens in the greatest Stile.[102] The Attitudes are admirable, so well done that while we behold them we forget they are inanimate. We tremble; we almost hear them howl. 6 feet by 8. Job's Friends bringing him Presents by Guido in large in his brightest Manner.[103]

The exposition of Cyrus, by Castilione, a most capital Picture.[104] Abraham's Sacrafice by Rembrandt: this is fine.[105] The Painter has avoided all the horrors of the Story by making Abraham cover the Boys Face to

[96] Hubert Le Sueur, active between 1610 and 1643, worked in France and England as a sculptor of tombs, equestrian statues etc. Murray and Murray, *Penguin Dictionary of Art and Artists*, p. 233.

[97] Bartolomé Esteban Murillo (1617/18–1682), the leading painter in Seville after Velazquez left for Madrid in 1623. *Ibid.*, pp. 285–286.

[98] Carlo Maratta or Maratti (1625–1713), an eminent painter and etcher. *Ibid.*, pp. 261–262. A printed guide to *Houghton Hall* (Derby, 1976), p. 12 states that he was the favourite artist of Sir Robert Walpole.

[99] Philipp Peter Roos, called Rosa da Tivoli (1657–1705). He mainly worked as an artist at Tivoli, near Rome. Bryan's *Dictionary of Painters and Engravers* (new enlarged edn., London 1904), IV, p. 274.

[100] John Michael Rysbrack (1694–1770). Born in Antwerp. With Roubilliac he was the most eminent sculptor in England from 1730 onwards. Murray and Murray, *Penguin Dictionary of Art and Artists*, p. 369.

[101] Sir Robert Walpole was a great collector of paintings and sculptures from all over Europe. He had acquired at least 400 paintings by 1736. Many of these pictures were displayed in the Gallery at Houghton. His grandson sold this extraordinary collection to Catherine the Great of Russia in 1778. Most of the pictures are still at the Hermitage, Leningrad. J. H. Plumb, *Sir Robert Walpole: The King's Minister* (London, 1960), pp. 85–87.

[102] A Rubens painting of a lioness and two lions hung in the Gallery at Houghton Hall. *Aedes Walpolianae*, p. 84.

[103] The original of 'St. John Receiving the Gifts of the People' is in Notre Dame, Paris. It is one of Guido Reni's most famous works. It was commissioned in 1601 and completed in 1635. A small copy was formerly at Houghton Hall. D. Stephen Pepper, *Guido Reni: A Complete Catalogue of his works with an Introductory Text* (Oxford, 1984), pp. 272–273 no. 157 and plate 183.

[104] Castiglione's painting of the Exposition of Cyrus hung in the Gallery at Houghton Hall. *Aedes Walpolianae*, p. 86.

[105] Rembrandt's painting of 'Abraham's Sacrifice of Isaac' (1635) was formerly in the Gallery at Houghton Hall and is now in the Hermitage. *Ibid.*, p. 88; Pierre Descargues, *The Hermitage* (London, 1961), p. 132 and colour plate on p. 133.

hide from himself the horrors of the Scene. The Adoration of the Shepherds by Guido is inferior to none: the beauty of the Virgin, the delicacy of the Child, the awe of the Shepherds and the Chiaro obscuro of the whole picture which is in the finest preservation are incomparable.[106] You see, you almost hear the Shepherds crying out Deus! Deus! ille! Menalca![107] Two fine Landscapes of Claude. But the most valuable and capital of all this Collection and perhaps the most valuable of any in Great Britain is the Doctors of the Church contemplating the immaculateness of the Virgin, who is above in the Clouds; the expression, drawing, design and colouring wonderfully fine.[108] The Virgin is in white and before her a sweet little angel flying. 8 feet 11 Inches by 6 feet wide. After Sir Robert had bought this Picture Pope Innocent 13[109] demanded it back as too fine to be let go out of Rome. But on hearing who had bought it, he suffered it to be sent off; value 3000 Guineas. The Prodigal Son by Salvator Rosa (8 feet by 6½) is vastly fine.[110] The last Supper by Raphael is in high preservation; 20 Inches by 8 Inches; immensely valuable.[111] There are besides these a surprising number of most capital pieces too many for Description.

From Houghton we went to Wells a little paltry dirty illy built Sea Port with a tolerable good Key. Here we stayed this Night.

March 27th 1776   3rd Day

We took a ride this Morning a few Miles to Holkam, the celebrated house of the Countess of Leicester.[112] The first objects which strike you are a few clumps of Trees which catch all your attention and give you a warning of an approach. They sketch out the way to a triumphal Arch under which the road runs. The Structure is in a most beautiful Taste and finished in the most elegant manner. It is extremely light, and built of a neat light colored

---

[106] This painting is one of several on this subject by Reni. It was painted in 1639–1640 and was purchased from Houghton Hall for the Imperial Collection of the Tsars of Russia. It is now in the Pushkin Museum, Moscow. Pepper, *Guido Reni*, p. 287 no. 190 and plate 221.

[107] God! God! It is he! Menalcas!

[108] This painting, by Guido Reni, was in the Gallery at Houghton Hall. *Aedes Walpolianae*, pp. 76–79.

[109] Michael Angelo Conti was Pope Innocent XIII from 1721 until 1724.

[110] Salvator Rosa's painting of the Prodigal Son hung in the Gallery at Houghton Hall. *Aedes Walpolianae*, p. 80.

[111] Raphael's painting of the Last Supper hung in the Gallery at Houghton Hall. *Ibid.*, p. 93.

[112] The Countess of Leicester (1700–1775) was the widow of Thomas Coke, 22nd Earl of Leicester (1697–1759). Holkham Hall was designed by William Kent and completed by 1761. The grounds of Holkham were laid out by Capability Brown in 1762. Cokayne, *Complete Peerage*, VII, p. 561; Pevsner, *Buildings of England: North-West and South Norfolk*, pp. 200–204.

brick, only one Story high. But that is of a great height and the Windows mostly Venetian are in a Stile proportionable. Before we reach the house we see a narrow plantation on each Side. A broad Vista leads from hence to the Obelisk which is a Mile and $\frac{1}{2}$ distant.[113] At the Foot of the Hill on which the Obelisk stands are two Porters Lodges, which in America we shall call very capital Structures. Half way between the Lodges and the obelisk you come to a place where are 8 Vistas: the grand Front of the house, Holkam Church[114] a beautiful object, the town of Wells, the triumphal Arch and others to distant plantations. From the house you have still a more beautiful, rich and extensive as well as a fine contrasted View. From the Front a little distance is a fine Lawn, in the middle a Lake surrounded by Trees at a distance, and beyond these Hills and Vallies soft, pastoral and delightful; and thro one of these pleasant Vallies you see the Ocean. On another Side the Park which is a most charming Scene full of Vistas and a multitude of objects, a Bridge with several Arches over a beautiful artificial River, to which the Ground is very judiciously sloping. Beyond it the Stables, which an American would mistake for a palace and over this a most picturesque and enchanting Country.

The house consists of five Quadrangles: the Center and the four Wings. Of the two fronts the South is most beautiful, the approach to it is grand, and it is as light airey and elegant a building as can be viewed. The Portico is magnificent in a fine Taste, supported by Corinthian Columns exactly proportioned. This Front in short is all Lightness, Elegance and Beauty. But however Grand the outside of this house may be, the inside is still more so and in point of Convenience is allowed by *Conoseurs* to be preferable to any in the Kingdom.

You enter what they call the great Hall, and here you feel every possible degree of Astonishment and Surprize. The Beauty and Grandeur of the Scene are almost too much to bear, and I'm sure I felt such an Exuberance of Joy, that I had no power to restrain me from a Behaviour quite ridiculous. It is a Cube of 48 feet supported by 18 very large and magnificent Ionic Pillars of Marble, their Pedestals resting on a marble Passage around it, 10 feet high, from the Area at[115]

[113] The Obelisk, which is eighty feet high, was put up in 1729 in axis with the house but a good distance from it. Pevsner, *Buildings of England: North-West and South Norfolk,* p. 204.

[114] This lies on a mound in the extensive park of Holkham Hall, not far from the lake. Though heavily restored in 1870, it was originally a Saxon or Norman church dedicated to St. Withburga. *Ibid.*

[115] The sentence tails off here.

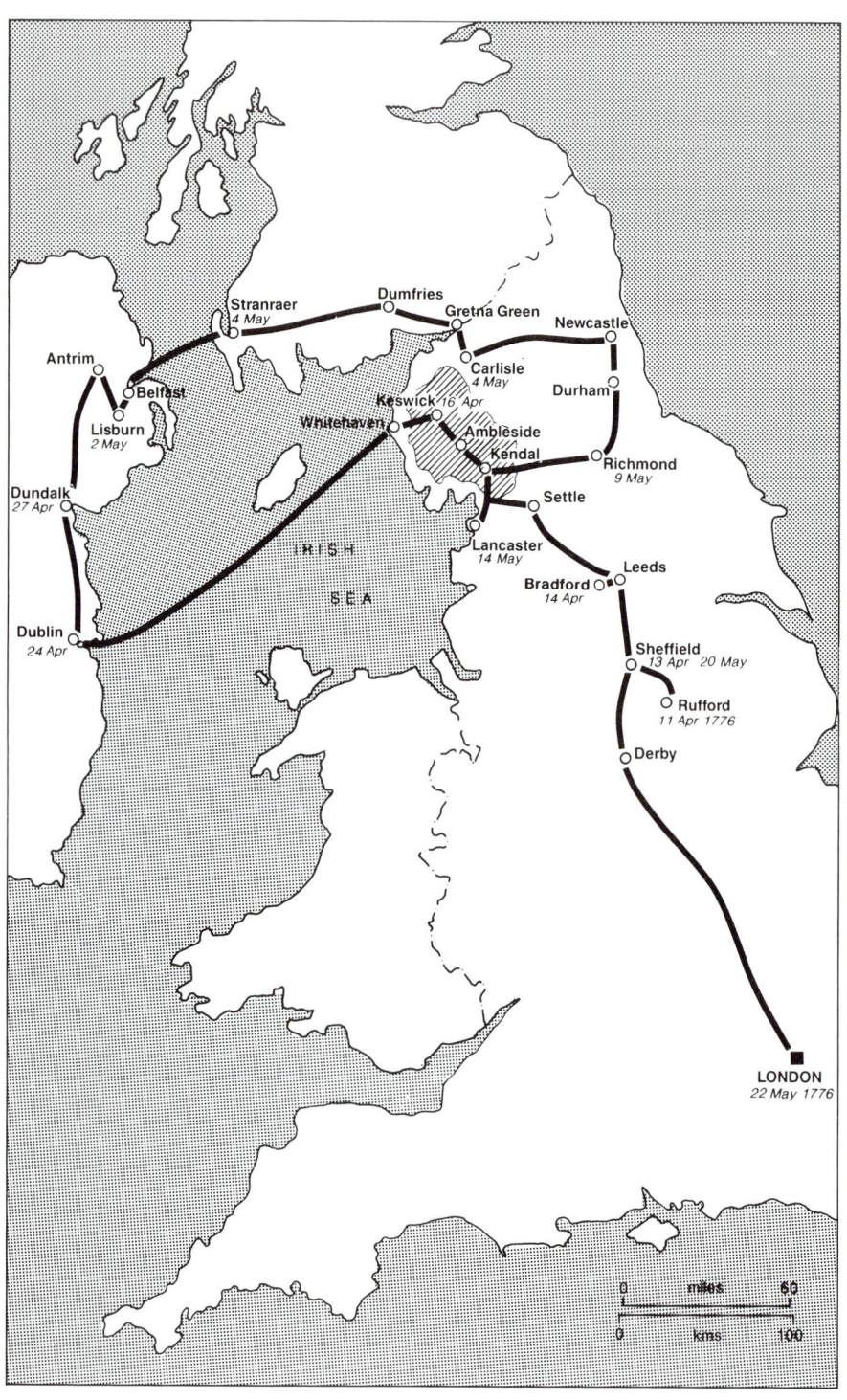

JABEZ MAUD FISHER'S TRAVELS, 11 APRIL - 22 MAY 1776

April 11th 1776   5th Day

Upon an expedition to see a great String of the Seats of Dukes Dutchesses Knights and Squires we mounted and first went to Sir George Saville's house at Rufford,[1] not half a Mile distant from the Inn at which we lodged. We enter the Gate and are conducted by a long Row of Yew Trees to the Stables which are commodious and clever and thro the Yard are led on to the house, the Entrance of which is rather awkward. The inside is convenient and the Rooms are spacious; the Hall is large but without any Decorations. The Gallery is a fine large Room and on one Side is filled with some excellent Portraits, by the best Masters. There is a good Collection of Paintings in the other Rooms, and some Tapestry.

Tho the house be very large its appearance is far from being magnificent. 'Tis a Building of the old fashioned kind, and wants many modern improvements to give it the Air of Lightness and Elegance. Its Situation is however extremely advantageous, the Lawn before the Front, terminated by a pretty River over which there is a light Chinese Bridge, and beyond this the rich pastures bounded by hills of agreeable declivity and those Crowned with Trees of various Sorts give it a pleasing appearance. The Gardens which consist of 4 different inclosures of high brick Walls intersected by Streams of Water which run thro them are neat and beautiful; a beautiful fountain which pours forth a vast Quantity of Water, and the Lakes which it feeds are pretty objects, and the Bath is convenient.

From the Park we have a fine view of different Plantations, and a pretty verdant Country, whose appearance Receives great addition from the Stream.

Our next Decampment was for Thoresby a most famous Seat of the Dutchess of Kingston[2] only 4 Miles distant from Sir George's. Its first

[1] Rufford Abbey, the seat of the Saviles from the seventeenth century. It was a large rambling house built at several different periods. Pevsner, *Buildings of England: Nottinghamshire* (London, 1951), pp. 152–153.

[2] Thoresby was enclosed out of Sherwood Forest in 1683 by William Pierrepont, 4th Earl of Kingston. Nothing remains of his house, destroyed by fire in 1745. The second house, built by John Carr between 1767 and 1771, was a modest red-bricked structure. A new stone mansion was erected on the site in 1868–1875. *Ibid.*, pp. 183–184.

appearance by no means raises the expectation. We rather prepare for a Disappointment as we see only the End of the Building. But after entering the Park and passing the Mausoleum we are all Surprize. A variety of Objects contend for a Preference, but as we approach the house, the Strife ceases, and our Choice is fixed. The Front is peculiarly striking and beautiful. The first Story is of a Stone of a Quality superior to the Portland. Above is Brick. The Middle of the House as far as the Hall extends on each Side of the Door is ornamented with Doric Columns the whole height of the house. The Windows are very capital and the whole Appearance is magnificent. The Offices and Stables are spacious and elegant consisting of 3 Courts or Areas, the Quadrangles of which are uniform and handsome.

When we come to the other Side of the house, a Canal which falls into a Lake by 50 Steps immediately catches all your attention, till it be called away by other objects not much less pleasing. The Hill at the Foot of which this Cascade falls gently rises for a great Space, and all the way up it is planted with Clumps of Trees at different Distances and of different Sorts and Sizes, which give them a Shade and richness which one would hardly believe them capable of. Thro these are a Number of Avenues where the Sight is always relieved by some or other object.

Between this River and the house we are presented with a confined view of a beautiful Garden, where Flowers of every Class and Odour meet our Sight, and scent the very Air. On one Side this Garden is a large pretty Building, which they use for an Assembly Room, and joining to this are the Green houses. On the Lawn runs a row of Bowers the whole length of the Building, under which you walk, and on every Side of you the branches are so thick as almost to deprive you of the Light of the Sun.

From this place we ride through a part of the Park, cross a Stone Bridge which is a good object from the house, and ride along a Canal near half a mile to the Menagerie, where is a mere City built for the accommodation of the Birds of the Air. Here are Streets of houses with Court Yards and pleasure Grounds inhabited by the more beautiful and curious of the feathered Tribe, Pheasants in abundance of almost every different Clime, and from the Linnet and the Lark to the Eagle the King of Birds, you may here gaze on.

From this place on our return towards the house, we cross the Canal by a beautiful Chinese Bridge quite a Semi-Circle which you ascend by Steps to a Mill which is built in imitation of a Castle with several Towers. Contiguous to this is the Flower Garden, where the Taste of the Dutchess has been exerted with great Success to form something as compleat as any of the kind well can be. Without the studious Art of Form and Regularity, without any regard to Uniformity this Garden is planned as if Nature in her more pleased moments had resolved to throw something together to put

Art to the Blush. The walks are Serpentine, the Beds of an hundred different Size and different Shapes, the walks sometimes Grass smooth as a Carpet, at other times more rank and sometimes a Gravel walk receives your Tread. Here a purling Rivulet, there a little smooth unruffled Lake, now a meandring Stream, then forgetting its importance to the Soil runs strait away till it recollect itself and instantly it returns to the very Source from which it first flowed.

Time did not permit us to go into the Minutia of this place, otherwise Days might have been spent here and every hour with fresh Delight. The last objects we see as if the Genius of the place had determined our impressions in its favor should be irrascible are a fine Image of an Harlequin,[3] and a sleeping Venus of excellent Statuary brought from Italy. She is reposed on a Rock, and laying in a pleasing Attitude her robes decently attiring her. In short tis the most beautiful Spot imaginable. The fragrant Bower, cool Fountain, shady Grove all strive to enchant.

The next place to which we bend our course is Clumber the magnificent Seat of the Duke of Newcastle.[4] To this we ride several Miles thro the Dutchess of Kingston's Park, which joins this place. It is not long since all this was like the rest of Sherwood Forest, a mere Chaos of Furze, inhabited only by the timorous hare and the Rabbit. Some few places furnished Food for the fleecy Tribe, but now everything is in order, everything blooms. Clumps of trees planted around us constantly meet our Sight. Rivers are made where there were no Rivers. Bridges are built where there was no need. A verdure smooth as the Surface of the Water spreads itself in hills and vallies for Miles on every Side and every thing that a Luxuriant Imagination could suggest are thrown together for the Gratification of the Eye.

We go round about to come to the house, that in the access no Part of its Beauty may be lost. Its front is of a fine white Stone inferior to none. Two Venetian Windows add much to its Beauty. It wants only some Pillars to make it compleat. The inside is very capital and magnificent.

The Hall which is a spacious and elegant Room has some fine Paintings among which are the Lion and wild Boar by Rubens, the finding of Cyrus, Joseph and Rebecca by Ditto. The dining Room has likewise some excellent Paintings, some good original Drawings and some fine Crayons of

---

[3] A Pantomime character, in tight-spangled dress, with visor and magic wand. *OED*, VI, pp. 1119–1120.

[4] The Clumber estate was part of Sherwood Forest until in 1707 licence was given to John Holles, Duke of Newcastle (of the neighbouring Welbeck Abbey) to enclose it as a park for the Queen's use. A house was built in 1770 for the 1st Duke of Newcastle (of the Pelham-Clinton family). It was considerably embellished in the nineteenth century but pulled down completely c. 1938. Pevsner, *Buildings of England: Nottinghamshire,* pp. 52–53.

the Ruins of Herculaneum.[5] The Large Library is a splendid Room but not yet quite finished. The Little Dining Room has a good Collection of Miniatures, some excellent Prints, and a large parcel of impressions of Roman Coins. In the Duke's Dressing room are two fine Landscapes by Claude, some good Portraits, fine Venetian Views and some choice Alto and Basso Releivo's. The great Stair Case is exceedingly grand, with Iron Banister richly ornament and enamelled. At the Foot are some good antique Urns and vases with inscriptions, and some Busts. In this house the Furniture is in general most superb and there are two looking Glasses which are the largest in England. Cost about 1200 Guineas each and imported from France, as there are more made in this Kingdom by much so large.

Near the house is an artificial River over which there is a grand Stone Bridge of 5 Arches but as it stands rather too near the house to give it the most pleasing Appearance the Duke is about to pull it down and build a still more elegant one at a further Distance. If we could see the Stables without first seeing the house we might easily mistake them for the Palace. They are grand spacious and beautiful, consisting of 3 Quadrangles, which you enter one after another. They contain as much Ground and have as much Building as many Villages with which we meet.

We now ride thro the remainder of the Park; and went to Worksop to dine, a Town which takes its Name from the Duke of Norfolk's Seat,[6] contiguous to which it is situate. We then went thro a capital lodge entered the Park of Worksop, the Duke of Norfolk's magnificent Seat, and here we see a Paradise which the foregoing places can scarcely vie with: Lawns, Fields and Woods, delightful Groves, pastoral hills, a thousand Deer skipping along the Vallies, a hundred Groups of Trees, disposed with a Taste and Happiness unparalleled. The Road to the house is smooth as a Bowling Green, Hills and Vallies far and near, and every variety of Scenery which fancy can dictate.

We come to the House after passing several Areas and Courts, all magnificently built of a beautiful hewn Stone. The Front surpasses any thing of the kind; the Color of the Stone forms a fine Contrast to the Verdant Trees which surround the house. Its appearance is very stately and magnificent. We ascend a broad Row of Steps into the Hall, before which

---

[5] Herculaneum, about five miles from Vesuvius, was destroyed by the eruption of Vesuvius in A.D 79.

[6] This was Worksop Manor. Its building began in the early sixteenth century under the 4th Earl of Shrewsbury. By the late seventeenth century, the manor devolved by marriage upon the Dukes of Norfolk. The 8th Duke modernised the house, but this building was consumed by fire in 1761. It was replaced by part of a Palladian composition by James Paine. Pevsner, *Buildings of England: Nottinghamshire*, pp. 214–215.

are a beautiful Row of Doric Pillars, to the top of the Attic Story. A Large Pedestal which extends the width of the Hall is richly ornamented with some fine Statuary. In the Center stands an Image which represents divine Virtue. On the two Ends Stand Peace and Plenty, a Horse Lion and Dog. The first represents Ardor, the second Strength and Power, and the latter Fidelity. The Motto *Sola Virtus invicta.*[7] Over the whole is a Balustrade covered with Urns.

After passing the Hall we go thro several Rooms which are well furnished and contain a considerable Number of good paintings to the Stair Case, which besides the wide Passage and the Curious Stone of which the Steps are composed, and besides the richly ornamented Banisters, contains the best imitation of Basso Releivo that I ever saw. They are done by *de Bruyn*[8] and with such art, that the nicest Critic would be deceived.

In this house are a tolerable Collection of Paintings, and a glorious parcel of superb Furniture. Here too is the Bed in which the Present King was born, the best Collection of Tapestry in England, some Good pieces of Titian and Rubens, and a great Number of fine Portraits.

From this Place we came to Welbeck the Seat of the Duke of Portland.[9] Here we entered between two Rows of the Offices, and realy thought we had got to the Mansion house. However our Mistake was soon after rectifyed, and going to the further end of this Street of out house we came to a capital Court, round which are the Stable, and in the middle of which is a Fountain for the watering of horses. The Duke keeps about 130 horses. His stables inside are cleaner and neater than a Scotsman's Parlour, and the outside might well pass for an American Governor's Palace.

The house is finely situated, not on the Top of the Hill to catch every Breath of Air that Blows, but on a plain surrounded by Hills, and near to a beautiful piu of Water. But whether the River be a natural or an artificial one I can't say. It is so common for the Owners of the great Seats to make Rivers in dry Places and to say 'Let there be Waters' that it is impossible to

---

[7] Virtue alone conquers.

[8] Theodore de Bruyn (1730–1804), a decorative historical painter who later painted landscape views. He was born in Amsterdam, studied at Antwerp, but was brought to England c. 1768 to do decorative work for the Duke of Norfolk at Worksop. He later exhibited landscapes at the Royal Academy. Ellis Waterhouse, *The Dictionary of British Eighteenth Century Painters in Oils and Crayons* (Woodbridge, Suffolk, 1981), p. 64.

[9] William Henry Cavendish Bentinck (1738–1809), 3rd Duke and 8th Earl of Portland from 1762. He was a politician who was twice Prime Minister (5 Apr.–Dec. 1783 and 31 Mar.–Oct. 1809). His seat was Welbeck Abbey, a large private estate of nearly 3,000 acres, which was created out of Sherwood Forest after the enclosure of Thoresby Park in 1683. Welbeck Abbey was originally a medieval mansion but extra building took place at various times between the sixteenth and nineteenth centuries. Cokayne, *Complete Peerage*, X, pp. 593–594; Pevsner, *Buildings of England: Nottinghamshire*, pp. 194–199.

say when Art or when Nature has been the Architect. However a beautiful Rivulet runs along near to the house, a Lawn only between, beyond it Rising Ground filled with the proud Elms, which rear their lofty Branches high in Air.

This is an old fashioned house and tho it have Size and Grandeur yet it wants some modern embellishments to give it a title to elegance. The inside is however exceedingly grand and spacious. The Hall is a perfect Curiosity, being an entire piece of Gothic Architecture uncommonly light and beautiful. Between the Tops of the Windows and the Ceiling which is richly stuccoed, are some Paintings of horses; among the rest one that was bred at this Park whose mane drags on the Ground. There are besides this many good Rooms and a pretty Collection of Paintings.

The Gardens are at a Distance from the house, but they are very capital.

From this we marched to Balbrough Hall, a famous old fashioned place belonging to Cornelius Heathcot, now Rodes, besides his last Name given him by Act of Parliament, as he fell heir to the Estate but not gain it, without that addition.[10] Here we were entreated most hospitably and elegantly. The Place stands near the Summit of a hill and affords you a beautiful Prospect of the Country round. The house is Stone, the Park is large, and Lands belonging to it rent for £25.00 per annum.

April 12th   6th Day

In Company with the Parson of the Parish, our Landlord and our Friend Watson of Lancaster,[11] we took a Ride to a fine Palace belonging to the Duke of Devonshire.[12] This house was built in the reign of Queen Elizabeth by the Countess of Shrewsbury[13] and for want of somebody living in it is now mouldering into its native Dust. There is a fine Collection of Tapestry and a great Quantity of rich silk flowered Velvet, now all tattered, torne, and in Ruins. Some of these Rooms are exceedingly grand,

---

[10] Cornelius Heathcote (d. 1825 aged 70) assumed the name and arms of Rodes, and took over estates at Barlborough Hall, erected in 1583–1584 by Sir Francis Rodes, a judge in the Court of Common Pleas, who was patronised by the Earl of Shrewsbury. Barlborough Hall is an Elizabethan mansion of compact, almost square plan. John Burke, *A Genealogical and Heraldic History of the Commoners of Great Britain and Ireland* ... (London, 1834–1838; reprinted Baltimore, 1977), III, pp. 563, 565.

[11] Possibly one of the partners in William & John Watson, merchants, Lancaster. Bailey's *British Directory* (1784), III, p. 653.

[12] Chatsworth, originally begun by Sir William Cavendish and his wife Bess of Hardwick. Later building was carried out mainly under William Cavendish (1640–1707), 4th Earl of Devonshire and 1st Duke from 1694, and under the 6th Duke, between 1820 and 1842. Pevsner, *Buildings of England: Derbyshire* (London, 1953), pp. 81–93.

[13] Elizabeth Talbot, Countess of Shrewsbury (1518–1608), known as 'Bess of Hardwick.' *DNB*, XIX, pp. 309–311.

and the Gallery a fine Room of 150 feet by 50 is well stored with some good Portraits. This Situation is vastly pleasant and healthful and overlooks a very beautiful Country, but it wants Water to improve it. The Park is large and pretty and contains a great Number of Deer.

Our next Visit was to Bolsover a Castle of excellent workmanship, great Conveniences, and a delightful Situation for Prospect.[14] But for want of Inhabitants, of whom it is quite bereft, it is mouldering into Ruin. At a Church in this Town are fine Monuments erected in a superb manner to the Memory of the Cavendish Family.[15] After viewing these wonderful things we returned home to Balbro a new road.

April 13th   7th Day

We left Balbro in the Rain and were fortunate enough to be accompanied by it to Sheffield, when we found ourselves thoroughly wet. No sooner do we enter the Town of Sheffield than the voice of industry is heard in the Streets and every house is a manufactury where the hammers strike Unison with our horses feet. The Mills the Furnaces and the busy Car all join in the harmony, and make it the most busy Scene imaginable, but as we intend to visit this place on our return I shall at present wave every observation, till my return.[16]

We dined with our Friend John Barlow the famous Cutler and maker of the Barlow Penknives.[17] From Sheffield we came on to Barnesly in the Neighbourhood of which is Lord Strafford's famous Seat.[18] Near the Road we pass by a great Number of Towers and a wall with Battlements, now in ruinous appearance and built by him, to serve as an object from the Seat. From Barnesly we came on to Wakefield, where stayed all Night. Here is one of the best Inns in England. The Front is very grand and the back buildings are like a little City.

April 14th   1st Day

We set off early and got to Leeds to breakfast and the 15th 2nd Day we left Leeds in Company with William Fisher and got to Undercliff to Breakfast

---

[14] A castle was erected at Bolsover by William Peveril soon after the Norman Conquest. Rebuilding took place in the early seventeenth century, but ruins were already evident from the reign of Charles II. Lewis, *Topographical Dictionary of England*, I, p. 201; Colvin, *History of the King's Works*, II, pp. 572–573.

[15] St. Mary's Church, Bolsover. The Cavendish Chapel, with monuments belonging to the Cavendish family, was added to the east end of the south aisle in 1624. Pevsner, *Buildings of England: Derbyshire*, pp. 61–62.

[16] See below, pp. 241–242.

[17] John Barlow (?1724–1799), a Sheffield cutler who invented the Barlow penknives. He married in 1752 and had six children. *DQB;* Robert Eadon Leader, *Sheffield in the Eighteenth Century* (Sheffield, 1901), p. 290.

[18] i.e. Wentworth Woodhouse.

at the House of John Hustler in the Neighbourhood of Bradford. From this place we were accompanied by Edmund Pickover[19] to Skipton all the way along Side of the great Canal which leads from Liverpool thro the Kingdom a distance of 113 Miles to Leeds.[20]

A Mile from Bradford at Bingley are three Locks where is a fall of 36 Feet. By these Locks the Vessels are brought down into the lower Canal with only a detention of 5 Minutes at each Lock. Half a Mile further on there is another Set of Locks, 5 in Number and a fall of 60 feet.[21] Along Side of the Locks runs the superfluous Water, which is a pretty object and makes a fine Cascade. Here the Vessels are detained 25 Minutes in their Passage.

We ride these 20 Miles on the Bank which is made for the horses which draw the Barges. These Barges carry from 40 to 60 Tons burthen, are conducted when the wind is not fair by a horse who goes 2 Miles an hour. This Canal goes thro a most fine Country on each side richly improved, and the lower side of us is a pretty River which runs winding along the Valley 50 feet lower than the Surface of the Canal.

We ride sometimes over the Turnpike Road, where there is a subterraneous passage frequently made for it, and sometimes under a Bridge over us on which the turnpike road runs. Sometimes we ride over aquaducts where Rivers and Rivulets murmur on. The Canal is here remarkably strait being from Bradford to Skipton a less distance than the turnpike Road; it is cut for the most part on the Declivity of a hill, which was favorable for the Design, but in some few places, where Bogs and Sands rendered it expensive and difficult. In these Cases immense Quantities of Lime have been planted at the Bottom of the Canal, which have made the Sand of a proper Consistency to hold Water, otherwise it would have absorbed the whole body of water. And besides being of a flux Nature it would soon have filled up, and counteracted the Designs of the Navigation.

Over this Canal are many bridges built at almost every quarter of a mile distance, as it would be inconvenient for the masts of the Barges to be struck every time they came to one of these Bridges. They have a Sort of

[19] Edmund Peckover (d. 1810 aged 53) was a prominent Bradford Quaker involved in the wool business and, from 1792, a banker. Hodgson, *Society of Friends in Bradford,* pp. 51–52.

[20] The Leeds–Liverpool Canal was begun in 1770 but was not completed until 1816. It cost £800,000 and was 127 miles long. Hadfield, *British Canals,* pp. 86–89.

[21] The Bradford–Bingley locks are on the Bradford Canal, which commences in the Leeds and Liverpool Canal, near Shipley. The locks are three miles in length, with a rise from the Leeds and Liverpool Canal of 86 feet by 10 locks. The Bradford Canal was finished in 1774. Joseph Priestley, *Historical Account of the Navigable Rivers, Canals, and Railways of Great Britain ...* (London, 1831), p. 84.

Swivel on which they turn round to let the Vessels pass, and this is done with great ease by having a Shaft at one End to project far out, and without the least delay.

It is at immense Cost and by encountering innumerable Difficulties that this Canal is now so nearly finished, besides the inconceivable Disadvantages which have occurred in cutting thro Mountains of Rocks and Hills of Sand in raising beds for the River to lay on where Vallies interposed in planting a new kind of Soil, where the natural would not do. Great opposition has arose from a variety of interests and inclinations clashing in the mode of carrying it on, and the places where it should come, and the Land which Owners who were averse to the Plan had refused to give up for the Purpose, and a multitude of other inconveniences with which the Proprietors have met. It is now however nearly accomplished, by the public Spirit of Men in every part of the Nation, who from truly patriotic Motives, and its great Utility have begun and prosecuted it in derision of all Opposition. But the father of this Canal, and to whom we must attribute the Execution of it is John Hurstler. The last few years of his Life have been devoted wholly to the perfection of it, and he is now likely soon to experience the Benefits of it, being all finished but about 40 Miles. The Expences will amount to about £350,000. The Irish and German Ocean will then be open to each other and advantages innumerable will flow from so laudable a plan to every part of this Empire.

Skipton is a Snug Market Town and from the Canal being brought thro the Town must considerably increase. On one Side is a large Castle and Seat belonging to Lord Thanet[22] who only resides here a little while in the Year. It is situated on a perpendicular Rock, has a happy Prospect but no Park or Garden. At the foot of it, or rather at the foot of the Rock on which it stands is a pretty murmuring brook and a little further a Cut from the Main Canal, which runs up a hundred yards to a Rock of Lime Stone from which vast Quantities are brought by which means Bradford Leeds and several other Towns are supplyed with Lime.

From this place we came to the very Romantic and sequestred Town of Settle. Till now the Country bore a very fertile and pleasing aspect, a continued Succession of Hills and Vallies, seldom a Spot, since we left Sheffield, but what bore the highest Marks of Cultivation. Seats without Number, inclosures without End, Trees sufficient to add Variety and to give Beauty to the Scenes around. But now a sudden Change insues, Mountains begin to rear their high and bulky heads, crowned with Crags and Precipices dire, Great Vales between losing the Sight with Avenues

---

[22] Sackville Tufton (1733–1786), 8th Earl of Thanet from 1753, was a Whig in politics. His seat was Skipton Castle. Cokayne, *Complete Peerage,* XII Part I, p. 697.

without End, and hills whose Declivities feed black Cattle, and Dales alive with all the bleeting kind.

Settle is placed in a Valley with all humility and diffidence. Its Spires and Turrets reach not a tenth so high as the Top of the lowest hill we can find in all the Brotherhood. The Prospect from it is however pleasing, and the inhabitants are civil, courteous, obliging besides being industrious frugal and notable.

April 16th   3rd Day

Unattended by a beautiful glittering golden eyed Morn, with a plenty of Rain we set off from Settle in Company with our Friend John Birkbeck junior[23] and thro a hilly Country, tolerably well chequered with the little humble habitations of the Cottagers. Sometimes a more stately Fabrick throws itself in view. We got to Kirby Lonsdale a little market Town where we breakfasted; but I forgot to make mention of a curious Spring with which we met in the neighbourhood of Settle, which ebbs and flows very suddenly sometimes a few inches and sometimes a foot or more in the Course of a very little time.

Thro a Country of much the same Sort of Features and Complexion we landed at Kendal a place which I have already fully described.[24] At Kendal we took a Dinner at the house of our Friend Isaac Wilson,[25] where we left horses and took a chaise to Keswick. A few miles only we passed before we came to the famous Lake of Windermere. Here Beauty Grandeur and Horror unite in forming a variety of views, pastoral elegant and grotesque. Mountains piled on Mountains sometimes by a gentle Slope approaching the Borders of the Lake, sometimes a perpendicular Rock rears itself from the water's Edge to a stupendous height, down which the rude Cascades fall dreadful and shake the watery element while its sound resounds from Shore to Shore and almost rends the vaulted Skies, whilst echoes reverberate with pleasing Awe.

---

[23] John Birkbeck, Jr. (1747–1808) was a partner with his brother, William, in a Settle firm that combined banking with the business of woollen merchants. He married in 1780 and moved to London, where he carried on an insurance business. In 1782 he became a partner in the Lynn branch of the Norwich Bank. Robert Birkbeck, *The Birkbecks of Westmoreland* (privately printed, 1900), pp. 110–111.

[24] See above, pp. 78–80.

[25] Isaac Wilson (1715–1785), a Quaker living at Kendal, married Rachel Wilson (1720–1775) in 1740. R. Seymour Benson, compiler, *Descendants of Isaac & Rachel Wilson: Photographic Pedigree* (Middlesborough, 1949), I, p. 1; John Somervell, *Isaac and Rachel Wilson, Quakers of Kendal, 1714–1785* (London, 1924).

April 16th   3rd Day
Cumberland

The Road kept us in Sight of this *great* Lake, till we reached Ambleside, a little Town on a River which is the Source of Windermere Water. We took a walk about half a Mile to a Waterfall which the Landlord gave us a most curious Account of and of which John Buncle has taken so much pains in the Description.[1] However we found neither the Romantic View of the Country, the dreadful Cataract of Water which rushed down with such Fury, neither the Stately Oaks which lifted their lofty branches high in the Air, nor the endless mountains which projected their craggy heads on every Side, striking terror into the Beholder. None of these are by any means competent to the Description. A little Rill ran trickling down a trifling precipice and emptied in a Pool, which as a Duck Puddle would have made some figure, but surely Buncle's Enthusiasm got the Better of his Reason when he called it a mighty Lake.

Our Ride afterwards became more and more romantic. We got into a Country full of Mountains, sometimes in a Dale where Avenues were open before and behind us, always terminated by monstrous hills and beyond them others still higher, with still more lofty ones behind them, losing their heads in mist and involved in the rolling Clouds. A continued roaring of Water resounded on every Side, falling with great rapidity from the Tops of the Cliffs by many precipices into the vallies below, which were finely mantled by Spring's delightful Garb. A Country like this accompanied us to Keswick, with new objects ever rising in view, always pleasing, always grand. But the prodigious height of these enormous mountains occasions almost a perpetual Rain. Not a Cloud floats in the Air but is broken by them, and it often pours down on the Hills when the Vallies are dry.

Keswick lies in the Vale of St. John, hemmed in by Mountains, through which a brook runs murmuring in many wild meanders, watering the fertile Soil, and washing inclosures of rich Cultivation, which stretch far on both

---

[1] A reference to a waterfall at Stonemore, in the fells of Westmorland, where rapid water comes headlong down in a fall of 140 feet. *The Life of John Buncle, Esq* ... (4 vols., London, 1770), II, pp. 28–29.

Sides the rising Hills. The town is in the midst of this Vale, the Mountains forming a grand and stupendous Amphitheatre around it. Enclosures of Grass and Corn Fields take up one third of the ascent. Above these the Fleecy tribe and the Cattle of a thousand Hills graze unheeded and unattended; above are barrens where Vegetation dare not make its appearance, save only in little Crevices, where Wood branches out and climbs up Shade above Shade. Their Brows are covered with a Sort of Heath and now and then a crest of Crags exalt their rugged battlements above them all and give a Silver hue to their appearance. Beneath is laid a plain of some miles in Diameter, diversied with Plots of Corn, delightfully mingled with the meadows and here and there a little Copse of Wood. Near it are two lakes. The small one has nothing particularly striking when compared to the large one, though the Sides and declivities above it, which shut it in from all the World, and the Mountains piled on Mountains make an awful Circle, and were it not for the other Lake would merit a particular Description.

The town itself is mean and dirty without Trade or manufactures to support it, though it serve for [an] object at a Distance and have a good effect. The Market place is a very droll and original piece of Architecture, honorable only from its Age, and intituled to respect, only because a little rough Usage would demolish it.

But it is not necessary that the Town should charm us, without one Elegance of Art, without Semblance of a Refinement of Taste. The Rough uncouth hand of Nature has left objects sufficiently sublime, sufficiently awful to claim our Admiration, to excite all our Astonishment. You have a vast Amphitheatre of great Circumference, in the midst of which is the great Lake adorned with a Variety of woody Islands, some in Cultivation, others in ab origine rudeness. One Side presents you with a view of rich and beautiful Landscapes: cultivated Fields rising to the Eye in fine disordered inequalities with Groves of Oak and Elm and Ash happily dispersed and climbing the contiguous hills, Shade above Shade in all the Wildness and rural softness of an Elysium. One Side gives you a view of Rocks and Cliffs of stupendous weight hanging almost over the Lake in glorious Grandeur and irregularity, an immense height, whose steep and shaggy Side never was stamped with human vestige. On heights like these Hutchinson says the Eagles build their nests secure from the vengeance of the Injured and far removed from the Danger of their Enemies.[2] A variety

---

[2] William Hutchinson wrote that, on the cliffs above Keswick Lake, 'eagles build their nests, far removed from gunshot, and undisturbed by men' (*An Excursion to the Lakes in Westmoreland and Cumberland; with a Tour through part of the Northern Counties in the Years 1773 and 1774* [London, 1776], p. 149).

of Water Falls are seen pouring down on every Side from the Summits and tumbling in vast Sheets down the declivities of the Hills forming a strong and lively Contrast as it falls from Rock to Rock, with the russet background, and giving it a rude and terrible appearance.

Whilst objects like these strike you, they only give a little Relief to the Eye and divert them from Scenes abundantly more grand and far more terrible, for on all Sides round this immense Amphitheatre, the lofty mountains rise round and pierce the Clouds in all the Whimsical and fantastical directions which Nature could contrive. These Mountains, unlike to others, unlike to the American Alleghanas,[3] do not continue in one long range, but stand independent of each other, and are all pointed with Spires or Turrets, or perhaps a more regular Cone. The lake being defended by these vast hills and sheltered from the rugged Gales is seldom seen with a Dimple. Its smooth surface doth not often curl to the Wind, so that the inverted Landscape is seen in the watery Mirror to great Satisfaction, and almost perfect as the reality. The Lake often receives bold projections of the Rocks which form capes and promontories of romantic Aspect. At other times retiring as if ashamed of its own Countenance forms a fine Bay. In other places they open abruptly their Charms or Cliffts through which you see the hand of cultivation making repose on the Vallies and over their head Mountains, rising over mountains, among which new prospects rise, fill the Eye with wonder and lose the Senses in a Maze of Perplexity.

The natural variety of colouring which the various objects produce is no less wonderful than pleasing, the ruling tints of the Valley being those of azure and green yet ever various arising from the Wood the Grass and the Corn. These are finely contrasted by the grey Rocks and Cliffs, and the whole is heightened by Streams of Light, the purple hues, the misty azure of the mountains, and the Beds of Snow which are scattered here and there. Sometimes you see a clear and serene Sky, but for the most part you see Clouds involving their Summits, resting on their Sides or descending to the Base, and rolling among the vallies in a vast Furnace. In clear weather the Landscape is all beauty. Islands, Woods, Fields, Rocks and Mountains all combine to delight the Eye.

The Perfection of this place consists in beauty immensity and horror. The Powers of Claude, Salvator and Poussin are requisite to paint them as they are. The first should throw his delicate Sunshine over the cultivated Vales, the scattered Cots, the Groves and the Islands and the Simplicity of the Shepherds should receive the soft touches of his Pencil. The Second

---

[3] The Alleghenies form part of the Appalachian mountains, which stretch for 1,300 miles from Cape Gaspé, on the Gulf of St. Lawrence, to Alabama.

should dash out the horrors of the rugged Cliffs, the Steeps, the hanging Woods and foaming Waterfalls, while the grand Pencil of Poussin should crown the whole with the majesty of the impending Mountain.[4] In short, the Variety and Beauty with which this Spot teems are too many to be described as they are too beautiful to be painted.

At Keswick the Northern Yearly Meeting[5] was held and attended by a vast Concourse of people of all Persuasions and Societys. It lasts 3 days. I met with a Number of my Acquaintance from all parts, spent my Time agreeably and on

19th April   6th Day

With R*obert* Ormston[6] of New Castle added to our Party we left Keswick and came through a Continuation of that country to Cockermouth, the Mountains not so high and more appearance of population. As we approach Cockermouth, we come into a pretty Country, hills and Vallies but no inaccessible heights except those which are at some Distance. This Town is regular, watered by two pretty Rivers. On one Side of it is an Elevation on which stands the Ruins of an ancient Castle belonging to Lord Egremont.[7] The Prospect from the Towers of this Castle is particularly fine. The more contiguous Parts are rich inclosures of Grass and Corn Fields intersected by several Streams and finely interspersed with Villages on every hand, the View one way extending to the Sea, and the other terminated by distant Mountains whose heads are mingled with the Clouds and lost in Mist and Darkness.

We here dined with our Friend Richard Pike[8] and in the Afternoon, taking High Field in our Way, we called to see our worthy Friend Hannah Harris. With her we drank Tea and in the Evening arrived safe at Whitehaven, a place in point of Regularity inferior to none in the

---

[4] These two sentences are copied verbatim from John Brown's *Description of the Lake and Vale of Keswick* (Newcastle, 1767): see Moir, *Discovery of Britain,* p. 149.

[5] The Yearly Meeting comprised all the Quakers living in a defined area of country, and was the highest source of legislative authority in the Society of Friends for the membership within its boundary. It met annually, received reports from the Quarterly Meetings, and dealt with the constructive problems of the entire body of membership. Rufus M. Jones, *The Later Periods of Quakerism* (2 vols., London, 1921), I, p. 111.

[6] Probably a partner in Ormston & Lamb of Newcastle: see p. 303.

[7] Cockermouth Castle, built in the mid-thirteenth century, belonged at this time to George O'Brien Wyndham (1751–1837), 3rd Earl of Egremont. Cokayne, *Complete Peerage,* V, p. 37; Pevsner, *Buildings of England: Cumberland and Westmorland* (London, 1967), pp. 107–108.

[8] Richard Pike lived at Cockermouth until he and his family moved to Lurgan, Ireland, in 1780. Margaret F. Young, 'The Shackleton Letters, 1763–83,' *Journal of the County Kildare Archaeological Society,* IX (1918), p. 167.

Kingdom, the Streets running in right Lines and dissected by others forming right Angles. The Streets are well paved, the houses neat and well built of Stone, but for the most part covered with plaister. It is a place of great Trade, particularly in the Coal Way, having 200 Ships employed in exporting that Article.[9] There are Seven good Piers which project far out and conveniently accommodate all the Shipping. These Piers are all built of a pretty hewn Stone procured in the Neighbourhood. The Harbour is situated in the bottom of a fine bay, but the Vessels are all obliged to lay on the Ground which is a hard Sand, for two thirds of the tide.

At the East Side of the Town is an elegant new Building, the seat of Sir James Lowther, but not being quite finished he has not yet got his rich Furniture nor his paintings removed here. Sir James is said to be the richest Commoner in Great Britain, having an Estate of £50,000 per Annum. On the other Side of the Town are his Collieries, which are wrought to the greatest Advantage of any in England, the Pitts being so near to Navigation, and the veins of Coal so near to the Surface in some of them, that they are brought up at an easy Expence and carted by a Descent on Waggons without horses.[10] They ascend back, and it is therefore necessary to have a horse for this purpose. He keeps 500 horses employed. The Coals are brought to a large Warehouse, on a perpendicular bank, where the bottom of the Waggon is in one instant taken out and the Coal is started into a trough thro which it runs directly into the hold of a Ship, which lies at a key underneath. By these means a Vessel of 200 Tons is loaded in 3 or 4 hours.

April 21st   1st Day

Our being so contiguous to Ireland, an opportunity offering directly for Dublin and the Company of our Friends *Catherine* Phillips and *Lydia* Hawkesworth[11] were sufficient inducements to take a trip over, not intending to stay in that Island above a Fortnight. This Day immediately after Dinner we went on board, being attended to the Key by a huge multitude. The Wind was directly against us, so that we made little Progress that Night. At 12 O Clock the next Day we found ourselves about 20 Miles from Whitehaven, passengers almost all but myself very sick. The

---

[9] Whitehaven's coal exports to Ireland grew from 49,968 tons in 1739–1740 to an annual average of 196,900 tons, probably about one-third of the Irish trade, in the years 1803–1814. Flinn, *British Coal Industry: The Industrial Revolution*, pp. 222–223.

[10] The Lowthers dominated the economic life of West Cumberland in the eighteenth century, especially the coal industry. The two nearest Lowther collieries to Whitehaven were Howgill and Whingill. J. V. Beckett, *Coal and Tobacco: The Lowthers and the Economic Development of West Cumberland, 1660–1760* (Cambridge, 1981), p. 42.

[11] Lydia Hawksworth (1733/4–1788qv). *DQB*.

wind still continued a head and at 12 O Clock the next Day we had progressed on about 20 Miles further. A perfect Calm and a very fine Day; the Passengers in good health and Spirits and able to eat an hearty Dinner of Mutton which we broiled on the Coals and of which we made a most tasty Dish. Our Vessel was a Sort of Snow or Hermaphrodite Ship, about 180 Tons burthen laden with Coals called the Lowther and Senhouse and commanded by Captain Hine. Her name is taken from the two Candidates who contested the last Election for the County.[12]

April 24th   4th Day

At 12 O Clock yesterday it fell quite calm and continued so till towards Evening. The Sea was like a Pond unruffled by the least breath, and not the least Swell to disturb the Repose of our bark. About 6 in the Evening came on a Gentle breeze sufficient to urge us on though at a very slow pace. This Breeze increased by slow progression till it forwarded us about 3 Miles an hour. We came all along Side of the Isle of Man, near enough at times to see the houses and inclosures of Grass and Corn Fields. The Parts next to the Sea appear to be barren. Further on are the improvements and beyond these Mountains unadorned by any improvements. On the island are three Ports, the principal of which is Douglass, near which we passed but could not see it, being situated in a Valley and eclipsed by a high Hill.

At Day Light this morning we saw the high Lands in the Neighbourhood of Newry. At 12 O Clock the little Islands North of Dublin Harbour appeared in Sight. We made a comfortable Dinner of Mutton Stakes which we broiled on the Coals not having a Gridiron nor any other implement of Cookery. We by Dusk got close in with the Harbour, but the wind coming a head and the Tide against us we could not get in that Night and indeed found a Difficulty on the 25th 5th Day to get over the Bar, the Water there being very shoal and the Channel narrow except at high Tide.[13]

We remained a good while in a State of Suspense, not a little disagreeable as the Cottages and Farms were thickly scattered around us and before us at no great Distance the famous City of Dublin rearing its gilded Spires and lofty Towers. At length however we passed the Bar and came up within about 3 Miles of the City where we run ashore on a Mudbank, the Tide not permitting us to make further Progress. We had now a

---

[12] Humphrey Senhouse of Netherhall, Cumberland (?1731–1814) had stood for the county in 1768 jointly with Sir James Lowther, but was defeated. He later became M.P. for Cockermouth, 1786–1790, and Cumberland, 1790–1796. Namier and Brooke, *History of Parliament: House of Commons 1754–1790*, III, p. 421.

[13] In general, streams set roughly north and south through Dublin Bay. Southern gales cause high tides in the Liffey and northern gales low tides. Reed's *Nautical Almanac 1989* (New Malden, 1989), Section 11, pp. 233–234. I have omitted a draft of Dublin Bay.

Task to procure a Landing, the Water in the Harbour being rough, and timorous Women to encounter the Danger of the Waters. However mustering all that Resolution which most People have a Share when there is a necessity, we embarked with all our Baggage on board the Ships Boat and combated the Waves and Tide for one Mile to a place called the Pidgeon house,[14] where we were carried on Shore on the backs of our Seamen, there being no Pier or deep Water near the Shore convenient for Landing.

Here neither the magnificence of the Structure, the elegance of the Rooms, the Costliness of the Furniture, the Assiduity of the Landlord, or the Alacrity of the attendants could be compared to some of the capital English Inns, particularly those of the Bath and London Road. The house was dirty; the inhabitants as much as the Furniture little better; and in short it exhibited a Striking Contrast of the Neighbouring Kingdom. With great entreaty and with many supplications we at length got a Breakfast, sent up to Dublin for a Coach and entered in our tattered Chariot the great City. The Road to it is by a Causeway for two Miles, and we then entered the most beggarly part of the Town and went through some of the most dirty and insignificant Streets to Joseph Pike's[15] in Meath Street. The Entrance by no means left many favorable impressions of its Grandeur, but we were afterwards agreeable disappointed in finding a great Number of capital Streets, which for Beauty elegance and regularity would vie with most of the London Streets.

Dublin stands on the River Liffi, a little pitiful Stream which intersects it in the Middle, and whether we consider its Breadth Depth or Extent, we are amazed to think of the Buisness which it carries on. Tho the vessels which come up to the town be small, and draw not much water, yet to look from the Bridge down among them, the Forrest appears as thick and the Path thro it as narrow as we behold them in the Thames. But if we compare this River to some of the American Creeks, it becomes quite insignificant and mean. There are several Bridges over it; the lower one is a good Epitome of London Bridge.

This City is about $\frac{1}{4}$ as large as London and in many Streets it would require the Assistance of very little imagination to conceive yourself walking in that Metropolis. The Mall is a very fine long Street, the houses

---

[14] The Pigeon House was a place on the breakwater where passengers arriving by packet at Dublin usually disembarked, owing to the difficulty attending the passage up and down the river. Constantia Maxwell, *Dublin under the Georges, 1714–1830* (rev. edn., London, 1956), p. 294.

[15] Joseph Pike (d. 1792) was an Irish Quaker who married Elizabeth Pim in 1748. Mary Leadbeater, *Biographical Notices of Members of the Society of Friends who were resident in Ireland* (London, 1823), pp. 308, 314.

high, regular, uniform and elegant; the Pavements good clean and as broad as we could wish. Merrion Square is very capital; the houses round it are grand and the Green is beautiful; but the finest Part of this Town and in which it may defy any City in Great Britain is St. Stephen's Green, a large and beautiful Square 1 Mile in Circumference planted round with stately Trees and a pleasant gravel walk all round it. Between the Grass and the Walk runs a pretty Stream which surrounds it, walled inside and out by a pretty hewn Stone. The houses on each Side this Quadrangle are particularly superb and in a fine State and the wide Pavements for Passengers of a large square Stone add much to its Appearance and its Convenience.[16] There is a number of very magnificent public Buildings in this place; some grand Churches; but St. Patrick's[17] is the only one which has a Spire of considerable height. St. Nicholas is a neat Front with large Doric Columns.[18]

The Parliament house is a spacious and grand Structure of fine Portland Stone.[19] The Rooms for the members are nicely decorated and *flog the British Senate house all hollow*. The Royal Exchange[20] is not entirely compleat. This will be the most capital of all. The two Fronts are amazingly magnificent, with Corinthian Pillars of 40 feet. The Situation is particularly favorable as it terminates a grand Avenue which leads from the Bridge, and the large Dome is inferior only to St. Pauls. The Colledge[21] is a very noble Pile of Building consisting of three Quadrangles very compleat and built of fine Stone, besides a number of Offices and a splendid Library, with a laboratory, a fine Collection of Anatomical Preparations of Wax, which are said to be the first in Europe. In the Museum is the Skeleton of a Man who measures 7 feet and a half. Beyond these Buildings are fine academic Groves, with Walks and other objects to heighten the Scene. At the Bottom runs a little Rivulet walled in with Stone.

There are great Numbers of Hospitals in this place (besides houses of

---

[16] St Stephen's Green, a large square, was laid out in lots for building in 1663. The largest and most magnificent houses of eighteenth-century Dublin surrounded this Green. Various celebrities and members of the nobility lived there. Maxwell, *Dublin under the Georges,* pp. 57, 78; *Hibernian Magazine,* July 1777, p. 491.

[17] St. Patrick's Cathedral, built about 1190. Maxwell, *Dublin under the Georges,* p. 96.

[18] This church occupies the entire northern end of St. Patrick's Cathedral. It was dedicated to St Myra. Lewis, *Topographical Dictionary of Ireland,* I, pp. 549, 556.

[19] This building, mainly in the Ionic order, was begun in 1729 during the administration of John, Lord Carteret. Walter Harris, *The History and Antiquities of the City of Dublin, from the Earliest Accounts . . .* (Dublin, 1766), pp. 410–412.

[20] This solid structure stands on Cork Hill near the castle. It was built between 1769 and 1779 in the Corinthian style. Maxwell, *Dublin under the Georges,* p. 63.

[21] Trinity College, part of the University of Dublin, was founded in 1591. *Ibid.,* p. 63.

Industry), the most principal of which are the Royal Hospital[22] and the Foundling Hospital.[23] But the lying in Hospital is preferable.[24] The Walks Groves and Shrubberies behind are charming. The Stately Elms with here and there a Seat and now and then an Image make it a beautiful Scene. On one Side of a Bowling Green is a fine Rotunda used for Concerts of Music for the Benefit of the lying-in hospital. The Ornaments within are fine, the carved Work and stucco elegant, a grand dome, and the Diameter of the whole Building is 300 feet.[25]

The Hall for the Sale of Linnen Yarn is a Spacious Building, with separate apartments for all those who have any to dispose of. But the Linnen Cloth Hall is much larger and of more general Use: a Building three Stories high and all divided into small Rooms where the Goods are exposed to Sale.[26] But of all the Buildings in this Place the Barracks[27] is the largest, capable of holding a great Number of Men with Stables and every other accommodation. This is the largest and most extensive Range of houses for the Purpose of any in Great Britain or Ireland. The appearance of it is beautiful.

From Dublin to Limerick a Communication is now opening by a Canal.[28] It is carried already about 12 Miles from Dublin and is now going on with Spirit. It is the widest, the deepest, and the prettiest canal I have

[22] The Royal Hospital of Kilmainham for old and infirm soldiers, built between 1680 and 1687. *Ibid.*, p. 57.

[23] The Dublin Workhouse, set up under an act of 1703, was divided into two parts in 1772: a House of Industry and a Foundling Hospital. The objectives of the latter were to preserve the lives of deserted or exposed infants and to educate them so that they could become servants or apprentices in trades and good Protestants. *Ibid.*, pp. 156–157, 159.

[24] The Lying-In Hospital, in Great Britain Street, was originally a small private infirmary opened in 1745. A new building was constructed on the site in 1750. Lewis, *Topographical Dictionary of Ireland*, I, p. 562.

[25] The Rotunda Gardens and Assembly Rooms (an imitation of Vauxhall and Ranelagh combined) were opened at the same time as the Lying-In Hospital. Concerts, masquerades, card parties and balls were held in the gardens. Maxwell, *Dublin under the Georges*, pp. 63, 114–115, 168.

[26] The Linen and Yarn Hall, erected in 1728, was modelled on Blackwell Hall, the great market of the drapers in London. Some 492 of its 557 apartments were used for the storage of linen; the remainder were used for yarn. The Dublin Linen Hall slowly decayed and was already deserted when the Linen Board was abolished in 1828. *Ibid.*, p. 257; G. N. Wright, *An Historical Guide to Ancient and Modern Dublin* (London, 1821), p. 329; E. R. R. Green, *Irish Linen Halls* (Belfast, 1951), pp. 3–4.

[27] The garrison of Dublin was quartered in various barracks but the largest and oldest was the Royal Barracks, situated on an eminence overlooking the Liffey between the city and the principal gate of Phoenix Park. Lewis, *Topographical Dictionary of Ireland*, I, p. 545.

[28] The Grand Canal, begun in 1772. By 1800 it had not quite reached the Shannon. R. B. McDowell, *Ireland in the Age of Imperialism and Revolution, 1760–1801* (Oxford, 1979), p. 19.

seen. A fine Gravel Walk on both sides planted with Trees and sufficiently wide for two Carriages to go abreast. Now and then is a Bridge over it, of pretty architecture.

The Streets in this City are for the most part indifferently paved. But some late Regulations are adopted and all the old Pavements are to be immediately taken up and new pavements laid like those of London. The People of that Place are the most hospitable and sociable and rare Drinkers of Claret. They have Hackney Coaches and almost all the other Conveniences of London: the same Luxuries, the same Diversions, the same places of public Resort. But it must be owned every thing of this kind are but humble imitations of London Refinements.

April 27th   7th Day

This Morning at 4 O Clock we marched away to our Coach, having (besides our Friend William Pyke)[29] an honest Irishman and two original Italian Musicians, who were engaged by a Candidate for representing the Town of Newry in Parliament, to come from Dublin and attend the Entertainments which are to be prepared for the Freeholders. These Musicians are to Entertain them with a Species of Music of novel Construction, curious in its appearance and as much so in its Effects. To such low Practices are the Sons of Britannia and Hibernia descended. Would not American Virtue revolt at the Idea! Would she not blush at such low devices! We were now and then serenaded with their Voices but in a Language unintelligible to our Ears; and at dinner we were regaled with an operation on their Musical implements. Such was the Medley of our Coach Company, and if we had no other Charms to make them desirable, we had the Charms of Novelty.

We breakfasted at an Inn on the Road called the Man of War, about 12 Irish or 15 Scots Miles from Dublin.[30] Our next Stage was at Drogheda 14 miles further on, where we changed our Steeds. Drogheda is in a Situation uncommonly pleasant on a Declivity whose foot is washed by the Crystal Stream of Boyne over which there is a neat Bridge. This for Size is the fifth or Sixth City in Ireland; in point of situation and as a Manufacturing Town will yield to none. As we passed through it was high Market Time, and a most plentiful Quantity of eatables of all kinds it exhibited. The Town

---

[29] An Irish Quaker who lived at Lurgan. William and Thomas Evans, eds., *The Friends' Library: Comprising Journals, Doctrinal Treatises, and other Writings of Members of the Religious Society of Friends* (Philadelphia, 1837), I, p. 435, VI, p. 317.

[30] The legal mile in England is 1,760 yards. The Irish mile of 2,240 yards is still in rustic use. The obsolete Scottish mile was longer than the English and probably varied according to time and place; one of the values given for it is 1,976 yards. *OED*, VI, p. 436.

Hall[31] is a neat Stone Building but there is no other Building that can be called elegant. The Walls round the Town are nearly perfect; in some places they begin to moulder and in many places are mantled with Ivy. We enter the Town by a Gate which appears to have the Vestiges of Antiquity, with a pretty large Tower. We leave the Town by another Gate exactly like it.

A Mile or two North is an obelisk raised to the Memory of the Heroes who fell in the famous Battle of Boyne.[32] Our next Stage was at Dundalk a very considerable Market Town of great Trade, and well adorned with Houses of neat appearance. Here we dined and came to Newry in the Evening, having this Day travelled 68 Miles, the first 50 of which was thro a fine fertile Country, without one Spot of uncultivated Land. A thick settled and well improved Country inclosed much as England is with hedge and Ditch. Its features are good, its Complexion pleasing, tinged with Springs most pleasing Mantle, the Creation just emerging from its torpid and lifeless state, and smiling in all its variegated verdure. The meads wear an aspect more beauteous than those in England, Vegetation being more forward, and the Corn Fields are more advanced in their Growth.

We passed thro the Counties of Dublin, Meath, Louth, Armagh and Down. The three first are in the Province of Leinster, the two last in Ulster. Newry is a beautiful Town and a place of great Trade and very populous. A Canal is cut from it to Lock [Neagh] a fine Lake about 50 Miles distant.[33] This gives it a fine inland Navigation and the Sea is not far off. Some of the small Vessels come up to the Town but the large ones lay about 5 Miles distance at the head of Carlingford Bay. Besides the Canal there are two small Branches run into the Town, one of which turns some Mills. The Streets here are not so well paved as could be wished; otherwise it would be a remarkably clean town being on a gentle Descent. The houses are good, all built of Stone, and many of them plaistered as are almost all in Dublin, in Drogheda, Dundalk and in most of the Irish Villages. These houses being of a whitish hue form an agreeable contrast with the herbage and in the country always look chearful and pleasing.

---

[31] The building where the Drogheda Corporation conducted its affairs was not referred to as the Town Hall in the late eighteenth century. Fisher probably saw either the Mayoralty House, built by the corporation in 1765, or the new Tholsel, completed in 1770. The former was where the Mayor of Drogheda resided and held official functions; the latter was used as a court house. James Garry, 'The Tholsel, Drogheda,' *Journal of the County Louth Archaeological and Historical Society,* XVII (1971), pp. 164–165, plus helpful guidance from Mr Hugh Comerford of the Drogheda Branch Library.

[32] William III defeated a largely Roman Catholic army here in 1690. This marked the end of James II's attempt to regain his throne.

[33] The Newry Canal, built between 1731 and 1742, was designed to carry coal from the Lough Neagh region to Newry for shipment to Dublin. L. M. Cullen, *An Economic History of Ireland since 1660* (London, 1972), pp. 88–89.

The last 18 Miles of this Days journey were through a different Sort of Country. We now and then have the View of a pleasing Landscape, but never for any Continuance. The Hills are barren and craggy, the Vallies boggish yield only Turf for the Hearths of the inhabitants who reside in this part of the Country. This Land is however valuable as no Coals are ever brought into these parts. All sorts of Provisions are cheap here yet we are constantly meeting in the Road with the most miserable objects of Distress; and we never leave an Inn but the Doors are surrounded with humble Supplicants of every distorted Feature and dreadful Malady. An ignominy on this Country that some pains be not taken to put a Stop to so shameful a Nuisance, and alleviate the Distresses of their Fellow Creatures, multitudes of whom must perish for want of Necessaries which with management and Oeconomy might be furnished at a small expence.

Journal I
1–9 May 1776

Ireland
May 1st   4th Day

Their Hut was humble, with but one Room. The Floor was the naked Earth. The Ceiling of Straw thatch'd. The Sides were a composition of Earth, which adhered to a few pieces of Timber which composed its Frame. The house was full of Children, and Father Mother and all were comfortably seated round the hearth, where a little turf Fire was lighted. The women were spinning, talking and singing, although the Fire scarce afforded any light.

The Neighbours seeing us stop at this house were soon collected. The Room was well filled, all could not find Seats. Some took the Floor and others stood, as the greatest Civility they could pay us was a Fiddle. The Fiddle was brought out and the ragged Clown and bare footed Lass tripped the Floor according with the Music. An intermission sometimes took place, then were all busy in inquiring about America, eager to go there, and wishing an End to the War.

The People seem happy contented and are remarkably chearful, poor things! They had nothing to offer us to eat or drink. They had not even a Dram of Whiskey, an Article used here in lieu of Rum. It is distilled from Malt, and is an exceedingly wholesome and strong Spirit. They had not even a Candle to compliment us with, but there was a Sort of heartiness in their Manner which added to the Novelty of our visit made our Stay quite pleasing.

We bid them Adieu with mutual wishes for each other's Welfare, and by the help of a charming Evening where bright Cynthia shed her Silver beams, we came to Antrim about midnight where we lodged. Here the Candidates for Parliament were indulging their nocturnal Revels.[1] The whole Town was in an Uproar.

---

[1] Antrim was a 'potwollaping' borough. It returned two members to the Irish Parliament between 1665 and 1800, when it was disfranchised under the Act of Union. The electors were Protestants only. The lord of its soil was the Earl of Massereene. At the general election of May 1776 Skeffington Thompson and Alexander Stewart lost to William and Chichester Skeffington, two of Lord Massereene's three brothers. A. P. W. Malcolmson, 'Election Politics in the Borough of Antrim, 1750–1800,' *Irish Historical Studies*, XVII (1970–1971), pp. 32–57.

May 2nd   5th Day

By Daylight we mounted and set off for Lisburne. A fine wind offering itself made us eager for setting off to Scotland. But alas! poor Tobias, the Steed which my Friend Handcock[2] rode, again gave out. So we left him to come on as fast as he could get his Beast. By and by my Friend Oxley's[3] Patrick likewise resigned his Strength, whilst my little Nag of about 11 hands high performed admirably.

I rode on before to procure a Chaise to take us to Belfast. As no Chaise could be got, so we again mounted and came to Lambeg a little Village charmingly situated, and famous for the best blankets, the best Paper, and the best Linnen of any manufacturd in this Kingdom.[4] Here I met with my Friend and fellow Citizen *Abraham* Usher.[5]

From thence to Belfast, a large populous and beautiful Town, situated at the head of Carrickfergus Bay. The Streets are good, the houses well built, and a place of great Trade. The infirmary here is a large neat Building[6] and the Barracks spacious.[7] Here we dined, and took a Post Chaise for Donnaghadee. At Belfast I met with a Man and his Wife who had just returned from Philadelphia in a Vessel to Derry. They gave me the information of our House being shut and advertised as Enemies to their Country.[8]

In the Chaise we came along over Belfast Bridge which has 22 Arches and the longest in Ireland, in Sight of the Harbour in sight of Carrickfergus thro Bangor to Donnaghadee, and by this time the wind had got so high that we could not venture on the Sea, so we are made Prisoners for the Night.

The Country from Lisburne hither is as fine as any part of the Island and delightfully scattered with Trees, houses, Water, and several very

---

[2] Possibly Jacob Hancock of Lisburn, county Antrim. *DQB* under Thomas Hancock M.D. (1783–1849).

[3] i.e. Joseph Oxley: see above, p. 35.

[4] Lambeg is about 1½ miles from Lisburn, which was the cradle of the linen industry in Ireland in the late eighteenth century. E. R. R. Green, *The Lagan Valley, 1800–1850* (London, 1949), p. 28.

[5] Probably Abraham Usher, a Philadelphia merchant who was in his late thirties in 1774. Richard Alan Ryerson, *The Revolution is Now Begun: The Radical Committees of Philadelphia, 1765–1776* (Philadelphia, 1978), p. 283.

[6] The Belfast Infirmary was part of the Poor House established by the Belfast Charitable Society. Construction began in 1771 and the building was opened in 1774. Clifton House (as it is now known) is the oldest complete surviving building in Belfast. R. W. M. Strain, *Belfast and its Charitable Society: A Story of Urban Social Development* (London, 1961), ch. 6; Paul Larmour, *Belfast: An Illustrated Architectural Guide* (Belfast, 1987), p. 1. This reference was provided by the Irish and Local Studies Department of the Belfast Public Libraries.

[7] These infantry barracks, built in 1737, were situated in Barrack Street. *The History of the Town of Belfast . . .* (Belfast, 1823), p. 99.

[8] For the significance of this to the Fisher family see above, p. 6.

principal Seats. We are now at the Eastermost point of Ireland, whence Scotland may been seen, and anxious to leave it.

Ireland is in Length 300 and in Breadth 150 Miles, its Proportion to England and Wales being 18 to 30. It is computed to take up 11,067,712 English Acres, which is to an Irish Acre as 16 to 21.[9] There are four Provinces, which are Ulster, Connaght, Leinster and Munster. These are divided into Counties making in the whole 32. The Healthfulness of the Air is not inferior to that of England, and if we may judge from the appearance of the inhabitants, we should suppose it more healthy. The People are more bulky and tall and a remarkable Phenomenon attending this Air is that there are no venomous Creatures on the Island. The Soil is abundantly fruitful and fit to be employed either under pasturage, Meadow or Tillage. It therefore accounts for the multitude of Cattle which it breeds not only for their own Consumption but exportation. An historian who spent some Years in it calls it a Land flowing with Milk and Honey, and again says from 8th Chapter of Deuteronomy that it [is] 'a Land of Brooks of Water of Fountains and Depths that spring out of Vallies and Hills; a Land of Wheat and Barley, wherein thou shall eat Bread without Scarcity and shalt not lack any thing.'[10]

No Country in the World abounds more in fine Bays and Harbours than this Island, and yet no Country receives less Benefits from Trade than this, owing perhaps to its Restrictions. It abounds in Lakes, and adorned with several fine Rivers joined together by Canals. The Discouragements laid on Ireland by the Acts of Navigation, and other Laws made in England, are so many, that it cannot be expected to flourish so much as its Situation, extended Coasts, its Rivers, Bays and Harbours should seem to promise.[11] Its exports are Linnen Cloth, Yarn, Lawns and Cambricks, Beef, Pork, Butter, Cheese, Tallow, Lead and Copper Ore, Herring and Salmon. With regard to the Antiquity of this Kingdom, Cambden in his Britannia says 'they fetch their Beginning from the most profound and remote Records of Antiquity, so that in Comparison of them the Antientness of all other Nations is but Novelty as it were of Yesterday.'[12] Tacitus says Ireland was

[9] In 1691, Sir William Petty noted that 121 Irish acres make 196 English statute acres. *OED*, I, p. 118.

[10] Deuteronomy ch. VIII, verses 7–9.

[11] The Navigation Acts of 1671–1685 forbade the importation of many products into Ireland except indirectly from England. Among these commodities were sugar and tobacco.

[12] Camden's *Britannia* was originally written in Latin. Fisher may have provided his own translation here, or he might be quoting from memory. Richard Gough translated this passage: 'For they begin their histories from the remotest period of antiquity, so that compared with them all other nations are of modern date, and but in a kind of infancy.' William Camden, *Britannia: Or a Chorographical Description of the Flourishing Kingdoms of England, Scotland, and Ireland . . .* , ed. Richard Gough (3 vols., London, 1789), III, pp. 464–465.

never conquered by the Romans, tho many from Spain Gaul and Britain retired there to withdraw themselves from the Roman Subjection.[13]

The Irish have made no other considerable Conquests than of Scotland, for they themselves were originally Scots.[14] Their Country was called Scotia Major. They called Scotland Scotia Minor.[15] The greater Part of the People here remain Papists, and though such Pains have been taken to extirpate the Religion by every oppressive Act, they have hitherto proved ineffectual, a striking Proof of the impolicy of Persecution.[16] Had the Catholics been left to the Enjoyment of their Religion, and more free Communication kept up between them and the Protestants probably that rigidity would have abated; though it must be owned the Barbarity of that Sect was such in former ages as intituled them to little Quarter.

There are now 2 Arch Bishops and 20 Bishops.[17]

Ireland is said by best computation to contain 2,500,000 people. City of Dublin 20,000. Cork 8,100. Waterford 2,628.

May 3rd   6th Day

Cease rude Boreas blustering Railer! Thy Wind prevents our bidding Hibernia's Shore Adieu, and we can illy spare the time; England's Charms await our Arrival, the Converse of social beings invites us away. Let thy Rage cease, or we cannot venture upon the Surface of the great deep, for a Sea high as the Mountainous Billows of the Biscay Bay is raised by thy Blast. How shall I tell thee to repose! What offering make for thy

---

[13] Tacitus describes Ireland in chapter 24 of his *Agricola* but implies that it was not captured by Agricola during his Roman campaigns of exploration and conquest in Britain between 78 and 84 A.D. A. J. Church and W. J. Brodribb, *The Agricola and Germany of Tacitus* (London, 1877), pp. xiv–xv, 23–24.

[14] The 'Scots' were Irish immigrants who settled in Dalriada, the modern Argyll, under Fergus, son of Erc, c. 500; they united with the Picts in the kingdom of Alba. Donaldson and Morpeth, *Dictionary of Scottish History*, p. 194.

[15] From the eleventh century, Caledonia (i.e. Scotland) began to be called Scotia minor and Ireland retained the name of Scotia, with the addition of major or vetus until the fifteenth century. William Camden, *Britannia: Or a Chorographical Description of the Flourishing Kingdoms of England, Scotland, and Ireland ...* (2nd edn., enlarged by Richard Gough, 4 vols., London, 1806), IV, pp. 224–225.

[16] The Penal Code existed for most of the eighteenth century in Ireland. It established social, political and, to a considerable extent, economic monopoly in the hands of a narrow group of the population who were usually descendants of English settlers and invariably members of the Anglican Church of Ireland. Edith Mary Johnston, *Ireland in the Eighteenth Century* (Dublin, 1974), pp. 17–18.

[17] I have cut a sixteen-line Latin description of Ireland plus a sixteen-line English translation.

appeasement. But entreaties are vain and Prayers of none effect. However having a Number of Correspondents I sit down and hold epistolary Confab with them, but for this my Patience would have been worn out, or received a Shock with which it could not easily dispense. Here then we are destined to remain all Day and all Night.

May 4th   7th Day

Borne by Zephyrus[18] o'er the Irish Sea to Caledonian Shores we seek our Way, whither we were wafted on the good Sloop Charlotte in three hours. We had a rare Company of about 20 Hibernians who gave themselves up to Merriment and singing, save those whose Stomachs became qualmish and whose moans were lent to keep time with the joyous Songsters.

We landed at Port Patrick a place where a Number of boats are kept for carrying Passengers across the Ferry, this being a great Thoroughfare over to Donnaghadee. The Last Land we see in Ireland is a little artificial Mount, raised on the Brow of a Hill in the time of the Danes.[19] This was a fortification and of this Sort there are a great Number all in Sight of each other from North to South and from the East of the Island to the West. These little Fortifications being raised in the most conspicuous places and inclosed by an Entrenchment, if the Enemy made any advances the Signal was immediately given by hoisting a Beacon, then the next gave the same Signal to the next, and by these means the whole Country was very soon alarmed and had an opportunity of preparing for their Defence, or for sending Succour to their Bretheren.

At Port Patrick we took a Chaise and without any Stoppages except now and then to change Chaises and procure a little cold Collation we came to Carlisle. Our progress was too rapid to be particular respecting the Country we pass. Suffice it to say that we came through Stranrawar, and Glenluice[20] and Newton[21] and Gatehouse[22] and Carling work[23] to Dumfries; that the Country thus far is dreary and barren; that it is the worst part of poor Scotland; that those Villages and Towns are but indifferent tho the accommodation at the head Inns be good; that nevertheless this Country is now likely to be brought into good Cultivation, some experiments having been tried with Lime in many places where the

[18] In Greek mythology, a personification of the west wind.

[19] This was probably erected some time between 940 and 1111, for the Danes ravaged and plundered Downpatrick several times in that period. *A Guide to Belfast and the Adjacent Counties* (Belfast, 1874), p. 166.

[20] Glenluce.

[21] Newton Stewart.

[22] Gatehouse of Fleet.

[23] Carlingwark.

Soil has become fruitful and Luxuriant, when before nothing but Crags and Stones appeared; that the people are getting into the planting of Trees; and that there is a prospect of this e'er long being fertile and populous. That after leaving Dumfries which is a large neat and populous Town, we come into a beautiful and rich Country; that there are here many Rivers which empty themselves into the Solway Firth; that we pass thro Anan and Longtown and several smart Villages; that we pass thro Gretna Green, a famous place for runaway Marriages, where the Woods, Walks and Fields aid Cupid and add Votaries to Hymen; that we at length arrive safe at Carlisle to an early Dinner, and having taken a late Breakfast the Day before in Ireland and travelled the Distance of 150 Miles, in the Space of 28 hours.

At Carlisle we went to view the Castle, the Church, and the blind Man which last is the greatest Curiosity in the North, but having given his Biography in a former Volume tis now needless.[24] I had a good deal of Conversation with him and found he knew the formation of the world its motion Revolution and indeed the whole Newtonian System.

We drank Tea at our Friend Dockroys[25] and spent the Evening with Thomas Irwin.[26] But before we leave Ireland as if the Genius of the Land had determined to impress on our minds those traits which have characterised her Sons; and as if their Titular Saint had abetted her Design, the instant of our departure an old Man came along crying his halfpenny Pamphlet. The dismal moan of his elegiac Voice, and the tattered Garbs which he bore, rather out of Charity to his Poverty, than a Curiosity to see his Books, induced us to make the half penny purchase and it did not a little divert us to find the following Title to the Work:

The Dying Words

Of the late Reverend Mr John Willison
to his Wife and Children
found among his Papers
after his Death.
To which are added
His dying Ejaculations
Written by himself
some days before he dyed.

---

[24] See above, pp. 77–78.

[25] See below, p. 300.

[26] Between 1702 and 1749 three different Thomas Irwins were born to parents belonging to Carlisle Monthly Meeting. This was probably the Thomas Irwin born in 1748. *TRE.*

May 6th   2nd Day

What a little Spot is England. With a little lean Pony, worne almost out with Grief we ride from the Irish to the German Ocean in a short day. A Kingdom like a dot on the Globe, and hardly magnified by the Reality. And shall this diminutive Spot give Law to the Continent of America, one of whose Lakes would immerse it in its Bowells? Well might the Indignation of America be roused. Well might her Pride startle at the thought. Scarce 60 Miles across. How is it lost in a view with some of our Provinces. With more propriety we might compare it to one of our Counties. Yet this little Kingdom has shewn us her power and Strength. Empires more formidable than ours has she bid defiance to; and over Kingdoms more populous has she rose victorious. Long has she enured herself to the horrors of War! She has taught her Children to forget what Fear is. With the wisdom of Ages she has profited herself and by their experience hath she rose to Eminence. Scarce a Foot of Ground but has been the Theatre of some Campaign. Scarce a Lump of Earth but has been deluged with blood! Her Surface has been covered by the Ashes of her dead. How many thousands of our Forefathers have been slain, how has Britain been strewed with their mangled Limbs! Shocking Reflections!

Ambition, 'tis thou who has made this havock! May future Ages banish thee for the deed; may thy Name be obliterated, and thy effects be no more known by the human Race. So shall Peace like a Cherub rule thy Land, and her fair Sister Plenty by her Side pour forth of her Blessings throughout the whole Earth. Who can pass this Road without Reflections of this Sort. This Wall now mouldering into its native Dust was once the Barrier of contending Powers when internal Discord reared her savage head. Unnatural! Inhuman Barbarity! Art thou not content with ravaging distant Worlds! Not satiated by making foreign Climes the object of our Rage, but thou must teach Children of one Kingdom to lift up the Spear against each other. Forshame!

From Carlisle to New Castle we ride all the way along the Picts Wall.[27] In some places its traces are difficult to be found. In others they cannot be seen at all. But in some they are perfect. We see the motes not yet filled up, and now and then the wall of hewn square Stones quite perfect. For the first thirty five miles the Country is but thinly settled, the Land uncultivated and the Soil but indifferent, for the greatest Part covered with Furze. This Part of the Country being the Boundary of the Scots and English, and the Settlers continually subject to depredations and alarms, it is no wonder so large a tract should remain without improvement.

---

[27] i.e. Hadrian's Wall (see above, p. 77, n. 107).

However the Cause of Strife being removed, some beginning is now making to alter its Countenance and we may expect e'er long to see it like other Parts of England teeming with Beauties.

After this we come into a Country where Nature seems to have poured forth her best Gifts. The Tyne's water the Fertile Soil, the Hills bow down to receive the grateful Streams. Vegetation is all alive. Every object is animate. No longer the Desert Waste throws itself in your view and shews its poverty and nakedness to the pitying Traveller. Reviving Herbage bursts from its Confinements; no longer will it be pent up and congealed by Winter's rugged Winds; she spreads the Fields in variegated Green. Plenty pours from her horn on the verdant Carpet all her Treasures, and the profuse hand of Liberality suffers not the declining Hills to appear without the thick sprouting Foliage of a chearful Spring.

At New Castle we arrived about 6 O Clock in the Evening and moved from our Inn to the house of my worthy hospitable Friend Ormston. Here we spent the Remainder of this and the next Day wholly in going round among my old Acquaintance. Notwithstanding I have now seen almost all the principal Cities and Towns in this Kingdom, New Castle in point of Size and number of inhabitants, London excepted, is nearly equal to any of them. But having when here before given a sufficient Description of this place, any thing now is needless.

May 8th   4th Day

The Weather certainly has a great effect on a Mans Spirits, or why should I have felt such Dejection and Reluctance on mounting my horse at New Castle. No! it was not the Weather. A little Rain and a little Wind surely would not have cast me down. I am so inured to ride in wet and dry, both by day and by night, and feel so little inconvenience from it, that were it not for darkening the Prospect, and depriving me of a View of a Country which I can never behold without Delight, I should hardly form a wish, for an azure Sky, tho it might rain ever so abundantly. But it was leaving a social Family whose kindness had endeared them to me, leaving them without an hope of ever seeing them more. The Reflection made me then, as it hath often besides, extremely melancholly. When a sufficient acquaintance has taken place to feel a Kindred of Spirits, to be torn away for ever is dreadful. However we bid them Adieu, crossed over the Bridge of the Tyne and came on by Lumley Castle, a fine Seat belonging to Lord Lumley,[28] through *Chester in the Street* to Durham, without any Deviation from our Road, except a short distance to see a poor unfortunate Wretch

---

[28] George Augusta Lumley-Saunderson (1753–1807), styled Viscount Lumley until 1782, of Lumley Castle, Co. Durham. Cokayne, *Complete Peerage*, II, p. 513.

hanging in Chains. His Flesh seemed perfect and he could not have been long executed. One would suppose from the Number of these distressing objects which throw themselves in our way in almost every Common in England, that it would have had some effect in ridding the Kingdom of those frequent Robberies which are committed in every part of the Country. However this and every other terrible Example have failed. They haunt the Moors as much as ever and there is scarce a Night but we hear of these highway Robberies and Government seems to be defied to suppress them, notwithstanding the utmost vigilance and assiduity.

At Durham we dined and took my old Friend William Paxton along with us to Sedgefield, adjoining to which is the famous Seat of Squire Burdon going by the Name of Hardwick.[29] We approach the Lodge by a fine Grove of proud and lofty Elms, which extend from it to the Road about a quarter of a Mile; we then enter through a magnificent Gate, and instantly are charmed with one of the most pleasing parts of the Creation, a fine Canal of Water directly before us, a beautiful Bridge terminating it, which is so thickly cloathed with Foliage as to hide all but the Arch. On one Side of us a smooth Lawn descending gently to a small but beautiful Lake, whose Surface unruffled by the Breeze, discovers the most perfect Mirror in which we view the Trees which surround it inverted, and almost as lively as the original.

In the midst of this Lake whose Sides are indented by Capes and Bays stands old bearded Neptune with his gilded Trident. This Image is reflected in the Water, and being white as Snow forms a fine Contrast to the Herbage, and to the water which being surrounded by such a variety of Verdure is green as the Lawn which leads to it. At the further End of the Lake stands the Bath a fine object indeed, being of white hewn Stone and on each Side of it a Yew Hedge.

On the other Side of us is one of the finest Groves imaginable, with Trees of every Size and of every Shade, from the mock-orange to the stately spreading beach. And under these a Profusion of the flowering tribe grows thick, gives the Carpet the richest variegation, and scents every breath of Air we inhale. Hence we walk to the Bath, which is not only an elegant Building outside and a pretty distant object but it is within very convenient; a Stair Case leads to a Room above, from whence we have a less contracted view. On our passage here we pass a number of fine Busts of the Poets Philosophers and Historians of the British Augustan Age.[30]

---

[29] The owner of Hardwick Hall from 1748 was John Burdon. The house dates back to at least the seventeenth century. Pevsner, *Buildings of England: County Durham* (2nd edn., London, 1983), pp. 300–302.

[30] The Augustan period in England covered the years from c. 1680–c. 1750.

The Yew which adjoins this Fabrick is to eclipse a Lake which lies below, of which we have no View till we enter close upon it. This Lake is supplied by Water from the one above it, by a fine Cascade which tumbles on 6 or 8 different Rocks before it reach the Body of Water. At the Bottom of this Lake which is thickly inclosed with Circles of Trees stands a pretty Summer house delightfully sequestered from every other part of the Grounds, and where Contemplative mind might meet with a Spot more contemplative than itself.

We next go thro Groves of Sycamores and Elms by a Serpentine Walk, where the Violet the Ranunculus the Hyacinth and a hundred other fragrant odours meet our Senses, where the purling Rivulets which feed the happy and fertile Soil, in many a Rill, runs murmuring where the Rook rocks her young over our heads. And her Caws resound with pleasing thrill through the nodding Branches where the feathered Choristers with every varied tune swell their throats and make the Elysium more Elysian.

Thro these Scenes we come to the Bona Retirons, a Place from which we have an elevated Prospect of all the Grounds. From thence thro a Continuation of Rural Beauties to an imitation of an old Castle in Ruins. This is an agreeable addition to the number of fine Objects, and a particular Ornament to the View from the Banqueting house, a most splendid Building surrounded by 30 Pillars of 20 feet height and built on an Artificial Mount. The principal Room is indeed magnificent. The Windows, the chimney piece, the Ionic Columns at each End of the Room, the Paintings on the Ceiling, the Busts of the Roman and Grecian Orators and Poets placed in Alcoves round the Room, and the rich Furniture make it one of the first apartments we meet with. From this place is the finest Prospect of any of these plantations. We not only have a perfect Sight of all the objects which are planted around, the Lakes, Canals, Lawns, Woods, Gardens, but the Eye has dominion over a great Extent of Country on every Side, where the Mountains at a vast distance give the finished Shade to the Landscape. The Banqueting house is the last place we visit and thro a delightful Grove we come to the same Gate we came in at.

This Place has been compared to Studley Park,[31] but certainly with very

---

[31] Studley Royal was the house of John Aislabie, a Yorkshireman who rose to various lucrative positions at court. He was Chancellor of the Exchequer at the time of the South Sea Bubble, but was expelled from parliament and retired to his estates, where he laid out beautiful grounds between 1720 and 1740. Studley Royal borders on the grounds of Fountains Abbey. Pevsner, *Buildings of England: Yorkshire: The West Riding* (London, 1959), pp. 495–496. See also Patrick Eyres et al., *Mr. Aislabie's Gardens: Three North Yorkshire Gardens Landscaped during the Eighteenth Century by John Aislabie (1670–1742) and his Son, William (1700–1781)* (Leeds, 1981); Patrick Eyres, *Studley Royal and Hackfall: The Classical and Sublime Landscapes of North Yorkshire* (Leeds, 1985); and W. T. C. Walker, 'Studley Royal: the Eighteenth-Century Water Gardens and Deer Park', *York Georgian Society Annual Report* (York, 1974).

little Justice; the Extent of Ground in the latter is so much larger, its natural advantages so much superior, its mountains so much more grand, and the Streams of Water so far more abundant, as give Studley every Advantage, and then Art has in proportion equally kept pace with Nature. As the Grounds of Studley are 5 times more extensive, proportionate to this have been the improvements. Her are 20 fine Cascades (Hardwick has but one). Here are Obelisks, Rotundos, Pyramids, Pillars, Grottoes, Summer houses, and 20 other objects which are to be seen from one another thro the Avenues of Trees, and all which Hardwick wants; but the finest Object of all, and which entitles Studley to a Preference to any thing I have yet seen, is that grand and amazing Ruin of Fountain's Abbey, inferior to nothing of the Kind in Great Britain if it can be equalled at all.

This Evening we reached Darlington having once or twice missed our Road; we made our home for the Night at my old Quarters James Backhouse's; and now having passed through the County of Durham twice, I pronounce it a fine County.

May 9th   5th Day

And so is Yorkshire. I never entered it without pleasure. It affords every Sort of Variety, and has a vast deal of American Grandeur, lofty Hills and towering Mountains, and has as great a Share of Cultivation, and contains as many objects worthy the Notice of a Traveller as any County in England.

We got to Richmond to Breakfast. A Situation full of Grandeur, and from the Number of Churches, Towers, and other objects its Entrance is very striking. The Town is large, placed on two Declivities which meet at the Bottom. The Market hall is commodious,[32] and the houses form part of Circus. And if some houses which stand in the middle were removed it would put us in mind of the Circus at Bath.

On the Borders of the Town stand the Ruins of Richmond Castle a most awful and magnificent Pile now mouldering.[33] But its Situation is as awful as the Building, being placed on the Brow of a fine Hill, one Side of which is nearly perpendicular, and composed of the roughest Crags. Under it

[32] The Town Hall at Richmond, on the south side of the Market Place, a long two-storeyed building erected in 1756. Pevsner, *Buildings of England: The North Riding* (London, 1966), pp. 295–296.

[33] William the Conqueror granted Richmond to Alan the Red, a relative of the Duke of Brittany, and Alan is said to have begun the castle in 1071. Most of it was built in the twelfth, thirteenth and fourteenth centuries. *Ibid.*, pp. 292–294; Colvin, *History of the King's Works*, II, p. 806.

runs a pretty River[34] whose Bottom is smooth as the work of Art, and has the appearance of a regular Pavement. A Bridge is on one Side and on the other a pretty cataract. In the neighbourhood are several neat and elegant Buildings of which this Castle commands a good Prospect.

[34] River Swale.

Yorkshire
May 9th   5th Day (continued)

At Askrig a little Market Town we dined; and from thence thro Bainbridge to Wenseldale, than which a more romantic Spot cannot be well conceived. At the further End of this Dale lives A*lexander* Forthergill[1] with whom we drank tea, and where I met an old Acquaintance, A: Freeman of London. After Tea we took a walk to a very beautiful Cataract about a Mile from the house. The particular Situation of the Rocks from which this Water falls and the little Rivulet by which it empties itself into the Lake below give it a rude but beautiful appearance. Unfortunately the late Rains were scanty, or I could have been gratified with a pretty Specimen of American Magnificence. The Stream was almost exhausted; only a very small Column of Water ran trickling down. The Prospect from the Brow of the Hill on which is this Cascade is exceedingly grand. The Hills form a spacious oblong Amphitheatre. The Valley below is partly taken up with the Lake, which is a beautiful piece of Water, and partly by some rich Meadows intersected by several Serpentine Streams and divided by many inclosures into a variety of pastures.

The Declivities of the Hills are in good Cultivation and chequered with multitudes of Cottages; and black Cattle innumerable graze here. The Summits are sometimes craggy, sometimes verdant, and every where covered with Sheep. Besides this pretty Cataract, there are several others of less Fame, all of which tumble into Rivers which give Succour to the Lake. My old Fellow Passenger E*lizabeth* Robinson[2] lives on the same side of the Dale. With her we spent the Evening and lodged there that Night.

---

[1] Alexander Fothergill (1709–1788), surveyor, attorney, farmer and diarist, was a member of the fourth generation of a Quaker family who lived at Carr End in Raydale, Wensleydale. They lived a mile from Countersett where there was a Quaker meeting house. Marie Hartley and Joan Ingilby, eds., *Alexander Fothergill and the Richmond to Lancaster Turnpike Road* (North Yorkshire County Council, 1985), p. 5.

[2] Elizabeth Hoyle (1729–1804) of Burnley, Lancs., married Joshua Robinson (n.d.) of Wensleydale in 1754. In 1778 she married George Gibson. *DQB*.

May 10th   6th Day

This Country so much abounds with Scenes of Beauty and Romanticity
that a multitude of them must pass unnoticed. Harbour Fall however is too
striking an object to let pass without just setting it down. We went one Mile
out of the way to see it, our Curiosity being much raised by the Account
Buncle gives of it,[3] and by the less exaggerated Description of the
Neighbours. However, we were fully repaid for our Trouble. The Rocks
are awful and stupendous, the height about 50 feet and the body of Water
which pours perpendicularly down into the River below considerably.

Thro Sedbergh over Hills and Vallies without a Tree to hide its
Nakedness we came to Kendal.

May 20th   2nd Day

I am now 10 Days behind hand in my Journal. Too much time has elapsed
to be particular in my transactions all that time. So shall content myself
with a Short Epitome of my Adventures. At Kendal I spent near three
Days altogether in gadding about to see my Friends. I then left it and set
off for Lancaster taking in my way Jane Crossfield,[4] where I breakfasted.
At Lancaster we dined, drank tea with some of her celebrated Damsels,
spent the Evening and lodged there one Night.

The next morning with our Friend William Dilworths[5] two Daughters
we set off for Settle and dined at Ingleton where they met their Sister. At
Settle we arrived early in the Afternoon, soon after which we took a walk
to a Cascade about 3 Miles distant, where I met with John Birkbeck,
Deborah Birkbeck,[6] *Benjamin* Jowit[7] and *Hannah Harris*. From this we
went to a very beautiful Fall where a considerable Body of Water pours
down by 3 different Cataracts into a delightful River below. From hence
we returned to Settle and made preparation for a very capital expedition to
view some of the wonders of the North.

The next Day, which was ushered in with a charming Sky, we all

---

[3] See above, p. 159.

[4] Jane Crosfield (1713–1784) was the wife of George Crosfield of Preston Richard,
Westmorland. She visited America in 1760 and was a member of the Kendal monthly
meeting. Henry J. Cadbury, *John Woolman in England: A Documentary Supplement*
(Supplement no. 32 to *JFHS*, London, 1971), pp. 50, 83, 138; Gummere, *Journal and Essays
of John Woolman*, p. 543.

[5] William Dilworth of Lancaster (1716–1787) served as Clerk to the London Yearly
Meeting in 1753 and 1773. Dilworth Abbatt, *Quaker Annals of Preston and the Fylde,
1653–1900* (London, 1931), p. 45.

[6] Deborah Birkbeck, a widow, lived at Settle. She was a sister of Rachel Wilson (see
above, p. 158 n. 25). FLL, Thomas Pole Journal (1775–1776), p. 219.

[7] Probably Benjamin Jowett (b. 1739), the youngest child of Richard and Elizabeth Jowett
of Holbeck, near Leeds. *TRE.*

mounted our Rosinante's, having a Party of 3 Dulcinea's and 4 Knights in quest of adventures.[8] After mounting the Summits of those mighty hills which seem to contend for height with the Skies, by Roads almost trackless, and over the most craggy and steep hills, we ride several miles. On these rude and grotesque heights we are not a little surprised to find a Spacious and beautiful Lake several Miles in Circumference, abounding with Fish and protected by Mountains higher than itself and altogether supplied with a variety of Springs which run in many little Rivulets thro the fertile Fields into it. Here are Cattle without Number and though these mountains be of such amazing Size, to the very Crest they are luxuriant and fruitful, most charming verdure over the whole Surface, chequered only by the points of white Cliffs of Limestone which grows here in great Profusion.

We soon arrive at Malham Cove, a most curious perpendicular Rock like a Wall built to keep the Earth on the Mountains from rolling into the Valley below. This Cove forms a Sort of Horse shoe and is very stupendous. To go to the bottom of this curious Cave the Women dismounted and we undertook to lead their horses, but they soon made their escape from us, and we had a most hazardous Chase over the Mountains for some Miles before we could overtake them. However we at length accomplished the arduous Task. We then went to a little Village and called at a little Inn where we regaled ourselves; and from thence went to Gorsdale where one of the most Romantic and pleasing Scenes in the location presents itself. A Rock burst asunder by the hand of Nature gives vent to a small but delightful River which rolls down over the rude Rocks till it meet a massive Mountain of prodigious height. But deriding all Opposition it has perforated a Passage through a vast Chasm in the Cliffs, from whence it tumbles sometimes perpendicularly and at others rolls over the crags, for some hundreds of Feet, till at length it gain a soft Bed in a beautiful River under mountainous Rocks which project their rude and awful heads directly over us. We seated ourselves down to a comfortable Repast. We made ourselves Seats of heaps of Stones and finding a convenient Rock we spread a Table Cloth and with some cold Tongue and Mutton we made a most hearty dinner.

After viewing these Romantic horrors and spending a sufficient Time in contemplating them, we called at a little Village and had a comfortable Dish of Tea and returned home in the Evening greatly delighted with our Expedition. The next Morning we bid the good Family Adieu, rode on to

---

[8] In Cervantes' *Don Quixote*, Rosinante is the name of the ex-carthorse that Don Quixote chooses for his high and noble adventure, and Dulcinea del Toboso (in fact, an ugly peasant girl called Aldonza Lorenzo) is the beloved he idealised.

Skipton to dine, and from thence came on to Bradford alongside of the Canal,[9] where for want of more interesting Converse we counted the Bridges, Gates &c &c. In that distance we met with 50 Gates. We past by 31 Bridges which by a Swivel turn round to let the Boats pass by. We went under 4 Stone Bridges over which the Turnpike Roads go and came over 22 Aquaeducts. At Bradford we drank Tea with Dr. Walker and called at Undercliff to see our Friend John Hursler. At Leeds we arrived before Dark. Here we spent 2 or 3 Days and from hence went to the Famous Seat of Edmund Lascells Esquire, a most beautiful and magnificent Building of modern Structure.[10] The Stone is a neat lively yellow with a grand Entrance thro Corinthian Pillars which support a rich Pediment. The outside of this house is light airy and elegant, the Plan beyond the Criticism of the nicest Conoiseur, and allowed to be as well executed as any in the Kingdom. The inside is equally elegant and equally pleasing: the Furniture rich gaudy and light, the Gilding and Carved Work and the inlaid Decorations inimitable, all in the Adelphi Stile.[11] The Stucco and the Paintings on the Ceilings are done by the best Artists and are superb beyond Description. In short, the Eye meets with all it can wish, the Judgement is pleased and however grand the Expectations may have been which we have formed of the Buildings and its furniture, we are sure of having our Ideas more than realised.

The next Day we went to Undercliff in a Chaise with Jane Fisher[12] and went in the Morning to Bradford Meeting; in the afternoon took a walk with John Hursler along the Canal near which he has a Quarry of peculiar Stone, being remarkably hard, yet running in the most direct Veins that sometimes pieces of 30 feet in Length and half as much Breadth are brought out whole, and the Surface without hewing is sufficiently smooth for any Purpose. Here the flat Stones are procured of which they make Slates for covering all the houses in the neighbourhood. On the Side of the Canal are 12 Spacious Lime Kilns, to which the Marble is brought and burnt. In the same range are some Dwelling houses arched over for the workmen. We came to Leeds again in the Evening and supped with the Batchelors of that famous Place.

[9] Skipton was skirted on the south-west by the Leeds and Liverpool canal. Lewis, *Topographical Dictionary of England*, IV, p. 94.

[10] i.e. Harewood House.

[11] The only sustained town planning completed to the designs of Robert and James Adam in their lifetime was the Adelphi, 4–6 Royal Terrace, Westminster, London. It became the focus for a new style of decoration and architecture. The Adelphi was built between 1768 and 1772 and demolished in 1936. Geoffrey Beard, *The Work of Robert Adam* (Edinburgh, 1978), pp. 15, 63 and plates 112–116; John Summerson, *Georgian London* (new edn., London, 1988), pp. 116–117.

[12] See above, p. 41.

This Morning we embark for London thro Wakefield, where my poor Quadruped discovered some Signs of indisposition. However, sometimes walking and sometimes leading, we got on to Sheffield where we met with our hospitable Friend John Barlow at whose house we were politely entertained, and where we lodged that Evening.

This Day we passed by the famous Seat of Lord Strafford.[13] The house is spacious and elegant, the Situation magnificent and beautiful, the woods Groves and other Objects very delightful. We came into Sheffield about the going down of the Sun. The Entrance to it is not exceeded by any thing. On the East we see all the Riches that Cultivation can give: Declivities gently rising from a fertile Valley a great height and intersected by numberless inclosures of the most exact regularity, before us the Town with a Cloud of Smoak over its head, and to the West an elysian Valley dissected by a fine River and bounded by distant Hills and mountains beyond those, with still more distant Brows of mountains further on.

May 21st 3rd Day

Scarce had we left Sheffield when my poor horse, unable to bear my weight, stopt short. I dismounted and led him, but now the poor Fellow was hardly able to support his own Frame. With difficulty however and frequently pausing to give him a little Breath, I got him on to a little Village called Grindle Ford Bridge, where I was obliged to leave him, and as I could get no other horse, I undertook to walk to the next Stage some Miles distant. However I had not progressed on far when a Man who was riding one and leading another horse overtook us. I prevailed on him to let me ride his led horse and put my own Saddle on and came with him to Middleton, where I procured a nice Nag.

We had now but a few Miles to go before we arrived at Chatsworth, the Seat of the Duke of Devonshire. This Place we approach without any Preparation for such a Change. The Country before us is a continued Wilderness without the trait of Vegetation but in the Valley's. This Spot however is too delightful to need such a Country as the generality of Derbyshire to set it off to advantage. Had Fancy traversed over the wide world in quest of some Spot superior to all the rest, she would have seated herself here at last. Whatever is beautiful, whatever is elegant, whatever is magnificent Chatsworth without the Aid of Art could boast. Nature has been profusely lavish in her Charms. She has with all her Bounty imparted every Sort of Beauty. Forgetting that it was her Duty to be impartial, she has extravagantly bestowed every Gift upon this favored Seat. But

---

[13] The seat of William Wentworth (1722–1791), 4th Earl of Strafford from 1739, was Wentworth Woodhouse. Cokayne, *Complete Peerage*, XII Part 1, pp. 331–332.

generous as She hath been, here Munificence hath met with every grateful Return of Taste, in which Nature in all her Luxuriance seems to be rivald. At least it is difficult to determine on which Side the Superiority lies. They both vie with matchless zeal for the Preference and the more you contemplate the more you are bewildered in the decision.

After passing thro a little straggling wood composed of Oaks and Elms bent with reverend Age into fantastic Directions, under which the Grass spreads a smooth and lovely Carpet, we come into a Scene where nothing eclipses the Variety of Objects which crowd upon the Senses, all striving to overpower them with their Charms. On the left a high Mountain lifts itself into the Sky. Its Crest is cloathed with every Species of the vegetable Tribe; its declivities covered with the more stately Princes of the Forest, hanging head over head with every variegated tint and hue.

As we come nearer the plain these romantic wonders cease, Chaos is dissolved, all is Mechanism, Order and Regularity. The Trees no longer growing up in their native Wildness and in their common disorder are all in uniform Rows: now they advance, then they retire, here they open a fine avenue, there they are closed by some enchanting object. Here too are fragrant Bowers, spouting Fountains without Number. Before us falls a Cascade down a hundred different Steps, and when it arrives at the Grass it loses itself, you know not where. The further part of this Waterwork is at a beautiful Stone Building with a Spiral Cone. At the Top of this the water gushes out and pours over the Cupula into a delightful Bason below. On the Top of this Building lie 3 Images to represent the Naiads pouring out Water from their Vases. Two Lions at the Corners spout it from their Mouths. In the Front of the house are two Whales from whose Nostrils vast Quantities are poured forth. On each Side the Steps sit two Dogs who foaming with rage send forth their Torrents at each other. These furnish the Cascade the Bason in the midst of which gushes out a little Fountain, where the Water is thrown up in a Column a great height.

We are next conducted to a place where Avenues are opened through several passages to a variety of objects. While we are here beholding the Beauties of distant Prospect, in an instant an Olive Tree from every Branch spouts out a vast number of Columns of Water, which they shoot a great Distance, when the Falling in some places forms Rainbows, and in the others every Drop of Water represents a Diamond of exquisite Lustre. Near this spout Fountains from the Earth of less Consequence. We are next led to a fine Lake whose Bottom and Sides are composed of hewn Stone. In this is a pretty Fountain where the Water is thrown up in a perpendicular Direction 60 feet. From hence we go to a little Pool of Water, near the South Front of the house, where 6 Sea horses are swimming from all of whom the Water is thrown up a great height and in the midst of them a Mermaid blows up a Column of Water from a horn which she holds to her Mouth.

While all these enchanting Objects surround us, at a little distance we behold a fine Lawn which leads down to as Beautiful a River as any in this World over which is a grand Bridge with elegant Palisadoes, and between the Arches are little Nitches in which stand 4 Images of excellent Sculpture. Beyond the Bridge the opposite Hill ascends gently to an astonishing height which is all covered with the darkest Verdure and interspersed with an hundred Clumps of Trees. The whole Scene is one continued Extent of Beauty mingled with Magnificence. The house is built of a hewn Stone nearly allied to the Bath Stone. One Front is adorned with Ionic Pilasters, another with Columns; the others are Corinthian. There is a fine Balustrade, and ornamented with Urns of the richest Workmanship.

We pass through a very capital Court in which is a pretty Fountain and are thence conducted thro a Hall in which are many good Paintings to the Chapel. The Ceiling is adorned with Scripture, historical paintings. The Sides are curiously stuccoed with Plaister of Paris, the Floor and the Altar all Marble, and the latter more beautiful than we any where did meet with. On each side of it are two Angels and near these two other Images to represent Peace and Plenty all of fine Marble. The Tapestry in several of these rooms cannot be equalld, but the Paintings in general are not extraordinary except the Portraits. The Furniture in antient Stile is grand, the Rooms are spacious and the house is convenient. There is a great Quantity of the most curious Carved Work over the Chimney Pieces which in general are fine.

Filled with astonishment at these wonders we depart for Scenes more romantic and rude and arrive at Matlock about 4 O Clock: as beautiful a Spot tho of a different Sort as the one we had left. Its Situation Prospect and its Baths occasion a great Resort of People the whole Year.[14] The Bath houses, the Inn, the Church are on the Brow of a hill on one Side which falls perpendicularly down a rocky Cliff of Chalk, at the foot of which runs a beautiful Stream, the murmuring of which is heard at a distance and has a happy effect on the awful Scene. On the opposite Side rises a white Cliff like the Wall of some antient Ruin. A great height here and there is a Crevice out of which jut out Trees of almost every kind, which seem not to have the least Earth to nourish them. The Top is crested by an irregular row of Trees which form a fine Contrast with the White Rocks. We took a

---

[14] The waters at Matlock were first applied to medicinal use about the end of the seventeenth century. Three springs and three baths were built, with hotels and lodging houses for visitors. The season at Matlock lasted from April to November. Lewis, *Topographical Dictionary of England*, III, p. 271.

walk a small Distance on that Side on which the houses are; called to see several manufacturers of Spars.

The Country here abounds with Petrifactions, Crystalisations and Spars, which are manufactured by the inhabitants into Urns, Vases, Obelisks &c and sold to the People who resort here.[15] We descend the Hill by Steps which are cut out into the Rock to the River below, over which we crossed by a Dam. At this Place are several Lead Mines which run a great Distance into the Earth.[16] The Engine to bring the Water up is turned by the Stream. We now take a walk alongside of the River thro a thick and beautiful Wood, where a fine Serpentine Path has been cut, the Trees over our heads locking their Branches together and almost hiding us from the face of Day, here and there a little avenue opening to give us a Prospect of some pleasing object, sometimes a beautiful Cataract tumbling down the opposite Rocks by many falls, at others in one great Stream pouring over a Projecting Cliff, murmuring with its Rage and shaking the adjacent Hills with its gushing Fury. Here are Seats for the contemplative Traveller to employ his Reflections.

After walking near a mile, we come to a path which leads up to the Summit in meandring Courses. By this we ascend. Half way up is a beautiful Arbour whose back and Sides and Top are covered with Ivy. Above this are several places to sit down and at the Top is a windsor Chair with a beautiful Lawn before us on one Side and on the other a terrible Gulph, beyond which is a most wild and romantic Scene. All this Neighbourhood with Beauty though County in general is poor and barren. However there are some rich Lead Mines. Here we stayed all Night; supped in the long Room with a large Company.

May 22nd   4th Day

This Morning we went into the hot Bath.[17] The Conveniences for bathing here are capital, the water being by Fahrenheits scale at 70 and never varying above 1 or 2 degrees. The Phenomenon of these hot Baths has occasioned much Speculation, the Philosophers having differed much in their accounts

[15] Urns and vases formed of spar, marble and alabaster were commonly obtained in Derbyshire. *Ibid.*

[16] Derbyshire lead mines were located mainly in an area bounded by the River Derwent to the east, Castleton to the north, Buxton to the west, and Wirksworth to the south. This field of lead mining was probably the most productive in eighteenth-century England. Roger Burt, 'Lead Production in England and Wales, 1700–1770,' *Economic History Review*, 2nd Ser., XXII (1969), p. 251.

[17] The medicinal springs at Matlock have a mean, slightly tepid, temperature of 68 degrees fahrenheit; they issue from an elevation of 100 feet above the river; at higher or lower points the springs are cold and possess no medicinal properties. Lewis, *Topographical Dictionary of England*, III, p. 271; White's *History, Gazetteer and Directory of the County of Derby* (Sheffield, 1857), p. 432.

of the Cause. Some say the Warmth arises from some subterraneous Fire; others, that the Acidity of the Water oozing thro Strata of Lime Stone effervesces and occasions the heat. However the matter remains disputable.

From this place we went to Derby a pretty neat well built Town of considerable Size situated on a neat River and watered by a less one which runs through the heart of it.[18] These Rivers furnish a number of Mills; two of which are of very curious and surprizing Mechanism, setting to work several hundred thousand Wheels for twisting doubling and reeling Silk.[19] Here we took our Places in the Coach for London and about 6 O Clock mounted the Machine. We came along all Night now and then changing our horses, passed through Leicester and Northampton shires, part of Bedfordshire Buckinghamshire Hartfordshire and arrived at Lad Lane London about 8 O Clock in the Evening.

May 26th   1st Day

This day commenced the Yearly Meeting where I met with a great Number of my Acquaintance from all Parts of the Kingdom and Ireland. The meeting continuing one week kept me in London without once leaving it.[20]

June 3rd   2nd Day

Early this Morning with *Samuel* Galton[21] and William Rathbone I set off for Hertford where was held the Quarterly Meeting, dined and spent the Afternoon with Baron Dimsdale.[22] The next Morning called on several of

---

[18] The River Derwent and the Markeaton brook, the latter running into the former at the eastern end of the city.

[19] One of these was Thomas Lombe's Silk Mill, established in 1717, the first and largest of its kind erected in England. It was situated on an island in the River Derwent. W. H. Chaloner, *People and Industries* (London, 1963), pp. 8–20.

[20] The London Yearly Meeting usually started in late May and often extended into June. 'It was an important assemblage, attended by representatives from all over the country who during its sessions dealt with nationwide problems of concern to the Society of Friends.' Corner and Booth, *Chain of Friendship*, p. 30.

[21] Samuel Galton (1753–1832), the son of Samuel and Mary Galton of Birmingham, was educated at Warrington Academy, married in or before 1778, and carried on a large gun business in Birmingham. He was disowned by the Society of Friends for his involvement in gun-making. M. E. Hirst, *The Quakers in Peace and War* (London, 1923), pp. 233–240; Barbara M. D. Smith, 'The Galtons of Birmingham: Quaker Gun Merchants and Bankers, 1702–1831,' *Business History*, IX (1967), pp. 132–150.

[22] Thomas Dimsdale (1712–1800), a Quaker who became expert in the process of inoculation against smallpox and the subsequent care of the inoculated. He visited St. Petersburg secretly in 1768 and inoculated the Empress Catherine and her son Alexander, a delicate boy of fourteen. The Empress honoured Dr. Dimsdale with gifts and with the title of baron. Dimsdale later established a banking house in London under the management of his sons and devoted himself to his medical work in a private hospital in Hertford. Thomas Dimsdale married twice. Corner and Booth, *Chain of Friendship*, p. 396; Namier and Brooke, *History of Parliament: The House of Commons 1754–1790*, II, p. 325.

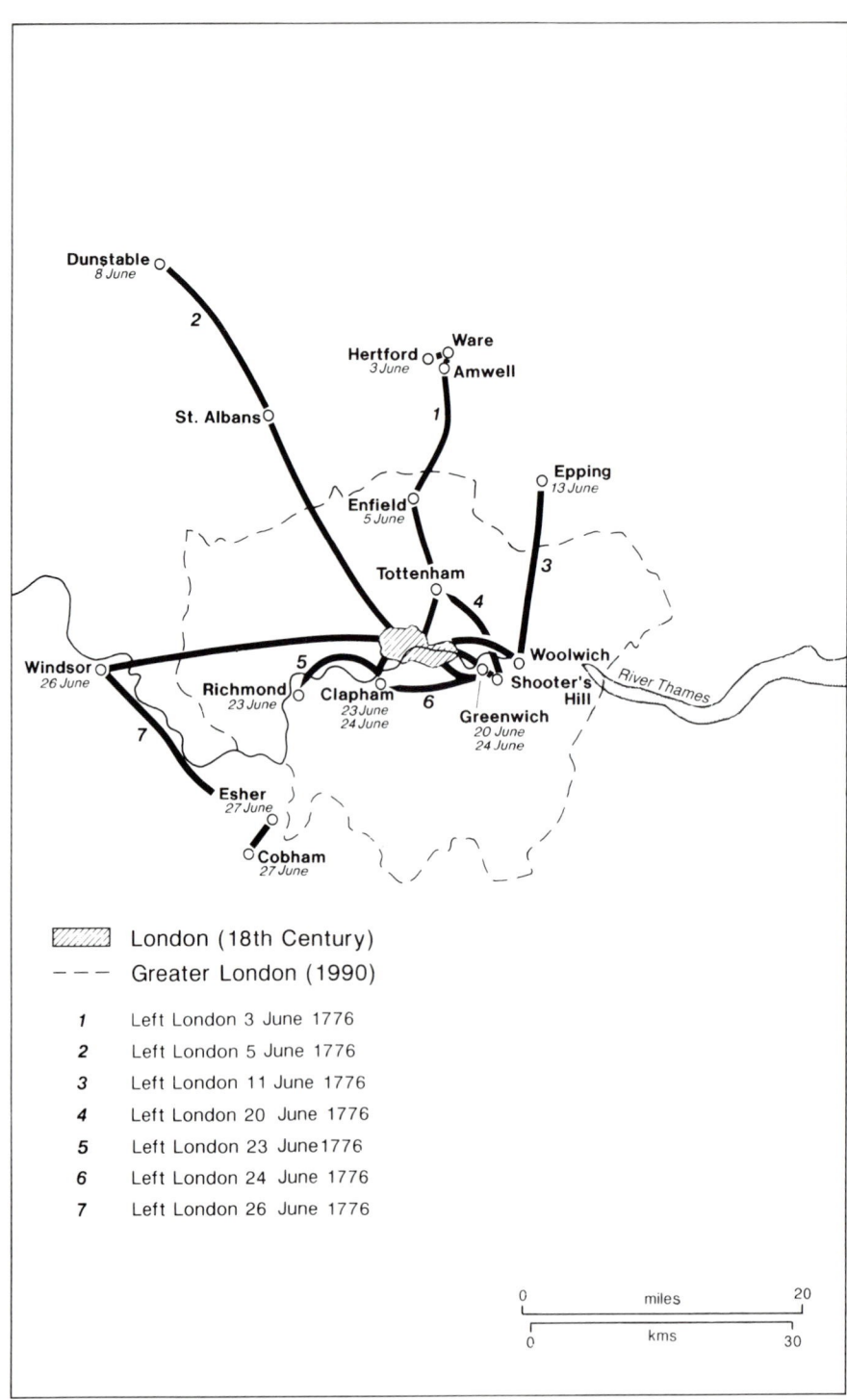

JABEZ MAUD FISHER'S TRAVELS, 3 - 27 JUNE 1776

our Friends, dined at Bangor [i.e. Bengeo], drank Tea at Dimsdale's and spent the Evening and lodged at Bangor.

June 5th   4th Day

Set off early for David Barclay's at Youngsbury where we breakfasted. From thence went to Ware to see the beautiful improvements of the celebrated Poet Scot, which have given rise to a fine Poem descriptive of his Situation, called Amwell. The Grotto here is very capital, the winding walks up to it pleasant, the Prospects rich, and the Taste of the Man far superior to his Fortune.

We next called at Enfield, which like all other places in the Neighbourhood of London is a Garden crowded with improvements. Here we called to see my Friend Thomas Weston, whose Situation is clever. From this place we came to Tottenham, where we dined with N: Morris; drank Tea with Friend Forster;[23] a Second Dish we took with Daniel Bell[24] at Stamford Hill and got to town in the Evening.

June 8th   7th Day

With Patience Chester[25] in a Post Chaise I set off this Morning for Dunstable. We got to St. Albans to dine, where Daniel Mildred[26] met with us and went to Dunstable to lodge where we met with Richard Chester. On the next Morning we went to Meeting about 2 Miles distant where were Samuel Spavold and Mary Brooks.[27] We came back to dine and set off for St. Albans where we lodged and the following Morning came out of the great London Road to see the Place of Richard Chester where we stayed an hour or two. The Country here is incomparably fine, chequered with

[23] William Forster (1747–1824) of Tottenham, a schoolmaster and a Quaker cousin of William Birkbeck, Jr. of Settle. Forster married Elizabeth Hayward in 1781. Cadbury, *John Woolman in England*, p. 88; Theodore Compton, *Recollections of Tottenham Friends and the Forster Family* (London, 1893), p. 68; 'William Forster on the American Revolution,' *Bulletin of the Friends' Historical Society of Philadelphia*, VIII (1918), pp. 74–5.

[24] Daniel Bell senior (1726–1802) lived at Stamford Hill and was a member of Tottenham MM. FLL, London and Middlesex QM: Burials; 'Letters from Joseph Gurney to Joseph Gurney Bevan,' *JFHS*, XX (1923), p. 86 n. 17.

[25] Patience Chester (1740–1802) married Richard Chester junior of Stoke Newington in 1759. *DQB*.

[26] Daniel Mildred (1731–1788qv) was for many years the clerk to the meeting of Devonshire House. He was a banker of White Hart Lane, Gracechurch Street, London. *Ibid.*; Frost, *Records and Recollections of James Jenkins*, p. 215; Gummere, *Journal and Essays of John Woolman*, p. 560.

[27] Mary Brook, the wife of Joseph Brook, a woolstapler, lived at Leighton Buzzard. She was brought up as an Anglican and became a Friend about 1753. Joyce Godber, *Friends in Bedfordshire and West Hertfordshire* (Bedford, 1975), pp. 39–40.

woods and Fields and beautified with Palaces and Rivers. We arrived at London in time to take a Dinner.

June 11th 3rd Day

Took a ride with *John* Miers,[28] S*amuel* Robinson[29] and some others to Woolwich about 8 Miles from London, a Dock yard and a Rendezvous for the India Men after their first Arrival.[30] We went on board one of them where I met with my old Friend Tom Wakefield.[31] We drank a dish of Tea on board and came back in the Evening.

June 13th 5th Day

At 5 O Clock in the Afternoon I set off with *John* Miers for Hackrell. We got a Dish of Tea in our Way there at Epping (delightful Country) and got to Hackrill at 9 O Clock. Supped with C*ornelius Heathcot* Rhodes Esquire and his two Sisters and in the Morning took leave of them and returned to London (by cross country indirect Roads) to dine.

June 20th 5th Day

A Party of 16 Young and old of both Sexes decamped for Greenwich early in the Morning. We had an excellent breakfast and took a walk after it to see that magnificent Pile of Building, Greenwich Hospital.[32] Its appearance on the Banks of the Thames is peculiarly striking and grand. Its front is adorned with fine Corinthian Pillars the whole height of the house and every other decoration that can add to its beauty. The Walks between the Buildings are kept in fine order and in the middle is a Square in which is a good Statue of Charles 2nd, the Founder of this Building.[33] The Hall

---

[28] Probably John Mier, tinplate and wine merchant, 50 Cannon Street, London. Bailey's *British Directory* (1784), I, p. 173.

[29] Probably Samuel Robinson (b. 1732), a Quaker who worked as a skinner in London. *JFHS*, XVI (1919), p. 59.

[30] Henry VIII built up the naval dockyard at Woolwich. An arsenal was created nearby in the late seventeenth century. Woolwich dockyard, distant from the sea and situated on a confined site, declined relative to the other yards throughout the eighteenth century. Bridget Cherry and Pevsner, *Buildings of England: London 2: South* (London, 1983), pp. 239, 241, 286–287; Morriss, *Royal Dockyards*, p. 2.

[31] Thomas Wakefield (b. 1750). *JFHS*, XVI (1919), p. 59.

[32] The Royal Naval Hospital, Greenwich, was built on the site of a Tudor palace. The foundation stone of the new building was laid in 1664. Mary (of William and Mary) made over the building to the purpose of a naval hospital. Various architects contributed to the building of this hospital, mainly between 1694 and the end of the eighteenth century. Pevsner, *Building of England: London except the Cities of London and Westminster* (London, 1952), pp. 145–150.

[33] A small error. The statue is of George II by Michael Rysbrack. It is eight feet high and was erected in 1735. Edward Gleichen, *London's Open-Air Statuary* (London, 1928), pp. 207–208.

contains on the Ceiling a very fine historical Painting with King William and Queen Mary seated under the Canopy of State trampling on Tyranny, Oppression and Persecution, with emblematic Figures of Agriculture, Architecture, Mathematics and the other Sciences finely displayed.[34] Round the room are painted Pilasters of the Ionic Order fluted; the deception is very capital, and you do not find the mistake till you almost touch the wall. There are likewise some other well executed deceptions. The Chapel is elegant and beautiful; the Altar piece has some good paintings.

The Rooms in which the disabled Seamen are stationed are large, clean and neat. They have each a Separate Apartment and live very plenteously. Adjoining to this Hospital is a spacious and delightful Park, where the Liberty is given for all the People of the Hospital to walk. This is finely variegated with stately Trees, sometimes planted in Rows, at other times in Clumps, here and there Seats Sub ? mine Fagi, hills and vallies all round it, and on an artificial mound is the observatory which commands a most noble Prospect. The City of London rises in all its Consequence and Lustre, the River Thames before and on each Side of us, and a Forrest of Shipping only interrupting its Charms; and an immense tract of Country opening all its Beauties to your view and terminated by distant Hills which lose their heads in mist and obscurity.

From this place we went to Shuter's Hill[35] about 2 Miles distant, where another most delectable View offers itself. The City of London with all its lofty Spires and gilded Crusts, the whole Retinue of Shipping, the Thames here advancing then retiring behind the indented Shore, Towns and Villages countless, Seats, Gardens and Elysium, Hills Vallies and Plains, Pastures and Meadows; in short a crowded variety of Beauties, with which the Sense almost aches. Here we had a most splendid Entertainment at an Inn much frequented by the Gentry adjoining which are Gardens and Shrubberies most pleasurably disposed. We returned home in the Evening, when *Samuel* Galton and myself immediately set off in our Friend Pym's[36] Coach for Tottenham. We lodged at Stamford Hill at *Priscilla* Wakefields.

---

[34] The centre of the ceiling of the Painted Hall at the Royal Naval Hospital is a Baroque ceiling painted by Sir James Thornhill between 1707 and 1717. The main representation is framed by an oval and shows William and Mary attended by the four cardinal virtues. Pevsner, *Buildings of England: London except the Cities of London and Westminster*, p. 149.

[35] Shooter's Hill.

[36] Possibly John Pim (1752–1829), a Quaker merchant and minister who settled in London in 1773. *Pen Pictures of the London Yearly Meeting*, p. 134 n. 9.

June 23rd   1st Day

Went to [?] Meeting this Morning where *Thomas Letchworth*[37] gave us a most excellent Discourse. Dined at J: Bocketts[38] near Clapham, and took a Ride with all his Family, E*dward* Jenston[39] and P: Horne and S*amuel* Galton thro that enchanting Park of Richmond, passed by Lord Bute's Seat[40] and got to Richmond Hill to Tea. There are so many fine Places in this Luxuriant and fertile Kingdom that I am at a loss for some new Words to give a Description with. All the Epithets I can find are hackneyed and half the lovely Scenes are left to be taken an Account of. My Journal will be a sad Jumble of Repetition; 'twill vex me to read it. However it will remind how often enchanting Objects have discovered their Beauties as I have passed along.

Richmond Hill is inferior to few places I have seen. It stands celebrated for the most delightful Spot in the neighbourhood of London. The View is very extensive, very rich. Windsor Castle[41] is a Crest to the nearer Hills, Groves on the opposite Sides, and hanging Woods if in which Taste have had little Share in Planting, She has certainly dictated the Spot where the house stands and from which we view this Paradise of Charms. The Thames washes at the Foot of the Hill. On its Banks are many capital seats, many pretty Gardens. The Mirror is interspersed with Islands; and there is nothing before us but an intoxicating variegation of Delights. After this I shall give no other Description of it than saying it is indescribable.

We returned to Clapham where we supped, set off for London and arrived there about 12 O Clock. A robbery had been committed on the same Road a few minutes before we came along.

---

[37] Thomas Letchworth (1739–1784), a Quaker minister from c. 1758 who lived in Southwark. He was the author of a number of tracts. *DQB*; William Matthews, *The Life and Character of Thomas Letchworth, a minister ... among the people called Quakers* (Bath, 1786).

[38] Probably a member of Bockett, Janson & Bockett, distillers and brandy merchants, Bridge Street, Blackfriars, London. Bailey's *British Directory*, I, p. 25.

[39] Edward Janson (d. 1813 aged c. 60) lived at Bishopsgate and belonged to Tottenham MM. FLL, London and Middlesex QM: Burials.

[40] John Stuart (1713–1792), Earl of Bute from 1723, was First Lord of the Treasury and Prime Minister between May 1762 and April 1763. He was a Ranger of Richmond Park from 1761 until his death. Because of this position, he was sometimes in residence at Richmond New Park Lodge. Cokayne, *Complete Peerage*, II, pp. 441–442; Colvin, *History of the King's Works*, III Part 1, p. 232.

[41] England's largest castle. The first stone buildings were erected between 1165 and 1179 and construction continued throughout the medieval period and later. Pevsner, *Buildings of England: Berkshire* (London, 1966), pp. 266–295.

June 24th   2nd Day

Took a Ride this Morning with Dr. Dimsdale, *John* Dilworth[42] and Wife and Sister Arthington[43] to Greenwich, where we went after viewing the Hospital on board the Yatch Caroline in which the present Queen came over to England. She is decorated in the most superb and gaudy Manner, has every Convenience that Contrivance and Ingenuity could invent. On our return to London we called at Deptford to view the Docks &c. Here are good conveniences for the Discharge of Ships, as well as for building and fitting out; and to this place are brought almost all the foreign Articles used in the different Kings Yards, and from this they are afterwards shipped off to Portsmouth Plymouth and Chatham, for which reason this is called the Mother of all the Docks, though it bear no Sort of comparison to either of the others.[44]

Soon after getting here I set off to Clapham to dine with 17 Gentlemen of London, where we had a notable repast on Turbut, and played Trap Ball[45] the whole Afternoon. Came back to London and set off with *Samuel* Galton to Newington and lodged with my Friends Hoare's.

June 25th   3rd Day

Took a Stroll with Molly Knowles[46] to the British Museum to M: Wright[47] who is working a most spendid Bed for the Queen. It is wrought on a rich Silk, the Flowers admirably executed and amazingly rich. This Art scene is brought to the Zenith of perfection; painting is outdone. However the Productions of this Lady's Needle do not quite equal *Molly* Knowles, who besides having done a Likeness of the King which might vie with the most capital Painters of the present Age, she has done some Flower Pieces, some Fruit Pieces and a Hare far superior to anything else.

[42] Possibly John Dillworth (d. 1830 aged 85), a Quaker from Yealand Conyers, Westmorland. Abbatt, *Quaker Annals of Preston and the Fylde*, p. 46.

[43] Phebe Arthington of Leeds (d. 1794 aged 53) married Benjamin Blesard of Bradford in 1765. They were both Quakers. Hodgson, *Society of Friends in Bradford*, pp. 113, 132.

[44] The navy's principal yard by the end of Henry VIII's reign. During the seventeenth century its relative importance declined but its situation, close to the centre of naval administration, retained for it a number of advantages. Cherry and Pevsner, *Buildings of England: London 2: South*, p. 398; Morriss, *Royal Dockyards*, p. 1.

[45] Trap-ball is a game in which a ball on a slightly hollowed end of a trap is thrown into the air by the batsman striking the other end with his bat, with which he then hits the ball away. Murray, *New English Dictionary*, X Part 1, p. 285.

[46] Molly Knowles (1733–1807) was an authoress and painter who was also known for her portraits in needlework. *DQB*.

[47] Mrs Wright (d. 1778) was well-known in her day for her needlework, including commissions from royalty. The bed which she worked for Queen Charlotte is still to be seen in the State Bedroom at Windsor Castle. Ralph S. Walker, ed., *James Beattie's London Diary 1773* (Aberdeen, 1946), pp. 107–108.

From this we went to the great American Wright famous for her Wax Work, who has a Number of excellent Busts of the principal Characters of the Nation and a great number of very interesting historical pieces. Her merit is great, allowed by all to be much superior to any other Person in that walk in England. But the most extraordinary part of her Character is that she from only seeing a Face once can take off the likeness in that admirable Manner.[48]

From hence we went to Sir Joshua Reynolds the most capital Portrait Painter now living. He has a vast many admirably fine Paintings of his own besides two fine Landscapes of Claude and several of Poussin and one of Raphael's about 18 Inches valued at £600. Miers[49] we called on next who is likewise a great Painter but inferior to Reynolds. We then went to Benjamin West,[50] the Raphael of the present Age, whose views are too well known to need any Comment.

June 26th   4th Day

In a Coach with *John* Dilworth and Wife, P*hebe* Arthington and Molly Knowles we set off for Windsor where we dined and then took a walk to the Castle, the magnificent Palace of our present Sovereign. This is a most spacious Structure, a number of Buildings abstract from each other in the Gothic Stile with Battlements, situate on a grand Eminence and command-ing as rich and extensive a view as almost any Spot in the Kingdom. From a Turret we have a clear Prospect of 13 different Counties, every Variegation of Hills and Vallies, Cities, Towns and Villages, Gentlemen's Seats, Parks, Woods, Rivers and every object which can diversify and delight. Here is an excellent Stand of Armoury all in good Order. There is likewise some most excellent Portraits of Vandyk, Rubens, history Pieces of Raphael, Guido and other great Masters. But the most celebrated Painting is of two Misers counting their Gold. This is done by [van Reymerswael], the poor

---

[48] Patience Wright (1725–1786), who used wax sculpture as a portrait art. Her subjects at her waxworks in London included Lord North, John Wilkes, the Elder Pitt and George III. She was a widow with teenage children when she came from New Jersey to London in 1772. She was an American spy during the War of Independence. Charles Coleman Sellers, *Patience Wright: American Artist and Spy in George III's London* (Middletown, Connecticut, 1976), pp. 15, 220, 225.

[49] E. H. Miers, a Dutch landscape painter, who settled in London, where he died in 1793. Bryan's *Dictionary of Painters and Engravers* (new edn., London, 1927), III, p. 337.

[50] Benjamin West (1738–1820) came from Pennsylvania Quaker stock. He learned to paint in America, was in Italy from 1760 to 1763, and then set up as a portrait painter in London. He produced many pictures of medieval history subjects. Murray and Murray, *Penguin Dictionary of Art and Artists*, pp. 441–442.

Blacksmith, and is allowed to have no Superior. The Projection, Chiara obscura and the Characters are astonishingly fine.[51]

From this we took a little Walk into the Park but this is so well described by Pope and so well known I shall omit any description.[52] We went next to Esher where we supd and lodged with our Friend *Joseph* Biddle[53] and took a Ride in the Morning to Squire Hopkins Gardens and Improvements known by the name of Cobham.[54] Here a fine Situation has afforded a man of great Taste to shew what can be done by Art. He has made Rivers where were no Rivers, raised Hills in the midst of Vallies and with Clumps of Trees disposed with the nicest Judgement, thro which the most enchanting Walks in many meanders lead us thro his pleasure Grounds. Now and then we come to Avenues where we see Temples Obelisks and Columns, Images, Rotundo's and other objects all lending their Charms to delight us. But the Place for which this is most of all famous is a Grotto which stands unrivalled for Beauty. We are conducted to it by a crooked Walk whose Sides are decked with the most gaudy Spars and Crystallisations of Cornwall and Derbyshire. The Floor is plaistered with white mortar. On entering it we are lost in Astonishment at its rude grotesque and beautiful appearance, regularly irregular.

[51] A picture of 'The Money Lenders' by Marius van Reymerswael (1497–1567), a Flemish artist. It is a genre subject, and was acquired by Charles I. C. H. Collins Baker, *Catalogue of the Principal Pictures in the Royal Collection at Windsor Castle* (London, 1937), p. 234 and plate 77.

[52] Pope's poem *Windsor Forest* (published in 1713) was dedicated to the Rt. Hon. George, Lord Lansdown. John Butt, ed., *The Poems of Alexander Pope* (London, 1963), pp. 195–210.

[53] Joseph Biddle was a Friend who lived at Esher. FLL, Thomas Pole Journal (1775–1776), p. 489.

[54] The manor of Mickleham, near Cobham, was in the hands of Benjamin Bond Hopkins from 1775 to 1780. Owen Manning, *The History and Antiquities of the County of Surrey* (3 vols., London, 1804–1814), II, p. 654.

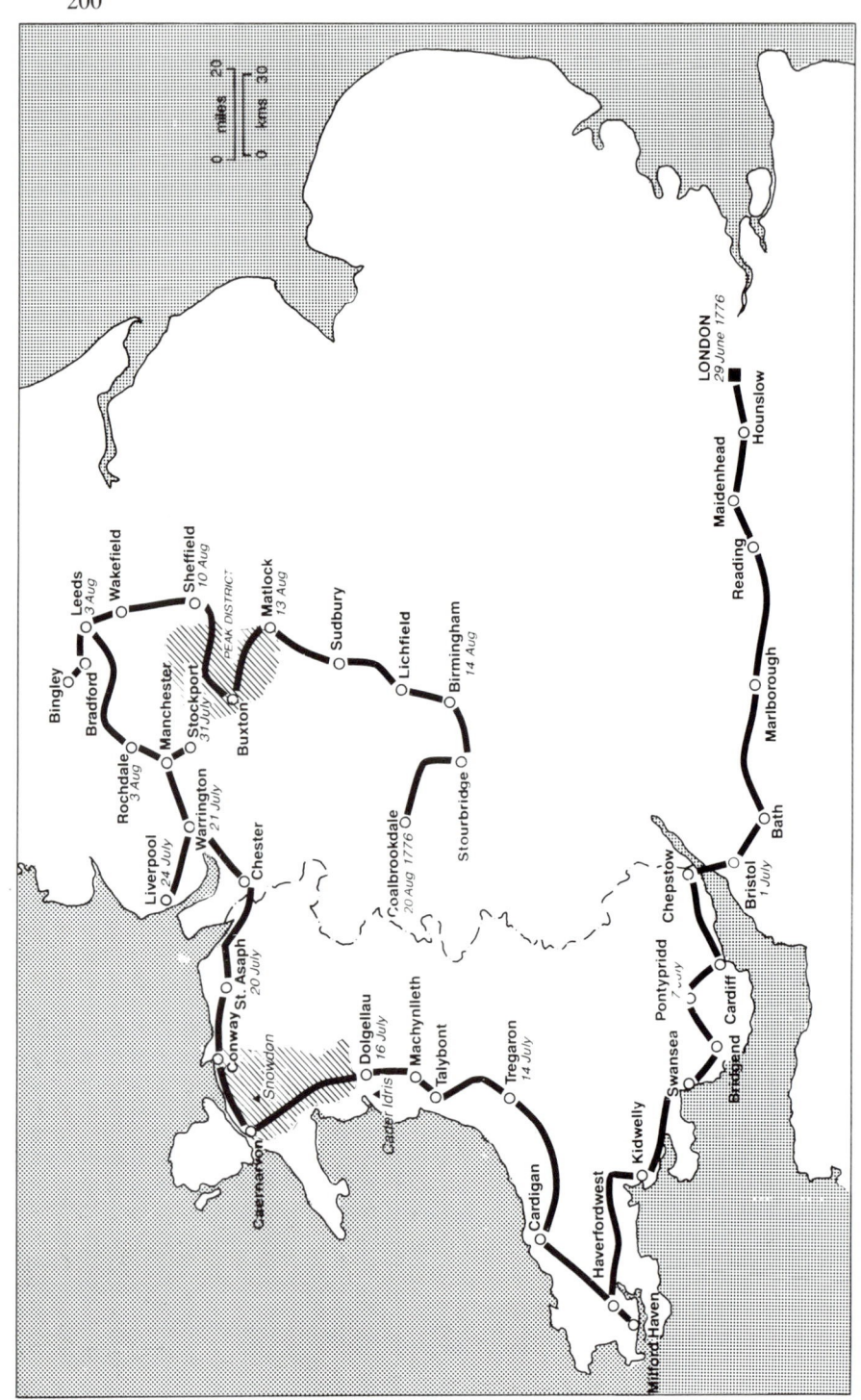

JABEZ MAUD FISHER'S TRAVELS, 29 JUNE - 20 AUGUST 1776

June 29th   7th Day

Having now a long Excursion before me, I mounted at Hyde Park Corner attended by *Joseph* Gurney of Norwich. With our Le Fleur behind us we got to Hounslow to dine, drank tea at Maidenhead and arrived at Reading in the Evening. Here we called on our Friend West, Brother to the Painter,[1] who with Speakman[2] and another Friend came and smoaked a Pipe with us.

June 30th   1st Day

We stayed. Meeting at Reading. Mounted immediately after and dined at a most capital Inn about 1 mile from Newbury. From this place we have a most rich and extensive View. We took a dish of Tea at Hungerford and got to Marlborough early in the Evening. All the inns on the Bath Road are amazingly grand. The Attendance of the People and their Assiduity can only be equalled by the grandeur of the Houses, the elegance of the Furniture, and the Convenience of the apartments. But this Inn is superior to all the rest. Not only the house, but the Gardens would grace the Seat of a Nobleman, which indeed the Castle here once was.[3] The Pleasure Grounds, Walks, Groves and Shrubberies are neat and beautiful. Here is a large mount in the Garden once probably the Tumulus of the ancient Druids who buried the Ashes of their dead in Tumuli of this Sort, and of which there are many in the Vicinities of this place. Up this mount is a pleasant walk, meandering round the Hill, planted on both Sides by Hedges, and by this Serpentine Ascent you gain the Summit after walking half a mile, from which the Prospect fully compensates your Trouble.

We lodged here in Beds of State and came on the next morning to Bath, thro Calne, and stopping in our Way, at the Seat of Paul Methuens

---

[1] Thomas West (1716–1792), half-brother of the American painter Benjamin West, lived at Reading. Robert C. Alberts, *Benjamin West: A Biography* (Boston, 1978), p. 524.

[2] Thomas Speakman (c. 1745–1823) was a Quaker minister at the Reading Meeting. *Pen Pictures of London Yearly Meeting*, p. 48.

[3] See above, p. 120.

Esquire[4] who has a very elegant House, grand Woods, and elysian Fields. He has likewise a finall but excellent Collection of Paintings of the best Masters.

When I saw Bath before the Ground was covered with Snow. I have therefore two Reasons for being better pleased with it than then, first because the Season is in all its Pride and Glory so that the Prospect which it affords is an hundred times more charming. And Secondly, because it is the last time, for Bath is so elegant and uniform a City, that the more often you see it, the more it will captivate and delight.

We dined here and got to Bristol in the Evening, but too late to go to our private Lodgings so we took up our abode for this Night at the Inn. Here we stayed a day or two, took several Rides out, one of which was to our Friend Mark Harford's at Stoke Bishop.[5] In the attempt to get there we missed our road and rode to Frenchay 9 Miles out of our way. However the Ride was so pleasant, the Country so delightful, abounding with the most enchanting Prospects, that we have no Reason to regret our having lost the Road.

The Situation of Mark Harford's house is particularly fine, the view exceeded by few. We drank Tea here with our Friend *Philip Debell* Tucket and Wife[6] and *Sarah* Champion in a little Summer house at bottom of a Lawn on the brow of a noble Hill overlooking a lovely Copse, beyond it a fine range of Pasture terminated by the Avon over which is a grand Landscape, but the objects too distant minutely to trace. Another ride was to Clifton, as beautiful a Village as any in England (Heath only excepted)[7] whether we consider its charming Situation for Health and Prospect, or the Neighbourhood of well built and elegant houses, among the foremost of which I may [mention] my Friend Goldney's.[8] This from a superb Summit overlooks an immense Country. The City of Bristol makes a fine object on one Side. On the other the barren Heath's of Redland Moor

---

[4] Paul Methuen of Corsham House, Wiltshire, was the cousin of the diplomat and politician Sir Paul Methuen (1672–1757), who had acquired a fine collection of pictures on the continent. The collection began moving to Corsham Court in the 1770s. *DNB*, XIII, pp. 312–313; Iain Pears, *The Discovery of Painting: The Growth of Interest in the Arts in England, 1680–1768* (New Haven, 1988), pp. 178, 264 n. 71. For a detailed description of the paintings at Corsham House see G. F. Waagen, *Works of Art and Artists in England* (London, 1838; reprinted, 1970), III, pp. 90–108.

[5] Mark Harford (1700–1788) was a Bristol Quaker. Alice Harford, *Annals of the Harford Family* (London, 1909), p. 156.

[6] Philip Debell Tuckett (1749–1816) was a haberdasher in Bristol by 1774. Later he was a grocer and merchant there. He was twice married: to Esther Champion in 1774 and to Elizabeth Wright in 1800. *DQB*.

[7] See p. 43.

[8] Gabriel Goldney (1704–1786). P. K. Stembridge, *Goldney: A House and a Family* (4th edn., Bristol, 1982), pp. 23–25.

whose Side are the roughest production of Nature's unpolished hand; through a fine Valley the pretty Avon winds her Silver Stream, displaying all her Charms before us, rich inclosures and the thick foliage of an extensive Wood.

His improvements are tasty and elegant, though contracted. His Fish Pond, Rows of Trees, Orangerie, and Images are pretty objects through Avenues of Trees well disposed. But his Grotto is the most capital of his improvements, and is perhaps equal to any in the Kingdom.[9] On entering we are struck with admiration and Surprise; the gaudy variety of the Shells scattered with such finished Taste in so fine a Form; the Gothic Arches by which the whole is supported; the nitches in the Wall; the Pillars; the Den before the Entrance of which sits a Lion in the most frightful Attitude, and within the Lioness equally to appearance alive. All vie with similar Success for a Preference. But what most claims our attention and what most captivates our Senses is a River God of excellent Sculpture, seated on a rude Rock up a distant Avenue of grotesque Craggs, down which from a Vase he pours a plenteous Stream of Water which falling by many pleasing Cataracts into a Silver Bason below in which the gold and silver Fish glitter and swim. The Light strikes so happily on every object as to make them all appear to the highest Advantage.

We called at the Hot Wells. This place (being now the Season) is crowded with the unhappy Sons of intemperance and disease, some of whom fall Victims to the rage of Disorder while a few receive benefit from Drinking the Water. This Water is well and justly celebrated for many peculiar Quality's, but nothing is more extraordinary than being keepable for years without becoming putrid. The Situation of this place is pleasant, situate at the foot of a pretty River, by which all the Vessels to Bristol pass. The romantic Rocks[10] above impend in a striking Manner.

July 5th　　6th Day

Soon after Breakfast we decamped for our Welch expedition. We went to Meeting at Kings Weston; and called afterwards to see the beautiful Seat of Lord Clifford[11] than which nothing can be more pleasingly situated; every

---

[9] The Goldney family purchased a house, garden and orchard on Clifton Hill, Bristol, in 1705. Thomas Goldney (1697–1768) enlarged his property and gardens. His first major garden project was a grotto built between 1737 and 1764. It includes a spectacular pattern of shells. *Ibid.*, pp. 17, 19.

[10] St. Vincent's Rocks.

[11] Edward Southwell (1738–1777), 20th Baron Clifford from 1776. Known as Edward, Baron de Clifford or Lord Clifford, he was Tory M.P. for Bridgwater (1761–1763) and for the county of Gloucester (1763–1776). He lived at Kings Weston House, Gloucestershire. Cokayne, *Complete Peerage*, III, p. 298; Namier and Brooke, *History of Parliament: The House of Commons 1754–1790*, III, pp. 457–458.

Side affords a very charming Prospect, but that Front next the River is preferable. The Park interspersed with Clusters of Stately Oaks and Elms begins the view. This extends to the Severn about half a mile distant where a Number of Ships are constantly riding: the Avon here empties itself into this noble River. On the other Side the Severn Wales discovers a thousand beauties, at first low rich Lands and extending itself further on is crowned with lofty mountains. The Shrubbery here is admirably laid out, the walks thro it a mere Paradise. The House is elegant, but not equal to many I have seen. But here is a choice Collection of Paintings of the most eminent Artists: some fine Titians, Rubens, Rosas and two Claude's. The decorations and Furniture of the house are nothing more than clever.

We dined at King Weston and came on thro a lovely Country to the New Passage across the Severn. The wind and tide being both against us, we concluded to leave our horses till tomorrow. We according marched into the boat rowed by two men and with immense labor gaind the further Shoar. The tide flowed in with such rapidity that we could hear it roar at a great Distance and in some places it formed a mere Cascade. The Water here rises near 60 feet in a common Tide and in Spring tides much more.[12]

We now land safely on the delightful Coast of Wales which seemed to greet us welcome with as fine an Evening as I ever remember. We drank tea at a little Inn; and walked across the Fields perfumed with every varied Scent, chequered by an hundred inclosures, variegated by Gardens, Woods, and Meads and intersected by several fine Streams. But the Genius of the place determined to give us the most strong impressions of its beauty had created the most gaudy temporary Scene. The Sun just leaving the hither Earth had tinged the western Sky with the richest Beams. The Clouds favored the Prospect, the Edges were all tinged with Vermilion, the Ether seemed itself to partake of the lively hue and all the horizon was more gloriously beautiful than Language can describe. We calld at a little Ale house and drank some beer, when we proceeded on our walk and reach Chepstow about 9 O Clock.

July 6th   7th Day

The Situation of Chepstow is rurally Romantic, on the declivity of a fine Hill by gentle Descent to the charming River Wye over which there is a noble Bridge as long as that of London. The Pillars are of Stone but the Top is Timber. Both sides of the River are formd of perpendicular white and red Cliffts, on one Side many hundreds of feet high. On the Chepstow

---

[12] The River Severn is estuarine and tidal beneath the city of Gloucester. A high bore, or tidal wave, for which the Severn is notorious, is capable of reversing the flow as high up as Tewkesbury. *Encyclopaedia Britannica*, XXIV, p. 723.

Side stand the Ruins of a large and magnificent Castle,[13] covered with Ivy and forming one of the grandest and most awful Objects. The Battlements are almost invisible. The windows are generally perfect, but screened by the branches of the Ivy which run up on every Side and almost hide the whole Wall. We took a ride about a Mile from Town, where we left the Chaise and entered the Wood of Squire Morris (now Governor of St. Vincents).[14] The first Object is a little cleared Mount on which is a house formerly a Wind Mill, but now fitted up for a Summer house. From the upper Story we have a delightful View of the Country, Rivers, and Farm houses far and near.

By a winding Gravel Walk dark with Umbrage, where the Branches interlocking each other, shut us up from the Sight of Day, we are conducted to an Alcove, where there are Seats, from which we behold the River Wye directly under us winding in beautiful meanders with a thick hanging wood leading down to a very perfect view of the magnificent Ruins of the Castle of Chepstow and the Town, the perpendicular Crags on the opposite Shore forming a fine Contrast with the verdure which spouts out of a thousand Crevices in the Sides. The distant meadows, Woods Hills and Vallies, beyond them the River Severn, and beyond this, the Shore of England losing itself by its distance in Mist and Darkness. Conducted by other Walks further on where Trees of every Size from the diminutive Shrub to the proud Oak are on each Side of us inaccessible, now and then a bench to sit down on, we reach a little inclosed rail with Seats round it which they call the Stage. Here is another delightful View. The same objects as in the last, but from a different point of View, yet no less pleasing. A little further on is a pretty Grotto, inlaid with beautiful Stones. From this an Avenue is cut thro the Branches to the opposite Shore where the Rocks rise higher than anywhere else and with more boldness and sublimity being near 1000 feet perpendicular. No object can exceed this.

From this place along a Road made at a great expence cut through a solid Rock on the Summit of the Hill, we go to the Chinese Rails.[15] This is

[13] The first castle at Chepstow was built by William Fitz Osbern (d. 1071) in the early part of the Norman Conquest (1067–1071). Much of the castle survives. Chepstow Castle was partially dismantled in 1690. John Clifford Perks, *Chepstow Castle* (HMSO, London, 1955), pp. 5, 32; Colvin, *History of the King's Works*, II, p. 607.

[14] Valentine Morris was Lieutenant Governor of St. Vincent from 1772 until 1776 and Governor between 1776 and 1779. St. Vincent, one of the Lesser Antilles in the Caribbean, was ceded to Britain by the Treaty of Paris in 1763. David P. Henige, *Colonial Governors from the Fifteenth Century to the Present* (Madison, Wisconsin, 1970), p. 169.

[15] A reference to the landscape improvements of Squire Morris at Persfield, between Tintern and Chepstow. These included a winding precipice cut in the form of a zigzag. William Gilpin, *Observations on the River Wye, and several Parts of South Wales, &c. relative chiefly to Picturesque Beauty; made in the Summer of the Year 1770* (London, 1772), pp. 39–41.

on a Rock directly over the River, 300 feet looking down with the greatest Pride on the enchanting Landscape below. We next go to a little Spot inclosed in not above 100 yards from the house. This View exceeds all the rest. The River winding in almost a perfect Circle immediately below, the delightful Peninsula opposite us, the many winding Meanders of the River which appear on both Sides of us, the points of Land projecting into it, the high rocks which rise perpendicularly from the waters Edge, the Hills at a distance which lift their Brows one over another, and an avenue which opens itself directly opposite, with the River Severn beyond all these, and still further off the Land of England, are all objects which strike us with peculiar Force from this enchanting Spot.

We now take leave of these Gardens, Woods, and Shrubberies and ride several miles thro a most romantic Country where the road is so narrow as barely to admit of one Carriage, and the Trees embracing each other from the opposite Sides, to Tintern, a little Village where stands that noble pile of Ruins called Tintern Abbey, being in length 77 yards and in breadth 56.[16] The principal Pillars are all standing. The Eastern Window where formerly stood the Altar is in choice preservation as also most of the capital Arches. But the Roof is entirely fallen in. The whole is overgrown with Ivy, as are all the Walls which inclose it and the neighbouring outhouses. This is only inferior to three Ruins which I have seen, Fountains Abbey, Kirkstall[17] and Whitby.

At this place is a great Manufactury of Wire,[18] the Iron being manufactured from the Ore, a furnace to make it into Barrs from whence it is taken to the tilting Mill, where it is lengthened out into long rods. It is then drawn thro the holes of the different Sizes till it be reduced to the desired fineness. This whole operation is performed by water by the addition of very little Labor.

We dined at a little Alehouse in the Village the situation of which is in a most sequestered vale, watered by a living River, which empties itself into the Wye. Returned to Chepstow where our horses were ready when we set off for New Port, a considerable market Town on a wide River which we

---

[16] Tintern Abbey was founded in 1131 for monks of the Cistercian order. Most of today's ruins date from rebuilding in the thirteenth and fourteenth centuries, when Tintern was at its zenith. O. E. Craster, *Tintern Abbey* (HMSO, London, 1963), pp. 3–5.

[17] Kirkstall Abbey was a Cistercian foundation whose main buildings were completed c. 1175. It was probably founded in 1152 for monks from Fountains Abbey. Pevsner, *Buildings of England: Yorkshire: The West Riding* (2nd edn., London, 1979), pp. 340–347.

[18] At the beginning of the eighteenth century, there were already two furnaces and two forges near Tintern which were reputed to make the best malleable iron in Britain. The iron ore was 'made into Wyer, by Water Mills, and other ingenious Inventions brought here by *Germans* many Years since.' Nathan Rogers, *Memoirs of Monmouthshire* (London, 1708), pp. 33–34.

pass by a very long timber Bridge. The Walls of the Town are yet standing. The Castles which are at the Gates of each End of the Town are in Ruins. From hence we came to Cardiff and got in before 10 O Clock.

This Day's ride for Prospects of the sublime and beautiful exceeds all my others. The road from Chepstow hither is one continued Scene of enchantment. We rise on Noble Hills, where Views interminable on every Side meet our Eyes, with every Sort of Variety with which the Sense could be gratified. Rivers and Sheets of Water without Number, Hills and Vallies cloathed with the most delightful Verdure, varied by the gaudiest tints, and interspersed with Clusters of Trees and the finest hedge Rows. Not a Spot but discovers the richest Culture.

July 7th   1st Day

Cardiff is a pretty Town, well pavd, placed on a Stream which supplies it with Fish, besides adding to its beauty and Convenience. It stands most reputed for containing the Ruins of an ancient Fortification, with several watch Towers, of Gothic Structure.[19] A small distance from this is the Ruin of an old Palace, inclosed within an high wall.[20] Cardiff is walld in and in days passed there has been a mote round it, which is now filled up and the wall like the Castle is mouldering to a Caput Mortuum.[21] For the first time we now ascend the Welch Mountains and having missed our way, we ride over Hills almost inaccessible but being repaid by the astonishingly fine Prospects they exhibit, we are emboldened to soar on others.

After riding about 10 Miles over these Gigantic Hills, the Vallies below being thick with Farm houses and Huts, we arrive at Caerphilly a small but beautiful Market Town, on one Side of which rise the stupendous Remains of one of the most magnificent Buildings of Antiquity.[22] This Castle with its Towers Barracks and other appertenances takes up a Mile in Circumference. It has a deep mote round it and has in days of yore had every Sort of defence. There is not now remaining one whole wall perfect. Monstrous pieces have fallen down which lie in different parts piled one on another in grand Confusion. One Tower is leaning over many degrees and

[19] Cardiff began as a motte castle, raised by c. 1080. It was converted from an earth-and-timber motte castle into a stone fortress. There were various medieval additions including a thirteenth-century Black Tower and an octagonal tower of c. 1420. Fry, *The David & Charles Book of Castles*, p. 335.

[20] A reference to the episcopal palace at Llandaff, destroyed by Owen Glendower and never restored. Lewis, *Topographical Dictionary of Wales*, I, p. 500.

[21] Capital of the Dead.

[22] The building of this castle was begun in 1271 by Earl Gilbert de Clare, Lord of Glamorgan. During the fifteenth century the castle fell into decay and by 1536 it was a ruin. *Caerphilly Castle* (HMSO, London, 1958), pp. 1–2.

seems ever ready to crush the very Earth with its enormous weight; others stand upright but their Crests are mouldering to dust, and supplanted by branches of Ivy, which suspend in most awful Majesty.

The immense theatre expanded to our view of the lofty mountains on every Side at first lessen the effects this prodigious pile might be expected to occasion, but on entering the Walls and contemplating the immense labour with which these walls must have been reared, reflecting on the yawning Cavities which open here and there in the building, the Chasms torn by the hand of old Time through Walls 15 feet in thickness, we are lost in astonishment at the wonderful Scene. This is the most Spacious Ruin in Great Britain and perhaps no Fortification of so great Antiquity can equal it in extent, yet this is of no Consequence since the Use of Fire Arms has been known.

We stopped at a little Ale house opposite to it and from which it appears in all its Grandeur and Sublimity, heightened much by the Ivy Mantle which is thrown over it. Here we drank some Ale and afterwards set off for Pont du Pree. We rode part of the way over an excessive stony Country, and some high Hills. At last came to the Side of a pretty River, by which we had a pleasant ride for several Miles. At length tempted by the Romantic appearance of the opposite Side we made an attempt to ford across and with some difficulty gained the Shore, the water running with great rapidity. Here we rode along a little foot path by the Side of the River through brambles, thorns, and thickets, and at least what little Vestiges we before had, disappeared; and we went on into such boggy Ground that we got swamped before we thought of retreating, when we precipitately dismounted and dragged our horses up a Hill almost perpendicular for a great height and with difficulty at length gained the Summit.

A Country more like America than this I have not seen since I crossed the Atlantic. Here are woods in all the Wildness of uncultivated Nature. The great Oaks of the Forrest with every little subject Shrub. The Mountains have all the Magnificence of America, and the rude Craggs which peep out of the Side, and the tumbling Cataracts in the River exactly resemble it.

We dined at an Ale house, near the wonderful Pont du Pree, a Bridge of the most curious Construction, being a Semi-Circle of 142 feet Diameter, the most light and beautiful as well as the largest Arch in the Universe. The Landscape under it of neighbouring and distant mountains is very fine. A view of this Scene has been published by Richard Wilson.[23]

---

[23] Richard Wilson (?1713–1782) was a Welsh artist mainly known for his landscape paintings. This is a reference to Wilson's painting of the 'Great Bridge over the River Taaffe.' The painting has disappeared, though it predates 1766. A print by Peter Charles Canot exists in the British Museum. The bridge was built in 1756 by William Edwards, a Welsh stonemason. The Welsh called this structure Pont-y-ty-Pridd (new bridge). David H. Solkin, *Richard Wilson: The Landscape of Reaction* (London, 1982), p. 98 and no. 121, pp. 223–224, 228–229.

The Landlord informed us that the Road from this place to Llantrissent was level and smooth; however we were sadly disappointed. It was excessively mountainous, rough, Stony, and difficult to find.

At Llantrissent is a fine Ruin,[24] but it is much decayed and the walls in some places are difficult to be traced. We came from thence to Bridgend, which we arrived at with some difficulty, the road being intricate and the People we met with only able to let us know they did not understand English. Dimi Saisenic[25] was always their Answer. A few Miles further led us to Pile, a little Village where we lodged. The house here was full. Every Room exhibited a busy Scene. The jargon of the welch was to us as unintelligible as the Confusion of Babel.

July 8th   2nd Day

We mounted early, passed by a famous seat of Morgham belonging to the antient Family of that Name.[26] The Prospects from the different Spots in these Gardens are very capital, and here is the first Collection of Orange Trees in the Kingdom. We passed by Aberavon a place where there is a large Copper works and to which the Ships come up. We stopd at Briton Ferry to breakfast. Our Landlady was conversible and intelligent. Crossing this Ferry is a fine Landscape a little Epitome of Mount Edgcombe[27] on a Scale of an Inch to a Foot. We rode from thence along the Sea Side on a fine bed of smooth Sand 6 Miles to Swansea.

The Town of Swansea is situated on a pretty River[28] at the Spot where it empties itself into the Sea. The Water is deep enough at low Tide for Vessels to be afloat, altho it flow 16 feet. In the Neighbourhood is a Number of Coal Pits. The Coal is brought down in Barges and shipped on board in the Harbour. 800 Ship Loads are sent off annually, besides the immense Quantities consumed at the Copper and Lead Works, of which there are several within a mile or two of the Town. The most considerable belongs to the Bristol Company,[29] one of whom is William Philips, who is

---

[24] Llantrissent Castle dates from the early thirteenth century when it was constructed with two buildings, the inner smaller than the outer. Fry, *David & Charles Book of Castles*, p. 364.

[25] i.e. 'No English.'

[26] There was a Cistercian Abbey at Margam. At the Dissolution of the Monasteries, the site was bought by Sir Rice Mansel who, in 1552, built a mansion partly on the site of the abbey. This was taken down c. 1782. Lewis, *Topographical Dictionary of Wales*, II, pp. 194–197.

[27] The seat of the Earl of Mount Edgcumbe, Cornwall (see above, p. 94 n. 73).

[28] River Tawe.

[29] The Bristol and Brass Copper Company established a new copper smelting site at White Rock, near Swansea, in 1737. This became one of the principal smelting works of its area during the eighteenth century. Joan Day, *Bristol Brass: A History of the Industry* (Newton Abbot, 1973), p. 68.

now here. We spent half a day with him in viewing the various operations, and the different Processes which the Ore undergoes before it becomes malleable. The Ore is all brought hither either from Cornwal or Anglesey. The Vessels in which it is brought belong to the Company, and they take Coal back. Thus the Copper Works in Cornwal are supplied with that Article. The Lapis Caliminaris[30] with which they mix their Copper for making Brass is brought from Ireland. Here are 43 Furnaces constantly in Blast, all employed in their proper departments, and 150 Men who appear like what we might conceive of the Inhabitants of Pandaemonium. The greatest decorum is however preserved; they all move like a Machine.

Up to this Spot the Vessels come to discharge the Ore, and there is a trough by which the Coal is put in the hold of the Ship. Besides this, there is a less famous one a few hundred yards distant and about a Mile further there is a capital Lead Work.

We took a walk with our Friend William Philips and William Padley[31] to a high Mountain at the Foot of which his works stand. From this Summit we have a grand View of a most fertile and rich Valley, dissected by a beautiful Stream, chequered with Cottages, Gardens, Fields of Corn and verdant Meadows, beautifully inclosed, and mingled with several pretty Woods, bounded by a long range of Mountains, over which more distant ones appear and form an awful Crest to the nearer one's. The Copper Works under us, those contiguous, and some distant one's near Neath, vomit out vast Columns of thick Smoak, which curling as they rise, mount up to the Clouds, with which they mingle and are lost in the immensity of Space. These have a most pleasing effect on the Landscape, and together with the Shipping in the Harbour very much enliven the Scene. On the other Side the boundless interminable Ocean rises to our view, the murmuring Surge plays on the Shelving Beach, its white Crest rolls on in constant unceasing Succession, and a number of Ships like Specks in the great Theatre appear in view. A vast promontory on one Side runs out to the Sea, and on the other, a few high Mountains separated by a little piece of Water from the mainland (calld the Mumbles) while we see at a vast distance the Island of Lundy peeping its head out of the Surface of the great deep, scarcely distinguishable from a Cloud. We descend this Mountain by the Side next the works, a declivity formerly crowded with the thickest Foliage but now bereft of every Species of Verdure and

---

[30] i.e. Calamine.

[31] A Swansea alderman. In 1726 he married one of the six children of Mary Bevan (1698–1784). Audrey Nona Gamble, *A History of the Bevan Family* (London, 1924), p. 24.

without the least appearance of Vegetation, so great is the effect of the Smoak from the Furnaces.

Provisions here are cheap. The Market is amply supplied with Salmon Turbut and other choice Fish at a reasonable rate. The Town is tolerably well laid out containing 500 houses, and is one of the largest in Wales consisting chiefly of two Streets. Here is an excellent place for bathing. This Town like all the others in Glamorganshire has the Ruins of a famous Castle.[32] William the Conqueror having given a Commission to 12 of his Captains who came over to England with him, to make what Conquests in Great Britain they might think proper and appropriate all the Advantages to their private Emolument, landed in this County, took possession of it, and were afterwards called the 12 Knights of Glamorgan.[33] But being in constant Terror of Invasions from the Welch, and being sorly pestered by their little incursions upon the Farms, were obliged for their own Security to build these Fortifications, which being now of no Use are daily approaching to Annihilation. This County is called the Garden of Wales, and were the Farmers as assiduous and careful in the Cultivation of their Lands as they are in some Parts of England the whole Kingdom could not produce a tract of Land equally extensive, so richly variegated with Hills, Vallies, Prospects and Rivers.

July 10th   4th Day

Having stayed a Day and a half at Swansea, viewing the Curiosities of the place, and the remainder of our Time with its Inhabitants, we set off this Morning about 7 O Clock, attended 20 Miles out of Town by Captain Bacon and Syl*vanus* James.[34] But I ought not to omit mentioning the Age of Elizabeth Philips[35] a woman now retaining all her Faculties and Senses, except her hearing, in good Perfection. She is now 94 years of Age, is personable, bulky, and as little wrinkled as the generality of People at 75. Her Eye Sight is remarkably good, and at this day she is capable of writing Poetry, in Sentiment and Stile not of the inferior Order. Another Person of great Age is Friend Inman[36] a sister to Timothy Bevan, 84 years of Age.

[32] There was a motte castle at Swansea, built by Henry Beaumont, Earl of Gower. It was attacked and burned in 1115–1116. Fry, *David & Charles Book of Castles*, p. 380.

[33] Robert Fitzhamon and his twelve Norman knights were invited to Wales c. 1100 by two Welsh noblemen, Encan and Jestyn, to assist them in dispossessing some of the neighbouring Welsh princes. *UBD*, II, p. 639.

[34] Sylvanus James (1753–1813), born at Penzance, became a shopkeeper at Redruth. *DQB*.

[35] A reference, in fact, to Esther Phillips (d. 1778 aged 97). She lived at Swansea and was the widow of Richard Phillips. FLL, Herefordshire, Worcestershire and Wales General Meeting: Burials.

[36] Priscilla Inman (1690–1781) was a sister of Timothy Bevan (1704–1786). She lived all her life in Swansea. Gamble, *History of the Bevan Family*, pp. 24–25.

She is a little deafish, otherwise retains all her Faculties and Senses quite perfect. She is remarkably chearful and conversible and is likewise a Poet.

We all got to Llughor[37] a little Ale House to breakfast, and from hence came to Kidwelly to dine. Here we took leave of our Friends and stopped at Carmarthen to drink Tea. Kidwelly and Carmarthen are both neat well built Towns and have both in them the Ruins of Castles.[38] We came on to a little Village where we supd and lodged. The Country thro which we have this day passed is not equal to the last County. It is however far from being a disagreeable County. The black Cattle graze here in great Multitudes, and Prodigious Flocks of Sheep are fed here.

July 11th   5th Day

The Road from the little Village at which we lodged to Narberth is finely interspersed with that Sort of Variety which always makes a pleasing Landscape. Hills and Vallies are necessary, but unless they be well cultivated they dont answer. Woods are absolutely essential; and inclosures and Cottages; yet all these without Water are like a furnished Room without a Looking Glass. All these we had and sometimes a little Sheet of Water to compleat the View.

We breakfasted at Narberth, a Place much more pleasant for its Situation, than the neatness of the Buildings, or the Spaciousness of the Streets. This Town standing on the Side of an Hill makes it a pretty object at a Distance. The whiteness of all the houses in Wales has a good Effect in the Contrast it forms with the Vegetable Class but what adds most to the beauty of this place is a Castle in Ruins.[39] The Sides are almost even with the Ground but the Towers stand nearly perfect. The ragged battlements over grown with Ivy look very pleasing and chearful.

We breakfasted at Narberth and came along to Haverford West by a most beautiful and fertile Valley watered by pretty Streams, and thickly inhabited. We passed a noble and magnificent Ruin, over which was cast in beautiful grandeur an unfading Mantle of Ivy.

The Welch Tongue contains 27 Letters. Besides the English are ch, dd, ff, ng, ll, ph, th, seven being double.

---

[37] Lougher.

[38] The first stonework of Kidwelly Castle is of the 1270s, though it was originally a Norman earthwork castle of c. 1106. The first notice of Carmarthen Castle is c. 1116. It was in ruins by the eighteenth century. Fry, *David & Charles Book of Castles*, pp. 359–360; Lewis, *Topographical Dictionary of Wales*, I, pp. 190, 443.

[39] The ruins of a stone castle built at Narberth in the thirteenth century are near the site of a Norman motte castle of c. 1100, which had been destroyed by the Welsh in 1116. Fry, *David & Charles Book of Castles*, p. 367.

A, is sounded as in English: Man, Can, Dan.

B, as in English, Book.

C, as in Can, come, never as in Cistern.

CH, as X in the English.

D, as in English Door.

DH, as Th, This, thou.

E, as in Men, Ten.

F, as in have, Love.

EF, as in Fowl.

G, as in Get.

NG, as in Long.

H, as in hand.

I, as in Beer.

L, as in Law.

LI, has a Sound peculiar to the welch, very difficult.

M, as in Man.

N, as in None, can.

O, as in gone.

P, as People.

PH, as Fool.

R, as Ramble.

S, as Sick.

T, as Hat, Tattle.

TH, as thick.

U, as I in English, this.

W, as O, to, who.

V, as in English U, further.

The Grammar is systematic, copious, and the welch say more independent than any other.

July 12th   6th Day

Attended by our good Friend Abram Clibborn with Son, we mounted after an early breakfast and rode through a very charming Country to Hubberon[40] a pretty Sea Port of inconsiderable Trade, situate on the River Milford, contiguous to a safe and commodious Cove, where the Vessels belonging to Haverford West generally lie for a fair wind. Here we got the King's barge, and were attended by 10 Men. The wind and Tide were both in our favor, so that we were not long in sailing up the River about 11 Miles. A [more] beautiful River cannot well be conceived, in some places widening out to 2 or 3 Miles width, then again contracting itself to about

---

[40] Hubberston.

half a mile, the Shore steep and bold, either richly cultivated or cloathed with the most lovely hanging woods; Cottages dispersed on every hand, a number of little Villages on the declivities of the Hills, several Gentlemen's Seats, a beautiful Fortification, and a fine Castle far decayed, all present themselves to our view. The Promontories and Capes jutting out into the River, the Land then again receding and forming large and small Bay's, the Number of Creeks which empty into it, afford the finest Harbours in the World for Shipping, and the Water is sufficiently deep for any Ship in the Navy to lie afloat at low Water, and the Tide flows about 16 Feet.

100,000 Vessels may lie here with the greatest Ease Convenience and Safety. From the particular Formation of the Land, and its repeated projection far out, as well as the Serpentine Direction of the River, always hinder us from seeing half a Mile either way, so that we are continually preserved in a Sort of Bason, and the Prospects always varying are beautiful beyond description. We took a Quantity of Shrimps down in the Boat by which we were regald till our Return, which was not until 6 O Clock, having been near 7 hours on the water. We landed at Hubberson, and made a most capital Dinner on some Mackarel and Fowls. We mounted soon after and came back to Haverford by a Road different from the one we went to it by, and got home in good [time] to sup with our Friend Clibborn, where I set up till towards Day.

The Origin of St. David the titular Saint of Wales.[41] When this Island was first enlightened with the Beams of Christianity several episcopal Sees were instituted, three of which were Archbishopricks.[42] That which comprehended the Principality of Wales was established at Caerleon in Monmouthshire where Dubricius[43] presided as Metropolitan: he was succeeded by St. David his Disciple who was no less famous for his Piety than his Valour. He was Son to Xantus,[44] Prince of Wales and Uncle to

[41] St. David (d. c. 601) is commemorated on 1 March. He seems to have been a leading figure in the monastic revival in the Celtic countries of Europe in the sixth century, but the details of his life are clouded in legend. Jones and Dixon, *Macmillan Dictionary of Biography*, p. 225.

[42] i.e. Canterbury, York, Caerleon.

[43] Dubricius was a sixth century Welsh ecclesiastic. He appears with the authority of a bishop in various South Wales monasteries 'but with no hint furnished of the place from which or the sphere within which he exercised his sway.' John Edward Lloyd, *A History of Wales from the Earliest Times to the Edwardian Conquest* (2 vols., London, 1911; 3rd edn., new impression, 1954), I, p. 147.

[44] Xantus, according to legend, was the father of St. David and Prince of Cereticu (Cardiganshire). Geoffrey of Monmouth makes St. David the uncle of King Arthur. Ivor H. Evans, ed., *Brewer's Dictionary of Phrase and Fable* (London, 1974), p. 302.

King Arthur.[45] These Endowments endeared him to the Welch, and the Signal Victory he obtained over the Saxons on the first of March gained him the greatest Veneration.[46] The Saxons in this Overthrow wore Leeks in their heads to distinguish them from their Enemies. But the Welch animated by the Conduct of their Commander totally routed the troublesome Invaders and each of the Brave Britons graced his head with the Leeks of the vanquished Foe. That day is still greatly honored and called to his time St. David's Day.

[45] King Arthur may represent the folk memory of one or more Romanized British chieftains who, after the departure of the legions, put up a heroic resistance to the invading Anglo-Saxons.

[46] A slightly puzzling reference. Professor J. Beverley Smith, Department of Welsh History, University College of Wales, Aberystwyth, tells me that he knows of nothing 'in the authentic source material or in legend to explain the reference to a battle where St. David defeated the Saxons on 1 March. Saint David's day falls on that day, of course, but the whole emphasis of the material is on the Saint's sanctity and good works, and nothing of the Christian militant.' (Letter to me dated 14 July 1989).

Wales
July 13th   7th Day

We came to Haverford West without a single Letter, or without the Acquaintance of any one Person, yet such are the kindness and hospitality of the inhabitants of this Island that we were most courteously received by John Lewis[1] and Abram Clibborn[2] who divided us between them. My Companion went to John Lewis's and I made my abode at A*braham* Clibborn and it was with great difficulty we could this day get away from the place.

Haverford is a dirty irregular Town, built on the Side of an hill, illy paved; it is however a place of considerable Trade; has a good key; to which Vessels of 12 or 14 feet Water come up with Ease. But the Vessels belonging to this Port chiefly load in Milford Haven a few miles below. 800 Vessels load out of the Haven every year. The Markets here for Provisions are very abundant and reasonable. Fowls are sold for about 5d. a Couple of Ducks from 6 to 7d and all other Sorts of Produce in proportion.

After dining with my Friend Clibborn, we mounted at 4 O Clock. We had got a few Miles on the Road towards Cardigan when we through Carelessness or Absence missed our Way, and got into a boggy swamp. After passing it and jumping over Gates and Hedges we at length got into the road again, which led over the Mountains whereon the Clouds had made themselves beds of Rest; these Clouds eclipsed our Prospect, or we should have had an almost boundless View. The Prospect was more contracted yet pleasing from accidental Circumstances while the Summits were involved in mist and darkness. The Sun shone in the most brilliant manner upon all the Vales around, where the Corn Fields, Meadow Grounds and scattered Huts, with thatched Roofs made an agreeable variety. The Road was craggy, steep, and disagreeable, and the Stage 30 Miles made us feel rather uncomfortable on Account of our horses.

---

[1] John Lewis (1716–1789) was a Quaker minister from the age of twenty-one. *DQB*.

[2] Abraham Clibborn was a Dublin merchant who retired to Haverfordwest. He was a partner in a chinaworks at Bristol. Hugh Owen, *Two Centuries of Ceramic Art in Bristol . . .* (Gloucester, 1873), pp. 21, 23.

However, we called at a litle Ale house and drank a refreshing dish of Tea and got into Cardigan in very good time in the Evening.

Pembroke is a County where a greater Proportion of the people speak English than in any other County in Wales. We leave it, on crossing a Bridge, which leads over a little inlet from the Sea, by which Pembroke is separated from Cardiganshire.

Cardigan is in a fine Valley encircled by a spacious Amphitheatre of Mountains. The Town is tolerably well built, consisting chiefly of one Street: about 300 houses. We put up at a good Inn for this part of the Country, but our Beds were not quite free from Bugs. In this Town is a noble Castle, built on a Rock now tottering from its Case, and mouldering to Dust, though sheltered from the inclemency of the Air by a Garb of green Ivy.[3] There is likewise at Haverford a Castle[4] in the same Situation, and a Convent in still further decay,[5] which I forgot to note in their proper places.

July 14th   1st Day

This day impresses me more strongly with the Idea of being in a foreign Land than any since I left my native Country. The Face of the Country is totally different from the Part of Wales we have before seen, a rude succession of Mountains, whose Tops are uninhabited but by black Cattle and Sheep and here and there a little hut, but this seldom unless we descend into the valleys. There indeed are Clusters of humble habitations whose Walls are of Mud and Sticks, and whose Roofs are covered with Straw. Solemn Silence holds her peaceful Domain, uninterrupted but by the Shepherds Song, who are tending the Flocks on every hill. And if the Face of the Country wear a different Garb, the Aspect, the Features, the Dress, the mode of living, and the Language are as different. We several times lost our way, and when we found the stragling Traveller on the Road it was seldom he could sufficiently understand us, to know what information we wanted. However sometimes finding the Road, and at other times where it was difficult to trace losing it, and now and then

---

[3] There have been two castles at Cardigan. The first, a Norman enclosure of c. 1093, was destroyed in 1231. The second, built c. 1240, became the administrative centre of the new shire of Cardigan c. 1279. Repairs were carried out in later reigns. Fry, *David & Charles Book of Castles*, p. 335; Colvin, *History of the King's Works*, II, pp. 590–591.

[4] Haverfordwest Castle was first built in the early twelfth century. It is strategically placed on a ridge about 80 feet above the River Cleddau. Colvin, *History of the King's Works*, II, pp. 670–671.

[5] Not a convent, in fact, but a priory of Black Canons, originally founded by Robert de Hurlfordd, and situated on the western bank of the River Cleddau. It flourished until the Dissolution of the Monasteries. Lewis, *Topographical Dictionary of Wales*, I, p. 401.

getting into a boggy Swamp, we at length arrived safe at Llanbeder, having stopped at a little dirty Inn on the Road to get our breakfasts.

Llanbeder[6] is a very little Market Town not half so big as the Villages in England: the houses built of Stone or Mud and the Tops thatched. One great Fault of all the houses we find in Wales is the want of Window Lights. We are always as we are now obliged to sit close to the Window, the other parts of the Room not giving sufficient Light to write by.

At Llanbeder we dined from whence we came along a most delightful Valley all the way to Tregarron.[7] On our road we stopped at a little Church where the pious Pastor was offering up his Supplications; and if we may judge of the integrity of their hearts by an apparent devoutness, by their prostrate Posture, by the attention they paid to what was delivered, and the Sobriety and awfulnesses of their Countenances we must at least judge favorably of them, and indeed own that their Conduct in these Respects is worthy the Example of many other Societies of Christians more enlightened and less uncultivated.

At Tregarron we found ourselves reduced to the Necessity of staying all Night. The horses had a long day's Journey. There was no Stage in our way at less than 22 Miles distance, the Roads rough, difficult to be found, and very mountainous. The Inn we are at is indeed miserable in its appearance, but worse in its Contents: dirty Rooms, dirty furniture, and dirty Victuals, dirty Beds, and dirty People; shocking Stabling for our horses, no Straw for them to lie on; and not a handful of hay for them to eat. Nor could the whole Town furnish them with it, whether it was because the Man could not be credited with as much, or whether there was none to be had, I know not. The poor horses like ourselves must put up with some inconvenience; there is no travelling without it.

July 15th   2nd Day

We made tolerably well out last Night at the Inn, alias the Ale house, and after taking a draught of Milk we mounted our Rosinante's, when alas the Fatigue of the Journey and the enormous hills we had to ascend, together with the miserable Fare the poor Brutes had last Evening met with, my horse Galton was compleatly worn down. Our Guide (for we were obliged to take a Guide with us) having a nice little Pony to which I took a Fancy, I asked him the Price. He told me £6. I offered him £5.10 and took the horse instantly. Our Servant can lead Galton to Chester where I intend to dispose of him.

Over hills and Mountains on which the Clouds reposed their big

---

[6] Lampeter.
[7] Tregaron.

swollen heads, and thro a Country of not totally yet nearly uninhabited and almost uninhabitable, we came 12 Miles to a little Ale house worse by far than the one we last Night lodged at. We however got a very notable Breakfast. We next set off for Tallypont[8] a little Market Town consisting of about 12 houses, a much smarter place than the two last. Our Landlord kept an Ostler. The former Landlords we took for Ostlers and indeed an Englishman though an Ostler would be ashamed to appear half so shabby.

The Country grows more and more wild, its mountains still higher, and its general appearance far more romantic, abundantly less populous than I could have expected, the Hills inhabited by immense Numbers of Sheep and Cattle. In the lowly Vallies the Cottages of the humble peasants tell us that one half the World knows not how the other half live: thatched houses universally, and fortunate indeed are we to find an house Wall composed of any other Materials than Clay and Sticks, in most of which the Ruthless Storms and old relentless time have made sad havock. The inclosures for the most part are banks thrown up on some of which Hedges are to be found. The Vallies generally are watered by a Serpentine Stream and their appearance from high Hills is always pleasing. They give a Variety to the Scene. Mountains piled on Mountains in the most grand Confusion serve for Protection, and their Barreness makes the low Lands appear far more rich.

We do not find in Wales the same fine Clusters and Rows of Trees in hedges and about the houses that we do in England: and this makes the Face of the Country (except in the South part of Wales) much less charming and beautiful: yet we behold a prodigious Number of large Woods on the declivities of their Hills, so that Wales cannot properly be called a naked Country. But the woods are badly disposed, for want of being considered as an Ornament.

The Roads, besides being mountainous, are rough and craggy; crooked to an extreme. But Turnpikes are introduced and there is no doubt from the Advantages which England has received from this most capital Improvement but that Wales will universally adopt them.[9]

We had this Afternoon a most delightful Ride from Machynleth to Talypont, about 12 Miles distant in a lovely Valley, thro several very extensive Groves. On one Side, the high mountains raising their almost perpendicular heads, directly over us with hanging Woods of Oak. Below us, a fine fertile Valley watered by a plentiful Stream, and beyond it a fine

---

[8] Talybont.

[9] The first Welsh turnpikes were constructed in Monmouthshire in the 1750s. They were soon extended throughout South Wales. Moelwyn Williams, *The Making of the South Wales Landscape* (London, 1975), p. 148.

Chain of Mountains but with many a broken Link. Before us an Avenue of great extent, disclosing very enormous Mountains on each Side and terminating with more distant and fantastic Mountains till we come within 2 or 3 Miles of Machynleth, when Beauty added to the grandest Sublimity renders the Prospect compleat. The Road here is half way up a prodigious Cliff and 'tis impossible to say whether the perpendicular Rocks which suspend over your heads and threaten to crush the Globe itself with the Fall, or whether the dizzy height down which you look is most terrifying.

Between the Foot of these Mountains and those on the opposite Side is a Valley through which winds in the oddest Meanders a beautiful Stream, where several Vessels are now seen. This forms a delightful Carpet on every Side of which Chaos itself as if chained to Stability in its frantic Career rises into Dominion, and erects his craggy and conic Spires, in terrible Array, lifted on the Summit of the Mountains and involving itself in flames of smoking Clouds.

Machynleth is situated in this Amphitheatre. It is a pretty Town, and the Spot on which it stands can only be equalled by the Vale of Keswick; to which it bears a strong Resemblance. It is not a little remarkable that there should be so striking a difference between the People and their Customs and Manners of those who live in that part of Wales that we have for a few Days past been in, and that part contiguous to the great Post Roads.

We have this Evening got to an Inn, where there are every Convenience and Necessary, merely because it is in a road of great Traffic. The People can speak English, and there is a riddance of that dirt which we generally have met with in the Welch Inns. A Man would form a very different Idea of this Country by going thro the great Turnpike Roads only; he should make traverses to and fro.

July 16th   3rd Day

A Delightful Morning ushered in the Day, and gave us expectation of a fine Sky; but such is the variability of this mountainous Climate, that a few hours spreads the horison round with black and loaded Clouds. We however got a few miles on before it began; attended by a clear and beautiful River which runs in wild Fury, over the rude rocks we ride a few Miles. The Prospect is sublime and grand, perpetually changing.

We got off our horses two or three miles from Machynleth to look at a fine Cataract, where Nature has burst a Mountain of immense Size in twain to give Vent to a small but beautiful Stream. In its Course some ponderous and enormous Rocks which have rolled down from the craggy precipice above impede its Course for a Moment, when it receives fresh Fury and rolls down in a steep and perpendicular Cascade, foaming with rage and white with Agitation.

We are led on a few Miles further through a most enchanting Valley, where the Declivities are loaded with Woods, of every Size, and the Earth entirely hid from us by the underwood which grows in ab origine wildness. Here the Mountains rise in long successive Chains above the Clouds in the most awful and sublime Stile. They are dressed in all the horrors that the imagination can suggest and excite Terror in the Minds of the Spectator.

At length however we are destined to soar on more lofty heights. By a road rocky in its base, paved with small and sharp Stones, and sometimes so narrow as barely to admit our horses a passage we ascend the mighty hills, and after walking (for we can only walk) a few miles, we reach the Summit. But how great was our Surprise to find this Summit only the Foundation of the Gigantic Caddyr Idris (alias Arthurs Chair).[10] In the utmost irregularity and romanticity this Mountain which yields only the magnificent Snowdon rears its exulting head above the neighbouring Hills, and seems to glory in its Superiority. With great Ingenuity has Wilson taken off this mountain in a capital Painting and a fine engraving of it is published.[11]

Not without some perturbation of mind did we descend this frightful height and entered the Town of Dolgelly[12] about 11 O Clock; soon after which John Lewis junior[13] of Haverford called on us. We went to dine with him at Tydden y Garrig where he had lately married. The Family received us with great Politeness and would not let us think of departing that Night. We took a walk to a Brook half a mile distant from the house, where several pretty Cascades tumble over the Rocks in a most pleasing manner.

July 17th   4th Day

We rose early fully intending to take our departure, but the Family plied us with invitations in so pressing a manner that while we were hesitating whether to stay or not, a Message arrived from one Squire Vaughan for all the Family with the two strangers to dine with him. This we accepted. He has a fine Seat about 1 Mile from Dolgelly, with an estate of about £6,000 per annum.[14] He entertained us in the most splendid and hospitable

---

[10] Caddyr Idris reaches at its greatest elevation a height of 2,900 feet.

[11] Richard Wilson's painting of Caddyr Idris is in the Tate Gallery. It was completed c. 1765–1767. David H. Solkin, *Richard Wilson: The Landscape of Reaction* (London, 1982), pp. 223–224.

[12] Dolgellau.

[13] John Lewis junior (b. 1742) was the fourth child of John Lewis (see above, p. 216 n. 1), *DQB*.

[14] Evan Lloyd Vaughan (c. 1709–1791), of Corsygedol, Merionethshire, was M.P. for Merioneth between 1774 and 1791. Namier and Brooke, *History of Parliament: The House of Commons 1754–1790*, III, pp. 575–576.

Manner, were serenaded the whole day with the Harp, an instrument of Musick, more used here than all the others. We lodged this Evening at his house and Early the next Day say

July 18th   5th Day

Bid our worthy host Adieu and attended by John Lewis and a Servant Squire Vaughan had sent to shew us the Way, we decamped. Our first Visit was about 5 Miles over the Mountains to two grand and noble Cataracts; compared with which all the other Falls of Water which I have seen in Great Britain are trivial and dwarfish. These if they did not remind me of our boasted Wonder, the Niagara Fall,[15] they at least did of the Montmorency[16] and La Choudière,[17] to which they yield but trifling Superiority. The first (I know not the Name of *either* and if I did I should be ignorant how to spell it, and if I were to write it I should be puzzled to read it) the first we arrive at after descending a dangerous precipice of prodigious depth. But we are amply rewarded by the beautiful Scene which is now presented to our View with all its Graces. On each side two Mountains rise with peculiar Grandeur and stretch their Awful Summits into the Clouds, which form a becoming Mantle. While these Clouds like curling Flames decorate their heads, the declivities are adorned with hanging Woods of Nature's favorite Choice.

In this deeply sequestered Vale over Rocks and Crags runs the enraged Stream till it arrive at the dreadful Precipice which throws it about 20 feet perpendicular to another Rock's which receive it in its Lap. But unable to retain the bountiful Stream it runs to another, which, equally unable to bear the constant Supply, with chearfulness imparts it to the Gulph below, where it runs on over trembling Cataracts whose Consequence is dwindled to nothing on Account of the great Superiority of their parent Fall.

This Whole Scene is awfully sublime. The Cataract pouring over three successive Rocks all winding like a Stair Case as they descend gives a pleasing variety to the view. The first Fall is about 20 feet, the 2nd about 30 and the last about 25. The Water by the time it gets to the bottom by these repeated Agitations seems to have lost all its Properties as one element, but like a Confusion of the whole exhibits a very Chain white with Ferment and Rage. The Vapour rises into a curling Cloud and is lifted up till it

---

[15] The Niagara Falls are rather more than halfway down the Niagara River. They are in two sections, the American (167 feet high; 1,000 feet wide) and the Canadian (158 feet high; 2,600 feet wide).

[16] The Montmorency Falls, near the mouth of the St. Lawrence River and just above Quebec City, are 275 feet high.

[17] The Choudière Falls, 130 feet high, are four miles from the mouth of the St. Lawrence River, near Ottawa City.

mingle with other Clouds and becomes lost in the great immensity of Space. Not distant from this 200 yards is another very fine Cascade, more than equal to the last in Height, equal to it in Situation; but not in the Quantity of water, not in the manner of its tumbling. This Fall is not quite perpendicular. It here and there in its Progress down meets with a little projected Rock against which with incessant Rage it strikes. The pool into which it pours is deep; the placid and calm manner in which it steals insensibly away is charming. From this too rises a large column of Vapours like smoak from some great Furnace. This Fall is about 100 Feet. This and the other are on two branches of the same River which unite about $\frac{1}{4}$ Mile below.

From hence after ascending the Steep Rocks over Hills and Vallies thro a most Romantic Country we went to Tan y Bwlch, a little Village, to dine, situated in a lovely Spot and commanding a most distant View. A few Miles from this Place conducted us to the head of Cardigan Bay, at which place *John* Lewis parted with us, and we were obliged to procure a Guide to lead us across the Sand to a Bridge called Pont Aber Glass Lynn. This Bridge crosses a River which divides the County of Merioneth from Carnarvon. A more beautiful and romantic Spot cannot be conceived: on one Side the Sea expanding to our View a prospect boundless and interminable; on the other the proudest Mountains of Wales rise with Majestic Horror, piercing the Canopy of the Heavens with their pointed, craggy and irregular Summits. Half way up the Sheep and Cattle chequer the Landscape. Here and there a little Cottage, the Residence of some solitary and philosophic Peasant with smoaking Chimney excites our admiration. Above, Vegetation dare not disclose her sprouting Foliage. Black Rocks and enormous Stones against which the Clouds for Ages past have been beating have driven every particle of Soil into the Valleys. These only appear on the Mountains in huge Piles ready to roll down on the gaping Traveller, while the Yawning and shelving Sides threaten to close in and swallow us up for ever.

But let us extend our Prospect a little further on and behold the heads of other more distant Mountains rearing their crested heads in grand Gradation, one beyond another, wrapping their Summits in the Smoaking Clouds and above all these the Royal Snowden lifting his exulting Dome and raising the Envy of his Subject Hills, while they bow with humility before him conscious of their inferiority. At our Feet falls a beautiful Cascade, roaring under a fine Arched Bridge, shaking the Caverns of the Rocks and reverberating with Echo's from the craggy Sides. Of this Scene Wilson has made a most inimitable Landscape.[18]

---

[18] Wilson painted two versions of 'Snowdon from Llyn Nantle': one is in the Walker Art Gallery, Liverpool; the other is in the Castle Museum, Nottingham. Solkin, *Richard Wilson*, pp. 11, 225–226.

We have now a dark gloomy and dismal Road in a melancholly Valley where nothing meets us but black and frightful Mountains and at the Foot an hoarse murmuring Brook for several Miles to a little Village, where not an inhabitant could speak English and where we could not procure a dish of Tea. This is the most humble Inn we have yet accosted. However, Wales is famous for Ale, not a Cottage but can furnace us with it; and with the Ale and a Slice of Bread and Butter after our fatiguing Journey we made a most comfortable Repast.

We had yet 10 Miles to go; the Road was miserably stony and hilly. We passed by the Foot of Snowdon and should most certainly have ascended it but Night would have overtaken us in the Expedition, it being 5 Miles to the Top. Besides, the Clouds would have so much intercepted our Prospect as to have hindered our seeing the Valley's below. This Mountain is [1,190] yards perpendicular Height, by much the highest in Great Britain. As We did not ascend it we can only speak of the Prospect it affords on a clear day from the Accounts the inhabitants have given us. They tell us that Ireland, the Isle of Man and the Land of Scotland besides a most extended View of all Wales and a great Part of England may be plainly discovered. A Sight of this Sort would have detained us some Days, but the uncertainty of clear Weather in this very capricious Clime without any expectation of a Day suitable for our Purpose made us (however) not without Reluctance pass it by.

At its Foot is a pretty Lake of several Miles extent, on the Side of which a magnificent perpendicular Mountain rises in an awful manner. We got into Carnarvon about 8 in the Evening.

July 19th   6th Day

We embarked in a little boat across the River Abermenay from Wales to the Island of Anglesea distant from Carnarvon about 2 Miles; and on the Banks of the Island took a walk. Few Prospects equal, none can exceed this for an agreeable Mixture of the beautiful and Sublime. Wilson thought so when he saw it and painted it.[19]

Carnarvon is a pretty town, stands on the Conflux of the Abermenay and a little Stream which empties into it. It is walled round and there is a Number of Turrets equidistant from each other in the Wall, some of which have decayed and are covered with Ivy. The part of the Wall next us runs along the River on a fine Stone Key, which is made use of for a Parade. On a little Mount at the very point of the two Rivers stands a magnificent and

---

[19] Richard Wilson painted three pictures of Caernarvon Castle (dated c. 1744–1745, c. 1764–1765 and c. 1765–1766). It is not clear which of the three Fisher knew. *Ibid.*, pp. 148–149, 223, 226.

spacious Castle of Sexagonal Form, and with six lofty Towers.[20] The Arches are Gothic. The County of Carnarvon gives £200 per Annum to keep this Castle in Repair; but Alas! Old time will not be bribed for £200 a year to stay his Depredations. Some of the Towers have already experienced the obstinate Power of his destructive hand. Several Arches have fallen in, the Battlements are losing their Form, and the Ivy is weaving it Cloathing. This is a delightful Object and forms a fine Contrast with a thick Wood which is just beyond it, a River only between darkened by the Verdure of the Copse, and creates the most perfect Mirror imaginable in which we view this noble Castle inverted, in the highest Perfection.

A little further to the right is the Brow of a beautiful Hill projecting itself into the River and on the Summit is a Summer house which has a fine effect. But what most of all adds to the Grandeur of this Scene are the distant Mountains piled one on another in grand disorder and above them all once more we see the Lofty Snowden, and half way up, the Clouds resting on his Lap; and to compleat the View and leave it wanting no accomplishment a fine Cluster of Vessels ride at Anchor in the Harbour, and others are sailing to and fro in the Silver Lake.

We returned to Carnarvon and mounted about 12. It is a true Saying that People who enjoy an uninterrupted Succession of Health Know not the value of it. I never was more sensible of the Difference between good and bad Roads than now, and never more highly enjoyed a smooth and level Road; and therefore concluded that People who always travel the turnpike Roads in England know not the benefit of them.

We have now a most lovely ride along the beautiful Banks of the fertile Abermenay, a fine River from one to Eleven Miles in width, sometimes promontories jutting out towards the opposite Shore, at other times retiring and forming a fine bay. The Country richly improved and rising with exact regularity from the Waters Edge; the distant Hills occasion a proper back Ground and add to the Beauty of the Prospects: no longer Walls of Stone, sad token of wretched Land, but verdant inclosures of the Hazel the Thorn and the Alder. Several Gentlemen's Seats and Parks we meet with in our progress.

We dined at Bangor one of the four Bishopricks of Wales,[21] a tolerably

---

[20] Caernarvon Castle, the town with its walls and gates, and the quay to which most of the heavy building materials were brought by coastal shipping, seem to have been part of a single building operation begun under Edward I in 1283. A. J. Taylor, *Caernarvon Castle and Town Walls* (HMSO, London, rev. edn., 1964), p. 6; Colvin, *History of the King's Works*, I, pp. 369–395.

[21] The see of Bangor was founded in 550. The first bishop was St. Deiniol. The three other Welsh bishoprics are St. Asaph, St. David's and Llandaff. *Imperial Gazetteer of England and Wales*, I, pp. 101–102.

well built Town. The Cathedral[22] is inferior to the common run of the English Churches. At this Place is kept the great Ferry for Passengers who come and go, over from, and to, Ireland by the way of Hollyhead. Still continuing in Sight of this Noble River, with the Island of Anglesea on our left, disclosing great Luxuriance, and a whole fleet of small and large Vessels gliding on the Surface of the Stream we arrive at Aber Conway, a pretty Town on a River at high Water a mile in width, but now not 100 Yards. This is a walled Town, has three or four Gates by which we enter it, and 15 or 16 Towers in different Parts. At one Corner is a noble Castle; which like all the Castles in Wales is in a State of Decay, being built before Fire Arms had found their way into the world.[23] They are now for the most part defenceless, and are therefore permitted to crumble to their Native Dust. The brave Welch however refused to admit Tyrant Oliver into their City till he had demolished one of the principal Towers of this Castle.[24] The broken Sides have fallen down and lie at the Foot of the Mountain on which the Castle is erected. The standing Part, as it projects over the Foundation, looks very Frightful.

From this Castle we have a fine view of Water, Meadows, Woods, Mountains and several Gentlemen's Seats. We had here the Ferry to cross in which we were detained near an hour and when we got over had half a Mile to ride over very dangerous Quicksands. From this Side, the Castle, the Walls of the Town, and a fine Wood behind it look grand. The Castle is just in sufficient Ruin to make it a pleasing object in the Landscape. The Stone is white. This forms a proper Contrast with the Ivy which is carelessly thrown over the Battlements and the back Mountain of hanging Woods.

We had now 10 Miles to ride and the Curfew had tolled. On the Banks of Denbighshire, which overlook the Irish Sea, we ride along. Nought disturbs the silent Night but the gentle Murmurs of Surge which plays upon the Beach and sometimes echoes from the Rocks. We arrived at Abergely[25] at 10 O Clock and after eating a comfortable Supper and

---

[22] Bangor Cathedral is probably situated on the site of a monastery founded by St. Deiniol in the sixth century. It was originally built in the period 1120–1139, and is now a mixture of pre-Reformation and Victorian work. M. L. Clarke, *Bangor Cathedral* (Cardiff, 1969), pp. 9–39.

[23] The building of Conway Castle began in 1283. In that year the English armies of Edward I completed the conquest of Snowdonia and terminated the rule of the Welsh princes. A. J. Taylor, *Conway Castle and Town Walls* (HMSO, London, rev. edn., 1961), p. 5; Colvin, *History of the King's Works*, I, pp. 337–354.

[24] The town and derelict castle of Conway were held for the King throughout the First Civil War. Colonel Carter's Parliamentarians overran the town on 9 Aug. 1646 and the fortress surrendered on 18 Nov. 1646 after a heavy bombardment. Peter Gaunt, *The Cromwellian Gazetteer* (Gloucester, 1987), p. 189.

[25] Abergele.

smoaking a comfortable Pipe we resigned our Bodies to forgetting Morpheus. For the first time for many a long year I layed in a Wicket Cradle.

July 20th   7th Day

We divided our March today into two Stages and therefore took our Breakfast before we decamped. The Road now appears very different from what it did a few days ago. Three Coaches and Chaises are now at the door of our Inn, and having for many Days been where a Carriage was never dragged, the Sight is altogether a Novelty. The Country too losing its wildness assumes a soft and pastoral Aspect and tells us of our approach to the more favoured part of Britain's happy Realm.

We came through St. Asaph. Its dwindling Situation would make one believe its being a Bishropric did it little Service. It is a little Town indeed not containing one hundred houses. The Cathedral[26] is a very paltry building and if my Lord Bishop were proud of outward Appearances, its insignificance would wound his Pride not a little.

The River Dee now opened all its Charms. A fine range of cultivated Land led down to it. Beyond Lancashire appeared but at too great a distance to investigate any of its Beauties, the River Mercey only varying its appearance and throwing one Gleam of Light into the dark undistinguished Mass. By the Side of the noble Dee we rode on to Holywel where we dined at a very capital Inn. From hence we came to Northop, when considering that we had now rode 600 Miles on horseback in the last 3 Weeks and that we had not indulged ourselves in that Space of time with a Chaise, we absolutely considered ourselves a little fatigued and agreed Nem: Con: to treat ourselves to a Post-Chaise. We accordingly got one and I dont remember to have enjoyed a Luxury of any kind with greater zest than I did this ride of about 12 Miles, though in the Execution of it one of our horses fell down, and some ugly Consequences had nearly ensued.

A Mile from Chester is the Boundary between Wales and England. Wales, Farewell. Long may thy Sons and thy Daughters experience the blessings of Peace and Plenty, may the Virtues of thy Inhabitants continue, and may they banish those Vices which the Remains of Barbarism and Uncivilisation only have left among them. May Trade and Commerce flourish among you and may the Arts and Sciences attend them. Farewel! And Farewel!

---

[26] It is believed that a monastery and episcopal see were founded at St. Asaph c. 560. The bishopric later fell into abeyance, but was refounded in 1143. The cathedral was rebuilt in the period 1284–1381. Edward Hubbard, *The Buildings of Wales: Clwyd (Denbighshire and Flintshire)* (London, 1986), pp. 435–444.

Few Nations have exhibited greater instances of their Courage and perseverance than the Welch; but whether the Motives for which they endured all the horrors of repeated Wars and for which they suffered every Species of Calamity could warrant them in the Eye of Policy is much to be doubted. It certainly would have been more consistent with their true interests to have entered into Alliance with the English long before they did. Their Country would have been more highly cultivated, more populous, and the inhabitants would have long since emerged from that State of Barbarism and Ignorance which Candor obliges us to own are too predominant.

The Men of inferior Station are Brutal in their Exercises and Amusements. Those whose Circumstances would admit a more refined Education remain unlearned. Few Charitable institutions are formed. No Academies for the Education of Youth. Those few who receive an Education are sent to England. No Arts or Manufactures are established among them except of Minerals and a trifling Manufactury in the Neighbourhood of Dolgelly for a woolen Cloth worn by the Soldiers.[27] Lands remain uncultivated. Those which do not evidence a want of Oeconomy and Management. The Usage those poor unhappy Sons of Wretchedness experience who are driven by Storms on their Coast witness their want of humanized Feelings.

Their Language wants much methodizing; it is uncouth in its Sound. The most difficult of all others to pronounce, there are 27 Letters in it, some of which can be of no Use, as all Sounds may be brought about without them.[28] They have a great Number of irregular Verbs. They have no Articles like the English or the French, but like the Latin their Cases are known by the termination of the Substantives.

They are generally dirty, and the Itch is a Disorder prevalent among them, and Care is necessary lest the Traveller should receive some inconvenience from its contagious Property.[29] Ignorant as the poorest Wretch among them is, he knows that the Welch are the only People of Great Britain who can boast a pure uncontaminated Blood unmixed with Saxon and Danish. They too know how much to value themselves for this immaculateness, but I doubt whether this have been any advantage to them. The English, by their mixture with other Nations, have got rid of

---

[27] The woollen industry was active throughout North Wales and each district had its own speciality. 'Strong cloth' or 'high country cloth' was made in the neighbourhood of Dolgelly. All types of wool were used to manufacture this cloth on the loom. The fabrics were woollens made from short, carded wool. A. H. Dodd, *The Industrial Revolution in North Wales* (Cardiff, 1933), pp. 235, 237, 238.

[28] For the letters of the Welsh alphabet see above, p. 213.

[29] i.e. scabies.

many peculiaritys in their Sentiments and Tempers. A Sort of Liberality has pervaded that part of the Kingdom which the Welch know nothing of.

The Welch have one Characteristic which distinguishes them and to which there is among them scarcely an Exception: their quick, Fiery Resentment, and their implacable unappeasable Disposition when it once has become determind. All other Faults I could forgive them, but the Consequences of this are too mischievous to be palliated.

They seem more than any other people to disregard the transactions of their Rulers. While every other Part of the Kingdom is distracted with the public Situation of Affairs, a Civil War raging throughout America, while this is a Topic of every Circle in England or Scotland, Wales, regardless of the great Machine of State, wisely leave their Superiors to settle the Din of Arms and philosophically resolve to trouble their heads not at all about the Matter; and they know as little as they care.

Their Language bears a great Affinity to the French. Many of their Words are of the same Signification, the same pronunciation. The Men are well made, have good Complexions, and do not want Courage. Their Women I cannot say much of, not having seen a Beauty among them.

We arrived at Chester time enough in the Afternoon to take a walk round the Walls of the Town and to see some of the principal Streets. Chester is placed on the River Dee, which is navigable for large Ships up to the Town.[30] Over this River is a Bridge with four Gothic Arches. Above it is a pretty Cascade over a Damb where there are two fine Mills. The Town stands on an Eminence in the midst of a flat Country of great Extent. The Buildings are irregular, old fashioned and inconvenient. The Streets are used only for Carriages and horses, there being a walk up one pair of Stairs on a boarded Floor for Foot Passengers. Here you are entirely protected from the Rain, having a good house over your heads and a dry Path with Rooms under you. You have now and then Steps to go down into the Streets. The modern houses have not this Convenience. They have a good Market House and plentifully supplied.

Being a great Provision Country and the most famous County in England for Cheese, there are several Churches, two of which have lofty Stone Spires of Gothic Architecture. The other has a large Tower and has been a fine piece of Workmanship but the soft Stone of which it is built has greatly dissolved, as have most of the public Buildings in the place. Here is a pretty large Castle built on a very substantial Rock mounted with

---

[30] Acts for the improvement of the River Dee up to Chester were passed in 1700, 1733, 1741 and 1744. T. S. Willan, *River Navigation in England 1600–1750* (London, 1936), p. 153.

Cannon.[31] The Walls round the Town are in nice repair. We walk on Top of them. On one Side is a Rail and on the other is a Wall, so that our passage is secure. The Terrass is nicely paved with large flat Stones; and the Walk affords a pleasing Variety of Prospects. On one Side the River washes the Foundation of the Walls and the Banks on the opposite Side are finely decorated with Cultivation. On another Side we have a pretty view of the principal Gardens. On another the Canal glides along,[32] in which is a Number of Barges and over it are several well turned Arches. On the other, the Race Ground which is a very beautiful Spot, even as a bowling Green, and beyond it a fine Range of Meadow Grounds covered with Tribes of Sheep and Cattle.

There are several Infirmaries and Hospitals in this place.

July 21st   1st Day

On our way to Meeting this Morning we met very unexpectedly our Friends *George* H*arrison*[33] and M*ichael* S*aunders*. We all dined together at Upton a little Village about two Miles from Chester and afterwards set off for Warrington, where George Harrison and Michael Saunders are to met us a few Days hence. We drank tea on our way at Frosham[34] a small Market Town and got to Warrington early in the Evening. The Road hither was level; the Country flat; a sandy Soil, yet yielding abundance of Provisions.[35]

---

[31] Chester Castle was founded by William the Conqueror on a site where there was probably a Saxon fortification. It became the seat of the Earls of Chester and the centre of government of the County Palatine. Pevsner and Edward Hubbard, *Buildings of England: Cheshire* (London, 1971), pp. 156–158; Colvin, *History of the King's Works*, II, pp. 607–612, III Part 1, pp. 238–242.

[32] This was the Chester Canal. Begun in 1772, it was intended to run from the River Dee at Chester to Nantwich and Middlewich to join the Trent and Mersey Canal. But this turned out to be an unsuccessful project, and the connection to Middlewich was not made for fifty years. Hadfield, *British Canals*, pp. 102–103.

[33] See below, p. 317.

[34] Frodsham.

[35] I have cut sixteen lines of poetry to Fisher's dying horse, Galton.

1776
July 21st   1st Day

We got into Warrington about 8 in the Evening. We had a flat sandy Ride from Chester. The next day and the day following we devoted to viewing the Manufacturies; for which Warrington is considerable. The Principal however is of Sail Cloth of which more is made here than in any Town in England besides. They have likewise a Glass house or two, and a few Miles from Town is a very Capital Looking Glass House, much superior to anything of the kind in the Kingdom and equal to those of France, which has long rivalled this Country in the manufactury of that Article, in so much that notwithstanding an enormous Duty on the importation of French Glass into England,[1] all the Capital Houses throughout the Nation are supplied from France. The Pin Manufactury is likewise carried on here, the making of which is curious; but as it is here on a very contracted Scale, I shall put off an Account till I come to a more extensive one. Buttons are also made here, but Birmingham rivals it. Some Checks of a peculiar Quality: more substantial than those at Manchester. Here is an Iron Forge for casting wheels &c. which are made to any Pattern and answer the Purpose as well as wrought Plate Iron.

Warrington is famous for Ale. They formerly exported considerably, but the Demand for London Porter has entirely, or nearly, stopped the Demand for this.[2] The best Academy for the Education of youth in

---

[1] At the time Fisher was writing, the rates levied on imported glass included 8d. per lb. on imports of Crown, Plate and Flint glass and 2d. per lb. on Green or other glass. 19 Geo. II c. 12 (1746): 'An act for granting to his Majesty several Rates and Duties upon Glass, and upon Spirituous Liquors. . . .' Glassmaking was a flourishing branch of manufacture at Warrington by the late eighteenth century. *The Statutes at Large*, VI (London, 1769), pp. 649–664; J. Aikin, *A Description of the Country from Thirty to Forty Miles round Manchester* (London, 1795), p. 303.

[2] The rise of porter brewing in London was one of the two major developments in the brewing industry in eighteenth-century England. Public taste did not begin to switch from porter to ale until about 1830. Peter Mathias, *The Brewing Industry in England, 1700–1830* (Cambridge, 1959), pp. 11–12.

England is at this Place.[3] The Building is neat, spacious, but very plain. The advantageous Situation of Warrington upon the River Mersey makes it convenient for Trade, and being a Thoroughfare Town from the West into the North, as well as the grand Avenue from Manchester to Liverpool, give it great Consequence.

July 24th   4th Day

We set off with George Harrison and Michael Saunders for Liverpool. On our way we dined at Prescot, a considerable Market Town and reached Liverpool in the Evening, tho we got wet thro on our way.

Liverpool for Situation is the first, for its Trade the second, and for Populousness the fourth Town in the Kingdom. Finely situated on a level Ground on the Banks of the Mersey but a few Miles from the Irish Sea of which we have a scanty Prospect thro the Mouth of the River. The noble Docks in this Port so admirably calculated for the reception of 3 or 4000 Ships, which may lie with perfect ease and Safety afloat; the keys for the Discharge of their Cargoes; the dry Docks for Careening them; the Expedition with which they may put to Sea, give it superior Advantages to any other Port. The only inconvenience is that the Harbour is larboard and there is not always sufficient Water for deep Vessels; so that these are sometimes detained till a Spring Tide when if the wind be unfavorable they cannot depart.

The Town itself is dirty, irregular, illy paved, and in general but indifferently built, though there be some good Streets and Squares. Liverpool being the Port for shipping of the Manufactures of Manchester, Warrington and other Manufacturing Towns in the Neighbourhood, being concerned largely in the West India Trade, in the Greenland Fisheries, and more largely in the infamous Affrican Trade than any other Place in England occasion a great Forrest of Shipping to be continually in Port. There are several noble institutions for the Poor, the Hospitals, Work-houses &c. The Merchants here are enterprizing and public Spirited which gives great Life and Vigour to the Town, and it is in a State as flourishing as almost any place in Great Britain. We stayed here 4 Days at the house of our very worthy Friend William Rathbone.

The Principal Buildings in this Town are the Exchange, St. Paul's Church, and the Hospital. The Exchange is a large stately Building of an

---

[3] Warrington Academy was the most illustrious of the eighteenth-century Dissenting Academies. It helped to introduce more liberal, scientific and utilitarian studies into English education. The most eminent of the Academy's tutors was Joseph Priestley, who taught at Warrington between 1761 and 1767. A. E. Musson and Eric Robinson, *Science and Technology in the Industrial Revolution* (Manchester, 1969), p. 90. See also H. McLachlan, *Warrington Academy: Its History and Influence* (Manchester, 1943).

excellent hewn Stone, adorned with Pillars and Pilasters in the Front, and supported with others in the inside; but the outside is very heavy and the inside so dark and gloomy that the Merchants prefer standing in the Street. The St. Pauls is a neat Church upon the model of St. Pauls in London, but the imitation is too paltry. The Hospital is a spacious Building, and contains 6 or 7 Persons. The Market is held in the Streets very inconvenient to the inhabitants, and troublesome to the People who have their goods to dispose of, as the place is a great Thoroughfare, and occasions a constant Assemblage of the mobility.

July 29th   2nd Day

We embarked in our Whiskey for Warrington attended by William Rathbone junior but stopped to take our breakfast at Prescot in the way. At Warrington we concluded to go by the Barge in the Duke of Bridgewaters Navigation to Manchester. We got an early Dinner and went about a Mile to London Bridge, a Rendezvous for Passengers who go to and fro. We got into the Boat, which we found admirably fitted up for the purpose of carrying Passengers. The whole is covered in from the Fore-Castle to the Quarter, of sufficient height for a Man to stand upright. Seats Fore and Aft, clean and neat, covered with Carpeting and a good Floor; Lockyers for the convenience of Passengers; and a Separation is made between the *Cabbin* and *Steerage* Passengers, the one paying 1/6, the other 2/6 for a Conveyance of $22\frac{1}{2}$ Miles.

We started at one O Clock, and found ourselves in an agreeable Circle of Acquaintance of both Sexes with whom we soon became very sociable. We were conducted by one Horse along a foot Path close to the Canal thro a delicious Country.[4] The novelty of this mode of Conveyance, the agreeable company, the variety and variations of Prospects: sometimes passing over Aqueducts while Streams of Water roll under the Canal; sometimes the Turnpike Road passes thro an Arch which supports the Canal; at other times we go under Arches while the Carriages thunder over our heads. The People who go in these Barges as Attendants carry for such of the Passengers as chuse, Tea, Coffee, Bread and Butter &c. We called for a Dish of Tea, which in a few Minutes was handed to us in all imaginable State. We made a most comfortable repast and after enjoying the Scene we arrived safe at Manchester about 6 O Clock in the Evening, having been near 5 hours on the water. This Canal unlike to the others in England is without Locks, so that there is no detention whatever, nor any Sort of impediment to the Navigation, till you get to Run Corn a few Miles from Liverpool where the Canal communicates with the Severn; here is a pretty Stair Case of Locks, being 10 in Number all together.

[4] A drawing of a horse-drawn barge has been omitted.

July 30th   3rd Day

An Invitation to take a Ride to the Duke of Bridgwaters Navigation at Worseley and Barton Bridge we accepted with a very formidable Party. At Worseley is a very curious Subterraneous Passage cut all the way thro a Solid Rock up to the Coal Pits.[5] The Passage is about 10 feet in Width, and above the Surface of the water about 6 feet. The water is deep enough for Vessels of 10 or 15 Tons of Coal to go up and down. The Cut is as strait as an Arrow for some miles up, and for the greater part of the way it is arched over with Bricks to prevent the Earth or Rocks falling in. A vast number of boats ply here, and from hence they supply the Town of Manchester chiefly with Coals.

This Canal is a little branch of the main one which leads from Liverpool, made merely for the purpose of going up to the Duke's Coal Pits. This too is without any Lock, though not effected without great expence and ingenuity, the principal Contriver of which was one Brindley[6] a poor illiterate Man, who merely from a Sort of innate knowledge of Mechanics and Hydraulics could at once contrive and execute, yet was so much in want of words as to be unable to communicate his Ideas, his intentions of prosecuting his plans, or the mode which he intended to pursue for accomplishing his Purposes. This Man by reflection and contemplation could not only tell what could and could not be done, but would always fall on the most feasible, expeditious and least expensive plan. The great Masterpiece of this great Man's ingenuity is an Aqueduct near Barton Bridge, where the Coal is carried across a wide Valley in the Foot of which runs a beautiful River of considerable width.[7]

Alongside of the Canal is a good Road. The immense weight which these Arches must support both of Water and Earth is surprizing; and a more beautiful Object cannot well be conceived than a Vessel sailing over these Arches, by her side a waggon or Cart drawn on the Road, and in the River below a Cluster of large and small Boats sailing to and fro. And added to all these an hundred yards from the Bridge is a fine Cascade tumbing over a Mill-Damb; and the Country round is delightful beyond Description. We had a refreshing Tea Drinking at Worseley; of the Party the Finality composing an agreeable Proportion.

[5] For a fuller description see above, p. 83.

[6] James Brindley (1716–1772) was one of the earliest English engineers to gain a great reputation in civil engineering. He was particularly important in the design and building of canals. In 1759, the Duke of Bridgewater called upon Brindley to advise on a project by which the produce of the Worsley coalmines could be cheaply transported to Manchester. Brindley produced a plan of striking originality including the construction of an aqueduct to carry the canal over the River Irwell at Barton. *DNB*, II, p. 1253.

[7] A drawing of the Duke of Bridgewater's Aqueduct from Barton Bridge is omitted.

This Evening we had a total Eclipse of the Moon. It began a little after 10 and remained till $\frac{1}{2}$ past 11 wholly shaded. The Night was as fine as possible; not a Cloud danced in the Firmament. The object was beautiful, the moon much more luminous than I should have expected. The Streets were crowded with Spectators, whose observations on the *Phenomenon* were not a little diverting.

July 31st   4th Day

We took a Ride with Gideon Bickerdike[8] and J*ohn* Lawrence[9] to Stockport, a beautiful Town about 6 Miles from Manchester. This Place finely situated on the declivity of a hill, at the foot of which several little Rills run on the water being converted in its passage to great Use in turning several Mills &c for the manufacturys of the Town. Here are several Button, Hat and Check Manufactures of considerable Consequence, but the Branch of Buisness for which this Place is most capital is the winding of Silk of which here are 5 large Water Mills, in each of which 300 People are employed.[10] The Machinery is complicated and curious; the model was brought out of Italy by [John Lombe]. The Water wheel of one of these Mills is 40 feet in Diameter, turned by about as much water as could go out of a Pint Mug. The wheel sets in motion many thousands of others; and the Sight of all this variety of motion is the most pleasing imaginable. We returned to Manchester in the Evening. The two following Days we devoted to viewing the Town, the manufacturies, and such of the public Buildings as are worthy our Notice.

Manchester is advantageously seated in the midst of a rich and very populous Country. The Soil round it is luxuriant; the Features happy for Prospect and beautiful with every Improvement; and its Neighbourhood crowded with Gentlemen's Seats. As a manufacturing Town it rises superior to any in the Kingdom, both for the variety of Articles in which they are engaged, and the Value of an enterprizing and Oeconomical Spirit seems to pervade all its inhabitants. The Voice of industry is heard on every hand. Idleness is disgraceful, and a Man without Buisness, or some

[8] Gideon Bickerdike & Co., merchants and cotton manufacturers, 13 Spring Gardens, Manchester. *UBD*, III, p. 795.

[9] John Lawrence, fustian and check manufacturer, Deansgate, Manchester. Elizabeth Raffald, *The Manchester Directory for the Year 1772* (Manchester, 1772), p. 26.

[10] By 1769, there were six silk mills at work in Stockport. The raw silk thrown in these mills was mainly prepared for the Spitalfields weavers. The cotton trade and the making of hats were also considerable manufactures in the town by the late eighteenth century. *UBD*, IV, p. 476; Aikin, *Description of the Country from Thirty to Forty Miles round Manchester*, pp. 445–446; J. H. Hodson, *Cheshire, 1660–1780: Restoration to Industrial Revolution* (Chester, 1978), pp. 151–152.

occupation, Manchester does not own. It is therefore no Wonder a place like this should be in a most flourishing State; it increases with almost incredible rapidity. The ingenuity of her Artizans is amazing. One would suppose they had already arrived to the Summit of invention, and had left nothing for Posterity to boast an improvement in. Yet we daily see some new and very important discovery in facilitating their operations, and in rendering Labour subservient to Contrivance. Already we see they have taught the dull feelings of wood and iron all their uses and powers. They have substituted these materials for mortals. They live, they move, and as if indeed with reason and reflection they guide and conduct all the mechanic Powers. Wool is carded from its fleecy knots into Sheets; it is then spun. This is done by Water. The Loom is managed with trifling Care. A man by moving one machine throws 40 Shuttles thro the Warps. In short every Process is so simple, and Labour is rendered of so little Utility, that it is almost time to call their *Manufactures* by some other Name.

With respect to the particulars of their manufacturies they are too numerous to mention. It were a Task almost as arduous as Linnaeus had experienced in the Arrangement of the vegetable World.[11] We must divide them into Classes, Genera, Species and Varieties. The Flax, Cotton and Silk are converted to a thousand different Uses, some beneficial to Society, others as they are Ornamental may perhaps be considered as Luxuries. Yet Luxuries have become politically necessary. A Pattern Card of Manchester Commodities forms as fine a Picture as could be composed from a Copy of Tulips and Ranunculuses. The great Choice of prints on the Jenets and Velverets vies with the Copperplate Cottons and Chintz. Their Damascus and Lorettes equal for Beauty and Elegance the most gaudy Silks of the Eastern Countries. Whatever Art, whatever ingenuity could invent aided by Taste and Judgement Manchester has effected. And among the most perfect of her Inventions is the mode of weaving the Quilted Coverlids and Petticoats. These are ornamented with Flowers of every Sort and of various Colours; some too are done in Silk. The Loom for this is upon the same general principles of the common kind, but several Shuttles are used instead of one, and there is great complication and trouble in adjusting the warp, as there is care in conducting the work afterwards.

Manchester for Size is equal to Liverpool or Birmingham. The Town is well laid out. There are a Number of good Streets and some very capital houses. Great improvements are making in a disagreeable Part of the town, where they intend to pull down many of the houses for the Sake of

---

[11] Carolus Linnaeus (1701–1778), a Swedish naturalist who evolved a system of classifying plants that brought order to scientific nomenclature.

enlarging the Street. The Hospital[12] is a large and elegant Building under excellent Regulation, with a Street of Water before the Door, and a fine walk with a pretty Row of Trees.

Here is a beautiful Gothic Church, almost new, of a neat hewn Stone.[13] In the Altar Piece are some good Paintings, and on the Eastern Window are Peter, James and John in stained Glass. The Charity School is a noble institution, having a fund for the maintenance of 60 poor Children, who are cloathed, fed and taught English and writing.[14] In the upper appartments is a capital Library left by a Gentleman who also bequeathed £200 per Annum towards purchasing what new Books were worthy of the Collection.

After viewing the Town, Vicinities, Manufactures, public Buildings, and experiencing the utmost hospitality and profusion of kindness from the very social inhabitants we decamped for Leeds on the Morning of the

3rd August   7th Day

The Country from Manchester to Rochdale is very populous as is indeed all Lancashire; that County only containing half a Million of People. The Neighbourhood of Manchester constantly puts us in mind of that of London, equally populous for several miles round the town and improvements in a very capital Stile. Rochdale is a large and considerable Market Town cheifly concerned in the manufacturing of Bays and Flannels. We came thro Ealand to Bridgehouse[15] where we supped and came on to Leeds about 12 O Clock at Night. We stayed at home chiefly the two first days and on

August 6th   3rd Day

We took an early Dish of Tea with *Sarah* Cowell,[16] and having formed an agreeable Party we set off for Lord Irwin's Seat,[17] a few Miles only from Town. The house is a spacious and old fashioned Fabric. The Situation is

---

[12] The Manchester General Infirmary and Dispensary, erected in 1755. Gorton, *Topographical Dictionary of Great Britain and Ireland*, III, p. 755.

[13] St. John's Church, St. John's Square, built in 1769. It no longer exists. Pevsner, *Buildings of England: Lancashire 1: The Industrial and Commercial South* (London, 1969), p. 268.

[14] A reference to Chetham's Hospital. The buildings of this institution were bought in 1653 by Humphrey Chetham, textile manufacturer and merchant, to found a school for forty boys. *Ibid.*, pp. 285–287.

[15] Elland and Brighouse.

[16] Sarah Cowell of Leeds. She married Thomas Rawlinson at Bradford in 1784. They were both Quakers. Hodgson, *Society of Friends in Bradford*, p. 114.

[17] Temple Newsome, four miles east of Leeds, was the seat of the Hon. Lady Viscountess Irwin. *UBD*, III, p. 541.

beautiful, commanding on every Side a rich and charming Prospect of a most lovely Country. The Park is very delightful, the noble Oaks and Elms disposed with the utmost Judgement, and the Lawn and rising and falling Ground form a most pleasing effect and create a happy Variety to the distant Scene, where the Golden Grain now verging to maturity appears in a hundred Fields [and] intersected by hedges spreads as beautiful a Carpet as Man could wish for. The inside of this house like the outside is old fashioned yet there is an appearance of Nobility and Hospitality in every appartment. Here are some very capital Paintings in the Gallery of Titian, Poussin, Rosa and some others of less Fame. In the other Rooms are some very good Portraits, but the Prospects from the Windows are as fine Pictures of Nature as the others are of Art.

The next Day we paid a Visit to John Hursler at his house near Bradford. He took a ride with us to Bingley along the Banks of the Canal: over the noble Aqueduct, much larger than that of the Duke of Bridgewater, having 3 Water Arches under which two Branches of the River run and thro which Vessels go up and down.[18] Bingley I have already described: the Number of Locks, the Facility and expedition of their being filled with a general Account of the whole Canal.[19] After riding thro the most populous part of all England and thro a Country which is not outdone by any in the world for Prospects, we returned to Under Cliff, had a late Dinner and got to Leeds in the Evening.

The Canal is just entering the Town of Leeds; the Bason is now making; a whole Square of houses is built. The new Cloth hall of spacious size is compleated and these improvements have all been made since I was at Leeds 12 Months ago.[20] The rest of the time we remained here we devoted to Society.

August 9th   6th Day

We rigged out our Whiskey with two horses one to go before the other, our Man Joshua on the foremost. This being a very genteel mode of Conveyance, we made no doubt a very respectable appearance. In our Whiskey we drove on to Wakefield, thus far accompanied by my old Fellow traveller *Samuel* Elam. At Wakefield we made no pause but stopped a few minutes at a little Ale house further on. The old Landlady was very conversible and gave us a full Account of the marvellous

---

[18] This eight-arched aqueduct, on the Leeds-Liverpool canal, carried water over the River Aire at Dowley Gap near Bingley. Charles Hadfield, *The Canals of North-West England* (2 vols., Newton Abbot, 1970), 1, p. 75.

[19] See above, pp. 156–157.

[20] See above, pp. 42–43.

Neviston,[21] a celebrated High Way Robber of a peculiar Cast who haunted this Neighbourhood about 80 years ago. Different from his Brethren in the occupation, he did not rob from want or from wantoness but from a charitable and, if not a laudable, a well meant motive. He took from the rich and distributed to the poor. He made no appearance of Gaiety and indulged in no Dissipation. His Dress as well as his manner was plain. He had long remained undiscovered and unsuspected, but he was at last detected and seized in this very house. The Chair was brought out in which he sat at the time the Sheriff paid him his addresses. We like other Travellers sat down in it for the sake of telling so remarkable a Circumstance.

This old Landlady (now in her 60th year) had never been 10 or 12 Miles from this her place of Nativity. She had twice visited Leeds, but had never been at Sheffield, yet she seemed as contented happy and chearful as if she had traversed over the great Globe. Contented with hearing of the great Wonders of the distant Countries she had no wish to see them. Her ambition had never aspired above her Circumstances. She had reconciled her mode of living to her own Convenience. Having with the hard earning of her own hands a competence, she wished for no more; and if she did not fill up a Station of Life important to Society, her example was worthy of imitation. She was an honest Woman which perhaps considering how little was given her, was as much as was required.

We dined at Barnsley, a place I have been at before and have before described.[22] A few Miles from hence on the Road to Sheffield is the very magnificent Seat of Lord Strafford,[23], to which we paid a visit through a park very Elysian. We rode about 1½ mile, where the most enchanting Groves of Sycamore and Elm and Oak were agreeably disposed on hills, vallies and here and there objects were scattered to add variety and give a Grace and Dignity to the Scene. A Canal mocking the River's natural wildness ran thro the whole [with] Bridges over it more for ornament than Use. Obelisks, Temples, Banqueting houses and whatever else could please, were mingled in the general View. From the Terrace before the grand Front, Art and Nature have strove with uncommon efforts to outdo each other in charming the Spectator. Tis impossible to say which claims the Palm with greater Justice. If Art have been defective, tis only when Nature needed no Decoration. If Nature were wanting Art has so

---

[21] John Nevison (1639–1685) was a Yorkshireman mainly active in robbery and horse stealing during the reign of Charles II. He was involved with gangs of robbers and ended up on the gallows at York. *DNB*, XIV, pp. 307–308.

[22] See above, p. 155.

[23] i.e. Wentworth Woodhouse.

concealed her Defects as to leave you without suspecting wherein she was deficient.

The Park first meets your Eyes. The [coating] of the Earth is stripped by Sheep and Deer and Oxen who feed indiscriminately. The Sheet of Water which intersects the whole is a fine Object. Some distance from this the Land assumes a subtle declivity and rises for a great Distance, scattered with Corn Fields, and grass ground variegated with Woods on the Top of the nearest Range of Hills, in a fine artificial Ruin. The Design is excellent, and the effect answerable. Beyond this rise distant Mountains, and the View if not interminable is lost in Clouds and Mist.

As the Country is very populous the Cottages which chequer the Landscape are pleasing and the Clumps of Trees at accidental Distances dispersed throughout are not a little advantage. The Pleasure Grounds and Shrubberies are delightful and the Wentworth Castle which gives a name to this Seat is a Ruin not very distant.[24] The Pleasure Grounds have some fine Obelisks and Monuments, on the Tops of which are some excellent pieces of Statuary. The capital Front of this Palace is elegant beautiful and splendid, built of a fine hewn Stone. A Parapet Wall without Balustrades, but it has a fine Pediment with Festoons of Fruit and Flowers of admirable Workmanship. The Windows are all gilt, yet still it has rather a plain elegance about it than a gaudy Magnificence.

First enter the Hall which is a noble appartment ornamented with Marble and some good Paintings. The Stair Case is prodigiously grand, in Geometric Stile, with gilded Iron Banisters. The Walls all the way up are adorned with Baiss Relievos, well executed. But the most capital of all these Rooms, to which the others bear no Competition, is the Gallery. The first Entrance strikes too forcibly immediately to note its particular Beauties. Our first feelings subside before we are capable of viewing it with composure: a long Room the whole width of the house (upwards of 200 feet) with four noble Pillars of Corinthian Order at each End and between these four very capital Pieces of Statuary in white marble. The Pillars are 18 feet in height, 14 between the Base and Capital, all in one piece. The two Venetian Windows at the Ends have a fine Effect as they are seen between the Marble Pillars. A beautiful Row of Windows in the Front throw a happy Light upon the fine Paintings which are ranged with great Judgement and of which there is a most eligible and costly Collection. The Chimney pieces in this Room are admirably curious. Two Billiard Tables are stationed in Copartments. The whole Glare within this Room and the beauty of the

---

[24] This is on the site of Wentworth Woodhouse. Its nucleus is the North Range, a seven-bay house of three storeys built c. 1670. Pevsner, *Buildings of England: Yorkshire: The West Riding* (2nd edn., London, 1979), pp. 546–548.

Country without are too captivating to describe. The Lady's dressing Room is fitted up in the Adelphi Stile, which now seems to prevail almost universally in the Ceilings, Stucco, Carved Work, Paintings and even in furniture. In a Closet adjoining is a beautiful Library. Tho inferior to the Lords, the State Bed Chamber and the succeeding Room contain as fine Tapestry as any in England.

We stayed here till near Dark when the rain began to fall heavily. However being protected by an Umbrella we made tolerably well out, and got into Leeds before 10 O Clock and removed far from us all Danger of catching Cold by smoaking our Pipes over a good Fire.

August 10th   7th Day

The Manufactures of Sheffield we judged of sufficient importance to devote one Day to which however we found hardly sufficient. The Plate Work with all its various modes of operation is brought to surprizing Perfection. The Tin Plate of about $\frac{1}{8}$th Inch thickness is sawdered to a block of Copper about $1\frac{1}{2}$ Inches. These blocks are taken to a rolling Mill, where they are rolled out, till they seem to be as thin as Paper twice or thrice folded. Then they are cut into whatever Shapes the occasion may require. If Buttons be wanted they are punched out with an instrument to the proper Size. Thence they are taken to the stamping machine where they receive whatever impression they think proper, having indented instruments for that purpose. This operation is performed by raising an Iron Weight which is fixed in a frame to make it fall in a proper Direction, an instrument wrought upon the same Principles as the Engine driving Pits. They are then filled with Tin or with Bone according to the kind. They afterwards receive a Polish and are then wrapped in their proper papers for Sales. The Single Article of a Button thus goes thro a multitude of different hands, each a distinct Trade. One man all the Days of his Life is engaged in punching, another in polishing, another in cutting the Bone, another in giving it the impression &c &c &c. By these Means each Person becomes expert in his particular Walk and carries on his Branch of Buisness with an expedition he never could acquire if his attention were diverted to numerous objects.[25]

In the Manufactury of Candlesticks Bread baskets Salts &c &c, as well as in all the different Branches of Cutlery the same Oeconomy and Management are observed.[26] These have been the means of bringing the

---

[25] Buttonmaking, silver plating, metalware and hardware were all important manufactures in eighteenth-century Sheffield. Robert Eadon Leader, *Sheffield in the Eighteenth Century* (Sheffield, 1901), pp. 62–88.

[26] Sheffield cutlery was of constantly increasing excellence throughout the eighteenth century. *Ibid.*, pp. 66–70.

manufactures to such perfection. In Cutlery the Situation of Sheffield gives it great advantages over Birmingham. The fine Streams of Water which wash the Foot of this place furnish her with the means of lessening Labour very much by doing many offices by Water, the Slitting, Tilting, Grinding being performed by Mills in which great Contrivance and Ingenuity appear. But in the manufactury of Hard Ware, in general Sheffield will stand no Competition with its Rival, for this reason: tho it increase considerably it is not by any means increase in the same Ration. The Town stands on little Ground, but contains near 40,000 inhabitants. Its natural Situation is quite delightful. For Prospect few places exceed it. The Country round about it yields superiority to none. But still the Streets of Sheffield are sooty, dirty, hilly, badly paved, the houses but indifferent. Besides the manufactures of Cutlery, Plate Ware and Gilding there is an extensive white Lead Manufactury and a large Silk Mill.[27] Yorkshire contains 1 Million Souls.[28]

---

[27] The silk mill was put up in 1758. It was twice burned down and twice rebuilt as a cotton mill before becoming a poorhouse. *Ibid.*, p. 324.

[28] I have cut some jottings on paintings owned by Lord Strafford.

August 11th 1st Day[1]
Sheffield

Setting off in the midst of an heavy Shower we had no other Consolation than the probable Prospect of its being at the worst and that if any Alteration should happen it would be for the better. However quite contrary to our expectation we had no sooner arrived on a dismal melacholly moor of a long extent without a house in which we might take shelter for 5 or 6 Miles, but it began to rain with intolerable Vehemence. Protected from its Fury by an umbrella and Apron we managed tolerably, kept the Bulk of the Rain off till we arrived at a little Village where we put up at an Inn. Here we found a Number of Friends who had been at a Village a few miles further on to a Meeting. They had walked from Sheffield 16 Miles, and were on their return caught in the rain and had all been wet to the Skin. The house could not accomodate them all and they had 10 Miles to go to their home. The laudable motive which had led them from Sheffield induced us to offer our Whiskey and horses to accomodate the Women, which they accepted and we tarried here this Night.

August 12th 2nd Day

We have now entered upon the Precincts of Derbyshire a County abounding with Prodigious of the most marvelous Species. Unable to the task of a thorough Description I shall content myself with making little more than a Catalogue of them, and trusting the particular minutiae to the frail Memory, which whether it will retain a proper Recollection I must leave to the issue of the Experiment.

After Breakfast we set off to Castleton. On one Side of it is the celebrated Cavern, known by the Name of the Devil's Peak.[2] The Situation of the Entrance into this whimsical Region is thro a natural Arch near the bottom of a perpendicular Mountain. The first objects which present themselves to our view are a parcel of little Cottages and a Ropery where

---

[1] I have cut three verses of poetry (24 lines).
[2] This large cavern is immediately under the walls of Castleton Castle. Lewis, *Topographical Dictionary of England*, I, p. 390.

Men Women and Children are busy as bees turning their Wheels and spinning and knitting. In this part of the Cave the inhabitants live very comfortably. We proceed a little further when the Passage darkens. We are now visited by the Matrons of the Cavern who bring us Candles to conduct our uncertain and bewildered tract. Now we find the way so low that we are obliged to stoop to gain further admittance. This is not the Case long; we soon find the Arch stretch its Gigantic Roof to an immense height. But alas! now a River impedes our Progress. But here the Pilgrim is proffered a Bark to conduct him across the River Stix,[3] but he carries no Provision with him on the Voyage. He lies flat on his back, not having room to sit up till Charron[4] or Neptune[5] or some River god have wafted him to the further Shore.

The Voyage is not dangerous; removed from the reach of blustering Boreas or Oolus,[6] and uninfluenced by the systematic Ordinations of Phoebe,[7] without a bottomless Depth to explore, or to encounter the rough billows of the great Deep, we are soon landed on a firm and solid Rock. Sometimes the irregular Roof falls near the bottom of the Place on which we walk, at other times it exalts itself into a mighty Dome. Sometimes a Gothic Arch is expanded over our heads, then some Catinarian Form[8] is stretched in wild Greatness, or perhaps some more Conic Shape lifts itself aloft, and sometimes a regular Circle which seems the Production of finished Architecture.

Pleased tho astonished at the wonderful Scene, while we are gaping with renewed Surprize at a great Chasm above our heads, at once a band of Songsters rush upon the Sight with lighted torches in their hands making the Face of Darkness blaze into Day, and chequering the glittering Sides with ten thousand brilliant Stars. The hollow Cavern now resounds with their harmony. Echo reverberates it to our Ears, Astonishment fills our Senses; horror and pleasure alternate rise in our breast. The thrilling Symphonies of their Music inspire Delight. The giddy height on which they stand strikes us with dread, while all the magnificent horrors present themselves in terrible Array, and freeze us into a belief that the whole is

---

[3] In Greek mythology, the River Styx was one of five rivers surrounding Hades, over which the ghosts of the dead who have been properly buried must pass.

[4] In Greek mythology, Charon was the ferryman who transported the souls of the dead (but only of those who had been properly buried) across the Styx to the Underworld.

[5] In Roman mythology, Neptune was the god of the sea. He came to be identified with the Greek Poseidon.

[6] In Greek mythology, the North Wind, the son of Astraeus and Eos, or of Aeolus.

[7] In Greek mythology, a Titaness. The name Phoebe became synonymous with the moon and with Artemis and the Roman Diana.

[8] Catenarian means 'of the nature of a chain, chainlike.' This is a reference to either a gradated natural curve or an arch with the shape of a chain. *OED*, II, p. 981.

imagination or the power of enchantment, but this Sensation soon subsides and we are convinced of its reality.

After this we are carried over many Pools of Water till we reach a Prospect of the Extremity which is 730 Yards from the Entrance. At this End a Man was working in blowing up the Rocks to seek some further Passage into the trackless Rock. Fortunately at the moment of our arrival at this Spot, he had loaded the Cavity and was ready to give Fire to the torch which was to cause the Explosion. The light in his hand produced a fine Effect as it reflected on the Stream which was lightly agitated, and this again was reflected from the Surface of the water on the Sides and Roof. The Guide gave the Command to the Labourer. He lighted the match. Instantly succeeded the most dreadful Peal of Thunder that I ever heard, which continued to a long frightful lingering Succession of rending rumors, shaking every Cavity, and making the very base tremble with Dissonance and Rage. A more awful and solemn Shock cannot be conceived.

Near this Spot a Cascade trembles down a little Precipice. The Noise has a fine effect among the Rocks. The whole of the Sides of this Cavern is composed of Marble in which is a great variety of Petrifactions, Shells of large and small Sizes and a thousand other marine Productions, some Snakes, a great Quantity of petrified wood. This marble is of a light greyish yellow, and much in vogue in Gentlemen's Seats for Tables, Door Cases, Chimneys &c &c.

We now return by the same passage we came; the longer we stay in it the more clearly we distinguish the grotesque Grandeur, and the wild Sublimity of this wonderful Object. The more we see the more we are surprized. But all the Preceding Wonders must yield to the gaudy Prospect we enjoy of the Sky when we first behold Day light after having been so long immured in the gloomy pit. The effect of this is unspeakably fine. We bid this Peak a lasting Adieu, without a hope or wish ever to see it more, or tho it be ever so grand, and equally curious, tis of that Sort that one Sight is enough in a Man's Life.

The Top of this Mountain stands a Castle,[9] but in so droll a Situation that it is of no Use in Peace or War. Time has not neglected it. The old Genius is hasting it to Nothingness with all Speed.

Castleton is a small Market Town, situated in a pretty Vale. Contains about 100 houses protected by the Mountains on every Side. From hence we go in quest of other Wonders, the first of which is Mam Tor[10] an high

---

[9] The most important castle in Derbyshire. Built by William Peveril during the reign of William the Conqueror. Peveril Castle has been in ruins since the seventeenth century. Pevsner, *Buildings of England: Derbyshire* (London, 1953), pp. 200–201.

[10] Mam Tor or 'Mother Hill,' 1,300 feet above the vale of Castleton.

Rock of a Scaly Stone on one Side sloping and regular to the Summit; on the other almost perpendicular, where the Stones are continually falling down into a deep Gulph below. This place forms a most Romantic appearance and has given rise to a fine print of the View. The Summit commands a very profuse and extensive Prospect of an immense Theatre. Multitudes of Mountains rise far and near, covered with Sheep and Herd, unless where the Lands are converted to mining, and for this, Derbyshire is famous, principally for Lead.

Two Miles from this place is Elden hole[11] near the Summit of a prodigious hill. This Place is too dreadful for Description. We must be present and fill the horrors which it inspires to form any Idea of its terrible appearance. On the declivity of this hill is walled in an Acre of Ground to prevent the unwary and benighted traveller from too near an approach to its verging precipice. In this inclosure is an oval Scissure as if the Earth had given way in the Center, to the weight of the Rocks which appear to our View on looking down this dark dismal and frightful pit.

The Guide who had led us hither collected a pile of Stones to shew us the effect their Falling would have. At first it makes a sighing Noise as if it were induced with the Passion of Fear, till the first stroke strike the astonished and wondering Ears. Thence it invades with greater Fury and resounding with louder Thunder through the Tartarean Shades,[12] which seem to groan forth horror at every Stroke till at last Echo tired with bearing the trembling Vibrations to the affrighted Sense cease to convey us any intelligence of its Progress. And how much further it may proceed, Supposition only can unfold. Some Traveller attempted to measure its Depth but the Serpentine Direction of the Cavity forbid him to make any Discoveries by fathoming its immensity. He then attempted *propria persona*[13] to explore its wonders and for this purpose by a Rope lowered himself down 80 yards. He found no Prospect of any termination to so uncertain a Voyage and retreated ingloriously without making any useful Discovery.

One Cotton a droll Genius, the identical numerical Poet who has burlesqued Virgil's Aneis, in his humorous translation, speaking of this Pit in the same Stile with his other writings, says:

[11] Eldine Hole is one mile south of Mam Tor and four miles east of Buxton. It is a perpendicular gulf or chasm, about forty yards long above ground. *The Life of John Buncle, Esq* ... (4 vols., London, 1770), p. 209.

[12] According to Homer and to earlier Greek mythology, Tartarus was a deep and sunless abyss situated in the lowest region of the Underworld. Here Zeus imprisoned the rebel Titans.

[13] In person.

Steep black and full of horror that who dare
Look down into the Chasm, and keep his hair
From lifting off his hat, either has none,
Or for more modish Curls, cashiers his own;
It were injurious I must confess,
By mine to measure other Courages;
But when I peep into't I must declare,
My heart still beats, and Eyes with horror stare;
And he that standing on the brink of Hill,
Can carry it so unconcerned and look so well
As to betray no Fear, is, certainly,
A better Christian or a worse than I.[14]

From hence in our way to Buxton we go within 2 Miles of Tydeswell a little Village, remarkable for a Spring that rises and falls without any periodical Certainty. The Ebb and Flow of this Spring are very considerable, and inconstant. The Cause however of this rise is not perhaps difficult to Account for. The Source from whence this Fountain orginaly flows is supplied by rains and these run to it thro a particular Stratum in the Earth which not being water Proof forms a Conductor, as the Rains fall without order either of time or quantity; according to the weight of Rain that falls into the distant Reservoir it is urged with greater or less Velocity and rises more or less at the Spring.

We at length arrive at Buxton, a Market which if it were deprived of its Inns would have no Inhabitants to buy Provisions, and as few to sell them. However the very many capital Inns give it a respectable appearance, and the Company constantly going and coming make it a busy Theatre. The Company come to bath and drink of its waters.[15] The Baths are an inferior Species of the same Genus as those of Bath, not so warm, but of the calcarious kind.[16] But what is more remarkable is that within a few feet of the warm Spring a cold one should blubber out, that two Sisters bubbling out of one Fountain should so differ in Constitution, that one should as it were burn with a Fever, and the other be chilled with an Ague. Cotton says

---

[14] Charles Cotton (1630–1687) is a poet known for his contribution to Izaak Walton's *Compleat Angler* (1676). He lived for most of his life in the High Peak. These words are quoted from lines 490 ff. of his poem *The Wonders of the Peake*, published in 1681 and dedicated to the Countess of Devonshire. John Beresford, ed., *Poems of Charles Cotton 1630–1687* (London, 1923), p. 28; John Buxton, ed., *Poems of Charles Cotton* (London, 1958), pp. xv, 66–71.

[15] Buxton was a spa town, with various baths arising from springs. The season at Buxton usually lasted from June until October. Lewis, *Topographical Dictionary of England*, I, pp. 325–326.

[16] i.e. baths composed of or containing lime or limestone.

Or that a Naiade, having careless played
With some male wanton Stream and fruitful maid,
Should have her silver breasts at once to flow
One with warm milk t'other with melted Snow.[17]

Here the Sons of intemperance resort more than to almost any other place.

Buxton is by no means an eligible Spot; the high Hills about it occasion constant Rains, the Country is barren, unpleasant and dreary. Contiguous to it is the famous and celebrated Pools hole.[18] The Passage is kept by two or 3 old women sad Historians of the dreadful Rocks, who are maintained by the humble Pittance they receive from the Traveller who finds his way thither. These good Matrons attend with their torches to conduct us thro this gloomy Cavern. We take leave for a little while of the light of Day and are soon removed from the most searching Ray of Phoebus. Thro a low narrow irregular and difficult pass by pointed Stones we urge our intricate progress into the awful Grotto, where we have Room to give Golia[t]h an upright Stand. Here the Sides glittering with crystal Drops emit a sparkling Light, and discover a rich enamelled Spectacle. Their Lustre is only borrowed from the Candles and must expire when they are gone. Now the Passage divides, one up the Steep Rocks where the footing is narrow slippery and dangerous, the other, along the edge of waters below on sharp and pierced Stones.

Our intelligent and learned expositors of the Miracles of this Fabric of Dame Nature fail not to give us every possible explanation of the uncouth Shapes which are formed in the Rocks, and which realy want little fancy to give them the pretended Figures. Here are *Men*, *Lions*, *Horses*, *Dogs*, *Tortoises* which are absolutely more like the Productions of Sculpture than the Chance medley of accidental Growth. An *Haycock* is extremely like Nature. A *Lady's Toilet* bids defiance to the Chizzels Art. All these Figures continue to increase by the Water falling from the Arch above, which crust by slow Gradations into transparent Stone, and would increase more rapidly did not every curious traveller who invades these Regions break off some piece as a trophy of his Visit.

After a laborious walk over lean and sharp stones of enormous Size, with an irregularly arched Roof, sometimes stretching its expanded Crescent a great height over us, again by fantastic Diminutions scarcely admitting our heads to pass without a Danger of hitting them, we after

---

[17] An excerpt from Cotton's *The Wonders of the Peake*: see Buxton, ed., *Poems of Charles Cotton*, p. 62.

[18] Poole's Hole is about three-quarters of a mile west of Buxton. It is a dark cavern, abounding with stalactites representing various natural forms. Lewis, *Topographical Dictionary of England*, I, p. 326.

walking about 600 yards hear the hoarse murmurs of a distant Cataract, resounding with awful horror thro the frightful Cavern. Here we stop, pause, ponder, and reflect on the astonishing wonders of this amazing Structure. At this Spot is Mary Queen of Scots Pillow, so calld from that Princess having schreend her Person there.[19] This is a very beautiful and transparent Pillar of the same brilliant Crystalization as all the rest of the Materials. Here Nature seems to contest the Prize with all the obelisks of antient Greece. The Chizzel never carved, the Pencil never drew finer and more natural Folds of Drapery. Here too are the representations of plants in the Rocks of a black bituminous Substance. The other representations of the Figures are formed by the dropping of water from the Rocks above which are Limestone. The Water partaking of this Quality generates a Sparry matter called Stalactites.

We now bid Adieu to the Bowels of this Mountain and traverse to our Inn. Drank a dish of Tea and set off for Bakewel a little Market Town about 14 Miles distant. This Day the Act of Parliament gave all qualified Persons Liberty to go in quest of Moor Game, a Bird very common in every part of England, of a very luscious Taste.[20] But Alas! great was the Disappointment of the Sporting Gentry to find the Morning was ushered in with an heavy rain, and that it continued to rain without Cessation till Night, by which many a fortunate bird had another Day added to his short lived Enjoyment.

August 13th   3rd Day

Like industrious Travellers we rose early in the morning and passing by a fine Country and a pretty Seat of the Duke of Rutland we arrived at Matlock in time to meet the Company in the Great Room at Breakfast. Matlock appeared more charming than ever. I recollected all its Features but I had almost forgot how beautiful it was. Many places please many people, but Matlock is one of those few places that please every body.

We spent the forenoon in walking about its Vicinities, crossing the River, admiring its wonders, traversing the Lovers Walk, seating ourselves in the Alcoves, and Summer houses, &c &c &c. At two O Clock the Bell summond us to Dinner. No place is under better regulation than this respecting the Company. We are all on a Footing. We seat ourselves without Distinction. We talk without Reserve and as every Man comes here for the Sake of Society they are generally of the most social Sort and

[19] The pillar of Mary, Queen of Scots, is at the extremity of Poole's Hole. *Ibid.*

[20] 16 Geo. III c. 30: 'An Act more effectually to prevent the Stealing of Deer, and to repeal several former Statutes made for the like purpose.' *The Statutes at Large* (London, 1776), pp. 516–521.

we frequently meet in so large a Circle with very sensible and entertaining Characters. There are few better Schools to acquire a knowledge of Men in than this. The only inconvenience attending this place is that Cards should be introduced as the mode of killing time. This is the false taste of the age. At the same time we must forgive them as Gaming is very little practiced.[21] Tho we cannot help wondering that rational Creatures should be so at a loss for Subjects of Discussion and Conversation from which Instruction might be derived, but as I can't reform the Age by repining, I will not grow dull upon the Reflection.

We took a walk after Dinner with James Peyton[22] to a Mill for spinning Cotton about one Mile from the Baths and made a very humiliating application to one of the Proprietors for a Sight of it, but all our intercessions were fruitless.[23] We were somewhat mortified at this Event, this Mill being the greatest Curiosity in the Mechanical Work in Great Britain. At this place the Cotton is carded with the utmost expedition, and it is afterwards spun. The Number of hands employed is trifling, as one Child can overlook a very great Number of Spindles. The Quantity of Cotton spun in this Mill is amazing. The Fabric is very spacious, and they have plenty of Water for keeping the Mill always going. All the movements of this wonderful work, we are told, are upon entirely new principles and the Mechanism is truly astonishing.

We bid Matlock its romantic Wonders, and all its Company Adieu, tho not without wishes to have dedicated a few Days to that Sort of Society. At the Inn we put up at they made up almost every Night 107 Beds, and there are two other capital Inns of not much inferior Fame besides these. There are many Day Visitors who do not stay all Night. The particular beauties of this Place I have mentioned in a former Rout.[24]

We ride on over hills and Dales to Ashbourn, a large and neat market Town where we lodged. On our way we had a view of Dove Dale but too distant to trace its Beauties. The Grotesque and wild manner in which the Rocks are thrown up is very curious. There are published some fine views of this Spot.

---

[21] Friends avoided most forms of diversion and took a stern view of any pastime which had no practical use or entailed a waste of precious time. This could become a matter of discipline in the monthly meeting. Frederick B. Tolles, *Meeting House and Counting House: The Quaker Merchants of Colonial Philadelphia 1682–1763* (Chapel Hill, N. C., 1948), p. 137.

[22] James Payton (1718–1786) lived at Dudley, Worcestershire. *DQB*; Frost, *Records and Recollections of James Jenkins*, p. 195.

[23] Fisher's visit here was to Richard Arkwright's Cromford, founded in 1771 as the first cotton spinning mill worked by waterpower. Pevsner, *Buildings of England: Derbyshire*, pp. 104–105.

[24] See above, pp. 189–191.

August 14th   4th Day

Ye Peakes! Ye Caves! and Grottoes now Adieu! No more shall I explore your dark Caverns, your dismal Cells, nor again ransack the Bowells of your rugged Mountains. And Derbyshire Adieu! Having gazed at thy Wonders and been inspired with all the Astonishment they could excite I am satisfied. Thy barren Mountains I leave without regret, be it the Miner's Cave to take delight in diving into the deep Recesses of thy Caverns. I have had enough. I envy him not his Feelings.

We now enter into the County of Stafford, and a most lovely Scene it displays to our Senses, Fertility, Improvement, Elegance, Taste already greet us into their Dominion. No longer dreary Moors, bleak Mountains, pointed Crags, and hills turned inside out, stare us in the Face; all is Symmetry and Beauty attired by the Graces, and consecrated to Harmony.

We breakfast at a little Village of Sudbury. Joining to it is a Noble Seat of Lord Vernon.[25] The house is not its principal Beauty, but the Grounds. They are laid out with admirable Taste and have the same appearance with hundreds of others in this Kingdom, where Art and Decoration have taught Enchantment to reside.

Hence we come for 8 or 10 Miles thro an inclosed Forrest of *George's*, fine Clusters of Trees, and Woods without Termination; covered with Sheep and Cattle, and Hare and Deer. The Road thro it is smooth as a bowling Green and the ride is all the way as delightful as Man could wish. The Prospect it commands of distant Hills and Vallies would make it sufficiently pleasing without its own Charms and its own Charms without those distant appendages are enough. United they almost intoxicate the Senses.

We dined at Litchfield a very pretty, regular, well built, well situated City, a River near it and a Canal not distant.[26] Several Churches, and a noble Gothic Cathedral;[27] remarkable for having no Dissenters in the whole Place. The present Bishop of this See is very famous for having been promoted merely for his Merit, without Friends, without Money; he is now

[25] George Venables-Vernon (1709/10–1780) of Sudbury, Derbyshire, 1st Baron Vernon, was created Lord Vernon, Baron of Kinderton, Cheshire, in 1762. Cokayne, *Complete Peerage*, XII Part 2, pp. 260–261.

[26] The River Tame and the Trent and Mersey Canal, the latter completed in 1777. Hadfield, *British Canals*, p. 82.

[27] The first cathedral at Lichfield was consecrated in 700. Much extra building took place in the twelfth century and throughout the Middle Ages. The cathedral was three times besieged during the English Civil War, and badly damaged. It was necessary to rebuild the fabric in the late eighteenth century. Pevsner, *Buildings of England: Staffordshire* (London, 1974), pp. 174–187.

Tutor to the Prince of Wales and the younger children of the present King.[28]

From hence we took a walk to a Country Seat of Friend Bourne her Son being an Acquaintance and her Daughter a fair Damsel of great Reputation. The Spot on which the house and Gardens stand commands a very lovely Prospect and there are many capital improvements: Walks, Woods and Lawns. We left this place about the going down of the Sun, had a rough and uncertain Road, and the Night coming on, and 16 Miles distance to ride, all which we accomplished without any Difficulty or Accident and got *propriis personis*[29] into Birmingham about 10 of the Night. Were deposited in a little *Closet* where we supped and smoaked one comfortable Pipe.

August 15th   5th Day

Our Friend George Boon[30] made us welcome to his house. We breakfasted with him. Took a walk with Charles Lloyd[31] and waited on my old Friend Samuel Galton. Our first Visit to the Manufactury's was to Clay's famous Paper Works.[32] The invention of this Article was about a dozen years since and the perfection to which it is brought is truly wonderful. They first place a paper on a board, which they wet with common Water, to prevent its adhering to the Board when the operation is over. On this are Papers one over another pasted. They are then baked to bring them to a firm body by a slow fire and are then sufficiently pliable to reduce to any Shape. In this State they are wrought into Form, and receive the impressions. They then

[28] Richard Hurd (1720–1808) was in good favour with George III, and was appointed preceptor to the Prince of Wales and the Duke of York in 1776. He was a moderate Tory and churchman who published tracts and sermons, and was Bishop of Lichfield (1774–1781) and subsequently Bishop of Worcester (1781–1808). *DNB*, X, pp. 314–316.

[29] Under our own steam.

[30] George Boone (1730–1785), born at Kettering, Northants., became an ironmonger in Birmingham. He was a regular attender at London YM. He represented Northants. QM in 1754–1755 and Warwicks. QM on many occasions between 1758 and 1784. *DQB*; Swinney's *Birmingham Directory* (1774), n. p.

[31] Charles Lloyd 'the banker' (1748–1828) began work in the family bank in Birmingham in 1775. He married Mary Farmer (?1751–1821qv) and there were fifteen children of the marriage. The Lloyd family owned extensive ironworks. *DQB*; Humphrey Lloyd, *The Quaker Lloyds in the Industrial Revolution* (London, 1975), pp. 145–249; Raistrick, *Quakers in Science and Industry*, pp. 119–121.

[32] Refers to the firm of Henry Clay, the inventor of papier mâché, who took out a patent on it in 1772. He was for twenty years the most important japanner in Birmingham and was also a button maker. He enjoyed royal patronage, gained by a judicious present of a Sedan chair to Queen Caroline. Samuel Timmins, ed., *Birmingham and the Midland Hardware District* (London, 1866; reprinted, 1967), pp. 566–567; W. H. B. Court, *The Rise of the Midland Industries, 1600–1838* (Oxford, 1938), pp. 235–236.

receive a Varnish, are scraped, varnished, scraped and varnished again, till they attain a proper Texture and Surface for receiving the Paintings and Gildings they put on. After this they receive several other Varnishes, till they assume the most rich and gaudy Lustre.

The Manufactury is very extensive and imploys a great Number of hands, Trays, Waiters, Decanter Stands, Snuff Boxes, Dressing Boxes and an hundred other Articles. They have an Advantage over metal. They are much lighter, not so subject to break or bruize, and the Paintings remain longer in higher Preservation. The ingenuity of the Artists in this branch is great. The Warehouse in which the goods are exposed to Sale is like a Nobleman's Room hung round with paintings: Flowers, Landscapes, Fruit Pieces, Beasts, Portraits and History are exhibited on the ware with nice and beautiful Taste, and in great Perfection.

We next went down in Friend Galton's Chaise to Soho the curious Residence of Bolton, the principal Manufacturer of this great Town.[33] His house is on a fine Spot. His Gardens are beautiful, interspersed with Canals, which are nothing more than his Mill Damb and his Races, which he has ingeniously constructed to answer the *Dulce* as well as the Utile. Over these he has bridges, and other good objects which are not a little beautiful.

A Quarter of a mile distant is his great and wonderful Manufactury.[34] The Front of this house is like the stately Palace of some Duke. Within it is divided into hundreds of little apartments, all which like Bee hives are crowded with the Sons of Industry. The whole Scene is a Theatre of Buisness, all conducted like one piece of Mechanism, Men, Women and Children full of employment according to their Strength and Docility. The very Air buzzes with the Variety of Noises. All seems like one vast machine.

The immense Number of Articles manufactured at this Town it would be idle to enumerate. Suffice it to say, that all Hardware of every Species and Quality are manufactured to great extent and to as great advantage as any other place in the world, and most Articles to *greater* advantage.

The manufactory of Bolton and Forthergill has not much to do with the less valuable Articles.[35] It consists of more costly and highly finished

---

[33] Matthew Boulton (1728–1809) founded the famous Soho Works in Birmingham in 1762. Pottery and metalware were produced and Boulton set himself to improve both the workmanship and artistic quality of his wares. Boulton entered a partnership with James Watt, the engineer, in 1772. *DNB*, II, pp. 916–917.

[34] i.e. the Soho works.

[35] Matthew Boulton had a twenty-year partnership with John Fothergill in the manufacture of jewellery and trinkets. Eric Robinson, 'Boulton and Fothergill, 1762–1782, and the Birmingham Export of Hardware,' *University of Birmingham Historical Journal*, VII (1959), pp. 60–79.

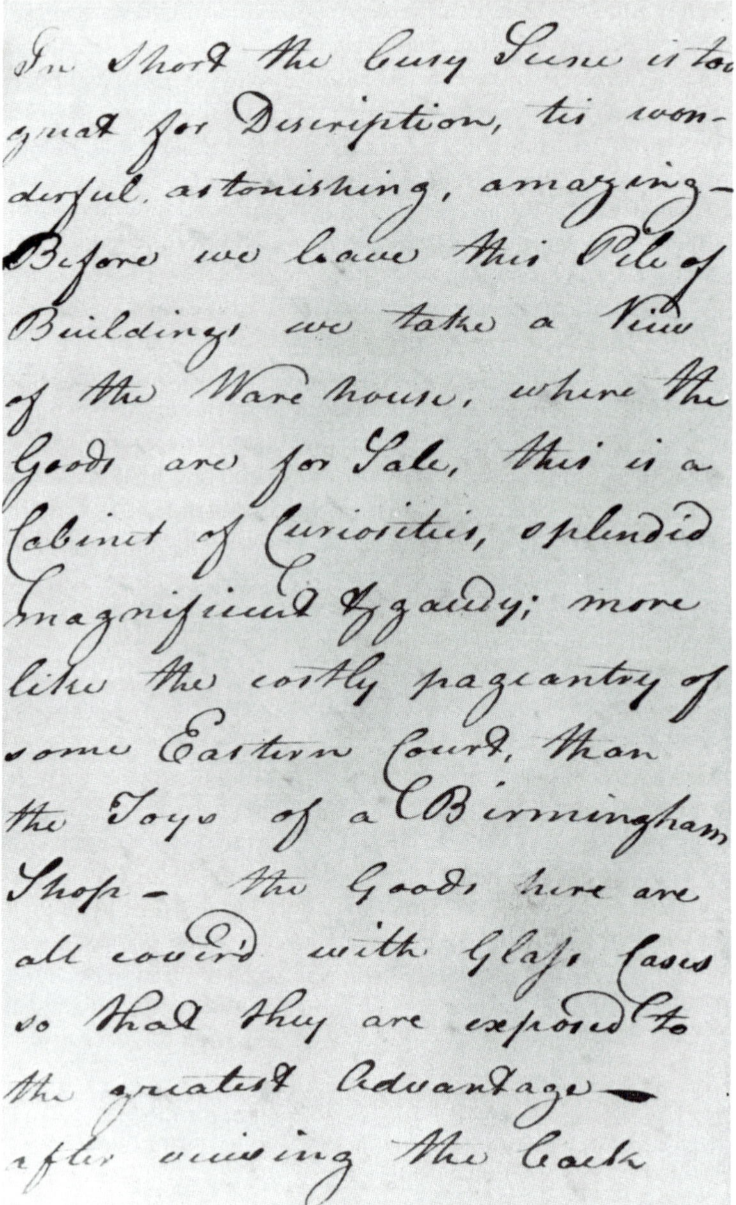

In Short the busy Scene is too great for Description, tis wonderful, astonishing, amazing—

Before we leave this Pile of Buildings we take a View of the Ware house, where the Goods are for Sale, this is a Cabinet of Curiosities, splendid magnificent & gaudy; more like the costly pageantry of some Eastern Court, than the Toys of a Birmingham Shop — The Goods here are all cover'd with Glass Cases so that they are exposed to the greatest Advantage—

after viewing the Cask

FIG. 5. Description of the Soho manufactory, Birmingham (15 August 1776).

Comodities. The making of Buttons of various kinds, plated, lacquerd, gilt employs a little Army of all ages. The great Contrivance and Ingenuity of the People here have taught them to produce some Articles for Sale at about half the price they could a few years ago be sold for. In Short the busy Scene is too great for Description. Tis wonderful, astonishing, amazing.

Before we leave this Pile of Buildings we take a View of the Warehouses, where the Goods are for Sale. This is a Cabinet of Curiosities, splendid magnificent and gaudy; more like the costly pageantry of some Eastern Court than the Toys of a Birmingham Shop. The Goods here are all covered with Glass Cases so that they are exposed to the greatest Advantage. After viewing the back Courts, the distant offices, the various Cells, Mills and all the appendages of these great Works we departed. The Architect of this whole plan, and the Conductor of all the Operation is Bolton (the partner of Forthergill). He is a sensible, ingenious, and enterprizing Man, who plans and executes with equal Expedition, but like many other great Men he has his hobby horse. He is scheming and changeable, ever some new matter on the Anvil to divert his attention from a steady pursuit of some grand object. He is always inventing, and by the time he has brought his Scheme to Perfection, some new Affair offers itself. He deserts the old, follows the new, of which he is weary by the time he has arrived at it. This Volatility prevents him from becoming very rich.

Birmingham is the most increasing Town in England (unless Manchester may be excepted) and contains as many inhabitants. Half the town is new, and they continue to build with greater rapidity than ever. The modern part of the town is most elegant, and they seem to have great Taste in regulating their Streets. Wherever Convenience is not sacrificed they have them regular, and they preserve great Uniformity in their houses. The Streets are wider than in almost any other principal place. The public Buildings consist of their Churches, their hospital and two Theatres. We cannot help lamenting that the Doors of Dissipation will have its Growth, Maturity, and Declension. As its Growth is greater or less, its maturity will be accelerated or protracted. The sooner it arrives the sooner it will decline.

This Reflection makes the human mind unhappy, but English Gloominess it distracts. In adversity they aggravate the Picture of their Misery, and fancy Destruction impends. In Prosperity they rack their brain for some Source of unhappiness and create Phantoms when they can find no Reality. This is too much the Case with Human Nature in general, but particularly with the November Spirited English.

Bolton has invented a Fire Engine of very curious Construction for which he has obtained a patent for 25 years.[36] The difference consists chiefly in making a better Use of the Steam by which he saves one half the Fire. There are likewise some little Jim-Crackeries about it, of considerable Utility.

One Great Advantage Birmingham derives over most other inland Towns is the Canal which comes to it from the East to the West.[37] They have on one Side an easy Communication all the way to the Severn, on the other by the Trent to the Humber. And although the Conveniences of this Navigation be great now, they will be much greater in Case of a War, when inland Navigation will be of more importance. They are supplied with Coal at a very cheap Rate, having only ten miles per Water to bring it to Market.[38] The little River at this place is converted to great Use, tho it could be wished it were not so trivial. Slitting Mills, Grinding Mills and Mills for boring Gun Barrels.

We took a Ride out of Town to our Friend Samuel Galtons Country Retirement.[39] He is happily situated on the Declivity of an Hill, commands a pretty not an extensive Prospect. Has a fine Lake of Water not distant from his house, which is not only an Ornament but is very beneficial to his Works as he has two or three Mills supplied by it. He has likewise some artificial Cascades in which a good deal of Taste is discovered. His walks, Shrubberies, and Gardens are well laid out.

He has a very capital Manufacty of Muskets, carried on in part at this place.[40]The Cheapness of this Article is almost incredible. A Musket to all

[36] In 1763, James Watt conceived the idea of a separate condenser; in 1769, he obtained his first patent for a steam engine. When Boulton and Watt began their partnership, an act of parliament granted Watt a monopoly in the manufacture of his steam engines for a period of twenty-five years in England, Scotland and Wales. Erich Roll, *An Early Experiment in Industrial Organisation Being a History of the Firm of Boulton & Watt, 1775–1805* (London, 1930), pp. 12, 13, 18.

[37] The Birmingham Canal was authorised by act of parliament in 1768 and opened in 1772. It was well connected to the existing canal system in the Midlands and was an important carrier of coal from Staffordshire to Birmingham. Hadfield, *British Canals*, p. 95.

[38] Birmingham was surrounded by coalfields and by an extensive network of canals. In the West Midlands, the canals generated competition that itself was responsible for lowering the price of coal. Flinn, *British Coal Industry: The Industrial Revolution*, pp. 14, 187.

[39] Duddeston House, on the outskirts of Birmingham, was inherited by Samuel Galton the Elder (1720–1799) in 1775. It passed to Samuel Galton the Younger in 1799. Karl Pearson, *The Life, Letters and Labours of Francis Galton* (2 vols., Cambridge, 1914), I, pp. 40, 49 and Plate A.

[40] From 1775 to 1800, there was a continuous demand for Birmingham's small arms and by the 1790s about three million muskets were produced in the city every year. There were fifty-one gunmaking firms in Birmingham in 1777. D. W. Young, 'History of the Birmingham Gun Trade,' (M. Com. Thesis, University of Birmingham, 1935), p. 24, and De Witt Bailey and Douglas A. Nie, *English Gunmakers: The Birmingham and Provincial Gun Trade in the Eighteenth and Nineteenth Centuries* (London, 1978), pp. 17, 27–60.

appearance well finished, of a good Size, is sold at about 6/–. We can only be relieved from our Surprize by observing how little Labour is applied to them, how great a part of the Execution is by Water, and by being informed that Men work at this Buisness for about 6/– a Week, it is not a little mortifying to observe how little the American Trade is valued by these People, and of how little Consequence our Non-Exportation Scheme is to the Manufacturers not only of this Town but of every Town I have been at in the Kingdom. Trade goes on without intermission to increase, a greater Demand for every kind of Goods than was ever known, the Price of Raw Material much advanced, and Labour near 25 per cent higher than for many Years.

Having received every mark of Hospitality from the inhabitants of this agreeable town and been highly entertained by the many curious and capital improvements in the Arts and Manufactures, we prepare to leave the Place uncertain whether I shall ever see it again.[41]

---

[41] I have cut five lines of an epitaph, some faded jottings and a few details of Fisher's accounts for his tour.

JOURNAL O
19–20 August 1776

August 19th   2nd Day
Birmingham

Jerry Vaux[1] escorted us to Hales Owen where we breakfasted (about 7 miles from town). A mile from this Village is the celebrated Retreat of Shenstone called the Leasowes.[2] We enter these Grounds after walking thro 3 or 4 fields, by a little Winding Path on the Declivity of a hill thro a thick Grove, which leads up to the house, from whence we have a noble and diversified Prospect. Hills and Vallies rise with peculiar Grace, the tufted Groves planted on the gay Lawns smiling with eternal Verdure, Cornfields tinged with gilded Age, and water in several near and distant Pools. We again enter the wood, and are conducted thro a sweet Grove; now and then a Seat under some umbrageous Branches; here and there an Image, perhaps, a Diana,[3] or a Pan;[4] sometimes where the Spot favors a more melancholic mood an Urn is erected to some one of his departed Friends; now we enter some moss lined Cell, then some still more humble Hermitage. Next under some fine Grotto a Cascade presents itself to our View, tumbling by many a little Cataract in a variety of Directions and rolling on impetuous, foaming with accumulated rage, it at last arrives at our feet; and while we are expecting each Billow will throw itself upon our Laps, it meets a subterraneous Passage, and as if it were desirous of paying us some Sign of Obeisance, it bows and is lost in the Earth; till it arrive at another opening where it again discovers reiterated Charms.

We walk further on by the Side of this irriguous Stream; a fine sequestered Spot where a Cascade offers its beauties to our Sight is

[1] Jeremiah Vaux (d. 1829) was a Quaker surgeon with a practice at 92 Moor Street, Birmingham. 'He was one of the first four surgeons to the General Hospital, also surgeon to the Militia, and a very experienced practitioner.' Joseph Hill and Robert K. Dent, *Memorials of the Old Square* (Birmingham, 1897), pp. 104–105.

[2] The Leasowes was a property that once belonged to William Shenstone (1714–1763), poet and landscape gardener, who devoted much time to beautifying the grounds there. *DNB*, XVIII, pp. 48–50.

[3] In Roman mythology, goddess of the moon, protector of the female sex, later identified with the Greek Artemis.

[4] A woodland god and god of pastures and of flocks. He lived in Arcadia and passed his days in comparative idleness, playing on his pipes and resting.

dedicated to Lord Stamford,[5] a place it seems he was particularly pleased with. Another spot on a more exalted Eminence where a rich but confined View of several tufted Groves, two pretty Cascades and a level Lawn expand their Charms is dedicated to Lord Lyttleton.[6] Dodesley[7] is not forgotten; he has a beautiful Scene. Thompsons's Memory is made sacred by an Urn with a beautiful Latin Inscription.[8] He has raised an Obelisk to the immortal Mars[9] and several other Poets might here find these Marks of his Regard and Gratitude.

The best Prospect about this whole Place is from an Alcove seated on the Brow of an hill. This is called the High Wood. Here the Prospect is too copious for the Eye, the Scene too great, the Variety too profuse. But if Hills and Vallies of happy Forms; if Woods and Clusters of Trees; if Lawns and Meadows chequered with Deer and Sheep, Cornfields of variegated hues, Villages, Spires, Cottages and Sheets of Water can make a view delightful this is most certainly so. On the back of this Alcove is the following inscription: Hic latis otia fundis / Spæluncæ, vivique lacus, hic frigida Tempi / Mugitus que boum, molles que sub Arbore Somni.[10]

At last we are led to a Cascade more grand than any of the former, at the foot of the great hill, immured among the Woods, and sequestered from the whole World. Here is a Number of Walks, Seats and Verses inscribed from various Authors suitable to the lonely solitary and contemplative Scene. At the foot of this Cataract, Venus de Medici as if just rising from the Stream, is placed on a Pillar, her Feet on the Surface of the Water. This spot is charming and here we bid it Adieu and Shenstone and all his improvements of Taste, Art and Elegance.

A Place like this I can view with pleasure. Here is nothing costly, nothing grand; yet for Taste in these improvements nothing can exceed it. 'Tis only a Farm; the Walks are laid out with little expence; the images and

---

[5] George Harry Grey (1737–1819) was 5th Earl of Stamford and Whig M.P. for Staffordshire between 1761 and 1768. His residencies were Enville Hall, Stafford and Bradgate House, Leicestershire. Cokayne, *Complete Peerage*, XII Part 1, pp. 224–225, 229.

[6] Thomas Lyttleton (1743/4–1779) was 2nd Baron Lyttleton of Frankley from 1773 and Whig M.P. for Bewdley in 1768 and 1769. *Ibid.*, VIII, p. 311.

[7] Robert Dodsley collected together and introduced the writings of his friend, William Shenstone. He paid tribute to Shenstone's memory by adding to his edition of the latter's works a *Description of the Leasowes* with a map. A. R. Humphreys, *William Shenstone: An Eighteenth-Century Portrait* (Cambridge, 1937), pp. 11, 89.

[8] Shenstone was distressed by the death of James Thomson, the poet, in 1748; 'though Shenstone had known him only two years, he felt the intimacy of a warm friendship, and commemorated it by erecting an urn in Virgil's Grove.' *Ibid.*, pp. 72, 83.

[9] In Roman mythology, the god of war. Later identified with the Greek Ares.

[10] 'Here (you will find) leisure by broad acres; grottos and sparkling lakes, a cool, delightful valley, the lowing of cattle, and sweet sleep beneath a tree.' From Virgil, *Georgics* II. 468–470.

urns are all that is superfluous. The Leasowes is a place which a Man of moderate Fortune may be Master of, and it is improved on a plan which a Person without an overgrown Fortune may imitate. The whole Ground is but 120 Acres, yet we are led in that round about way thro it, that 4 miles would barely make up our walk, the whole is Serpentine.

Hagley the beautiful Hagley is but 4 Miles from hence. Thither we went full of expectation loaded with wishes and impatience. We are taken into his Lordship's[11] Gardens; first thro four or five great Areas inclosed with high Walls, laid out in great Method, into strait Walks quite in the Parterre Stile.[12] These are old improvements which the fine fruit, gaudy flowers, and scented herbs scarcely make tolerable. The pinery, Vineyard, and all the rich fruit of the Indies can't make these beautiful, therefore we haste out of them.

But lo! here is Taste, true Elegance. Thro a Shrubbery composed of all the Class of the vegetable Kingdom that can add to its beauty, or give fragrance to the Sense, are laid out Borders for the flowery Tribe to gambol in; here every chequered plant which Flora[13] has in Store, she has scattered carelessly about, as if her Basket had been overset, or her wreath had fallen from her head. Full of mazes and intricacies are these walks, as the margins are full of flowers; and here you might stroll all Day and all Night too, with fresh enjoyment, but Scenes of different kinds haste us away; for Fame had not been silent respecting those Objects which this celebrated Spot has in Store for her Visitors to gaze at.

Adieu! Flora. Now Venus let us approach thy Idalian[14] Glades or Cyprian Lawns,[15] but why are they so soon terminated by Groves and Woods! But these are as beautiful as thy Lawns. These are the Objects which give them their Beauty. A Range of Trees semicircularly planted forms a Theatre, in the midst of which is a very Capital Monument with the Statue of the late Prince of Wales, Father to the present King.[16] This is a

[11] Hagley Hall was occupied by the Lyttleton family. It was about four miles west of the Leasowes, just over the brow of the Clent Hills. George Lyttleton, a friend of Shenstone, inherited the estate at Hagley in 1751. Humphreys, *William Shenstone*, pp. 30–31.

[12] 'A level space in a garden occupied by an ornamental arrangement of flower beds of various shapes and sizes' (*OED*, VII, p. 502). The Parterre style was an essential part of the formal, symmetrical manner in which English gardens were laid out at the beginning of the eighteenth century.

[13] Italian goddess of flowers and spring, and perhaps of love.

[14] One of the names of Aphrodite, goddess of sexual love, in Greek myth.

[15] Both Shakespeare and Milton refer to cypress lawn as a dark cloth from Cyprus. The cypress was a coniferous tree of sombre foliage planted in cemeteries in southern Europe as a symbol of death and mourning.

[16] Frederick, Prince of Wales (1707–1751), father of George III. E. B. Fryde et al., *Handbook of British Chronology* (3rd edn., London, 1986), p. 46.

good piece of Statuary and at the foot of it is a Seat which gives a very rich view of the Park, its Clusters of Trees, the House &c.

We now enter the wood, by a gentle Ascent climb a stout hill. Half way is an opening, at which is an Alcove, commanding a pretty Scene, of Woods, Waters, and Lawns. This is dedicated to Thompson; we next go along the same sort of Serpentine Path, pervade the thickest Woods, where all the Trees of the Forrest shoot most luxuriantly; presently come to Virgil's Alcove from whence a Variety of Objects thro Avenues in the wood meet our Eye, the most beautiful of which is a noble Gothic Ruin, cloathed with a rich Mantle of Ivy. We walk up to it and behold a most delightful Scene. After being delighted with all these enchanting Prospects, we arrive at the Seat of Contemplation. Here the Prospect is contrasted. What we see is wild uncultivated Nature without the touch of Improvement; Woods in ab origine Disorder exactly fitted for meditation. The Alcove is rustic. On the back is the Motto Omnia Vanitas. The former Parts of Hagley may be compared to the improvements of Solomon,[17] and this Motto is appositely introduced. All is Vanity.

While we are left in this thoughtful train, we are led on to an Hermitage composed of Crooked Limbs of Trees and Roots, the Cavities filled up with mud and over grown inside and out with moss. Here meditation holds her dominion, and is Monarch of the heart. If we chuse to stay here tis well our Thoughtful Frame will not be disconcerted, but if we go the Scenes of Pleasure that await us will dissipate all our Reflections. Of these no more! A Continuation of this lovely path leads to a Seat which is dedicated to Lord Stamford, of whose magnificent Seat we distantly behold some traces. The Prospect from this Spot is superior to all the rest. It is higher and the Country round is of that delightful Sort that the more you see of it, the more lovely is the View. Nothing is wanting to perfect the Scene. The Banks by a gentle Slope fall a great Distance. On their Declivity Clumps of Trees are disposed in such Order as to produce the most happy effect. Ourselves are immured in a Thicket, but it does not hinder us from seeing every distant Object.

The Season is never more delightful than at present. The Cornfields are dressed in their gayest attire. They have not yet assumed the Russet brown which they take upon them just before the Sickle has separated them from their mother Earth, when they seem to put on a Countenance of mourning as if conscious of their speedy end. Of these Fields we command

---

[17] This alludes to the wealth and magnificence of Solomon's court and to his passion for building. He spent thirteen years constructing a splendid royal dwelling and a complex of buildings.

unbounded Views, dissected by Hedge inclosures, interspersed with woods, and chequered with Cottages.

> These are thy glorious Works! Parent of
> Good, Almighty thine this universal frame,
> Thus wondrous fair, thyself how wondrous
> then, unspeakable to us invisible, or dimly
> seen in these thy Goodness.

The foregoing Lines are written on the back of this Alcove.

Hence we go to Pope's Seat[18] famous for a fine Echo which reverberates from an opposite Hill. Whether Lord Littleton meant by dedicating this Spot to Pope to allude to his poetical merit, I can't say. But there is some reason to suspect his Lordship had it in View. Pope's borrowing his Beauties from other Authors and having a want of invention that he was only the Echo of more ingenious and Sublime Poets.

One other Seat we arrive at in the Course of our Revolution round these Grounds. This being placed in a solitary Spot is dedicated *Quieti et Musis*.[19] The last Object of all is a Cataract which we view from a temple directly opposite it. In a small Valley, between two lofty and steep hills, whose Sides are crowded with the most stately Oaks, is a fine Lake watered by constant Streams which roll down the Mountains. This lake by a pretty Cataract about 12 feet in fall tumbles into a still larger one below. The foaming rage with which it pours makes an agreeable murmur, and the white waves caused by the agitation of the water forms a lively Contrast to the Mirror which is made green by the Reflection of the Woods that overhang it. This is the last and perhaps the most pleasing of the whole Catalogue of Improvements. We traverse thro the park, pass by the house, the outside of which is not particularly magnificent, of fine hewn Stone, spacious and elegant, tho rustic. The inside is well finished, well furnished, well contrived and contains some good Paintings. Near to the house is the Chaple, of some Use in the Life time of the late Lord; but now of no other use than a Fortification to a Town in time of profound Peace.

The Late Lord Littleton was a Man not only of the most shining Abilities, but of the most amiable heart.[20] Patriotic in his public, Affectionate in his domestic Life, a Scholar, whose Learning had ranked him among the most eminent, a Poet on whom Appollo had bestowed his

---

[18] A building dedicated to Alexander Pope, who visited and wrote about Hagley. *UBD*, II, pp. 246–247.

[19] To Peace and the Muses.

[20] George Lyttleton (1709–1773), 1st Baron Lyttleton, was a politician, author and owner of Hagley, which he rebuilt in 1759–1760. *DNB*, XII, pp. 369–373.

richest Gifts, whom the Muses had often invited to their Banquet, and to whom the Graces had imparted their secret Science. As a Senator he was great and great in the Field. In short he possessed all the great and all the amiable virtues, and died universally beloved as he was lamented.

Strange Degeneracy! The Son blessed with those natural Endowments which would by proper Culture have rendered him an Ornament to human Nature has by a strange and fatal perversion of his Talents become the most abandoned and dissipated Character of the Age; the very opposite to his Father in all that was amiable; and he has an indisputable Title to all the vices which disgrace and degrade the human Species. Effeminacy and Debauchery have marked him for their own, and infamy has stamped her indelible Print on his Brow. The unparalleled Conduct he has shown to his Lady, who is of unsullied Reputation, ranks him among an order of Beings inferior to Man. Yet with all his Frailties, all his Deeds of Darkness, he is made one of the Rulers of this Great Empire. What a Pity that such Characters should meet a Monarch's welcome to his Councils. That such Views should find a Reward instead of an Ignominy they merit and that such Men should be placed in a Situation which might excite the Envy of others and perhaps induce others to tread the same walk to arrive at equal honors.

Still Lord Lyttleton is a great Man, in his speeches, fluent, nervous, manly and argumentative. His manner is persuasive and fascinating; his Stile irresistably captivating. 'Tis only on great occasions he exercises these Powers and only to oppose the great Leaders of the opposite Party that he summons his Faculties to Exertion. When he does, he yields only to Mansfield.[21] Campden[22] and even Shelbourne[23] fear him. With all, in his political Character he has no Principle; the Vicar of Bray;[24] his Extravagancies drive him to seek the favour of the Court. His abilities make him an object of their Attention; as he is employed he acts.

---

[21] Sir James Mansfield (1733–1821), Lord Chief Justice of the Court of Common Pleas, practised both at Common law and in Chancery and was engaged in some state trials. He was M.P. for Cambridge University between 1779 and 1784. But 'in parliament he made a poor figure, whether in office or in opposition' and 'was a dull speaker, with an ungraceful delivery and a husky voice'. *Ibid.*, pp. 976–977.

[22] Charles Pratt, 1st Earl Camden (1714–1794), created Baron Camden of Camden Place, Kent, in 1765 and Lord Chancellor in 1766. He was usually a vehement opponent of Lord Mansfield in his political speeches in the House of Lords. *Ibid.*, XVI, pp. 285–288.

[23] William Petty, 1st Marquis of Lansdowne, better known as Lord Shelburne (1737–1805). He was M.P. for High Wycombe, 1760–1761, but took his seat in the House of Lords on the death of his father in 1761. He made many famous political speeches in parliament in the 1760s and 1770s. *Ibid.*, XV, pp. 1005–1013.

[24] *The Vicar of Bray* is the title of an anonymous eighteenth-century song about a parish priest who managed to keep his parish through every political and religious vicissitude. The name is thus representative of time-servers. Gillie, *Longman Companion to English Literature*, p. 854.

We dined at an Inn adjoining the Park. It rained heavily. We bid defiance to it, being secured and Protected by a commodious Chaise. We came through Stourbridge, a large neat manufacturing Town in the Nail Hardware and Glass Trade. Thence to Woolverhampton a still larger Market Town in the same Manufactures of Stourbridge. The Roads were indifferent till we came to Shefnal; intolerable and dangerous afterwards considering the Darkness of the Night. We now enter Shropshire, an old Welch County, but now left out of that Principality.[25] Call the People in this country Welch and you offend them: go into Wales and you can offer them no greater insult than to call them English. Is this Patriotism? Tis a Love of one's own Country that makes us think better of it. Happy for us we are so.

A Scene is now before us, for which I was by no means prepared. The effect therefore was more strong; it was unexpected and therefore more wonderful. When we arrive at the Summit of the Hill which overlooks Colebrookdale, we are presented with all the horrors that Pandemonium[26] could shew. Behold far below us an immense Theatre, lighted only by the Streams of Light which rise from the Furnaces, from the Mountains of Ore which are here and there scattered mixed with the Coal, and burning with prodigious fury; and from the heaps of Coal which are Scattered here and there on every hand which are involved in Flames being partly burnt to make Charcoal. While all these Etnas and Vesuvius's[27] are spread before us, the Heavens are dark and black undecked by a single Star. We descend the Hill passing thro the very midst of all these Flames; the Prospect is awful and magnificent. The curling Clouds rising in successive Columns add greatly to the Beauty and Grandeur of it and the Shape of the Hills around us which we can just discern, puts on the finish of Perfection. My lodging Room commanded a very extensive view of this great Theatre. From my bed I could look down upon the Craters of the burning Mountains; the house of my host being situated on an elevation which gave every desirable advantage to the novel Scene. We took up our abode with *Abraham* Darby[28] one of the principal Proprietors of these Works and the sole Superintendant.

---

[25] Throughout the Middle Ages Shropshire was a county where the Welsh and English tried to establish jurisdiction and frequently fought.

[26] The abode of the demons, a place represented by Milton as the capital of Hell.

[27] Etna, the chief mountain of Sicily and the higest volcano in Europe. Its elevation is c. 10,758 feet. Vesuvius, on the Bay of Naples, is the only active volcano on the European mainland. It has two summits, the volcano proper (c. 4,200 feet) and Monte Somma to the north (3,370 feet).

[28] Abraham Darby III (1750–1791) was a member of the Quaker family who owned the famous ironworks at Coalbrookdale, Shropshire. He was the grandson of Abraham Darby I (1677–1717) who disovered in 1709 a method of using coke instead of charcoal for the smelting of iron ore. Arthur Raistrick, *Dynasty of Ironfounders: The Darbys and Coalbrookdale* (London, 1953), ch. 1, 2, 3, 6.

August 20th   3rd Day

We decamped with A*braham* Darby to take a general Survey of the Furnaces, Forges, and other Conveniences for the manufactury of Iron. The Ore is brought a few Miles from the mine to the works. It is then laid on a great Pile with a Stratum of Coal under it, and a considerable Quantity of loose pieces thrown into the general mess. These coals are lighted and thus the Ore is first calcined, being purged of a variety of combustible materials before it is taken to the Furnace. The Coal for this business, as well as for the principal Concerns of these works, is burnt into Charcoal before it is used. For this purpose it is thrown up into a multitude of uniform hillocks and attended till it become of a proper Quality for their Use. The Coals are brought by Land 2 or 3 Miles on fine level Iron paved Roads. Down the declivities they use no horses. By the same Roads the Lime and Ore are also conveyed.

The old Furnace (nearest the house) has been in blast without the least diminution for 7 years last past. It continues to vomit out its Flames and emit a vast Column of Smoak. The great Number of Buildings for the Furnaces, Forges, Founderies, Warehouses &c and the habitations of the Workmen 200 of whom are imployed compose a little City. It is astonishing to think of the uses to which Cast Iron is converted. Besides common castings they make their Chimney Tops, their Window Cases, their Chimney Pieces, their Sashes, their floors, their Scantlen for their Roofs, Doors, Pallisadoes, Ploughshares, besides an hundred other Utensils for domestic Use of this permanent and durable material. The Arch over one of their door Cases which is 16 feet in Diameter is likewise of Cast Iron. But all these are trifling compared with the great Tools for which they have occasion in the progress of their Business. Their Boilers and Cylinders and above all, their Conduits for water to turn the Mills which they serve instead of Races, and answer much better, as less Water is wasted both by the exhalations of the Sun, and what the Ground would absorb. All these are of Cast Iron.

Their Water Wheels are likewise composed of Iron. The Crank of the great Wheel which sets the Bellows to work weighs 50 Cwt. The axes weigh 140 Cwt. and besides this the whole wheel is of Iron, even the Ladles and shroudings. The Diameter of this Wheel is about 25 feet. These Gudgeons turn on Friction Wheels, by which means much less Water is necessary to give Motion to the Machinery. There are to this Bellows three large Cylinders 78 Inches in Diameter. The Bellows in these rise 4 feet at a time. While one is up the other falls, so that the Air is constantly gushing through the Funnel with equal Force. The Funnel is 20 feet in length, at the Body of the Bellows about 30 Inches in Diameter, narrowing into a Cone; being only 3 Inches where it emits the Air into the mouth of the Furnace. It is impossible to conceive with what vehemence the Air Rushes into the Furnace or the roaring which it occasions. The Noise is like the rudest Blustering of Oolus, but greater and may be heard at a great Distance, though the general bourdon, which an hundred other Machines make, drown it in the confused Crush.

The slitting Mill which they are about is of Iron wholly. There is not a wheel in the whole Machine but is cast. The water wheel is 12 feet. This with all the Ladles and Shrouding is a Mass of Metal, the Cags, Rounds and every thing about it even the Flies which are 20 feet Diameter and the Troughs which furnish it with water.

But a far greater and more wonderful piece of Architecture is now in agitation by the enterprizing Owners of these works, a Fabric which England or the whole Globe cannot equal. This is an Iron Bridge across the River Severn to consist of one Arch only.[29] This will be a regular Circle. The Span from Side to Side is near [196] feet. A*braham* Darby has made a very elegant and compleat Model of the plan on a Scale of $\frac{1}{4}$ Inch to a Foot, by which it appears so easy, practicable and simple that an Act of Parliament is passed for his effecting it. The whole will be of Cast Iron without an ounce of any other Sort of material about it. It may be taken to pieces at any time, and should it ever become out of Order it will very easily be rectifyed.

These Iron Works for Perfection, for Extent and Convenience, are superior to any upon Earth. The Severn is at hand by which they transport their Pigs and Founderies to Bristol. The canal which opens into the Severn has a ready Communication to the inland Part of the Kingdom, and even to the Trent. London is supplied from hence. It has no Rival except the Carron in Scotland, where the same Perfection is by no means arrived at and from its Situation never will.

In the Afternoon we took a ride to see my Friend R*ichard* Reynolds[30] who lives about 5 Miles distant at the *Bank*, commanding a lovely view of a rich and extended Valley, and some distant Mountains. On the way here we stopped at a very capital Pig Iron Works, the Property of Reynells and Darby.[31] Here is one of the largest Fire Engines in the Kingdom, and

[29] This famous iron bridge, the first of its kind, was designed by Abraham Darby III and cast in 1778 by his Coalbrookdale Company. Pevsner, *Buildings of England: Shropshire* (London, 1958), p. 157.

[30] Richard Reynolds (1735–1816), a Quaker philanthropist and an iron merchant of Bristol. He became a partner of Abraham Darby II in the large ironworks at Ketley in Coalbrookdale in 1756. He married his partner's daughter, Mary, in 1757 and later assumed charge of the ironworks, then the most important of its kind in England. *DNB*, XVI, pp. 955–956.

[31] The Ketley ironworks were managed by Abraham Darby III and Richard Reynolds. Raistrick, *Dynasty of Ironfounders*, p. 90. The Darby-Reynolds group at Coalbrookdale is discussed in *ibid.*, pp. 83–99 and in Raistrick, *Quakers in Science and Industry*, pp. 122–146.

converted to as droll a Use as any thing of the kind I have seen. They have a pretty large Mill Pond, but not furnished by sufficient Streams to keep it always full. As the water runs into the Mill Tail, it is confined. In the bottom of this are fixed the Cylinders of the Engine which rise 30 Hogsheads of Water per Minute from whence it is conveyed by a Trough into the Mill Pond from whence it originally had its Source by which means the Mill for blowing the Furnace is kept constantly in ample Supply.

The next day we took a ride a few miles to a fine Farm belonging to Abraham Darby. The Situation is as delightful as any thing can well be. Its banks rise with great Regularity from the Sides of the Severn of which there is a pretty avenue for a great distance up and down the River, while a fine Range of Hills and Vallies and a richly improved and thick settled Country (not without its Copses) spread their Charms before us. The Gardens and Fruitery and Walks and every thing here are pleasant.

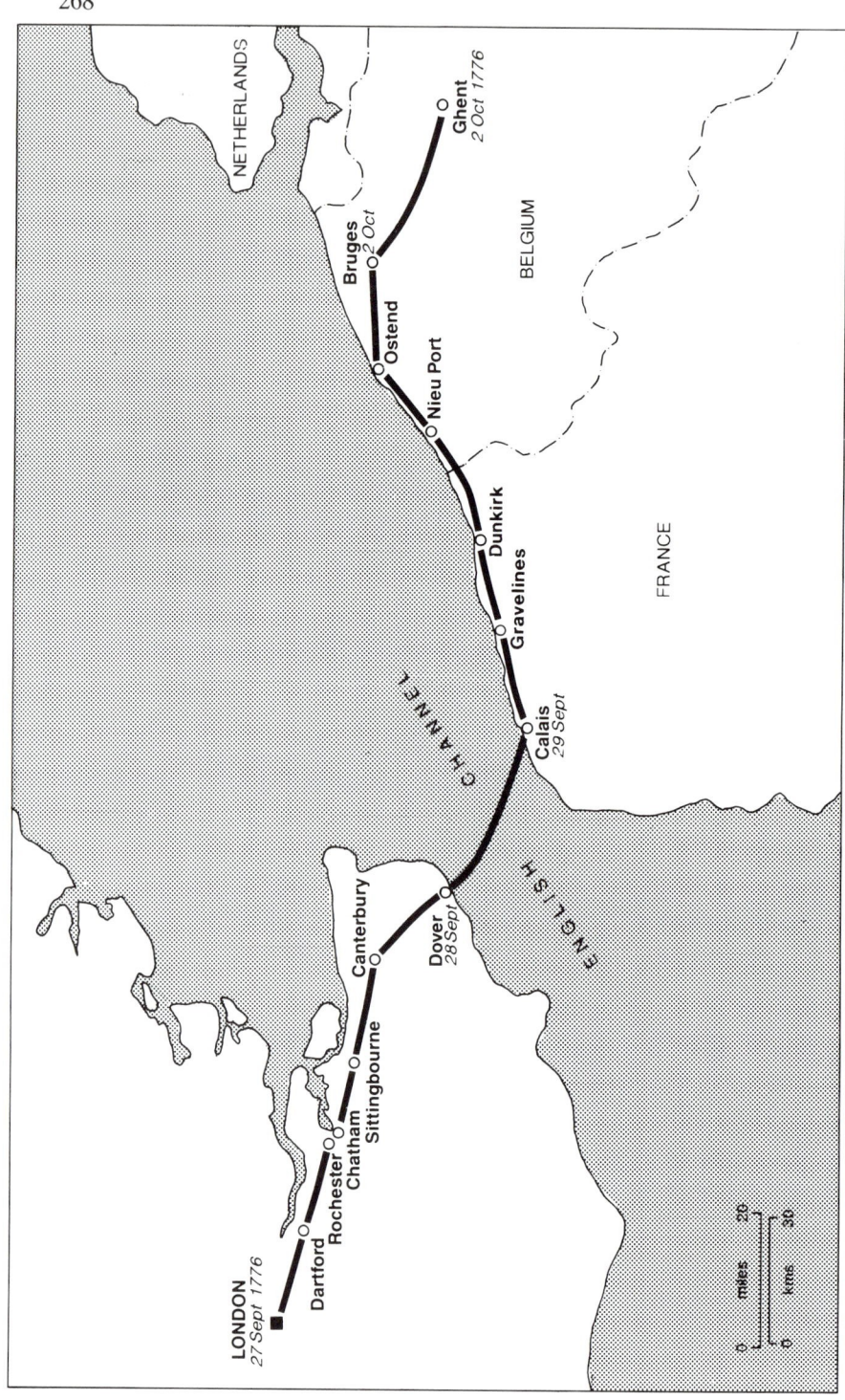

JABEZ MAUD FISHER'S TRAVELS, 27 SEPTEMBER - 2 OCTOBER 1776

27 September–2 October 1776

London to Dover September 27th, 1776[1]
6th Day

We left London (R*ichard* Philips and myself) about 3 O Clock. Came thro Dartford to Rochester where we lodged. No remarkable Event. A Country I had travelled thro before. Strood, Rochester, and Chatham three pretty large Towns lie in a String. The first is a Market Town, the two last considerable trading towns on the Conflux of the Medway and Thames. They both give Title to Earls. Chatham is one of the finest Arsenals for Shipping in the Universe.[2]

September 28th, 1776   6th Day

We left Rochester very early, stopped at Sittingbourne to breakfast and stopped a while at Canterbury a famous large old fashioned Town. The Cathedral is capital, having once had 26 Altars in it.[3]

We got into Dover in good Dinner time, and took a Passage in the Packet for Calais. We met with Ferguson an ingenious Gentleman of my Acquaintance from America, who being acquainted with the Laws, Customs, and Fashions of France politely offered us his Services and Attendance to Paris. We took a walk up to the Castle which stands on a noble Hill of Chalk, the Side next the Sea being perpendicular. This Castle

---

[1] I have cut a drawing of a barge on the canal between Bruges and Ghent plus a brief inscription, written in French.

[2] Chatham was a major dockyard for the English fleet in the sixteenth and seventeenth centuries. The dockyards were completely laid out anew in 1685 and the first twenty years of the eighteenth century saw a complete new set of administrative buildings and storehouses. John Newman, *Buildings of England: West Kent and the Weald* (London, 1969), pp. 196–200; Morriss, *Royal Dockyards*, p. 2.

[3] Canterbury Cathedral has been the seat of the Archbishop, Primate of All England, since St. Augustine's mission from Rome to reconvert the country, in 597. Between 1070 and 1077 Lanfranc, the first Norman archbishop, rebuilt the cathedral church but most of this, like the original Saxon cathedral, has virtually disappeared. Most of the core of the present cathedral was built from 1378 onwards in the Perpendicular Style. John Newman, *Buildings of England: North-East and East Kent* (2nd edn., London, 1976), pp. 170–227.

was first built by Julius Caesar but only a small Part of his Building is now standing. The well which is 360 feet is of his sinking.[4]

The Master of the Packet (Radcliff) told us he should go off about 1 O Clock at Night. We went down to the Sloop at $\frac{1}{2}$ past 12 O Clock. The Cabbin was full of Men Women and Children. We got into the After Part of the Vessel laid ourselves down against the transom put our Feet against some Boards and invoked Morpheus[5] till 3 O Clock in the Morning without Success when the Captain came to inform us that the wind was a head and he could not go that Night. We came to the Inn, went to Bed, and considering our Disappointment slept comfortably.

September 29th   1st Day

At 10 O Clock came the Summons for us to go on board the Packet. We had about 20 Passengers. The Cabbin was filled with a third of them. The rest came upon Deck. We had not been long on the Water before Neptune received the Tribute of plenteous Sacrafices. The day was fine. We had a pleasant Sail and came over to Calais in about 4 hours.

Calais stands on the Promontory of a piece of Low Land. There is no River or Bay and therefore they have run out two long wooden Piers, built on piles far into the Sea, which form an artificial River, by which we are conducted up to the Town. At the End of these Two Piers are two Forts of but little Signification. An hundred People met us at our landing. Before we could get ashore, Valets from all the Inns in Town came on board, each soliciting our Attendance, offering us their Services and begging a Preference.

We land at 12 O Clock. Every thing bore the Aspect of Novelty. We were escorted up to the Custom house, had our Trunks searched. The Officers finding nothing illicit were content with a Livre. From thence we were conducted to our Inn, the Land lord of which is Monsieur Dessin a Genius of some originality characterised by Sterne, particularly for his Eyes (or rather Eye for he has but one), and his Wig.[6] The Inn is capital. We ordered a Dinner of Quarante Sous per head. We had 2 Courses, drank some Burgundy and eat Fruit. They have no Ale here. We drink an ordinary wine instead of it.

Calais is a Town of considerable Size is clean and tolerably well built, walled in, and has a mote round it, a Square in the middle. Several

---

[4] Dover Castle was built in the Roman period, but considerable alterations have been made since. Colvin, *History of the King's Works*, II, pp. 629–641, III Part 1, pp. 242–248.

[5] In Greek mythology, Morpheus was the god of dreams who imitated human forms and voices.

[6] The Hotel Dessein is the setting for the opening scene of Laurence Sterne's *Sentimental Journey*.

Churches are in it and a Steeple of curious appearance.[7] They have also a Theatre, which we were called on with an invitation to attend though it was their Sunday.

We supped at home and went to bed, which was made up of 3 Mattrasses and a bed of Straw under all. Monsieur Dessin keeping a large Quantity of Carriages, he furnishes Passengers with the necessary modes of Conveyance, sometimes sells, sometimes hires, there being no Post Chaises in the Country at the different Stages, and horses are only kept by the Master of the Post houses. Other People can't hire them without a Licence. So we agreed with Dessin to take us (with our Friend Ferguson and another Gentleman) to Dunkirk which is 22 English Miles for 42 Livres.[8]

September 30th   2nd Day

France fills me with a thousand droll Ideas. The Novelty of the Thought, the Novelty of the Scene, the difference of the People in their Behaviour, Appearance, Manner, Custom and Language, the drollery of their Furniture, the oddness of their houses and every thing is so different, so new, that I have not yet had time to expand my Imagination for the conception of the variety of objects that crowd upon it.

The first Sight of their Diligence which goes from Calais to Paris set me a laughing for a quarter of an hour. Its shape was so uncouth and awkard, the Conveniences so indifferent, and its whole appearance so grotesque and queer and indeed every thing else is so novel that my Senses seem scattered. The *Voiture* or the *Diable* which Monsieur Dessin procured for us was a very whimsical Machine, more like a Landau than any thing else, but not like that neither. It carried 4 of us very agreeably. The Top was open and we sat face to face. Dessin has generally 2 or 300 of these Machines which he keeps for the accomodation of his Friends. These he will either sell or hire. His Coach Yard is a Cabinet of Curiosities. This Genius has made a Fortune of about £20,000 by the entertainment of English Gentry who for the most part resort to his house, tho there be many other Capital Inns in the place.

R*ichard* Philips and myself went to the Mass house, where the silly People and the more silly Priest were running over the superstitious Ceremony, counting their Beeds, crossing their Foreheads with the holy

---

[7] A reference to the heavily buttressed Tour du Guet, a watch tower built by Philippe de Boulogne in 1224. *Ibid.*, p. 91.

[8] The average rate of exchange for London on Paris in 1775 was 30.70 pence sterling per ecu (crown) of three livres tournois. John J. McCusker, *Money and Exchange in Europe and America, 1600–1775: A Handbook* (Chapel Hill, N.C. 1978), p. 97.

Water. In the Church are some tolerable Scripture Paintings. The Altar (as all their Altars have) has a good Effigy of our Saviour.

We mounted our voiture at 7 in the Morning. The first few Miles were sandy barren and dreary, the Country thinly settled. What few Cottages we see are humble Fabrics of Clay and Sticks covered but thinly with Straw. The Men and Children of these habitations devote their Summers to catching Fish. How the poor wretches live in the winter is matter of Surprise. They have no Coals, no Wood, and no Turf. Their Situation must subject them to great Asperity of Weather, for they have not a hill or a Tree to shelter them from unpitying Boreas. Cow Dung they burn but this is stealing from the Soil the Tribute due to it for the poor Gratuity they receive. The little Children yet unable to traverse the Sea for Fish ran out from every hut we passed by, begging with fervency, 'Charité, Monsieur! S'il vous plait.'

Even in this distressing employ, we cannot help remarking that uncommon digree of Chearfulness which characterises this Nation. They smile even in their Prayers for Relief. Happy People! Without the possession of one earthly blessing, without even the enjoyment of Liberty or Competence, they smile at Grief and bid Defiance to Care, while an Englishman with every blessing that heaven has in Store poured on him with unlimited Profusion is perpetually murmuring at his fate, poor amid Riches, unhappy while Peace and Plenty flow in upon him. Thus is Providence equal in all her Distributions. If she give the English the means of being happy, she denies them the power of enjoyment. If she deny the French the means she gives them the Disposition to laugh at their wants, so that the Fancy without the materials is equal to Reality without the imaginary possession.

As we approach Gravlines the Country is more populous, tho still open and the Soil barren. Gravlines is a strongly fortified Town with several Tasses, covered Ways, Motes and Walls round it.[9] We enter it by several Drawbridges and thro several Gates at which poor wretches are stationed who live by enquiring of the Passengers whether they have any Contraband Articles! And tho we had a Pass Port from Calais where our Baggage was searched, we are obliged to give them a few Sous, or endure another overhauling of our apparel. This same process we undergo several times at every Town we come to and we are sometimes called upon to give our Names to Officers who are appointed for that purpose.

Gravlines is one of the strongest fortified Towns in Flanders. It is well built, regularly laid out. The streets are well paved, the houses uniform, of

[9] Gravelines is an ancient fortress which preserves its sixteenth and seventeenth century ramparts. Robertson, *Blue Guide: France*, p. 91.

light colored bricks, and the Streets are abundantly cleaner than any in England. We breakfasted here and set off about 11 O Clock for Dunkirk. The Road continued much like the other part of the Day, sandy, tho the Country more populous. We got into Dunkirk about 3 O Clock, having passed the Mardick,[10] a little fortified town and come over a Plain where were the marks of French Encampments; the French having 30,000 Men stationed there in the last War sometime and where they built boats with an intention to cross over to England. But the scheme was too ridiculous to execute.[11]

At Dunkirque the Officers made us give them a few Sous and write our Names. Dunkirque is a place of great Repute from the Noise it made in the Politics of the last War and the Treaty of Paris.[12] It once belonged to the English but was sold to the King of France by Charles the [2nd].[13] By the Treaty the Fortifications were to be destroyed, but this is yet only in Part done, for in the same Treaty it was Stipulated that the English should pay the utmost regard to the health and Salubrity of the inhabitants, which could not be adhered to if the Sluice, which is the great inlet from the Sea, were to be demolished. And this Sluice is the principal part of the Fortifications and will always be a sufficient Defence as by it they may fill the motes and surround the Town with a great body of Water. The French alledge that if this were to be destroyed it would cost them a Million of Money to make the River navigable up to the Town, and that it would occasion such a body of stagnant and putrid Water as would subject them to the greatest want of health.

However a fine Bason which would have accomodated a great Number of large Ships is destroyed and some other Parts of the Fortification. The Arsenal is in good Repair. The town is a beautiful place, precisely regular and uniform, the houses neat and well constructed, the Streets paved of

---

[10] Fort Mardyck.

[11] The French war minister, the Duke of Choiseul, hatched a plan to make a direct attack on Britain during the Seven Years' War. But delay in constructing the transports caused a postponement, and in 1759 the English were informed and given ample time to take counter-measures. Walter L. Dorn, *Competition for Empire 1740–1763* (New York, 1940), p. 355.

[12] During the Seven Years' War, Britain was very concerned about the security of the Straits of Dover and therefore insisted that the fortifications of Dunkirk be dismantled. But the French persisted in rebuilding Dunkirk. This dispute was frequently discussed in the peace negotiations that concluded the war. Under Article 13 of the Treaty of Paris (1763), the French conceded the fortification of Dunkirk in return for regaining fishing rights off Newfoundland. David Ogg, *Europe of the Ancien Regime 1715–1783* (London, 1965), pp. 170, 177; Zenab Esmat Rashed, *The Peace of Paris in 1763* (Liverpool, 1951), pp. 84, 88, 90–91, 96, 194–197, 221.

[13] Dunkirk was sold by Charles II to Louis XIV of France for £200,000. Cassell's *Encylopaedia*, IV, p. 87.

excellent Square Stones. A kennel divides the Foot from the horse Road, but there are no Posts. There are two noble Squares, well adorned with regular and neat houses. The largest is called *Place Royale*. We were here introduced to Captain Frazer an English Officer very intelligent and sensible who afforded us all necessary information and behaved with great Civility. He walked round the Town with us and gave us ample directions for our future Rout.

This is a free Port, of course has considerable trade, especially as the Conveniences for Shipping are great and the Canals commence here, which afford a fine inland Communication by water into the heart of the Country. The Police of this place is like all the fortified Towns in French Flanders. The administration of Justice is impartial, tho from its very Nature liable to great Abuse. All contested Matters are submitted to the Reference of two Officers, first nominated by the People and afterwards appointed or rather confirmed by the King. In the Decision of all matters the Concurrence of the Intendant is necessary. And he being appointed by the King, the Democratical Weight in the Scale of Power is of no Consequence. In trivial matters where these Officers have acted, the intendant may reverse a Decree, and from hence there lies no appeal but in the King's own Person. In the issuing a writ these Justices act by sending for the Defendant and hearing the Arguments he has to offer. They then proceed in regular Process to decide; but the mode is tedious.[14]

We dined, supped and lodged here, having before concluded to take our Rout to Paris. On considering the little time we had to effect so long a Tour and the time it would take to pay Paris its Curiosities and vicinities a proper Respect and how very superficial our investigation of its Wonders must be, we determined to give that up and in lieu thereof to take Flanders and Holland in our way. By this means we part with my Friend Ferguson whose Company would have been highly entertaining and useful to us, as he has many times been that Road, and having lived some time in France is well acquainted with its Laws Language and Customs. We found him from the little time we had travelled together much of the Gentleman and Scholar, a man of great reading, entertaining and instructive.

---

[14] By the reign of Louis XIV, *intendants* had become regular, permanent officials of the central authority in the French provinces. There were thirty *intendants* throughout France in the eighteenth century. Their duties included recruitment for the army, the dispensation of justice, the apportionment of the *taille*, and responsibility for collecting direct taxes. J. O. Lindsay, ed., *The New Cambridge Modern History, VII: The Old Regime 1713–1763* (Cambridge, 1957), p. 153.

October 1st   3rd Day

Early in the Morning we rose and having agreed the Evening before for a Calash[15] to take us to Ostend we were calld for and mounted it. A curious Vehicle it is, in its principle not unlike the Canadian Calash, tho more convenient, having a Top and being lined and stuffed. We were drawn by two horses. Five Leagues we came along the Sea Side and after that left it till now. The Beach was hard, but here the Sand was deep and in spight of Monsieur le Driver's whip and all his oratory he could not get the horses out of a walk. The Traces which were of a hempen Cord and all the flimsey Harness remained firm and brought us to New Port without one Misadventure. Nieu Porte is a strongly fortified Town, has every possible means of Defence, constructed with great ingenuity. The French never wanted Engineers. Their Forts all declare this Truth. The town is pretty, regular, clean &c.

We got here at 12 O Clock, eat an hearty breakfast, and set out for Ostend. We rode 4 Miles along the Canal which goes to Bruges.[16] The Country now assumes a more smiling Visage. We see a pleasing Verdure and a number of little Villages with their Spires on every Side of us. We leave the Canal and have now a strait paved road to Ostend about 5 Miles in an exact right Line and as level all the way as a bowling Green.

We got into Ostend too late to dine and agreed to lose our Dinner and live on a dish of Tea till Supper time. Between these two meals we took a walk to see the Town Harbour and Fortifications, all which are objects of Beauty and Utility. The Harbour is most commodious for Shipping. There are 20 feet water at its Entrance. The Sea washes the Fortifications of the town, on which account they are secured by a sloping Dyke supported with Piles and Taxines. The other parts are kept in nice order. The Port is capable of receiving 3 or 400 Ships of War. The Bason is a fine object, being a noble artificial River fitt for the finest Navy in the world, dyked all round regularly and strong. The Workmanship of this Bason has been enormous and the expence prodigious. Tis well laid out.

Sas de Sliken a famous Sluice[17] is 1 Mile from the Town. In it are 3 Passages by which Vessels of 400 Tonns are admitted into the Canal, which is 150 feet broad and very deep. Contiguous to this are 17 Wind Mills for saving Plank. A Barge sets out from hence every day and carries

---

[15] A kind of light carriage with low wheels, having a removable folding hood or top. The French form is calèche. Murray, *New English Dictionary*, II, p. 24.

[16] The Bruges-Ostend Canal was completed in 1666. Naval Intelligence Division, *Geographical Handbook Series: Belgium* (1944), p. 505.

[17] The Slykens lock at the entrance of the maritime port of Ostend. This lock connects with the Ostend-Bruges Canal. *Ibid.*, pp. 399, 517.

Passengers to Bruges 4 leagues for 1/-. The town is clever clean, neat, and uniform. The great Square has an Inn, calld the *Maison de Ville*, which for Spaciousness is equalld by few in England. We got an excellent Supper in it for 1/- each of 3 dishes besides Plenty of Vegetables.

October 2nd   4th Day

It is inconvenient travelling in Flanders as the Gates of every town are shut as soon as it is dark and if we cannot reach the Town we have in View, we must be locked out and seek Shelter in an open Sky. 'Tis no better in the Morning. We must wait the hour of their being opened. For this reason we did not start till past 6 O Clock from Ostend, and we had afterwards a Ferry to pass which detained us some time. We came by the Sas de Slicken, the Sluices which I mentioned in yesterday's occurences.

The great Number of Windmills here is a pleasing Sight. These being contiguous to Navigation do a great deal of Business in the sawing of Timber. Flanders as well as Holland is a flat Country and having no Falls of Water all their Mill work is done by Wind. It is the same in France. I am informed there are 200 Wind Mills about the Town of Lisle. The Mills at this Sluice are large and well constructed. The Locks raise the Ships up about 10 feet when they are in the widest and deepest Canal in Europe, perhaps in the world.

We passed by 2 Ships on their way towards Bruges of about 300 Tons each. They are drawn with ease by 5 horses. The Canal is 150 feet wide and makes a Noble appearance. We rode all the way to Bruges in our Voiture along Side of it, there being excellent Roads on both Sides. The Country now affords very different Prospects from those we yesterday had. Tis highly cultivated and well settled. Trees which we had not seen since we left England were plenteously disposed.

We got into Bruges in time to take our Passage in the Barge which goes to Ghent at 9 O Clock, but we had no Breakfast. However we ran to one house and got some Roles and to another and got some butter, came on board and eat a tolerable Breakfast. Bruges is a very capital Place strongly fortified, and the Fortifications add much to its Beauty, the Motes being spacious.[18] We came thro 4 or 5 Gates at the Entrance and 2 or 3 on leaving it. There are several Canals pass thro the Town which add greatly to its Beauty as well as to the health and Convenience of its inhabitants. The town is clean handsome and regular, contains a number of Churches with some elegant Spires and Towers. It has several Convents. One in

[18] Bruges was an important medieval trading and political centre, with fourteenth century ramparts. *Ibid.*, pp.594–595.

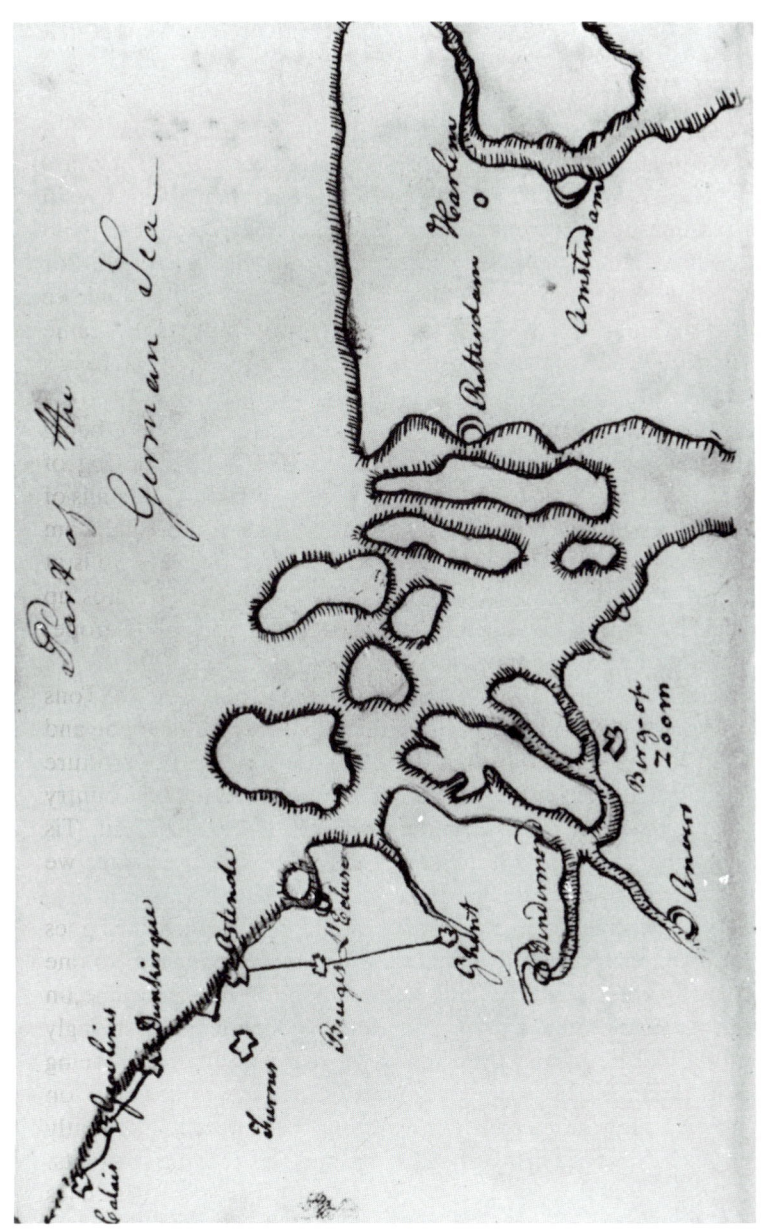

FIG. 6. Fisher's map of 'Part of the German Sea'.

particular of St. Augustine has an elegant Chapel of the Corinthian Order.
There is one Tour which makes a grand appearance long before we come
into the town. This is La Tour des Halls 300 feet high.[19] The Market place
is convenient and well supplied with Meat and Vegetables.

The Dress of the People now becomes a good deal dutchified. The Men
wear very large Breeches and very droll made Jackets. The Women have
either a straw [Beehive] Bonhat; or they have a square piece of black Cloth
thrown over their heads which comes down as low as their Wastes, which
gives them a monastic appearance. Their Dress however I prefer to that of
the French who affect a richness in every part of their Garb. Let them
be ever so poor, they chuse some tawdry fine Colour, perhaps a red, a
green, or a blue and every Man of any appearance at all wears his hair
powdered and in a bag, and this is often the Case with the very poorest
wretch, and not uncommon with Barbers and even Coachmen. A Sword or
Cutteau de Chase is likewise a very necessary appendage to a Man's
Dress. Without it he makes no figure and cannot always be admitted into
public Company. The Flemings however are very different. Their Dress
is more plain and substantial, more awkard than that of the English tho
this may perhaps be my Prejudice in favor of a mode I have been
accustomed to.

We embarked on board the Barge where we found a large Company
composed of various Characters and Complections, of different Nations
and Tongues, of different Ranks and appearances, and of different Sexes. I
divided my time between some uncouth Dutchmen who sat at one end and
some polished French Men who had the other End of the Vessel. If the
latter were more instructive, the former were more entertaining. I hardly
know a higher enjoyment than such a mixed Crew, where the Customs of
all were so novel.

At Dinner the Rich and the Poor were divided. There were dinners at
two Prices. We took the more grand Table and being Characters of a new
Stamp to our Companions we attracted their Notice and Attention. There
were 15 of us at Table. The Conversation was upon France and England,
their Languages and Populousness and drawing Comparisons between
London and Paris. The former they had never seen and the latter we had
only heard of.

Our Dinner was quite elegant consisting of 3 Courses of substantial
Dishes. The French use a Fork with 4 Prongs and this they use with their

---

[19] The thirteenth-century Halle, a large block around a courtyard, served for a long time
as the main market for Bruges. At one end of the Halle is the Belfry, the best-known and
most prominent feature of Bruges, 83 metres in height. John Tomes, *Blue Guide: Belgium
and Luxembourg* (6th edn., London, 1983), p. 155.

left hand. I attempted to adopt their mode but found myself too awkard to continue it. This Dinner with 1 Bottle of Burgundy and another of *Vin ordinaire*, besides beer of different Sorts, together with our Passages of 24 Miles, cost but 4/6 per head.

This Barge is upon Deck 90 feet in length and about 12 broad. She draws 5 feet Water. All the length from Stern to stern is divided into different appartments and offices. It is a compleat house, having every conveniency of an Inn, a Larder, a Kitchin with a noble hearth and Sack, Pots, Kettles, and Stews, le Privé, and a dining Room for the Common Passengers and at each end are two Rooms compleatly furnished with Tables Chairs and Looking Glasses. The Benches round are covered with Cushions of green Velvet. There are Windows all the way on each Side so that if the Weather be bad tis convenient being below.

The Canal is a noble one, about 50 feet wide, the water clear as crystal, the Banks gently rising, and covered with Grass. Where the Soil is loose there are Fascines made of hurdles drove down to keep the Earth from falling in. All the way there are two wide Roads, one on each Side and Rows of Trees planted with great Uniformity. We are drawn on by two horses who go a League an hour, but all distances here are by the hour. For instance if the distance be 8 Leagues, they say the distance is 8 hours.

The Country here is extremely populous. All the way tis like one Village. The houses in general are small, but they have an Air of Neatness and most of them being white forms a pleasing Contrast with the Verdure. The Country is as level as a Country can be. There is not a Mole hill for the whole 24 Miles, so that from the Deck of the Vessel we could see but a little Distance. But I frequently went to the Mast head, from whence I could command a pretty extensive Prospect. The Country is finely cultivated. Every field declares how industrious these People are. The Soil tho originally indifferent by proper culture is made fertile and yields abundantly of every kind of vegetable. Tis divided into small Fields and prettily inclosed with hedges or Rows of Trees.

The inhabitants besides paying great attention to Commerce and to the Cultivation of their Lands do a great deal in the manufactury of a coarse Sort of Linnen. We passed by a great Number of bleaching Yards and in many places the Banks of the Canal are covered with Linnen.[20]

We arrived at Ghent or Gand about 5 in the Afternoon, and on our

---

[20] The linen industry, stimulated by the invention of the flying shuttle, recovered in the Austrian Netherlands during the eighteenth century. There was a great stimulus in this period to the cloth industry in general at Tournai, Ghent and Courtrai. Naval Intelligence Division, *Geographical Handbook Series: Belgium*, pp. 106–107.

landing a crowd of the inhabitants came to the Shore whose Notice we by our Dress attracted. We came to the *Hotel d'Holland* a pretty good Inn, and took a walk in the Town from which we promise ourselves much entertainment tomorrow.[21]

[21] I have omitted some jottings written in French.

PLACES MENTIONED IN THE LIST OF GOODS

Bristol

Thomas Frank[1], Philip D*ebell* Tucket & John Waring[2] have lately entered into Partnership. They are all Friends and Men of Reputation. Have a good Capital and the best Connections in Philadelphia of any house in this place. At present they are not particularly attached to any house in Philadelphia and would willingly enter into Partnership with our house in a Ship between the two Ports as soon as the Trade shall open. Amongst various Articles which might be brought from Bristol in case we should establish a Ship in the trade, are the following which must be brought from thence at any Rate: Pewter, Nails, Shot, Rugs, Blankets.

Thomas Rutter[3], a very worthy, industrious Man, who wishes to form a few good Connections with Philadelphia but he does not want to extend them. He could purchase any Goods for us and could make Sale of a Cargo of our Produce to as much Advantage as any Person in Bristol; and would constantly give us the most authentic State of the Markets in England for Wheat, Flour &c &c.

John Dowell now Dowells & Gardner[4] are a very good house, in the manufactury of every Sort of Felt hats, and have lately set Foot an extensive Manufactury of fine hats which they will be able to sell at as low or lower Rates than they can be had from Manchester or elsewhere.

Liverpool

William Rathbone, a man of most excellent Character and Worth, well acquainted with Buisness, has every Convenience for Shipping, could

---

[1] Thomas Frank was a Bristol merchant (1738–). The date of his death is not at present traced. He married Elizabeth Fry of Bristol in 1764. There were two children of the marriage. *DQB*.

[2] 'Porter merchant and factor, Quay, Bristol.' Bailey's *Western and Midland Directory* (Birmingham, 1783), p. 31.

[3] Thomas Rutter (1741–1800), a bellows and brush maker by profession, was a minister from Bristol and an eminent Quaker preacher. Frost, *Records and Recollections of James Jenkins*, pp. 118, 335–336; J. G. Bevan, ed., *Piety Promoted* (London, 1811), pp. 142–145.

[4] Hat manufacturers, 35 and 40 Wine Street, Bristol. Sketchley's *Bristol Directory* (1775; facsimile reprint, Bath, 1971), p. 26.

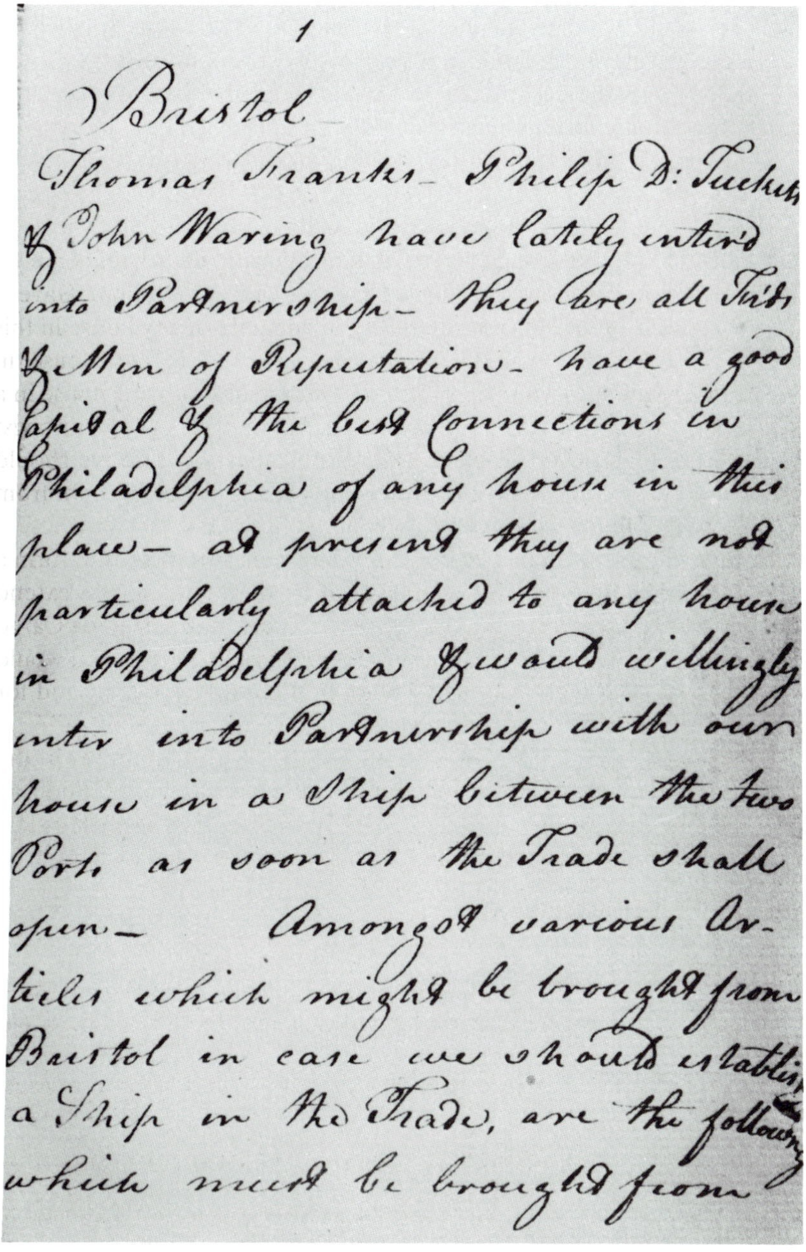

1

Bristol

Thomas Frankes — Philip D: Tuckett
& John Waring have lately enter'd
into Partnership — they are all Men
& Men of Reputation — have a good
Capital & the best Connections in
Philadelphia of any house in this
place — at present they are not
particularly attached to any house
in Philadelphia & would willingly
enter into Partnership with our
house in a Ship between the two
Ports as soon as the Trade shall
open — Amongst various Articles which might be brought from
Bristol in case we should establish
a Ship in the Trade, are the following
which must be brought from

Fig. 7. Extract from the List of Goods (Bristol).

Command great Interest in Liverpool and amongst the Manufacturers of Manchester in case we should establish a Ship in the Trade, in which he would willingly take $\frac{1}{3}$ or $\frac{1}{2}$ Concern. (He has a Son who is in all Respects clever and will in a year or two come into Business with his Father.) He is the best Person in Liverpool for the Sale of Lumber or Wheat and Flour, being himself largely in those Trades and having commodious Accommodations for landing and storing any Quantity of Goods.

Rawlinson & Chorley[5] do more Buisness than any house in Liverpool, but chiefly to the West Indies. A Connection with them would be no otherwise desirable than by having a Chance of their Recommendations from some West India Houses.

Manchester

Robert & Nathan Hyde[6] is a house with whom we have long had Connections. They are tolerably clever and being acquainted with the Trade of our Country can on that Account supply us with Goods on as good terms as any house in Manchester. The Goods we have usually had from them are as follows:

¾ Linnen Checks and Stripes
⅞ Linnen Checks
⅞ Cotton Ditto
Yard wide ditto
yard ⅜ ditto
Striped hollands
Cotton ditto
Dyed Jeans
Dyed Pillows all Prices
Cloth Coloured Corduroys
⁶⁄₄ ⁶⁄₄ and ½ and ⅞ Bed bunts
Striped Damascus
Cloth Coloured Threads
Light Coloured Ditto
Red and blue Ditto

    [5] Abraham Rawlinson (1709–1780) was a merchant in Lancaster trading to North America and the West Indies. Alexander Chorley (1746–1801) was an ironmonger who lived at various places in Lancashire, including Warrington between 1771 and 1776. *DQB*.

    [6] Robert and Nathaniel Hyde, Check and Fustian manufacturers and merchants, King Street, Manchester. *The Manchester Directory for the Year 1773 by Elizabeth Raffald* (reprinted Manchester, 1889), p. 29.

Stitching Ditto white Sorted
Quality and Shoe Bindings

They likewise deal in all other Sorts of Manchester Goods, for a more exact Account of which I must refer to their Pattern Book.

Robert Hamilton[7] is likewise precisely in the same Buisness and will always rejoice in having our Commands.

Gideon Bickerdike is in the Manufactury of various Articles and engages to supply us on lower terms than any Person who purchases them on Commission as Hydes &c &c. He is a Friend and is very solicitous of furnishing such Goods as he is in the way of, Vizt.

Jennetts of all Prices from	2/10	to 3/4
Velvets from	4/8	to 5/8
Quiltings from	5/3	to 6/3
Corded Dimotys	1/9	to 2/4
Cordonnett	2/	to 2/4
Snowdonnett	2/4	to 2/9
Pillows	11d	to 1/7
Jeans	2/4	to 2/6
Jennett	2/	to 2/8
Indianett	2/2	to 2/4
Cotton Jean	2/10	to 3/4
India Jean	5/	
Denims	3/7	
Sattinett	3/8	
Ribbs	3/4	to 3/10
Nockinetts	3/5	to 4/2
Cataloons	3/9	
Thicksetts	1/6	to 3/10
Cordeleur	1/8	to 3/8
Corduroy	2/9	to 3/
Siberian Cords	1/8	to 2/9
Velveretts	4/	to 5/3
Fine Velvets	6/	to 9/6

and some other Articles for which and for an Explanation of these I refer to his Pattern Card. As he does not deal in the generality of Manchester Goods it will be inconvenient for us to have a part from him; otherwise I should be glad we could serve him.

Edmund Radcliffe[8] is the greatest Manufacturer in England. The

---

[7] Fustian and check manufacturer, King Street, Manchester. *Ibid.*, p. 23.
[8] Merchant, 6 St. Ann's Square, Manchester, *Ibid.*, p. 40.

extent of his Trade and Correspondence to Spain, Portugal, France and the Mediterranean is prodigious. There is not a City of Note in those Countries but he has Connections with and he makes me very flattering offers of Interest and Introduction to his Correspondents there, if our house will have any of his Articles. The only Objection to this is that he is not in the Manufactury of one half the Goods we should have occasion for. However to make up in some Measure for this he says his particular Friends Samuel & Thomas Taylor[9] who are in the Linnen and Check Manufactury will furnish us on good terms with such Goods as he does not, and the whole shall be made out in one Invoice and the Remittances made to him. This would save us the Trouble of an additional Correspondent. Those Articles he sends are as follows:

	$\frac{1}{2}$ yard			$\frac{1}{2}$ Ell	
Cotton velvets	4/	10/		6/	14/
Velveretts	3/	4/6		3/6	6/
Summer Velvets and Corduroys	1/4	3/		2/	6/
Malzetts	1/3	3/6		2/	6/
Denims				2/6	5/
Sattinetts				3/	4/6
Cantons and Cataloons	1/6	3/		2/	5/6
Baragons	1/6	2/6			
Ribbs	1/4	2/			
Thicksetts	1/2	3/6		1/6	5/
Fustians	1/	2/		1/3	2/9
Drabbetts $\frac{3}{4}$ $\frac{1}{2}$		1/6			
Dyed Jeans	8d	2/4		1/	3/6
White Jeans	8	2/		9d	2/6
Cordinets	1/6	4/			
Corded Dimotys	1/	3/6	yard wide	2/	6/
Southwellets			$\frac{1}{2}$ Ell	2/	2/8
Draw boys			yard wide	1/10	2/9
Loom Quilting yard and Ell wide				6/	8/
Nankins $\frac{1}{2}$ yard				1/2	1/6
Turkey Stripes $\frac{3}{4}$				1/10	2/2
Bed Quilts					
Cotton Linings					

For further particulars see his Pattern Card.

Samuel & Thomas Taylor are plain honest Manufacturers of the following Articles:

[9] Check manufacturers, Calender Street, Manchester. *Ibid.*, p. 47.

Linnen Checks and Stripes ⎫
Cotton Checks |
Cotton Hollands |
Cotton Stripes |
Bed Silks and Bed Bunts ⎬ of all Sorts and Prices
Check handkerchiefs |
Blue Linnens |
Lorretos |
Damascus |
Saxes &c &c |
Printed Handkerchiefs ⎭

Linnen and Cotton Goods in imitation of India Silks, such as are sent to Africa.

Birmingham

Welch, Wilkinson & Startin[10] are the Persons we have hitherto been connected with. But as they are not in all Respects quite the thing, if an house who could serve us equally well should offer itself it might be well enough to leave them. They have sent us usually the following Articles:

Small and Spike Gimblets
Padlock and splinted Locks
Bright Augurs — different Sizes
Claw hammers
Wrought metal Buttons ditto groces
Vert ditto
Lacquered ditto
Common and dotted Awl blades
Shoe Tacks
Common Needles
White Chappell Needles
Paper Ink Pots
Leather Ditto
Shoe Hammers
Coffee Mills
Scissors and Shears
Sheap Shears

[10] Merchants, 32 Snow Hill, Birmingham. Pearson and Rollason, *The Birmingham Directory* (Birmingham, 1777), p. 52.

Plain Iron Candlesticks
Brass balled Ditto
Curry Combs
Carpenters hammers
Solid Checked hammers
Shoe and Knee Buckles all Sorts
Snuff Boxes
Handsaws
Steel Plate Ditto
Sleeve Links all Sorts
Ivory and horn Combs
Stock Locks 6 Inches to 10 Inches
Knives and Forks 20d 3/3
Burnt bone Knives
Seal End Penknives
Pistol Capt Ditto
Cutteaux Knives
Stag Penknives
Death head and Basket Buttons
Vest Ditto
Chest Locks
Brass Cocks
Shoe Nippers and Pinchers
Hinges H and H
Hand mill and x cut saws
Coffee Mills
Brass Candlesticks
Brass and Iron Wire
Spectacles
Frying Panns
Nails
Snuffers
Files of all Sorts
Plated Buckles Spurrs &c
Pocket Books all Sorts
Bellows
Fishhooks
Japanned ware of all Sorts
Tea Kettles and Urns
Silver and metal Watches
Cabinet Furniture and all other Sorts of hard ware
If Charles Lloyd be sufficiently acquainted with these Articles he would

gladly undertake it. If not Harvey Mariden & Frith[11] are very suitable Men.

Leicester

Chamberlain & Burgess,[12] an house from whom we had formerly some Goods, have now separated. They are neither of them over and above clever. Their Connections are not extensive and their Business wholly confined to the Country. The Goods manufactured here are of inferior Quality and Price to what are manufactured in Nottingham. The higher Prices we must get from thence, the lower we shall get on better Terms from this Place. Crafton & Colson[13] have them on the same terms we may procure them and they charge at least $7\frac{1}{2}$ per cent on all their Goods.

Joseph Bunney & Co. are a very capital house and are People of Reputation. I believe no Person could supply us with Cotton and thread hosiery on better Terms and they wish to form a Connection with us. They manufacture

Boys thread Stockings	10/–	20/–
Womens and small Mens	18/–	48/–
Mens	18/–	60/–
Boys white thread	10/–	30/–
Womens	18/–	60/–
Mens	18/–	72/–
Boy's Cotton	10/–	24/–
Womens	20/–	60/–
Mens	24/–	72/–
Mens patent Ribbed Brown and White	40/–	63/–
Boys worsted stockings	10/–	20/–
Womens	15/–	42/–
Mens	15/–	60/–
Worsted Mitts for Women	5/–	14/–
Worsted Breeches Pattern	2/6	8/6

---

[11] Merchants, 69 New Street, Birmingham. *Ibid.*, p. 23.

[12] John Burgess & Co., manufacturers of hose, and Chamberlain, Son & Markland, manufacturers of hose. Bailey's *British Directory*, II, pp. 385–386.

[13] Hosiers, 9 Great St. Helens, London. They traded with Pennsylvania and New York before the American Revolution. Kent's *London Directory* (1774), p. 46; Katherine A. Kellock, 'London Merchants and the pre-1776 American Debts,' *Guildhall Studies in London History*, I (1974), p. 122.

Cotton and Worsted Caps all Sorts
Men's thread Gloves

Though this house do something in worsted Goods they are not so extensive in that Branch as Carrs & Cumberland. People of excellent Character and Fortune. They manufacture

Boys grey and marbled Stockings	9/–	19/–
Black and white	same prices	
Womens black ditto	12/–	32/–
Womens blue chever'd with Coloured blocks	16/–	36/–
Mens black hose and white	16/–	59/–
Mens grey	17/–	61/–
Mens blue	20/–	63/–
Womens black and buff Mits	5/–	16/–
Breeches Patterns black	30/–	55/–
Blue and Grey	36/–	61/–
Mens Pack thread hose ribbed	22/–	26/–
Sham Ditto	26/–	30/–
Fine Ditto ribbed and plain	26/–	54/–

They can make Mens hoze as low as 14/ per Dozen and Breeches Pattern as low as 22/– per pair. These are 12 Months' Credit Prices. Discount is per Cent.

Settle

Shalloons	25/–	50/–
Tammy's and Durants	19/–	33/–
Calimancoes $^{15}/_{40}$ yard wide	25/–	29/–
Common Colours $^{16}/_{40}$ Ditto	28/–	31/–
$^{18}/_{30}$ Ditto	25/–	45/–
$^{20}/_{30}$ Ditto	27/–	35/–
But Blues Greens &c are 1/ more		
Boys and Girls yarn hose	5/–	8/–
Womens Ditto	8/–	15/–
Mens Ditto	10/–	20/–
Ditto	30/–	40/–
Mens ribbed worsted hoze or finer	20/–	48/–
Hardens yard wide 27 yards	12/–	14/6
$^9/_8$ wide 31 to 33	18/–	19/–
Ell wide 33	20/–	23/–
Twilled Sacking ½ Ell wide 24 yards	12/6	
25 Inches	27	16/–

The above Goods are manufactured by William Birkbeck & Co.[14] on whose Punctuality and Honesty we may place entire Confidence. We have been used to pay Cash for such of the above Goods as we have imported from them, but if it do not suit us in future it will make no odds. They likewise are concerned in a Manufactury of Threads with a House in Scotland and can supply us with this Article. Viz.

Kendal

Isaac Wilson & Son we have hitherto dealt with. A Correspondence with them will always be very desirable. Their goods are

Silk Rugs Spotted and green from 8/6 to 18/–
Negro Cottons 20 yards 18/–   24/–
Striped Lineys about 12
Cotton Ditto.   14d.
John Wakefield[15] is largely in the Manufactury of Kendal Cottons and Linery's. Thomas Crewdson[16] would be a good hand for Stockings, if Settle was not equally convenient.

Whitby

Is largely engaged in building and letting out Vessels on Freight. There are no Speculators among them except in the Coal Trade. Thomas Lindskill[17] who is a man of Property and Reputation would wish frequently to send his Ships to Philadelphia with a Cargo of Coals from NewCastle, but it would not suit him to load her with our Country Produce for a European Market. However if a probable Prospect of obtaining a Freight from our Port should offer and Vessels be plenty at Whitby, I think he woud always be willing to run the Risque. If this Buisness be worth our engaging in 'twill be well to give information occasionally.

Abel Chapman[18] is likewise a man of Property and Consequence with whom something in the same way might be carried on. John Chapman[19]

---

[14] William Birkbeck (1745–1805), a merchant and banker at Settle, Yorkshire. *DQB*; Robert Birkbeck, *The Birkbecks of Westmoreland* (privately printed, 1900), p. 106.

[15] Merchant and manufacturer of Kendal. Bailey's *British Directory*, III, p. 556.

[16] Thomas Crewdson (1737–1795) was a hosier and, later, a banker of Kendal. He married Cicely Dillworth of Lancaster in 1774. They had nine children. *DQB*.

[17] A shipowner of Whitby. Bailey's *British Directory*, III, p. 730.

[18] Either Abel Chapman (1694–1777) or Abel Chapman (1752–?). These were two Quakers who lived at Whitby. Lilian Clarke, *Family Chronicles* (Wellingborough, 1910), Section 2: The Chapmans of Whitby and their Descendants, pp. 10–11.

[19] See above, p. 49, n. 118.

manufactures Sail Cloth to great Extent but he is always engaged in Government Contracts.

Scotland

The only Place in this Country where we could form any Connections for procuring Goods is at Montrose. At Edinburgh no Manufacturies are carried on. At Glasgow and its Neighbourhood large Quantities of hosiery and some other Articles are manufactured. But I could find no body on whom we could rely to send us anything we might want.

Montrose

At this Place lives Henry Mill a very worthy young Man who would purchase the Manufactures of that Neighbourhood at $2\frac{1}{2}$ per cent Commission, having Liberty to draw for the Money as soon as he transmits the Invoice to our Friend in London. As Barclay's purchase these Goods in the same way (by means of their Friend) I think it will be our Interest to give our Orders to Henry Mill for all the Goods of which annexed is a List, being subject to great Allowances:

Tow Oznabrigs
Flaxen Ditto.
The Discount in the Measure of these Goods is $9\frac{1}{2}$ per Cent which is given by allowing two yards to each Score. They also purchase ⅞ white Linnen common Prices about 13d ⅝ Sheetings 13½ and on these Goods the same Allowances are made.

Portsmouth or Gosport

Erasmus Carver[20] of this place is concerned in a Rope Walk, at which they manufacture a kind of Cordage which they call twice laid. This is made of 2d hand Cordage which is sent from the King's Stores after a little wear. The Appearance of this Cordage is almost equal to the best Cordage made in any Part of England, and I am assured that it is equally serviceable with common Cordage and the Price being above ⅓ lower I think must make it answer well. It may at any Time be sent to London with a few Weeks Notice, or Vessels coming from London may touch at Portsmouth for it.

Erasmus Carver is a Man of Property and of good Character. His

[20] Erasmus Carver & Sons, merchants, Gosport. Bailey's *British Directory*, III, p. 655.

Conveniences for landing a Cargo of Rice are the best in the Port, and he is very desirous of serving us herein should we have occasion.

Whitehaven

A considerable Port but no great Foreign Trade. Their Vessels are wholly imployed in the Coal Trade and the Coals are of inferior Quality to the NewCastle Coals. A Disadvantage in Vessels coming here is that they ly ⅔ds of the Tide a Ground on a very hard Sand. The Expedition of Loading here is such that a Ship of 300 Tons can load in half a Day.

Skyren & Cowpland is as good a house I believe as any in this Place and if any Plan of Buisness can be fallen on for mutual Advantage, they will gladly embrace it.

Peter Pearson[21] is in the Manufactury of a coarse white Linnen but I think it comes too high for our Consumption. And he is also in the Manufactury of housewife Checks. These also come rather high though the quality be good. He is a very honest Man and would be glad to deal with us.

Sheffield

Broadbent & Bland[22] are the Persons with whom we have hitherto had Connections, but the Manner of their doing Buisness and their bad Observance of our Orders render them improper Persons for our Purpose.

John Barlow is a very desirable Man to purchase any Articles we might want, but he wishes to avoid any Connections with America, even if he had the Money in hand to buy the Articles we might have Occasion for. However he recommends Joseph & Benjamin Broomhead[23] as very honest Men in whose Integrity and Ability we may thoroughly confide. Those Goods which they do not themselves manufacture they will purchase for us at 2½ per Cent Commission and allow 6 Months. Their own Manufactury consists of Viz.

Bone Table Knives and Forks 22d   24d   2/6   3/–   3/6   4/–
Sham buck Ditto uncapt 20d
Ditto Capt 1/10   2/–   2/3   2/6   3/–

---

[21] A linen manufacturer of Whitehaven. *Ibid.*, p. 732.

[22] Thomas Bland, merchant, edge-tool, hammer and spademaker, Paradise Street, Sheffield. Thomas Broadbent (d. 1813) was a merchant who was also involved with his brother Joseph in a bank in Sheffield between 1774 and 1780. *Ibid.*, IV, p. 893; Robert Eadon Leader, *Sheffield in the Eighteenth Century* (Sheffield, 1901), pp. 89–90, 108–109.

[23] Manufacturers, Far Gate, Sheffield. Bailey's *British Directory*, IV, p. 893.

Real Buck 3/6   3/–
Real Stag 4/–   4/6   5/–
Red Wood 2/9
Black Ebony 3/–
Butchers Knives 2/6   3/–   3/6   4/–
Sickles are manufactured by William Staniforth[24] and in our Orders must be calld Philadelphia Sickles.

No. 1   3/6 ⎫
   2   4/6 ⎮
   3   5/6 ⎬ 5 per cent Discount
   4   6/6 ⎮
   5   7/6 ⎭

Besides which the Goods they purchase are

Scythes Strongbacks 42 Inches 22/–
Ditto   45 Inches 24/–
Weeding hoes 7½   Inches deep 9 wide 17/–
Ditto   8½   10   21/–
Knives and Forks of higher Prices
Shoe Knives 2/–   2/3
26 Inch Handsaws compleat marked White   54/–
Cast steel handsaws compleat   72/–
Stag Stafford Penknives 4/– ⎫
Ditto   Ditto   3/6 ⎮
Ditto   Ditto   3/– ⎬ Barlow
Buffalo and Sham Stag 4/– ⎭
Childrens   painted Whittles   4d
                     Burt bone   12d
Buck Pistol Capt: Knives 2/4   2/6   2/8
Buck Cutteaux 18d   1/8   1/10   2/–
Soft Seal Penknives 1/10
Hard Seal Ditto 2/–
Pistol End Ditto 2/–   2/3   2/6
Buffaloe com: Ditto 2/6 Ditto 3/– to 6/–
12 Inch Castard flat Files
9 Inch 3 Square Ditto
Handsaw Ditto 16/– to 18/– sorted
Rasps and other Files
    John Wilde[25] manufactures all sorts of Edge Tools Vizt.

---

[24] A Sheffield linendraper. Leader, *Sheffield in the Eighteenth Century*, pp. 181–182.

[25] Jonathan Wild and Son, penknife cutters, Kim's Court, Sheffield. Bailey's *British Directory*, IV, p. 899.

Bright Augurs from $\frac{1}{2}$ Inch 6/– to $1\frac{1}{2}$ Inches 18/–
Black Augurs from $\frac{1}{2}$ Inch 5/– to $1\frac{1}{2}$ Inches 15/–
Screw Augurs from $\frac{1}{2}$ Inch 8/– to $1\frac{1}{2}$ Inches 24/–
Drawing Knives from 14 Inches 12/– to 10 Inches 9/–
Spoke Shaves &c &c
Socket Chizzels from $\frac{1}{2}$ Inch 4/6 to 2 Inches 6/6
Socket Gouges $\frac{3}{4}$ Inch 4/9 to 1 Inch 5/–
Long firmer Chizzels from $2\frac{1}{2}$ Inches 8/– to 1 Inch 3/–
Short firmer Chizzels 2 Inches 5/6 to $\frac{1}{8}$ 18/–
Firmer Gouges 1 Inch to $\frac{1}{8}$ 2/2   1/6
Mortice Chizzel Ditto Ditto 5/–   2/6
Plane Irons $2\frac{3}{4}$ to $1\frac{1}{2}$ 4/6   2/–
Plane Irons of all Sorts
Turning Chizzels of all Sorts
Curriers Tools
Skinners Tools
Tanners Tools
Shoe and Heel Knives
Sheap Shears 7/– to 20/–
Steel long Saws 4 to 8 feet
        from 11/– to 24/– per piece $\left.\right\}$ Best
Steel Ditto 4 to 8 feet
        from 6/– to 16/– $\left.\right\}$ common
Best Steel handsaws 16 to 28 Inches
        from 36/–   50/– per Dozen
Common Steel handsaws Ditto
        from 12/– to 26/–
Tennant Saws $\left.\right\}$
Sash Saws
Dovetail Saws $\left.\right\}$ best and common compleat
Lock Saws
Pannel Saws $\left.\right\}$

These Edge Tools are all to Receive a Discount of 5 per cent if paid in 6 months or 10 per cent if paid in Cash and Joseph & Benjamin Broomhead are in all Respects calculated for us to purchase these Goods. John Hoyland[26] a very honest Man carries on a Manufactury of all Sorts of plated Goods.

---

[26] John Hoyland (1752–1831), a factor of Sheffield. *DQB*.

Norwich

The Manufactures of this City are in general high, the Goods being of better Quality than the same Articles manufactured at Durham and Yorkshire.

Nathaniel Springal is a very worthy Man and if any Goods from thence would answer our Purpose should be glad to have them from him. The Articles he makes are

Messinets	28 yards	34/–
Silverets		44/–
Silk Sagathys	30	75/–
Corded Poplins	28	28/–
Venetian Poplins	28 yards	28/–
½ Ell Poplins	36	68/–
½ Ell Beavereens	28	50/–
½ Ell Hairbines	28	68/–
Ditto patterns	26	25/–
Broad Ditto	40	75/–
Camblets		8d to 2/– per yard
Flowerd Russels	26	26/6
Ditto Worsted Damask	26	42/–
Bed Damasks	36	76/–
Fancy goods	from	1/– to 1/6
Coulourd and Mourning Crapes	10d	3/–
Yard wide Crapes	30 yards	50/–
½ yard Bombazeens		70/– to 120/–
½ Ell		120/– to 160/–

Camblettus plain striped and checked from 7d to 1/– per yard.

Nottingham

This Place is more suitable for the finer Sorts of Hosiery than the Coarser and I believe the higher Priced Articles may be had here on better Terms than at Leicester. Mark Huish[27] is very extensive in this Trade and is very desirous of opening a Correspondence with us. He wishes us at least to try one Parcel. And as he supplys Crafton & Colson who make a great Proffit and promising to supply us on the same terms I think it may be worth our

---

[27] Mark Huish & Co., merchants and manufacturers of hose in general at Nottingham. Bailey's *British Directory*, II, p. 411.

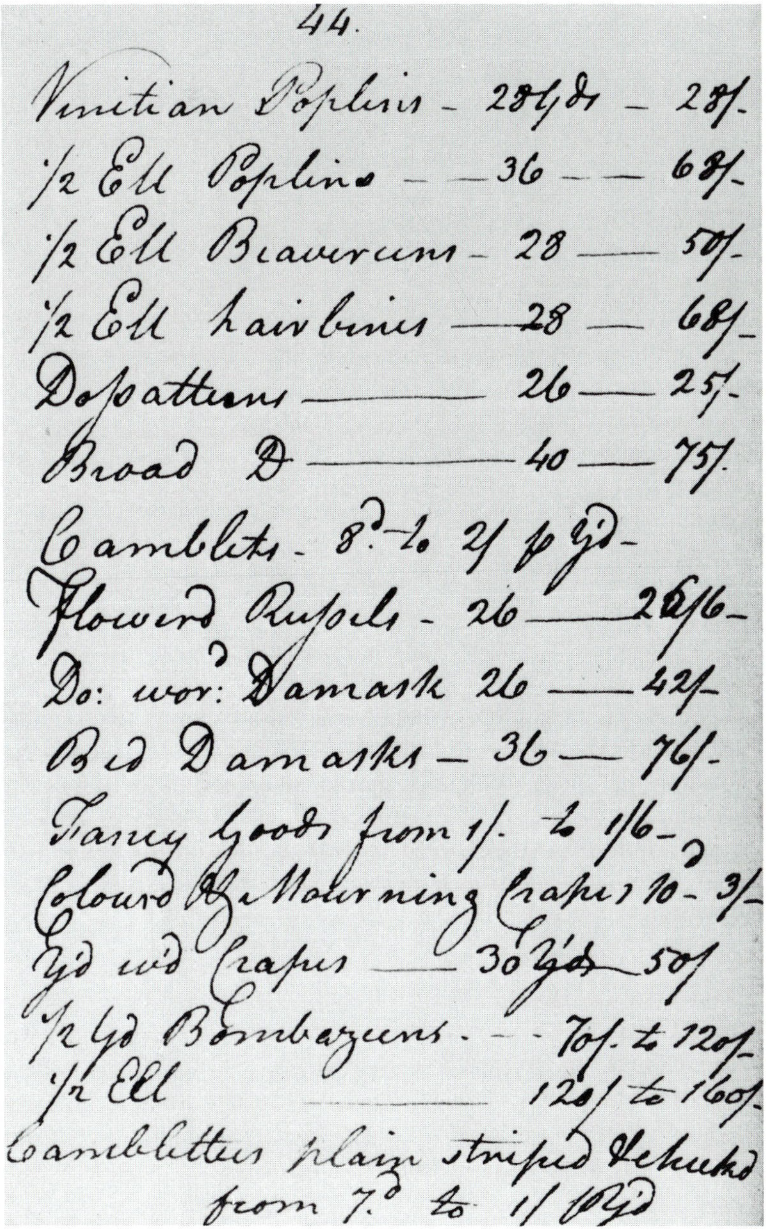

44.

Vinitian Poplins — 28yd — 28/.
½ Ell Poplins — — 36 — — 68/.
½ Ell Beavereens — 28 — 50/.
½ Ell hairbines — 28 — 68/.
Do patteens — — 26 — 25/.
Broad D — — 40 — 75/.
Camblets — 8d to 2/ p yd —
Flowerd Russels — 26 — 26/6 —
Do: wor: Damask 26 — 42/.
Bed Damasks — 36 — 76/.
Fancy Goods from 1/. to 1/6 —
Colourd & Mourning Crapes 10 - 3/.
yd wd Crapes — 30 yds 50/
½ yd Bombazeens — - - 7o/. to 120/.
½ Ell — 120/ to 160/.
Camblettes plain striped & checkd
from 7d to 1/ p yd

Fig. 8. Extract from the List of Goods (Norwich).

while to try an Importation. Boys Girls &c worsted hoze of all Sorts and

Colours	10/– to	18/–.
Mens Ditto	15/6	30/–
Mens Ditto	19/–	54/–
Small Mens of every Quality	3/– to	5/– a Dozen Less
Mens Silk and worsted hoze	61/–	67/–
Small Mens	6/– less	
Mens Cotton and worsted hose	34/–	46/–
Fine 2 thread black worsted Breeches or any other Colour	36/– to	45/–
Fine 3 thread	52/–	58/–
Fine 4 thread	63/–	69/–
Mens cotton hose	26/–	51/–
Womens Ditto	22/–	50/–
Boys and Girls	14/–	24/–
Mens br. thread hose	23/–	50/–
Small Mens	4/– per Dozen less	
Boys of all Sizes	12/–	20/–
Silk hose		
Caps &c		

Leeds

Emanuel & Samuel Elam with whom we have had a long Correspondence and who wish to keep it up are I think Persons as capable of serving us as any house in this Place. William Fisher is concerned in the same way of Buisness but is not quite so clever. Buck & Elam[28] are likewise in the same Trade and would exert themselves to serve us. But on the whole I think Emanuel & Samuel Elam are the most suited for us. The Articles usual had from them are

⁶⁄₄ Blue Coating	2/6	2/8
⁶⁄₄ Beaver Frizes	2/8	3/–
⁶⁄₄ Beaver Coatings	2/7	2/10
⁸⁄₄ Bath Coatings	5/6	6/6
Broad Cloths of all sorts		
Prices and Colours	3/–	7/6
higher we had not best yet at Leeds		

[28] Merchants, Burley Bar, Leeds, *Ibid.*, III, p. 561.

Calimancoes 40 yards 16 Inches of all Colours and for this last Article I think this best place.

This house is likewise concerned in a Manufactury of Camblets but not so low as John Starforth[29] of Durham tho the goods be better. They make a Discount of 10 per cent for Cash or less in proportion to the time of Payment.

Thomas Maud of Wakefield is precisely in the same line of Buisness, but having no Connections in America cannot be so well acquainted with Articles which suit us.

[29] A stuff manufacturer at Durham. By the 1790s, he was in partnership with Gilbert Starforth as stuff and carpet manufacturers in an extensive business, including accommodation for dyers and woolcombers and machines for spinning wool. They manufactured all types of cloth and had begun to make carpets. *Ibid.*, p. 523; *UBD*, II, pp. 868, 875.

List of Goods, Volume 2

Lancaster

Thomas Dilworth, Sons and Dockeroy[1] are a very good house from whom we have usually imported our Scan and Sail Twine. The different Sorts are:

No. 1 Turtle Twine   7/– per dozen
    2 Ditto   7/6
    3 Topt Scan Twine 8/6
    5 Soft Sail twine   12/–
    5x Fine ditto   14/–
    7 Mullet ditto   12

The kinds we import are Number 3 and Number 5.

John and William Winn of Halifax[2] is I believe the best house here tho I think Leeds in all Respects as good a Market for these articles. They make:

Broad Cloths all Colours 3/   9/
Plains and Forest Cloths 2/
⁶⁄₄ Frize 3/   5/6
⁷⁄₄   5/   7/
Duffils and Coatings 2/9   3/9 and 3/6   6/6
Kerseys Swanskins
They buy and finish
Shalloons Half thicks
Kerseys Bearskins
Common and German Serges
Serges de Nyms Lastings
Flannels Blankets
Strouds &c

---

[1] Thomas Dillworth (1713–1786) and David Dockroy (1732–1807) were Quaker merchants from Lancaster. Dillworth was a prominent member of the Lancaster meeting. *DQB*.

[2] William Winn was a merchant in Halifax. Bailey's *British Directory*, III, p. 531.

Haverfordwest

Summers and Clibborne[3] are a house of very great Capital and extent of Buisness. They are not concerned in any Manufactury but largely in the Trade of Flour and Wheat. Their Connections in the different Markets of Europe are great and it might be well worth our while to keep up a Correspondence with them. The Harbour in Milford Haven is inferior to none in the World for Safety and Space.

Willing and *Morris*[4] and several other Houses have ships to this Place for orders from them to a Market. I believe they would have no Objections to be equally concerned with us occasionally in Speculations of those Articles and we might probably enlarge our Concerns to more Advantage. They have had many Cargoes loaded at Philadelphia on their own Account and may have more.

They have very large Concerns in Shipping and of their Stability there is not the least Question.

New Castle

William and John Chapman a good house here willing to execute any Buisness for us to send Cargoes of Coal in their own Ships when a Prospect offers of a tolerable Price and a Freight back.

New Castle besides for Coals is a good Place for sundry Articles such as

Lead
Copper ass
Grindstones
Cordage
Quart Bottles
Crown Glass
Axes Nails &c

[3] Abraham Clibborn was a merchant of Dublin who retired to Haverfordwest. Richard Summers (d. 1796 aged 87) was a wealthy landed gentleman of Haverfordwest who lived in Bristol from 1759. Clibborn and Summers were partners with George Bush in a china works at Bristol. Hugh Owen, *Two Centuries of Ceramic Art in Bristol* (Gloucester, 1873), pp. 21, 23.

[4] Willing and Morris were a large shipping and mercantile firm in Philadelphia during the era of the American Revolution. Robert Morris (1734–1806) was the junior partner in this wealthy firm. He was elected to the Continental Congress in 1775 and was instrumental in promoting the Bank of North America, based in Philadelphia, in the 1780s. Thomas Willing, Morris's former partner, was in charge of day-to-day operations at the bank at this time. Doerflinger, *Vigorous Spirit of Enterprise*, pp. 38, 236, 297–305; Dumas Malone, ed., *Dictionary of American Biography* (New York, 1934), VII, pp. 219–223.

To give us an Idea of the Prices and Charges of shipping the following Invoices will suffice

Lead
1000 Pigs of refined Lead
    Fodder
    71.2.3. @ £13.17.6   £ 986.18
    Duty 1/ per cent or 21/ per   74.13.9
              Fodder
    All other Charges   2.15   77. 8.9
                                     £1064. 7

Commission is 2 per cent.
A fodder is 21 cwt.

Copperass
140 casks 100 tons £4.10   £450
Duty and Charges   23
                      473

Commission 2 per cent

Grindstones
120 Chaldrons Grindstones⎫ 18/   £18
    1 and 2 feet   ⎭
  50 Ditto 3.4.7 and 8   20/   50
  30 Ditto 5 and 6   24/   36
Duty and Charges   4 5
                            108 5
Commission 2 per cent   2 3 4
                        £110 8 4

24 Chaldrons Grindstones are computed equal to 1 Keel and 36 Stones of 1 foot make 1 chaldron

27	21
18	31
9	4
5	5
3	6
1	8
3	7

In the Measure of Grindstones 8 Inches are calld 1 foot and in large Stones they measure in the thickness as part of the Diameter.

Coals

120 Chaldrons coals	12/	£72
Duty	14/	84
Charges &c		13
No Duty on Coals to America		£169

but 3/9 Commission 2 per cent

NB. 1 Keel contains 8 Chaldrons New Castle Measure which weigh 21 tons 4 cwt and are equal to 15 Chaldrons London Measure.[5] Therefore the above Quantity may be as 225 London Chaldrons.

Cordage and Glass

Best cordage per Ton	£30
Inferior Sort	£26 to 28
Champain Quart Bottles	16/ Gross
Common Ditto	15/

the maker receiving the Drawback and allowing 5 per cent Discount for Cash

Best Crown Glass	38/6 ⎱	Crate of
Second Ditto	32/6 ⎰	12 Tables

Discount 5 per cent for Cash. Since these Prices an additional Duty has advanced the Price.

Nails lower than in London.

These People are likewise engaged in the Corn Trade and if we could propose any plan for their Interest they would adopt it.

Ormston & Lamb are concerned in the Printed Linen and Calico Buisness, but this will not answer our purpose.

Falmouth

George Croker Fox[6] is a considerable Merchant at this Place; has extensive Connections in all the Corn and Flour Markets in France, Spain, Portugal

---

[5] After 1700, the Newcastle chaldron settled down to a weight of 53 cwt. The London (or Winchester, or Winton, or Imperial) chaldron was used for the measurement of coal from the north-east in the London and south-coast trades. During the eighteenth century, the London chaldron was normally one half (26.5 cwt.) of a Newcastle chaldron. Flinn, *British Coal Industry: The Industrial Revolution*, p. 461.

[6] George Croker Fox (1727/8–1781), a Quaker living in Falmouth. He married in 1749 and had nine children. *DQB*. For a pedigree of the Fox family see Joseph Foster, *The Descendants of Francis Fox of St. Germans, Cornwall* (London, 1872), p. 11.

and the Streights and has had many Cargoes shipped by *Willing* and *Morris* at Philadelphia. Being very enterprizing and having several Sons who are Men of Buisness it may be worth our while to enter into some Connections with him and he will be much pleased with an opportunity when a Prospect of Benefit presents itself to open a Correspondence with us and I should think we might command a Preference in any Commission Buisness. From the Situation of this place, it may frequently suit us to stop here with Ships and take his Orders for a Market and we may always rely on his advising whatever may be for our Interest.

John Fox his Brother is precisely in the same Buisness and a man of great Probity, but his Connections are not on so large a Scale.

Poole

Moses Neave[7] of this Place hath heretofore had Occasion to send Vessels to Philadelphia to load with Provisions for Newfoundland with which Island the whole Trade of this Port is engrossed. *John Warder & Sons*[8] have executed this Buisness formerly to Satisfaction. I made him a tender of our Services and his making us any Consignments will depend on Circumstances. However we must write him hereon.

John Jeffery[9] and several other Merchants in this place I waited on, but found them all engaged with their several Correspondents in Philadelphia New York and Maryland and found little Encouragement. Every American that has come to England hath been here upon the Buisness of Solicitation before me.

Respecting the Employment of a Vessel by bringing Coals from England to America they did not seem to approve it without the Certainty of a Freight back. However of this Buisness we may have enough elsewhere.

Durham

John Starforth is the only Manufacturer here, having a large Sum lent him by the Corporation of this City for carrying on this Manufactury without Interest. He has it in his Power to make and dispose of his Goods on equal or lower terms than any other Person. His principal Articles are

---

[7] Joseph and Moses Neave were merchants at Poole. Bailey's *British Directory*, II, p. 428.

[8] A successful Quaker merchant firm active in Philadelphia before the American Revolution. Doerflinger, *Vigorous Spirit of Enterprise*, pp. 47, 119, 223.

[9] Jeffrey and Street, merchants at Poole. Bailey's *British Directory*, II, p. 427.

Jeans
Shalloons
Boars and Boaretts
Camblets
Camblettees and some other Stuff Goods

Lancaster

is a Place of very considerable Trade, chiefly to the West Indies. It sometimes happens that the Merchants here send their Vessels from thence to Philadelphia or New York to load with Provisions. I made myself known to many of the Merchants with offers of our Services.

Samuel Bradford[10] (Brother in Law to *Morris* Birkbeck)[11] is a considerable Merchant. He has had a Ship built and loaded by *Willing* and *Morris* and may have future Buisness to transact in Philadelphia. His Character and Fortune are unquestionable.

Lynn, Norfolk

This is a considerable Place for Trade in the Article of Corn. Should we have occasion for a Correspondent Joseph Pickover[12] is a very honest man and suitable for our Purpose.

Yarmouth

Nathaniel Symonds[13] is the most principal Merchant at this Port. Should we ever have need of a Correspondent for the Sale of any Article or in the purchase of a Cargo of Malt he is a very suitable Man and would gladly serve us.

For a Load of Malt this is the best place in England and 'tis a good Market for Tar or Turpentine.

William Thomas and William Palgrave[14] are equally clever and more extensive in the Malt Buisness.

[10] A Lancaster merchant. *Ibid.*, III, p. 557.

[11] Morris Birkbeck (1734–1816), a prominent Friend and noted bibliographer who married Hannah Bradford in 1762 (d. 1764) and Sarah Hall in 1776. He was a minister who was also involved in the insurance business. *DQB*.

[12] Joseph Peckover of King's Lynn was the brother of Edmund Peckover of Bradford (see above, p. 156). He joined John Birkbeck and the Gurneys in 1792 to form the Fakenham Bank. Raistrick, *Quakers in Science and Industry*, p. 329.

[13] Merchant of Great Yarmouth. *UBD*, IV, p. 949.

[14] W. T. and W. Palgrave, merchants, Quay, Great Yarmouth. Bailey's *British Directory*, IV, p. 929.

Birmingham

George Boone would execute any Buisness for a Commission of 5 per cent and allow all Advantages but on these Terms he must have the Cash and being determined to have no Connections with America, he must have the Orders given out by some Person here or a Remittance sent with the Order.

List of Goods, Volume 3

London

John & Robert Barclay[1] with whom Joshua Fisher & Sons have been long acquainted and whose Reputations are sufficiently known. The following is a List of all such Goods as they deal in.

Russia Sail Cloth
Russia Drabs or Drillings
brown white or dyed
Russia Sheetings yard wide and ⅞
Ravens Duck
Hempen Russia Linnen for Towells about 10 Ells in each
Flaxen Ditto finer 15 Ells
Flaxen Ditto broader 15
Russia Huccaback ½ Ell wide 18 Ells
Russia Diaper ¾ wide   18
German Flaxen Oznabrigs
German Ticklenburghs
Scots Oznabrigs
Brown Roles
White Ditto
Brown Hesses White Ditto
Brown Pomerania Linen
White Ditto or Princes Lawn
Dowlas ¾ wide   32 yards
Ditto   ⅞   64
Garlix   ¾   32
Ditto   ⅞   24
Brown   Silesia   36
White Ditto
Double Tandem Silezia   18
Single Silesia's   09
Pistol Lawns   8

---

[1] Merchants, 108 Cheapside, London. Kent's *London Directory* (1780), p. 14.

Hambro Long Lawns   32
Holland White   32
Gulix Hollands   30 Ells
Brown Buckrams   22 yards
White Buckrams   12
Dyed and glazed Linnens 24
Irish Linnens   ¾ wide
Irish Linnens   ⅞
Irish Linnens   yard wide
Brown Irish Sheeting   ⅞
White Irish Sheeting   ⅞
White Irish Sheeting   Ell wide
Yorkshire Huccabacks   ¾ wide
Ditto ⁶⁄₄ wide ⎫
Ditto ⁸⁄₄ wide ⎬   for Tabling 30 each
Ditto ¹⁰⁄₄ wide ⎭
Clouting Diaper
Damask Ditto
Hambro Diaper ⁶⁄₄   ⁷⁄₄   ⁸⁄₄   ¹⁰⁄₄
Setts of Damask containing 1 Cloth ¹⁰⁄₄ wide and 1 Dozen Naipkins to match
Blue and white checkd Scots handkerchiefs
White bordered Scots Kenting Ditto
Plain Silesia Clear Lawns 8 yards each
Flowerd or Spotted
Plain Scots Lawns 10 yards each
Spotted Striped or flowered Scots Lawns
Red ⎫
Blue ⎬   printed Bengal Stripe Linens for Waiscoats
Purple ⎭
Printed Linnens of all Sorts
Printed Cottons Ditto
Printed Calicoes Ditto
Printed Linen and Lawn handkerchiefs
India Nankeens
White Gurrah Calico 18 ½ yards each
Humkums ⁶⁄₄ wide 12
Cassacs ⎫
Tanjits ⎬   of all Sorts plaind striped or flowered
Mulmuls ⎭
Clear or book Muslin ⁵⁄₄ and ⁶⁄₄ 16 yards
Ditto or Ditto Handkerchiefs

Ditto or Ditto with red borders
India Dimities 12 yards each
White Moree Calicoes 14 yards each

French
- Cambricks ⅞ and yard wide
- Clear Lawns Ditto and Ditto
- dimy Packets Cambrick
- dimy Packets Lawn

Cotton Romalls
Ditto mixed } 15 handkerchiefs

Silk Lungie Romalls 16 handkerchiefs

New Silk Ditto
Pullicat Ditto } 15

Suktersay Ditto
Barnagore Ditto } 10

Mitchlapatam Ditto
Sastracundi Ditto } 16

Persian Taffaties plain Ell wide 10 ½ yards different Colours
Ditto Striped
Chints Patna ¾ wide 9 yards
Ditto   yard wide 12 and 14 yards
Ditto   ell wide   14
Bandanoes spotted and flowered 7
Ginghams 10 ½ Peniascoes 10 ½
Nillaes   10 ½ Chelloes   17 ½
Nickanees large and small 14 and 10
Tapseils 14 Photaes 14
Chints Amadavad 9
Dimy yard wide Chints printed in India 6 ½ yards each
Ell wide Superfine 7 each
Ell wide Ditto borderd 8
Blue Gro. India Long Cloth 18
China Taffities 15
British and Flanders bedtick
British Sail Cloth No. 1 &c &c.

In Russia Goods, Barclay's themselves are conscious they cannot always do so well as some others, though they say their Proffit is hardly equal to the Interest of their Money. They had rather drop this part of their Trade than continue in it. They have likewise done with their British Sail Cloth Manufactory, so that 'tis likely we can procure Sail Cloth of other Persons more advantageously.

    The Reputation of Barclay's house and the intimacy subsisting between us will always make it agreeable to keep up a Connection between us and the Power they have in procuring Recommendations may make it worth our while to carry this Connection to the utmost extent.

John Barclay lives a few miles out of London and is probably confined there for life. At present Robert is the principal Superintendant of the Buisness of which he is careful and assiduous. D Bell who is now in America will some day be placed in the house. He will be more in the Executive than the planning Branch.

Thomas Powell[2] is a worthy, honest, plain, industrious Man. The Experience he has had in Trade will give him great Advantages and tho he be not a Man of great Capital the Attachment of John Barclay to him will always render him adequate to any Occasion we may want of him in monied Matters. His Charges on Ships are more reasonable than any other Person's in London and no man is more equal to the Task.

In the purchase of such Goods as we may want in London he will be very suitable and his heavy Losses in Trade have determined him to transact Buisness in future in very circumscribed bounds. Upon the whole I think him the most suitable Man for our purpose in London.

John Roberts & Son.[3] The Father is an honest worthy Man. The Son's Character is hardly formed. They neither have much Spirit or Enterprise in Trade.

Cooke & Relph[4] are in all Respects clever. Their knowledge in Buisness, their Capital, and the extent of their Buisness all make it our Interest to remain connected with them; but especially if we should keep a Vessel in the Trade; and as they now consider themselves under obligations, a Preference to our house may always be preserved. They deal in the following Articles.

Tammys	Diamontus
Durants	Mecklinburgs
Calimancoes	Dorsetteens
Camblets	Silk Camblets
Taberets	Hair Ditto
Russels	Hairbines
Everlastings	Silk Sagathies
Antelloons	Allopeens
Shalloons	Rattinetts
Serge Denims	Kustres

[2] Merchant, 26 Philpot Lane, London. *Ibid.*, p. 139.

[3] Merchants, 109 Fenchurch Street, London. *Ibid.* (1777), p. 149.

[4] Cooke, Relph & Barnardiston, Mercers and Warehousemen, 71 Leadenhall Street, London. *Ibid.*, p. 43.

Duroys	Messinetts
Sagathies	Irish Stuffs
Worsted Damasks	Gazettes
Furniture Ditto	Brolios
Cheneys	Thread Sattins
Harrateens	Grograms
Morines	Norwich Crapes
Yard wide ⎱	Bombazeens
Worsted ⎰	
Stuffs ⎱	Italian hat Crape
all Sorts ⎰	
Starretts	Tiffanys
Barlycorns	Gauzes
Nonpareils	Princes Stuffs
Tobines	Prunellos
Worsted Shag	Spitalfield Handkerchiefs
or Plush	
Hair Ditto	English Persians
Venetian Poplins	Alamodes
Corded Ditto	Sarsinets
Masqueraded Ditto	Taffaties
Pelong Sattins	Brocades
Mantuas	Damasks
Lutestrings	Sattins
Armozerns	Tissuas
Durapes	Velvets
Paduasoys	Quilted Petticoats
Plain and ⎱	
changeable ⎰	Silk and Cloaks
Lutestrings ⎰	
Striped Ditto	Cardinals
Flowerd Ditto	&c &c &c
Tobined Ditto	

But many of these Articles can be had better from the Makers.

Crafton & Colson a very good house in the hosiery Way. But I apprehend their Goods may be had considerably better from Nottingham, Leicester and Settle.

Boys and Girls yarn hoze		
Womens plain and stamped Ditto	10/–	12/–
Mens plain grey yarn Ditto	11/–	15/–
Ditto ribbed Ditto	14/–	18/–

Mens milled yard hose		
Single milled yarn Caps		
Boys and Mens yarn Gloves		
Ditto Ditto Milled and Mitts		
Children Spotted worsted hose	4 Sizes	
Boys grey Ditto	6 Sizes	
Girls Clocks Blue Ditto	5 Sizes	
Mens wove grey worsted Ditto	16/–	50/–
Ditto French grey Ditto	30/–	52/–
Mens wove grey Drabs	18/–	42/–
Ditto marbled Ditto	18/–	42/–
Ditto clouded and figured	20/–	45/–
Ditto cotton and worsted	45/–	60/–
Ditto thread and worsted	40/–	60/–
Ditto Silk and worsted	63/–	75/–
Ditto plain white worsted	20/–	40/–
Ditto black Ditto	20/–	42/–
Womens pointed blue worsted	16/–	19/–
Ditto chevd.	20/–	25/–
Ditto with Silk Clocks	26/–	36/–
Womens white worsted	18/–	30/–
Ditto blue and black	18/–	30/–
Mens ribbed, grey marbled &c	25/–	36/–
patent Ribbed	36/–	60/–
black or white	36/–	60/–
Knit rib'd all Colours	26/–	50/–
Boys brown thread	20/–	50/–
Cotton	22/–	50/–
Mens random and marbled thread	26/–	36/–
Figured	42/–	60/–
Ditto Cotton	42/–	60/–
Mens brown thread	20/–	50/–
white	22/–	56/–
wove ribbed thread and cotton	30/–	42/–
patent ribbed ditto	48/–	63/–
knit ribbed brown thread	34/–	50/–
ditto white ditto	40/–	60/–
white silk hose	6/–	10/6
white marbled etc. spun⎫	6/–	17/6
Silk hose ⎭		
patent ribbed all Colours	12/–	15/–
Single striped worsted caps	3/6	12/–

Single and double, Green Scarlet, Crimson and marbled worsted Caps
Velvet Fashion Ditto all Colours
Striped Cotton Caps
White Ditto

German Town Ditto	8/6	12/–
Womens black, Cloth Coloured and sorted Colours		
unlined worsted mitts	6/–	8/–
Ditto Ditto Ditto lined	8/–	18/–
Boys Mens and Womens Gloves		
Womens brown and white thread Mitts	10/6	18/–
Ditto Ditto	12/–	20/–
Mens and womens Ditto Ditto Gloves		
Womens Gimpt black Silk Mitts	26/–	40/–
Ditto Cloth Coloured	29/–	44/–
Ditto white and sorted Colours	29/–	44/–
Silk Gloves and Mitts all Colours		
Patent Ditto		
Mens silk Gloves all Colours		
Black Worsted Breeches Patterns	2/6 to 9/–	
Cloth Colourd Ditto all prices		
Waistcoats all Colours and prices		
Silk knee Gaiters Ditto		
Checked Linnen handkerchiefs	3/6	24/–
Plain Lawns of all breadths	1/–	14/– per yard
Figured and flowered Lawns	1/2	7/6
Bordered kenting handkerchiefs	8/–	60/–
Flowered and needle work Lawn Apron		
Scots white and sticking thread	3/–	4/2
Ditto Ditto in ¼s	3/–	100/–
Scots Oznabrigs		

Wakefield Pratt & Miers[5] are all good Men, strictly honest, punctual and all acquainted with Buisness. They are the first house in London in the Irish Linnen Way, have Factors always on the Spot to purchase the Linnens unbleached. They are not desirous of forming any connections with America as this would if it were known materially affect their Interest with Barclay's house and many other American houses whom they supply almost wholly. Nor would they wish to credit any Goods to the Americans. However they will supply our house on Credit if requested. But if it should

---

[5] Merchants, 1 Lad-Lane and 15 Wood Street, London. *Ibid.* (1774), p. 179.

at any time suit us to lay out Money for this Article the Terms on which they do Buisness would make it worth our while.

They are likewise in the Stuff Way but in this, they cannot do better than Cooke & Relph.

They are the Proprietors of a new bank established between London and Dublin of great Extent and Capital.

Morris Birkbeck & John Blakes[6] have just entered into Buisness as Factors and Brokers. The first of these is a steady man, the latter an enterprising man. As they have good Connections, they will before long probably extend their Trade considerably.

They are Vendors of the most considerable Manufacturers of British Sail Cloth, with which they could supply us on as good or perhaps better Terms than Barclays.

They would be good Men to consign any Articles to, for Sale, and mean after some time to receive the Consignments of Ships or Cargoes. It would be in their Power to purchase Russia Goods for us on good terms for Cash.

John Chorley,[7] a very industrious honest Man in the Linnen Drapery Way, particularly Irish, German and Russia Goods. He is well acquainted with these Articles and assures me that having Cash in his hands, he could make occasionally some cheap purchases of Russia Articles.

Fludyer Marsh & Hudson, now Fludyer Hudson & Streatfield[8] are a good substantial House, having extensive Connections both in their Purchases of all Sorts of Woolens from the different manufacturing Towns and in their Trade to America. They furnish all the following articles:

Best Superfine Spanish Cloths
Best Supers
Supers, Table
Yorkshire Cloths
Forrest Cloths
Swanskins white dyed and spotted
White Bays and spotted ditto
Devonshire Kerseys
Yorkshire Ditto
Wiltshire Plains ⎫
Devonshire Ditto ⎪
Yorkshire Ditto ⎬ all sorts
Hunters Ditto ⎪
Prest and napped Ditto ⎭

[6] Factors, 48 Little Eastcheap, London. *Ibid.* (1780), p. 21.

[7] Linen draper, 30 Gracechurch Street, London. *Ibid.*, p. 39.

[8] Warehousemen, 79 Basinghall Street, London. *Ibid.*, p. 67.

Double Milled Drabs   ⎫
West Country and Yorkshire ⎬ all Sorts
West Country and Yorkshire
Coating of all Sorts. Plain and napped.
Fearnoughts. Norwich and Town made.
Spotted Ermines
Striped Lineys
Frizes, all Sorts and Prices.
Kendal and Yorkshire Cottons
white, dyed, plain and spotted
Flannells, white and dyed
Bath Coating ¾ all Sorts
Witney Coatings white and dyed
Latteens, superfine, narrow and broad
Bath Beavers ⎫ Yard wide
Lambskins   ⎭
German Serges   ⎫
Padua Serges
Long Ells
Shalloons   ⎬ all Sorts
Sagathys   Colours
Duroys, Druggets   and Prices
Serge Denims
Half Thicks
Honbys
Hair and Worsted Shags ⎭
Stripe and Shag Duffils
Indian Kersey Blankets
Embossed Serges and Flannells
Wilton Cloths
Cassmeres

    John Whitelock, a Man of great Fortune and Interest, with whom it might be worth our while to form some Connection, as he is frequently engaged in Shipping and Speculations, tho he deals in few Articles which it might suit us to have from him. He has taken his Son into Partnership. The firm is John Whitelock & Son.[9]

Pins and Needles
Osnabrigs thread
Bleached Ditto
Coloured Ditto

  [9] Merchants, 46 Lime Street, London. *Ibid.*, p. 185.

Sticking Ditto
Scots Ounce Ditto
Knitting Threads and Cotton
Sewing Silks of all Colours
Tapes and Bobbins
Dutch Lace and Nonsopretties
Quality Binding and Gartering
Silk and Worsted Knee Garters
Mohair Buttons and Twist
Metal Buttons
Buckrams
Dyed and glazed Linnens
Silk terretts
Ribbons of all Sorts
Black and blond Laces
Fans all Sorts
Womens and Childrens Stays cheap
Womens Stuff Shoes
—— Chip and Straw hatts
Scarlet and Drab Cloaks and Cardinals
Gauzes plain and flowered
—— handkerchiefs and aprons
Cat guts &c
Barcelona Silk handkerchiefs
Silk handkerchiefs of all Sorts
Persians
Sarsnets
Lutestrings, plain and figured
Bombazines and Crapes
Princes Stuff and Prunelloes
Gloves and Mitts of all Sorts
Shirt and Waistcoat Buttons
Millinery of all Sorts

DuBois & Lucas[10] are clever men, and men with whom we have heretofore transacted Buisness to great Satisfaction and Advantage. From all the information I can gain of them they are strictly punctual in Buisness and from my own Observation they are industrious and careful. Their Buisness is in sending British Goods to Forreign Merchants which they purchase of the Manufacturers. DuBois has travelled frequently through England and has very good Connections in the different manufacturing

---

[10] Merchants, New Basinghall Street, London. *Ibid.* (1774), p. 57.

Towns. They would be glad to receive any Orders from our house and can execute them well. And if our Connections with M: Daubarich & Co. should continue we must contrive to give them an Order now and then.

From their universal Character of Probity and Honour and the Stile in which they live I should suppose them People of Consequence and Fortune. DuBois is of Switzerland, but has lived 30 years in England. Lucas is an Englishman. They are both shrewd and sensible.

Horne & Kemp[11] I have kept up an Intimacy with. They are very Friendly People and extensive in the Coal Trade. They will always be willing to send one, two, or three Cargoes of Coals annually, while there is a Prospect of obtaining a good Price and Reason to think a Fit can be obtained back. They are upon the whole much pleased with the Connection they have had with our house, though they find some Fault with our having deviated from Orders in the Dimensions of the Arundel. She draws so much Water as to make her unfit for the Trade she was intended.

Captain Manson is in America.

William Atkinson[12] is in the same Buisness and connected with Horne & Kemp in several Concerns. He is willing now and then to send us a Cargo of Coals on the same Conditions but not so as to interfere with Horne & Kemp nor to glut the Market. In this particular he will always govern himself by our Advices. Captain Atkinson has left his Employ on some Difference between them.

George Harrison[13] Warehouseman and Factor is a clever honest Man who could supply us in several Articles of the Woolen Trade on good Terms. He is Factor for many of the Manufacturers in Wales where we have no Connections, and some of these come perhaps lower than any Goods in the Kingdom.

Welch Cloths calld
—— Plains
—— Penistones or
—— Cottons ⅞ wide 10 ½ to 17d. per yard
    these are white but may be dyed any Colour.
Yard wide Flannels 10 ½   2/– per yard
Drapery Bay   36/–   70/–
Scots hose   29/– to 60/– per Dozen
worsted Greys and all Colours

[11] Coal Factors, 12 Coal Exchange, Billingsgate, London. *Ibid.*, p. 91.
[12] Linen draper, Coventry Street, Leicester Fields, London. *Ibid.* (1780), p. 11.
[13] George Harrison & Co., Factors, Capel Court, Bartholomew Lane, London. Bailey's *British Directory*, I, p. 114.

Ditto from 30/– to 64/– white and brown thread
Kendal hose all Prices

These goods he sells at 6 Months Credit or 2 ½ per cent Discount.

James Phillips[14] Stationer is a very worthy Man and would supply us with every Article of Stationary as well as any Man in London. He sells his Goods at 12 Months or will make 6 per Cent Discount per Annum.

Paper of all Sorts Sizes and Prices
Books such as
Spelling Books
Psalters
Testaments
Bibles
Primers
All Friends Books
Ink Powder
Blank Books for Composition
Houses &c &c

William Cowpland[15] is a very clever Fellow and there are some Goods which at times he can ship us on perhaps better Terms than any house with which we have hitherto had Connections. The following are Goods of which he is a Manufacturer:

Persians of all Colours
Sarsinets
½ Ell Lining Modes
¾ Ditto
Ditto Rich Ditto
Pilong Sattins of all Prices and Colours
Rich Sattins Ditto
½ Ell plain and changeable Mantuas
¾ ——— Ditto Ditto
½ Ell and ¾ black Ditto
Black Barcelona handkerchiefs
Coloured Ditto all Prices
Culgie Printed Ditto Ditto
Black English Taffaties 15 yards
Ell wide black Persian   10 Ditto

[14] Bookseller and Stationer, 2 George Yard, Lombard Street, London. Kent's *London Directory* (1780), p. 136.
[15] Merchant, 11 Cannon Street, London. *Ibid.*, p. 46.

Morea Gowns
Sewing Silk and all other Silk Articles

He also ships East India prohibited Goods which at times he has an Opportunity of purchasing very low. And it frequently happens that these Goods meet a little Damage for which they are to Appearance no worse, but greatly lower in Price.

Kellam & Palmer[16] are men of great Integrity and are largely concerned in all Branches of the Tea Trade and there is no house in whom we may more safely rely for this Article both as to the Quality and Price. They sell this Article at 12 Months Credit.

Richard Bush[17] is a very capital Corn and Flour Broker if we had a mind to consign him a Cargo of Flour or Wheat. His only Charge is   per Cent for which he insures all Debts whatever. He is a very honest man and no Person is more capable of executing this Buisness for us. He would have no objection to take a Concern with us whenever a Prospect of Advantage offered.

Taylor,[18] a very good house in the same Buisness.

John Ewer.[19]

Thomas Everett[20] is largely in the Woolen Way, altogether able to serve us on the best Terms. And should any thing happen to stop our Connections with Fludyer's House, he would be a proper Person to supply their Place and deals in every Article which that house does. He is a very good Man and of great Capital.

Townsend & Giffin,[21] a house of the first Reputation, would supply us with every Article in the London Pewter way and would be much pleased to have any Connection with us.

Storrs & Christie[22] very honest People in the Manufactury of Castor hats. If London be as good a Place for this Article as Bristol these are the People.

Berthon Brothers.[23]

---

[16] Teamen, 154 Fenchurch Street, London. *Ibid.* (1777), p. 103.

[17] Merchant, St. Mary Overy's Dock, London. *Ibid.* (1774), p. 33.

[18] Abjohn Taylor & John Vickris, Corn Factors, 18 Lemau Street, Goodman's Fields, London. *Ibid.* (1776), p. 171.

[19] Walter & John Ewer, Merchants, 2 Little Lane, Aldermanbury, London. *Ibid.* (1780), p. 63.

[20] Blackwell Hall Factor and Warehouseman, 1 Castle Court, Laurence Lane, London. *Ibid.*, p. 62.

[21] Townsend & Griffin, pewterers, 136 Fenchurch Street, London. John Townsend's dates were 1725–1801. *Ibid.* (1774), p. 174; Gummere, *Journals and Essays of John Woolman*, p. 563.

[22] Storrs & Christy, Hat Makers, 5 Whitehart Court, Lombard Street, London. Kent's *London Directory* (1780), p. 165.

[23] Peter Berthon & Co., Merchants, 2 Laurence-Pountney Lane, London. *Ibid.*, (1776), p. 21.

APPENDIX I
Instructions from Joshua Fisher & Sons to Jabez Maud Fisher

Philadelphia 4 September 1775

Dear Jabez

Owing to the Distracted state of all human Affairs having not only continued since the day of thy departure but very rapidly increased and our minds having so sensibly felt on this Occasion, we have been prevented from furnishing thee with such Information and Instructions relative to our Business as we have long thought necessary and indeed had time allowed would have been much better if thou had taken them with thee, as thou will probably have visited many parts before this reaches thy hands, and should this be the case we would have thee go again to such places as thou imagines advantage may result from and thou can conveniently revisit. These Instructions are such as thou may by a Steady Attention to, improve thyself in a more extensive Knowledge of all the Branches of Business in which we have been concerned or hereafter may upon due deliberation engage in. And we are now induced thereto not by any Prospect of any advantage likely shortly to result therefrom, or that any of us *will* reap the Benefit, but as Youth is the time as well of acquiring knowledge and experience as of being active and diligent in Business, that part of thy time which may necessarily be employed herein will tend to make thy Journey more agreeable, enlarge thy Acquaintance among the more reputable People, keep thy Mind more usefully employed and if the present Storm should abate and go over, the knowledge thou may gain aided by thy two Brothers having gone before thee in the same Tract and conducted in all their Business with Reputation may be of lasting benefit to such of us as are or hereafter may chuse to continue in our Present Business.

We would have thee Particularly observe that we are not desirous of doing a great deal of Business, but to carry on our Trade in our usual Manner, endeavouring to procure our Goods from the several Merchants and Manufacturers upon the best Terms, to be connected in this Branch as well as all others in Shipping Consignments &c if possible in every Place with Persons of known Uprightness and Integrity, always giving the Preference to those of our Society, not from any degree of wrong Bias, but because from experience we have found them to merritt the Preferrence of any others in England. And if in the Course of thy Travels thou should have probable prospect of Advantage from Schemes or Plans of Business that may appear, or be offered to thee, we desire thou may weigh every circumstance well, and not to be concerned in any thing unless it not only meets thy own entire approbation but also are quite clear that it will also meet ours, as thou well knows our care and Anxiety. Nor be concerned in any kind of Business that may before the Conclusion of it involve us in difficulty and embarrassment. And in matters of this kind if thou dost not carefully attend thereto thou should consider that there will be some danger of our not executing them, if they should meet our Disapprobation. On these Accounts where time will admit to obtain our Concurrence, we should like it much best.

We would have thee visit the Manufacturing City's Towns &c generally, for altho as before mentioned two of thy Brothers have been before thee, yet it does not follow but thou may find some New Articles that may answer as well as to the means of our being supplied with others upon better terms than we have been, for we are ready to believe the Manufacturers &c will be as ready to be acquainted with and shew their Goods to the Americans as usual, knowing that when the present dispute subsides there will be the usual course of Trade opened for their Goods.

At Bristol we much want a good Correspondent. Richard Champion we think is by no means such a One as we would chuse, unless upon enquiry thou should find a better cannot be had there. If a Steady Friend of Reputation and Property can be had suitable we had much rather be connected with such a Person. R Peters is a Man whose Character we esteem much, but being by Trade a Baker is not a person sufficiently acquainted to transact any Business for us unless in the Sale of Flour and Wheat. And we desire thy Particular Attention to this Matter when in Bristol that we may hereafter reap the Benefit of thy Voyage in this Particular, as we have suffered in our Business for many Years on Account of our Connections there not being such as could place full confidence in.

At Liverpool we think William Rathbone is as good a Correspondent as can be had and tis probable our Connection with him may be enlarged to mutual Benefit if Trade should again get settled and if a Ship could be well employed between this and that Port to mutual benefit. We should like to have his sentiments thereon expressed to thee for our Government and we are the more pleased with this Connection, as he has a Son who is clever and likely to succeed him in Business.

Our Connection with DuBois & Lucas has been valuable and thy best Endeavours should be used to cultivate it. And as Captain Ord upon his return from Coruna informed us that our Friends M. Daubarich & Co. intended to have another Ship built for them in about 18 months from that time if things went well with them and that they intended employing us on that Account, we think thou may probably be the Means of fixing this matter either by conferring with DuBois & Lucas or writing to M. Daubarich & Co. or both, which upon considering thou may think best, for it may occasion us less trouble and save them something considerable in the Price by their forwarding their Orders early, the Carpenters being in a great measure unemployed, or building Ships on their own Accounts, so that we believe we might agree for a Ship by having the order in our hands previous to the Settlement of the present unhappy dispute much cheaper as tis probable the Prices will advance considerably presently after the Trade is opened. That thou may the more readily introduce the Matter to our Friends at Ferrol, we have inclosed our Letter to them, which after translating and shewing it as well as the One thou writes to accompany it to DuBois & Lucas thou should forward to them.

At London we are well satisfied that John & Richard Barclay should remain our Correspondents in the Manner that house long has done confining our Business in the Linnen way to them, except about half our Russia Goods, which we must endeavour to have bought for us for Cash in hand, as some of our Neighbours do and have been thereby enabled to undersell us. This we would not have known to them as we do it merely to keep our custom. Jonathan Brown has a Brother in London who used to do this business for him very well. He will not object to doing it for us, as Jonathan told us so some Years past. Thomas Powell may be qualified and we believe is to do it well and thou may know by enquiring whether DuBois & Lucas are sufficiently acquainted to do it. We mean to have a considerable part of our Linnens from Ireland as usual and that thou should be at Liberty to try any others in the Print way in London that thou thinks can do better either as to Price or Figures. We would not have thee be backward in asking John & Richard Barclay's Advice and Assistance in any Business that may occur, taking care in other respects not to be too much under Obligation to them. Thomas Powell we think will make as good a Correspondent in the Sale of our Consignments and purchase of some Articles for Ready Money as any we can have and his Commissions are very low. We take him a Blunt honest Man.

Crafton & Colson from whom of latter Years we have had most of our Hosiery we think cannot do so well for us, as we may be supplied by several at Leicester, particularly in All Sorts of Cotton Worsted and Thread except Knitt. Several Years ago we have had from Chamberlain & Burgess several parcels and from Joseph Bunney a small parcel. They both did well and we think Leicester Goods are better suited for this Markett than Nottingham, but thou should inform thyself at both Places as we never had any from the latter.

It is perhaps too late to say any thing about Scotland as tis probable thou will have been there and be on thy way to London before this can reach, yet hoping if this should be the case that thou hast made thyself acquainted with those Articles of their Manufacture which suit our Trade and with suitable persons for Correspondents. We need only say that we believe it may be well worth our trouble to have part of our Oznabrigs Ticking Thread Checkt Handkerchiefs Kentings Gauze and some other Articles from thence, as they come much lower, at least some of them than from London.

At Birmingham we are not so well suited with Correspondents as we could wish, knowing that Welch, Wilkinson & Startin do not supply us on as good Terms as some of our Neighbours are supplied. Yet would not chuse to drop them, as they are well acquainted with our Trade, till we have by experience found others to do better. Perhaps some of the Lloyds may be suitable and if they can do it well we should like to be connected with them, or if thou can find James Bringhurst's Correspondent we think he can do as well, if not better, than any we have knowledge of.

Broadbent & Co. will by no means suit us for Correspondents as we do not like them and therefore desire thou will endeavour to find an Active Man of Probity to buy for us the Manufactures of that Place and Neighbourhood on Commission with Money in hand. If John Barlow will undertake it and is well acquainted himself, or by thy Information with such Articles as suit our Trade, we should like him much. When at this Town don't forget Sickles.

At Newcastle, Shields, Sunderland, Whitby and Scarborough we Should chuse to be acquainted with the Mercantile People and particularly at the two latter, where there are many Friends largely concerned in Trade. At most of these Places there are SailCloth Manufactorys and perhaps some other with which it will be well to be acquainted if any of our Ships should go that way, or any People there should incline to send theirs here. Coal is very scarce and the first Cargoes that are admitted from Great Brittain will bring a higher Price than usual, as not only most of the Smiths, but also the Sugar Bakers are standing for want of them. If there are any Merchants of undoubted Character at Whitehaven, it may not be amiss to be known to them and to be acquainted with their Trade and the Neighbouring Manufactures.

At Pool there are many Merchants largely concerned in the Newfoundland Trade, where we should like to be better known, as they have frequent occasion to send their Ships this way for Provisions. It may not be amiss to inform them that they may always depend upon 18d. per Bushell for Newcastle Coal, in case of their having nothing better to induce them to send their Ships this way when they want Provisions. Moses Neave a Friend there is known to both of us and concerned in this Trade.

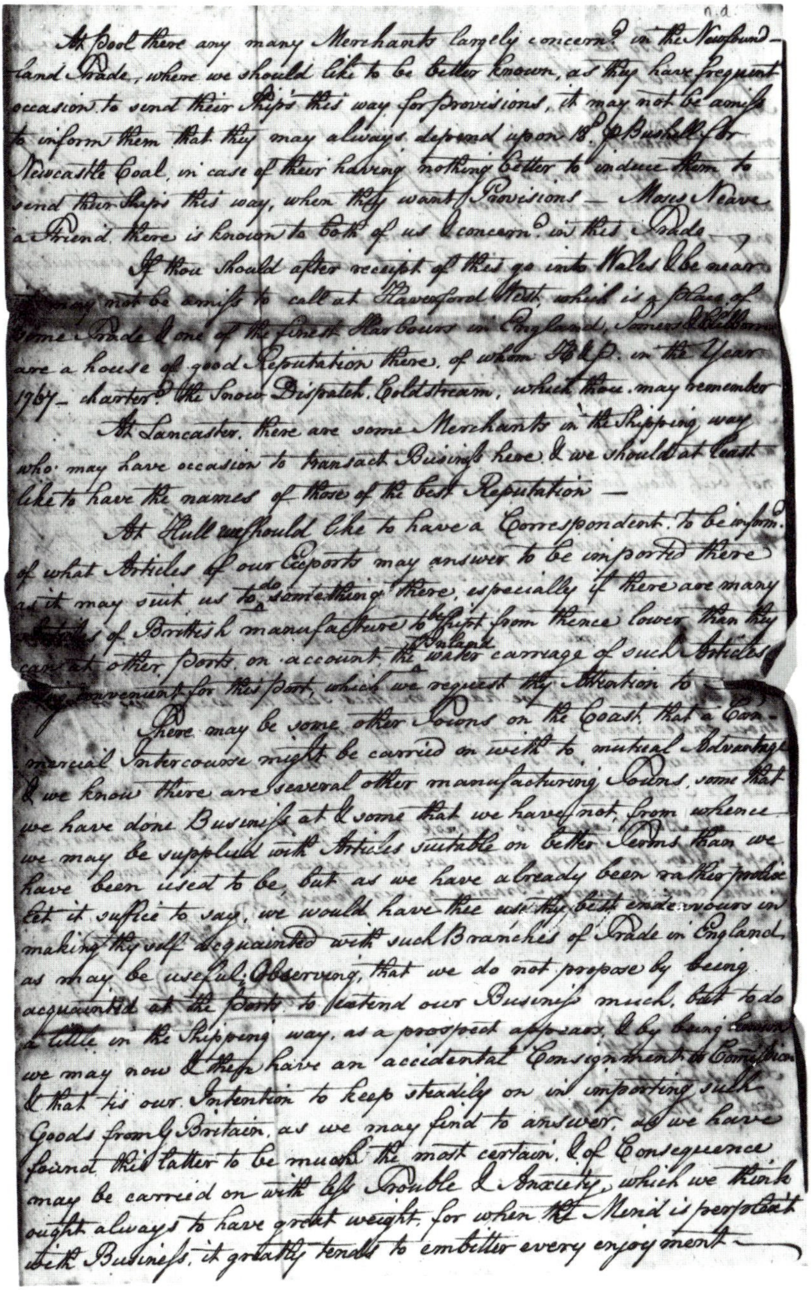

At Pool there are many Merchants largely concern'd in the Newfoundland Trade, where we should like to be better known, as they have frequent occasion to send their Ships this way for provisions, it may not be amiss to inform them that they may always depend upon B. Bushell for Newcastle Coal, in case of their having nothing better to induce them to send their Ships this way, when they want Provisions — Moses Neave a Friend there is known to both of us & concern'd in this Trade —

If thou should after receipt of this go into Wales & be near, it may not be amiss to call at Haverford West which is a place of some Trade & one of the finest Harbours in England, James & William ... are a house of good Reputation there, of whom H. & J. in the Year 1767 charter'd the Snow Dispatch. Coldstream, which thou may remember —

At Lancaster, there are some Merchants in the Shipping way who may have occasion to transact Business here & we should at least like to have the names of those of the best Reputation —

At Hull we should like to have a Correspondent, to be inform'd of what Articles of our Exports may answer to be imported there as it may suit us to do something there, especially if there are many ... of British manufacture to ... from thence lower than they can at other ports, on account the water carriage of such Articles ... convenient for this port, which we request thy attention to —

There may be some other Towns on the Coast that a Commercial Intercourse might be carried on with to mutual Advantage & we know there are several other manufacturing Towns, some that we have done Business at & some that we have not, from whence we may be supplied with Articles suitable on better Terms than we have been used to be, but as we have already been rather prolix let it suffice to say, we would have thee use thy best endeavours in making thy self acquainted with such Branches of Trade in England, as may be useful. Observing, that we do not propose by being acquainted at these ports to extend our Business much, but to do a little in the Shipping way, as a prospect appears, & by being ... we may now & then have an accidental Consignment or Commission & that tis our Intention to keep steadily on in importing such Goods from Britain, as we may find to answer, as we have found this latter to be much the most certain, & of Consequence may be carried on with less Trouble & Anxiety, which we think ought always to have great weight, for when the Mind is perplext with Business, it greatly tends to embitter every enjoyment —

FIG. 9. Extract from the Instructions from Joshua Fisher & Sons to Jabez Maud Fisher, 4 September 1775.

If thou should after receipt of this go into Wales and be near it may not be amiss to call at Haverford West, which is a place of some Trade and one of the finest Harbours in England. Somers & Clibborn are a house of good Reputation there, of whom H & P in the year 1767 chartered the Snow Dispatch Coldstream, which thou may remember.

At Lancaster, there are some Merchants in the Shipping Way who may have occasion to transact Business here and we should at least like to have the names of those of the best Reputation.

At Hull we should like to have a Correspondent, to be informed of what Articles of our Exports may answer to be imported there as it may suit us to do something there, especially if there are many Articles of British manufacture to be Shipt from thence lower than they can at other Ports, on account the Inland water carriage of such Articles being convenient for this Port, which we request thy Attention to.

There may be some other Towns on the Coast that a Commercial Intercourse might be carried on with to mutual Advantage and we know there are several other manufacturing Towns, some that we have done Business at and some that we have not, from whence we may be supplied with Articles suitable on better Terms than we have been used to be, but as we have already been rather prolix let it suffice to say we would have thee use thy best endeavours in making thy self acquainted with such Branches of Trade in England as may be useful; Observing that we do not propose by being acquainted at the Ports to extend our Business much, but to do a little in the Shipping way, as a prospect appears, and by being known we may now and then have an accidental Consignment or Commission and that tis our Intention to keep steadily on in importing such Goods from Great Britain as we may find to answer, as we have found this latter to be much the most certain, and of Consequence may be carried on with less Trouble and Anxiety, which we think ought always to have great weight, for when the Mind is perplext with Business, it greatly tends to embitter every enjoyment.

By the foregoing part of this letter, it may appear as if we are very anxious in this time of general Comotion to enlarge and Increase our Trade, which is by no means the case, for we would have thee to attend as many of Friends Meetings in the different Parts as thou conveniently can and let thy Business serve to fill up that time which might otherwise hang heavy upon thy hands. And in order that thy travels may as well be the more entertaining and pleasant to thyself, as more beneficial in a commercial Respect, we desire thou may particularly be careful to get well recommended to the several places of note which thou may visit, having no doubt but most of thy Friends will willingly assist herein.

By Captain Waid we forwarded thee an Abstract of all our Accounts in

England and desired thy settling the whole of them as fast as they became due and we had money in England to do it, which we doubt not but thou hast carefully attended to; we have been using our best endeavours from the time of Captain Osborne's sailing to pay off every thing we owe here, and hope in the Course of the present Month to accomplish the whole without drawing any more and as we shall look upon the Money we shall have in England when the Remittances from Lisbon and Cadiz get to hand (by rough Computation about £4,000 Sterling) of more value to us, if the present Troubles should continue very long, than what we have on this side the water. We request thou endeavour to be frugal in thy expences, for indeed at any time there is a satisfaction in a propriety of spending Ones Money that the Avaricious or Extravagant know nothing of.

B.Birkett expects to embark the end of this week per the Centurion Captain Allen for Newry per whom we shall again write thee, being with the united love of every Branch of our family

Thine Affectionately
Joshua Fisher & Sons

Flour 14/6   15/–
Wheat 5/– to 5/6
Flaxseed 10/–
Exchange 51½ to 55 per Cent

APPENDIX II
Glossary of Textile Terms

Alamode	A plain-weave, lightweight silk, usually black, much used for ladies' scarves.
Armozeen	A stout black silk used for clerical gowns.
Bandana	A kind of handkerchief.
Barragon	A corded stuff.
Beaverteen	A heavily wefted fabric of the moleskin type, used chiefly for heavy trouserings.
Blanket	A stuff, commonly made of white and coarse wool, to cover beds.
Bombasine	A stuff usually made of worsted and cotton.
Broadcloth	Fine, plain-wove, dressed, double width black cloth, used chiefly for men's garments.
Brocade	A textile with raised figures, originally in gold and silver, but later used about any kind of stuff richly wrought or flowered with a raised pattern.
Buckram	Coarse linen gummed for use as linings.
Calamancoe	A glossy stuff, chequered in the warp, whence checks appear only on one side. They are usually made entirely of wool, though some have a mixture of silk in the warp, and others of goat's hair.
Calico	Cotton fabrics of all kinds, usually coloured, imported from the East and later imitated in Europe.
Camblet	A stuff, sometimes made of wool, sometimes of silk, and sometimes of hair.
Cambric	A kind of white, fine linen.
Canton	A strong kind of fustian, showing a fine cording on one side and a smooth bright surface on the other.
Cardinal	A red woollencloth used for children's clothes.
Cashmere	Fabric made from the hair of the Cashmere goat (Northern India).
Check	Fabric woven or printed with a pattern of cross lines forming small squares, as in a chess board.

Chello	Indian cotton fabric.
Cheyney	A sort of worsted or woollen stuff.
Chintz	A painted or stained calico.
Coating	Coarse woollen material for coats.
Cord	Cotton ribbed fabric.
Cordeleur	Black and knotted silk neckerchief.
Cordonnet	Loosly spun thick silk thread or weak card made from waste or inferior silk and used for fringes, outlines of lace work etc. where strength is not required.
Corduroy	A kind of coarse, thick-ribbed cotton stuff.
Crape	A fabric sometimes made of highly-thrown and crimped silk; sometimes made of silk and worsted. Black crape was much used in mourning.
Damask	A sort of silk stuff originally brought from Damascus in Syria; having some parts raised above the ground, representing flowers or other figures.
Denim	A name originally given to a kind of serge.
Diaper	A linen fabric with a characteristic design of lines crossing diamond-wise with the intervals variously filled up.
Dimoty	A kind of cotton cloth, or fustian, wove full of ridges, like cards, manufactured in the East Indies and also in several European countries, but chiefly in some of the islands of the Turkish archipelago.
Dorsetteen	Woollen cloth.
Dowlas	Either a plain-woven coarse linen fabric used for clothing or a low-quality cotton fabric made of coarse rough-spun yarn, finished to imitate linen and used for towels, aprons etc.
Drab	Thick strong grey cloth.
Drabbet	Drab twilled linen used for making men's smock-frocks.
Drawboy	Figured woven stuff.
Drilling	A coarse linen or cotton fabric.
Duffel	Coarse woollen cloth having a thick nap or frieze.
Durant	Woollen stuff; a variety of tammy.
Duroy	A coarse woollen fabric of the tammy type, manufactured in the West of England.
Ermine	The white fur of the ermine (stoat).

Everlasting	Usually shortened to 'lasting' in the eighteenth century. A strong twilled woollen stuff, now also made of cotton.
Fearnought	The apt name of a rough woollen cloth especially used on board ships for outside clothing.
Flannel	A slight, loose, woollen stuff, not quilted but very warm, composed of a woof and warp.
Forest Cloth	Woollen cloth.
Frize	Woollen cloth or stuff for winter wear, being frized, or napped, on one side.
Fustian	Cotton stuff chiefly used for frocks or outer coats of men and boys.
Gauze	A very thin, transparent fabric of silk, linen or cotton.
Gingham	A cotton fabric, often woven in stripes, checks and other patterns.
Grogram	A coarse fabric of silk, of mohair and wool, or of these mixed with silk.
Harden	Coarse fabric made from the hards of flax or hemp.
Harrateen	A linen fabric used for curtains etc.
Hessian	A strong coarse hempen cloth, so called because it was originally made in Hesse, Germany.
Holland	A fine, white, even, close kind of linen cloth, chiefly used for shirts and sheets.
Huccaback	Originally hempen but later imitated in linen and cotton. A stout fabric with the weft threads thrown up alternately so as to form a rough surface.
Hummum	Plain white muslin, superior to fine quality, from Bengal.
Jean	Twilled cotton cloth; a kind of fustian.
Jennett	Imitation cotton fabric.
Kenting	A fine linen cloth.
Kersey	A kind of woollen cloth; manufactured in Yorkshire for export.
Lasting	Durable kind of cloth.
Lawn	A very fine fabric of the cambric type.
Loretto	A silk fabric used for vests.
Mantua	Silk fabric.
Mecklenburgh	Woollen fabric.
Morine	Stout woollen or woollen and cotton material.

Mulmul	A thin cotton cloth of the muslin type.
Muslin	A general name for the most delicately woven of all cotton fabrics, including many varieties.
Nankin	A yellow cotton cloth, originally made in Nankin, China.
Niccanee	Indian cotton fabric.
Nilla	Indian cotton fabric.
Nonsopretty	Fancy decorative tape used for trimming garments.
Osnabrig	A coarse quality linen.
Paduasoy	A strong corded or gros-grain silk fabric.
Peniasco	Mixed cotton and silk striped fabric of medium quality from Bengal.
Penistone	A coarse undyed cloth, usually classed with kersey.
Phota	Indian cotton fabric.
Plain	Plain cloth; a kind of flannel.
Plush	Refers to all sorts of textile materials, their common characteristic being a nap longer and softer than that of velvet.
Poplin	Mixed woven fabric consisting of a silk warp and worsted weft, and having a corded surface.
Prunella	Originally a strong stuff, so called from its colour, which is that of the fruit of the blackthorn.
Quilting	Cloth with a diagonal pattern suggestive of the appearance of an ordinary quilt.
Rattinet	A thin variety of rateen or thick twilled woollen cloth with a curled nap.
Rib	A fabric in which all the loops of alternate wales are intermeshed in one direction and all the loops of the other wales knitted at the same course are intermeshed in the other direction.
Romal	A silk or cotton square or handkerchief or a thin silk or cotton fabric.
Russel	A kind of woollen stuff.
Sacking	Closely woven material of flax, jute, hemp or similiar material, used chiefly in making sacks or bags.
Sagathy	Slight woollen stuff, being a kind of serge or ratteen, sometimes mixed with a little silk.
Sarsenet	A very fine and soft silk material.
Satin	A silk fabric woven in such a way as to give a very glossy surface to one of the sides.

Sattinet	A very slight, thin sort of satin, chiefly used by ladies for summer night gowns and ordinarily striped.
Serge	A strong wool stuff, either all-worsted or made with a worsted warp and a woollen weft.
Shag	A fabric with a long and coarse nap on one side, generally of worsted, but also of silk.
Shalloon	Closely woven woollen material chiefly used for linings.
Sheeting	Stout cloth of linen or cotton, such as is used for bed linen etc.
Silesia	A fine linen (later cotton) fabric.
Stay	A laced underbodice made in two pieces, stiffened by the insertion of strips of whalebone, worn by women to give shape and support to the figure.
Stripes	Striped textile fabric; usually linen manufactured from yarn.
Stroud	Blanket, originally from Stroud in Gloucestershire.
Stuff	A name normally used for fabrics made wholly or partially of combed wool (such as worsteds or half-worsteds).
Swanskin	A thick kind of flannel.
Taffety	Originally a thin glossy plain-wove silk. In the course of time, however, the word has been used about many sorts of materials, linen, woollen and cotton, the reason being that the original fabric possessed characteristics easily imitated in material other than silk.
Tammy	Strong sort of worsted stuff or woven manufacture.
Tanjib	A fine kind of muslin.
Tapseil	English cotton fabric of fine texture, with blue warp and white weft.
Tecklinburg	Coarse, strong linen fabric similar to Osnabrig, but broader and thicker.
Thick	Cloth made close in texture by fulling.
Thickset	Stout twilled cotton cloth with a short very close nap; a kind of fustian.
Tiffany	A kind of thin transparent silk; also a transparent gauze muslin.
Tissue	Rich or delicate fabric.
Tobine	A stout twilled silk.

Twine	Thread or string composed of two or more yarns or strands twisted together.
Velveret	A variety of fustian with a velvet surface.
Velvet	Rich kind of stuff, all silk, covered on the outside with a close, short, fine, soft shag; the other side being a very close tissue.

Sources: [Richard] Rolt, *A New Dictionary of Trade and Commerce* (London, 1756); Carolyn A. Farnfield and P. J. Alvey, eds., *Textile Terms and Definitions* (7th edn., Manchester, 1975); Leif J. Wilhelmsen, *English Textile Nomenclature* (Bergen, 1943); K. N. Chaudhuri, *The Trading World of Asia and the English East India Company 1660–1760* (Cambridge, 1978), Appendix 4, pp. 500–505; *OED*; D. C. Coleman, *Courtaulds: An Economic and Social History* (3 vols., Oxford, 1969–1980), 1, ch. 3; Nesta Evans, *The East Anglian Linen Industry: Rural Industry and Local Economy, 1500–1850* (Aldershot, 1985), pp. 169–170; Eric Kerridge, *Textile Manufacture in Early Modern England* (Manchester, 1985); D. T. Jenkins and K. G. Ponting, *The British Wool Textile Industry, 1770–1914* (London, 1982), pp. 332–353.

Index of Personal Names

A 'Q' after a name indicates that the person has been definitely identified as a Quaker.

Index of Places

Index of Commodities

Index of Subjects